P9-CMR-068

Ch

For Doug,
From a "bunch"
who have voted
"many ways"
The MacIntoshs

M W
& R

ON THE TAKE

ON THE TAKE

Crime, Corruption and Greed
in the Mulroney Years

STEVIE CAMERON

Research Associates
ROD MACDONELL AND ANDREW MCINTOSH

MACFARLANE WALTER & ROSS
TORONTO

Copyright 1994 © by Stevie Cameron

All rights reserved. No part of this book may be reproduced or transmitted in any form, by any means, without written permission from the publisher, except by a reviewer, who may quote brief passages in a review.

Macfarlane Walter & Ross
37A Hazelton Avenue
Toronto, Canada M5R 2E3

Canadian Cataloguing in Publication Data

Cameron, Stevie
On the take : crime, corruption and greed in the Mulroney years

Includes index
ISBN 0–921912–73–0

1. Political corruption – Canada.   2. Canada. –
Politics and government – 1984-1993.*   I. Title.

FC630.C35   1994   971.064'7   C94–932324–1

The publisher gratefully acknowledges the support of the Ontario Arts Council

Printed and bound in Canada

For David

Contents

PREFACE

T HIS BOOK IS NOT ABOUT POLICY; IT IS ABOUT CORRUPTION. Someday other writers will analyze the impact on Canada of the Conservative Party's legislation between 1984 and 1993. They will examine the Mulroney government's efforts to overhaul the country's social security networks, privatize Crown corporations, deregulate industries, and bring a more business-minded approach to government. Some books have already described the influence of the Republican administrations of Ronald Reagan and George Bush on this country during the Mulroney years. I have attempted none of these laudable goals. What this book is about is how the Mulroney regime caused Canadians to lose faith in their government and why voters crushed a party they had come to despise. Almost every Conservative interviewed for this book admitted that the party had earned its reputation for corruption and that the defeat it received on election night, October 25, 1993, was just. What the Conservatives did to deserve that reputation and that defeat is my story.

Almost all the political sources for this book were Progressive Conservatives. They include a number of former ministers in the Mulroney cabinet as well as some of their chiefs of staff, senators, members of Parliament, aides, fundraisers, lobbyists, campaign managers, field organizers, and PC Party staff. Most of them cannot be named, but they know I am grateful. In particular, I would like to thank former deputy prime minister Erik Nielsen, who was exceptionally generous with his time and exceptionally frank, even about his own role in some of the events that he describes. And I would like to acknowledge the help of a number of former Mulroney household staff members, including their former chef, François Martin. Brian and Mila Mulroney chose not to be interviewed, but some of their closest friends did agree to requests for interviews, and in particular I wish to acknowledge David Angus, Guy Charbonneau, Joe Stewart, and George and Helen Vari.

I owe Mordecai Richler a great debt. Not only did he spend time showing me the haunts of the Mulroney Tories in Montreal, but he shared his insights into their characters and helped me to understand the community in which they flourished.

Over the past year I have been given essential assistance by many bureaucrats who explained how events unfolded or how certain systems worked, whether it was the distribution of shoe quotas or the financing of the Export Development Corporation. It must be said that several bureaucrats who helped with this book suffered permanent damage to their careers during the Mulroney years for failing to carry out orders from their political bosses, and even today they do not want their names used. To all the public servants who helped me, I offer my deepest gratitude.

Among those who can be named, I would like to thank Suzanne Amos-Kinsella at the National Capital Commission; Heather Bradley in the House of Commons Speaker's Office; Bud Slattery and Elaine Martel at Elections Canada; Michele Currie and Yvon Deloughery of the Privy Council Office; Michael Swift at the National Archives; Maurice Cutler, former public affairs spokesman at the Auditor General's Office; Deputy Assistant Registrar General Howard Wilson and his predecessor Georges Tsai; Corinne MacLaurin and her staff at the Lobbyists' Registration Branch; and Jean-Guy Ieraci at Foreign Affairs. Among the political staff who helped, all long before the 1993 election, were the New Democratic Party's Vince Gogolek and the Liberal Party's André Tessier, Warren Kinsella, and Mark Laframboise. As always, Don Boudria deserves many thanks for keeping impeccable records and for sharing them with journalists.

I have no adequate words to express my appreciation to my fellow reporters across Canada who have stood behind this book project with facts, files, moral support, and hospitality. I must offer special thanks to Bob Fife at *The Toronto Sun* and Chris Cobb at the Ottawa *Citizen*, who never flagged in their encouragement. Andrew Mitrovica at CTV National News was always there, continuing a friendship that began when we worked together at the CBC's *fifth estate*. So too were Jim Littleton at CBC National Radio; Sean Moore, John Chenier, and Steve Chase at the *Lobby Monitor*; Charlie Greenwell at CJOH-TV in Ottawa; Ottawa columnist Claire Hoy; Stuart Langford at the Canadian Bar Association's *The National*; Annabelle King and Claude Arpin at the Montreal *Gazette*; Alain Gravel at *Le Point* in Montreal; Michel Vastel at Unimedia; David Vienneau and Linda Diebel at *The Toronto Star*; Gord McIntosh at Canadian Press; Anne Collins, my editor at *Saturday Night* magazine; and Michel Auger at the *Journal de Montréal*.

I would like to add a special word of appreciation to my colleagues at the *Globe* during the years I wrote for the paper. Many of the stories in this book were first researched during my years there. The person who worked most closely with me for almost all that time was national editor Sylvia Stead, one of the bravest editors I've ever known. Sarah Murdoch, the Focus section editor, edited most of my large investigative projects, made even the most complicated stories intelligible, and always left in the funny bits. Celia Donnelly is a gifted librarian whose investigative skills have been the backbone of countless *Globe* scoops; she is one of the reasons that the *Globe* library, under the direction of Amanda Valpy, is such a great part of the paper's strength. Library assistant Rick Cash and photo librarian Sonja Lindegger are two more reasons. Former newsroom colleagues who have made a difference on this project include Jock Ferguson, Bill Houston, Paul Knox, David

Livingstone, Linda McQuaig, Lawrence Surtees, and David Shoalts.

One former colleague in particular helped with several chapters in this book: my friend Richard Cléroux. Richard shared files, interview transcripts, and tape recordings that he has been collecting over the last decade. I am especially indebted to him for his help with the Mulroney trips abroad, the burglaries in Montreal, the Marin inquiry, Roger Nantel's contracts, and the history of Richard Grisé's escapades. Richard was always available when I needed help; his cheerfulness and generosity, and the kindness of his wife, Arlene Wortsman, have touched me deeply.

Halfway through this project I joined *Maclean's* magazine as a contributing editor. What we didn't know at the time was how little I would be able to do for the magazine until the book was finished. For their unfailing support, patience, and good humour, I thank publisher Brian Segal and editor-in-chief Bob Lewis.

Over the years, I have been grateful for the expertise of many academics. In particular, I would like to thank University of Toronto political scientist Peter Russell and Faculty of Law professor Jacob Ziegel for sharing with me their study of judicial appointments; York University political scientist Ian Greene for his help with conflict of interest; and Queen's University political scientist Doug Brown for helping Rod Macdonell, Andrew McIntosh, and me to launch our book project.

Before I began this book, I consulted with several of the partners and staff at Lindquist Avey Macdonald Baskerville Inc., the Toronto-based forensic accounting practice. Over the years I have found the people there, led by managing partner Bob Lindquist, to be extraordinarily generous to an innumerate journalist tumbling around in the bottomless pit of white-collar crime. In particular, I must single out Bob Lindquist, whose sense of fun — mixed with a passion for justice and the rule of law — is an example to me. Rod Stamler was also most helpful, as were Hazel de Burgh, who helped me sort out some mysteries in Saskatchewan, and Mario Possamai, another former colleague at *the fifth estate*. Bashir Rahemtulla and Cheryl Stewart provided invaluable guidance; so did Stu Allen in Washington.

Over this past year many other friends have rallied to make my research as pleasant and trouble-free as possible. Richard Reynolds, a dear friend, set up my computer, loaded programs, and was always cheerful about my late-night panic calls. Stephen Bornstein gave me the key to his house in Montreal, which became my second home. Donald and Florence Deacon made us welcome in P.E.I., while in Nova Scotia we were looked after by Sharon and Al Hollingsworth, Jim and Cheryl Littleton, Judy and John Langly, my brother-in-law Silver Donald Cameron, his wife, Lulu Terrio, George Anderson and Leslie Oyler, and Nick Pearce and David Barrette. Anita Neville, Bill Neville, and all their family and friends in Winnipeg have done much to make me feel like a member of a big and generous family. In Saskatchewan I am indebted to many people, most of whom must remain nameless, but surely Garry and Jaquie Wilson won't mind if I thank them for a great dinner. In British Columbia, my brother Chris Dahl and his wife, Judy, turned their home, telephones, and computers over to me. I thank also my fellow volunteers, especially Cameron and Marg Brett, Michael and Janice Barnes, Chip Pitfield, Sarah Band, and Ruth Dicerni, and all our guests at the Out of the Cold program at St. Andrew's Church. Our time together there last winter kept me in balance.

It took a dedicated and talented team to put this book together. First and foremost is my publisher, Jan Walter of Macfarlane Walter & Ross, who encouraged me to write it. Rick Archbold and Barbara Czarnecki improved the manuscript with their tactful and careful work, and I thank them, as I do my Toronto research team, which included Kate Robson, Doug Saunders, Heather MacKay, and Greg Sewell. And I wish to thank Jack Stoddart for all his support and Peter Jacobsen for his thoughtful advice.

I hope my friend and agent Linda McKnight and her staff at Sterling Lord Associates know how much I appreciate their hard work. Linda went far beyond the call of duty to work with me on the original outline.

I must add a special word about my research associates, Rod Macdonell and Andrew McIntosh, two of the finest investigative journalists in this country. When we began this book, we had no idea of the adventures and characters lying in wait for us nor of the fun we'd have sharing these experiences. I will miss the talks and the laughs and the excitement and look forward to the day when we can work together again. I thank too their respective partners, Shelly Potter and Carolyn Adolph, for their unfailing patience in seeing us through. Because of Rod's and Andrew's painstaking work, which included interviewing several sources and unearthing court records, deeds, coroners' reports, and corporate documents, our stories are better than any I could have accomplished alone.

Most of all I thank my own beloved family: my husband, David, and our daughters, Tassie and Amy, who took such good care of me.

SAYING GOODBYE

INUTES BEFORE BRIAN AND MILA MULRONEY LEFT THE PRIME minister's official residence at Harrington Lake for the last time, their household staff gathered outside on the drive to say goodbye. It was Monday, June 28, 1993, a hot summer morning, and the maids, the chef, and the butler were hoping for a few days off.

Unfortunately, their prospects were not good; the new leader, Kim Campbell, would shortly move into the old white farmhouse, which would serve as her headquarters for the forthcoming election campaign, and the Mulroneys' staff had promised to see her through the summer months. After that, who knew? If the Tories won again, they'd keep their jobs. If not, chances were they'd be fired, just like the political staff on Parliament Hill, to make way for a new Liberal government and its appointees.

But the Mulroneys' plans were set. They were off to the Riviera for the summer while their recently purchased Montreal home was gutted and renovated; after that, the former prime minister would be rejoining his old Montreal law firm. This morning, the limousine was packed and stood idling in the driveway, ready to take the couple to the airport for the flight to France. When Mila came out of the house, she was in tears. Her husband followed and solicitously handed her into the back seat of the car. Straightening up, he turned to the cluster of grim-faced servants and tried to smile. "We're just a phone call away," he muttered,

1

his eyes not meeting any of theirs, "just a phone call away."

No one knew what to say. Finally one young man, who had worked for them since 1989, mustered his courage. "What's the number, Boss?" he asked, a smile twitching at the corners of his mouth. There was no reply. "What's the number?" he asked again.

"Uh, just a phone call away . . ." Mulroney repeated, his eyes on the ground as he bent and slipped into the back seat beside his wife.

The door slammed and the limousine pulled away, followed by the RCMP escort car and watched in silence by the servants. As the Mulroneys' car slowly rounded the curve a few hundred feet down the driveway, it suddenly stopped. The staff froze. Maybe the Mulroneys were just having a last look at the house, maybe they'd forgotten something.

The tension was too much for one of the maids; she could not stifle a heartfelt shout: "Don't come back!"

The car started up again and soon it was just a speck in the distance.

The Mulroneys have not come back to Ottawa, but the taxpayer is far from through with them. Earlier that June, a long tractor-trailer had driven slowly past the iron gates at 24 Sussex Drive in the nation's capital, carrying a full load of furniture out to a local warehouse for storage. Other vans and trucks had pulled out of the residence in April and May, but they had turned east for the 125-mile drive to Montreal. At a warehouse there, workers unloaded most of the goods from two of the country's most famous houses, the official residences of Canada's prime ministers. Brian and Mila Mulroney's furnishings were placed in a safe section of the warehouse, one set aside for semi-permanent storage.

The movers organized the Mulroney goods carefully; there were no immediate plans to move them into the couple's new house. That would wait until after the renovations. And Mila Mulroney was buying new furnishings, such as the $15,000 dining-room table picked up from one Montreal antique dealer. So, until the couple decided what they wanted done with the old pieces, everything was to remain in storage — at the expense of the Canadian government.

The government has a rule when politicians leave official residences: the public pays for only one move in and one move out. Documents released by the National Capital Commission show the government paid $70,000 for a number of official moves, including the Mulroneys' moves from the official residences, but the documents are far from complete. They don't include the Montreal storage charges. A Toronto moving expert, when shown the figures, said bluntly that the Mulroney move alone had to have cost at least $100,000 and probably far more. He added that the invoicing was unusual; most movers charge by the pound and then tag and invoice each item they move. In the Mulroneys' case the movers sent separate purchase orders for each trip to the houses, for each set of workers and vans, and for each order of packing materials. That way, the moving expert said, the bills could be divided among several departments and no one would ever know what the Mulroney move finally cost.

What the documents do reveal is the sheer size of the operation. To store the furniture left behind in Ottawa, the National Capital Commission rented two bays of a warehouse from local developer PerezBramalea for $3,600 a month; the space was private and air-conditioned, featured its own washroom, and had twenty-four-hour security. The NCC gave the actual moving job to Boyd Movers and Storage of Ottawa, the company that has had federal moving contracts sewn up for decades. From April 4 to October 30, 1993, Boyd's staff made at least thirty-one trips with seventy-two vehicles, from cars to tractor-trailers. Some trips were to or from the official residences to pack and move goods; others were from the warehouse to Montreal. They booked ninety-five workers over the same period to pack 110 china barrels, 80 tea chests, 42 wardrobe cartons, and 768 standard cartons, from small ones for knick-knacks to large ones for paintings and antiques. The movers also built 23 specially designed wooden crates. They used 2,030 pounds of corrugated paper, 930 pounds of newsprint, and 695 rolls of bubble wrap.

How big a move does all this represent? "It's off the scale," said one mover who has dealt with large and complicated diplomatic moves. "I've been in this business seventeen years and those are the largest numbers I've ever seen." Moving an average household usually involves about 8,000 pounds and one van. Moving a diplomatic household, one that has been occupying a large embassy residence, might add up to 20,000 pounds and require slightly more than one van. The goods stored in the Ottawa warehouse alone totalled 40,000 pounds and took at least two vans. Most of the other vans went to Montreal, but there was so much furniture to relocate that the overflow spread as far as Toronto, where some pieces wound up in the apartment of Mila's sister, Ivana. Ivana Pivnicki's boyfriend has shown off a Quebec pine armoire from one of the residences that he was keeping in his flat.

Canadians could be forgiven for believing that they'd paid the last bill for Brian and Mila Mulroney when Kim Campbell was sworn in as prime minister on June 25, 1993. Alas, that was far from the case. They were still paying Mulroney's salary and expenses as a member of Parliament — about $85,000 annually — until he formally quit that job after the October 25 election. Then his indexed parliamentary pension kicked in.

The government does not reveal pension amounts for privacy reasons, but spokesmen refer the curious to the National Citizens' Coalition, which has calculated politicians' pensions using an annual inflation factor of 5 per cent. Based on Mulroney's six best years in Parliament, his pension works out to $33,535 every year. (This figure is far less than the pension some of his longer-serving cabinet colleagues are enjoying. Perrin Beatty, for example, now receives a pension of about $70,000 a year because he was elected in 1972 and served twenty-one years as an MP before being defeated in 1993. At age seventy-five, he will have earned $5 million in pension benefits.) By the time Mulroney is seventy-five, he will have been paid

$1,180,218 from his standard MP's pension. Things will be better ten years from now, when he is sixty-five and his prime-ministerial pension kicks in, giving him two-thirds of whatever the prime minister of the day is paid. Today, the prime minister's extra salary — on top of his MP's pay — is $74,000 a year for a total of $159,000. In ten years Mulroney's total annual pension, according to the Coalition, will be about $85,000 a year.

Then there is the expense of twenty-four-hour security provided by members of the Royal Canadian Mounted Police, which is costing the government at least $1.6 million a year, exclusive of travel expenses. On one trip to Toronto in late September 1993, the Mulroneys had dinner with Toronto financier Peter Munk, at his Highland Avenue house in Rosedale, to celebrate Mulroney's appointment to two of Munk's corporate boards. Two RCMP officers accompanied them from Montreal, two more met them at the airport, and two Metro Toronto police officers joined the four Mounties to protect the Munk house during dinner. Security is an unfortunate necessity for former prime ministers; Pierre Trudeau was also given protection by the RCMP when he returned to private life in Montreal, but he had a much smaller crew looking after him and the protection lasted only a short while. Six guards for one former prime minister at a Rosedale dinner party? Perhaps they knew something the rest of us didn't. What stuck in the minds of some of the neighbours that evening was that, in the same way U.S. presidents retain the title of "President" for life, police officers with Mulroney referred to him as "Prime Minister" while explaining the heavy police presence to baffled local residents. To this day, the Mulroneys are still followed around Montreal by RCMP officers. "He needs it," said one security expert grimly. "Whatever you think of a politician, prominent ones like Mulroney get a lot of nut cases threatening them. People have to be able to be in politics without fearing for their lives."

Canadians are footing some other bills as well. Back in Ottawa, a committee of Treasury Board approved a request on June 9, two days before Mulroney stepped down as leader of the Progressive Conservative Party, to give the National Archives an extra $1.475 million over five years to pay for handling all the personal and political papers of three retiring party leaders, Mulroney, John Turner, and Joe Clark. All three men were leaving Parliament, all three had been prime ministers. But Mr. Turner's prime-ministerial term lasted all of two and a half inglorious months in the summer of 1984; and Joe Clark had managed to stay in power for only nine months in 1979. Most of the money, admitted government spokespeople, was intended to handle nine years of Mulroney papers and to pay for a spacious Ottawa office at which he and two assistants would organize the material. Until Liberal MP Don Boudria started poking around in the archives arrangement, a private bathroom was planned for the Mulroney office, but it was hastily cancelled after Boudria's complaints. Even so, a facility as grand as this was a first for Canadian prime ministers.

Archivists had another worry with Mulroney's papers. By the end of the summer of 1993, Mulroney was discussing tax credits with government officials. He was not alone. After leaving his papers on deposit with the National Archives in 1984, Pierre Trudeau formally donated his papers to the archives in November 1993, taking a $1-million tax credit for them. Mulroney's hope was that if he too donated his papers to the National Archives, he would enjoy a similar tax break. (A number of his cabinet colleagues were also haggling with archives officials over tax credits.) In 1994, the National Archives finally agreed on a value for his personal papers before 1983, but they would not say what that value was or whether he was receiving a tax credit or payment for them. They are still sorting and evaluating the papers from his years in government.

So in mid-1994 the Mulroneys were costing taxpayers nearly $2 million annually in pensions, police protection, and archival support. It could have been worse. We could have paid the $150,000 initially granted to Mila Mulroney for the furnishings she left behind.

In a deal devised in March 1993 by the Mulroneys, Mulroney's deputy chief of staff, Marjory LeBreton, and the National Capital Commission's executive vice-president, John Hoyles (a former organizer for the PC Party who was put into the NCC when his predecessor was found to have some Liberal ties), the government discussed paying the Mulroneys about $170,000 for furniture, curtains, bedding, china, and other goods they were leaving behind them. The figure was based on the couple's assessment of the replacement cost for new goods, not on the value of the goods as used furniture. A letter dated March 19, 1993, to NCC chairman Marcel Beaudry says that "an expert" (who has never been identified) evaluated the replacement value of the furniture at $168,200 but that the prime minister had agreed to accept $150,000. The NCC deleted the name of the letter-writer when the letter was released in response to an access-to-information request. There had also been a discussion of tax credits in lieu of a purchase, but the issue was not raised in this letter.

When the deal was first proposed, Mila Mulroney provided the NCC with an inventory of goods she said she and her husband owned. She noted the value beside each item but did not provide any receipts or documents to show the original prices, when they were bought or from whom, or who actually paid for the goods. The NCC hired three evaluators to ensure that the prices were fair. The first evaluation was done over a week in March 1993 by Ottawa auctioneer Peter Walker, who has experience in resale value estimates. The second was carried out in April 1993 by Caris Interior Decorations, a well-known Ottawa firm, which was also given a week. The third evaluator, Mary Robertson of Robertson and Associates of Ottawa, was told by John Hoyles that she had to complete her assessment within twenty-four hours. Officials called her on Friday afternoon, June 18, and told her to visit the houses on Monday, June 21, to inspect the furniture and other goods for sale. An NCC work order confirms that the evaluation was to be on his desk by Tuesday, June 22. It was important to get the deal signed and sealed and the money paid before Kim Campbell was sworn in on June 25.

Robertson, who has been evaluating goods for the government for nearly thirty years, was dismayed; she protested that twenty-four hours wasn't nearly enough. The NCC relented and gave her a few more days; she hastily arranged for a number of antiques experts, including one who could photograph the goods, to accompany her.

But the NCC soon found it had another question to cope with while waiting for Robertson's evaluation: the ownership of the furniture. In his letter to the prime minister about the deal, NCC chairman Beaudry had referred to "your furniture." The correspondence was quickly changed to indicate that Mila, not Brian, was the owner of the goods. The Parliament of Canada Act prohibits the government from paying a member of Parliament for any goods or services beyond his or her regular salary and expenses. It is difficult to see how these amendments to the paperwork would have made any difference, since the act clearly bans all payments, either "direct or indirect."

What the NCC and aides in the PMO never counted on was someone finding out about it. By June 25, an individual familiar with the deal was ready to talk; calls to the NCC resulted in a flustered Beaudry defending it as a "bargain." He even declared he had dreamed up the idea himself and mentioned it to the Mulroneys at a social function. Interestingly, John Hoyles gave out the identical story about a social function, but in his version *he* was the one suggesting the idea.

Once Mulroney's PMO staff discovered that details of the secret deal were about to be published in *The Globe and Mail*, they issued a press release trying to control the spin on the mess and ensuring that the *Globe* would not have an exclusive on the story. Sure enough, puzzled newsreaders reported the arrangement on television that evening, but no one knew the background until the *Globe* story appeared.

Public reaction was swift and hostile. Why should taxpayers reimburse Mila Mulroney for used furniture? raged the talk-show callers and writers of letters to editors. No explanations, no talk of bargains, no excuses satisfied a weary public who had watched nine years of Mulroney excess and who were not convinced the Mulroneys had paid for the goods in the first place. In fact, Canadians were suspicious that someone else had paid for the stuff — maybe the Progressive Conservative Party, maybe themselves. Despite Mulroney's public promise that he would limit any expenses for furnishing or decorating to $98,000, at least $1.5 million of public money had been poured into the residences during Mulroney's first eighteen months in office, and much of that was for furnishings.

Incredibly, however, the government's own documentation on these purchases has been lost. Until 1987, the Department of Public Works was responsible for the official residences; after that date the residences moved under the control of the National Capital Commission. Records from 1984 to 1987 are completely missing, all gone. Making the trail even more difficult to follow and accountability more complicated was the government's creation in 1985 of a new organization called the Official Residences Council to oversee renovation work and furnishing of these government houses. It was run by the Privy Council Office, and PCO officials have consistently refused to allow NCC staff to see their records. The Mulroneys arranged for close friends — Montreal pals such as John Lynch-Staunton, Mulroney's comptroller for his 1983 leadership campaign, and Lynne Verchère, the wife of one of Mulroney's financial advisers, Bruce Verchère — to be appointed to the Official Residences Council.

Still, the furniture mess wasn't a story that was going to fade away. With a federal election just a few months off and a new leader struggling to establish her credibility with a public that had come to mistrust her party, Conservative strategists advised that the deal be killed quickly and cleanly. The NCC agreed. "We have respect for the views of Canadians. We heard the message loud and clear," said Suzanne Amos-Kinsella, the corporation's spokeswoman.

By this time, Brian and Mila Mulroney were vacationing with their family and one or two close friends in a borrowed villa near Cannes. In a petulant letter to Marcel Beaudry, dated July 15, 1993,

Mila Mulroney complained about her years of unpaid service to the people of Canada and told him to cancel the deal.

"Dear Mr. Beaudry," she wrote:

> Prior to leaving Ottawa, I accepted the NCC offer to purchase furnishings I own at 24 Sussex and Harrington Lake.
>
> Your offer was significantly below the independently appraised value and replacement costs of these items which I had purchased over the years to ensure that both official residences met standards appropriate for a nation like Canada.
>
> I am presently on holidays and have been advised that the transaction — which you and other leading public officials have described as "extremely advantageous" for the government of Canada — has been characterized by others as somehow being inappropriate.
>
> After a decade of public service, which I performed with pride and pleasure and during which I neither received nor expected to receive remuneration of any kind for any of my activities, I am of course disappointed by the suggestion — even from some partisan sources — that I might have sought to profit from this transaction. Accordingly, I have instructed my accountant to return immediately your cheque thereby terminating the agreement between us.
>
> I accepted your proposal to purchase my property in the genuine belief that such an initiative would benefit the Canadian taxpayer and lessen the burden on future prime ministers. I regret this gesture was misconstrued. So as not to inconvenience the Prime Minister, I will leave all of my personal effects now in both residences in place until such time as they can reasonably be replaced.
>
> Thank you for your kind attention.
>
> Yours sincerely,
>
> Mila P. Mulroney

A little sadder, a little poorer, the Mulroneys returned to Montreal in August. Their new house at 47 Forden Crescent in Westmount, Montreal's most exclusive residential area, wasn't yet ready so they stayed in a country house in the Laurentians and commuted to the city, he to set up a new practice in his old law firm, Ogilvy Renault, and she to decorate the house.

By August it was clear that the furniture issue was still sensitive, especially to the Tories trying desperately to hang on to enough seats to come back as the official opposition. Jane Billings, a senior official in the Privy Council Office, had been asked by PCO clerk Glen Shortliffe to ensure that 24 Sussex Drive would be in good shape to receive the new prime minister on October 26, the day after the election, even though a new prime minister does not move into the house until after his or her swearing-in, which occurs about ten days after an election. The NCC had brought in workers to do last-minute repairs and to touch up the paint on the walls and woodwork; cleaners had been scouring every inch of the place. Most important was getting the last remnants of the unsold Mulroney furniture out of the house before October 26. But Jodi White, chief of staff to Prime Minister Kim Campbell, wasn't taking any chances that reporters and photographers might notice more vans in front of the house and accurately conclude that the infamous furniture was making its exit. Such stories would only remind Canadians of the Mulroneys and sour them once again on the Tories. According to a memo from Billings to Shortliffe, White called John Hoyles to instruct the NCC "not to remove any furniture until after the election." In her memo Billings noted that she had checked this with Janice Charette, an aide to Jodi White, "who confirmed this direction and explained that the Chief of Staff wanted no moving trucks at 24 Sussex until after the election."

With Shortliffe still insisting that the house be empty of Mulroney possessions *before* the election, an accommodation was reached: most of the Mulroneys' remaining furniture would be removed in late

August, but the operation would be performed with unmarked vans at 6 in the morning. John Hoyles, who was working closely with Marjory LeBreton to coordinate events for the least possible embarrassment to the Mulroneys, turned up at dawn to supervise the movers personally.

As October 25 approached, there were still items belonging to the Mulroneys at 24 Sussex Drive. Organizers decided to choose election night itself for the deployment of one last van. As they expected, local reporters were too busy tracking the election returns to notice. On the same night that the Conservative Party was almost wiped off the electoral map, a final load was spirited out of 24 Sussex Drive, at a cost of $1,110.

Many of those involved in these manoeuvres surely breathed a sigh of relief that night, believing this was, at long last, the end of the Mulroney furniture saga. It was not to be.

It turns out that the sofas, vases, and *objets* that Mila had tried to sell to the people of Canada were left behind in the residences. It was almost a year before NCC chairman Beaudry or Prime Minister Chrétien's PMO staff discovered that most of those items were still there. Informed of the lingering lamps and tchotchkes by *The Toronto Sun*'s Bob Fife, Beaudry was irate. All year his office had been telling reporters that Mila's things were gone, and he realized he'd been misled. The Official Residences Council, its members appointed by Mulroney, had consistently refused to cooperate with the NCC or the PMO, and Beaudry was not kept informed. The furniture is there to this day.

And the whole affair refuses to die. In June 1994, Mila Mulroney went to the Federal Court in Ottawa to try to block the public release of the first appraisal, done by auctioneer Peter Walker. He'd based his evaluation on the resale value of the furniture, while Robertson and Caris had done theirs on replacement value. The legal argument was that releasing a resale appraisal could result in substantial financial loss to Mrs. Mulroney. If Canadians discovered that the auctioneer thought the stuff might fetch, let us say, $20,000 at auction, then why would any interested buyer pay more? Furthermore, a low resale appraisal might make Canadians wonder once again why the NCC had agreed to pay $150,000. Rather than taking the customary route of hiring a lawyer, the Mulroneys used their accountant, Alain Paris, whom Mulroney had appointed to the board of the CBC, to launch a court action to suppress the information. The case is ongoing, keeping government lawyers busy and billing to allow Mila to fight for the best possible price for her furniture.

The Mulroneys had left public life in the same fashion in which they had conducted themselves during their years in power: with an unshaken belief in their entitlement to the taxpayers' purse.

CHAPTER ONE

HAIL, HAIL, THE GANG'S ALL HERE

OW VERY DIFFERENT WERE THE EMOTIONS AROUSED BY BRIAN and Mila Mulroney when they first arrived in Ottawa ten years earlier. After Mulroney won the leadership of the Progressive Conservative Party in a close fight to a fourth ballot with Joe Clark on June 23, 1983, the city and then the country moved enthusiastically to support the new leader and his party.

Canadians were tired of the Liberals, and they were particularly fed up with Pierre Trudeau. He had held office for almost sixteen uninterrupted years, and even many Liberals were bracing themselves for a clobbering, admitting privately it was time for a change. Events moved quickly after Mulroney's leadership victory. In late August 1983, he won a by-election in the safe Tory riding of Central Nova, a Nova Scotia seat vacated for him by his close friend Elmer MacKay. Six months later Trudeau announced he was retiring from politics; by June 1984, the Liberals had a new leader, John Turner.

During that year as leader of the opposition, Mulroney and his closest advisers prepared for power. Conservative forces had made liberal and left-wing politics unfashionable in the United States and Great Britain; the same mood had permeated much of Canadian political thinking. And Mulroney was an attractive leader. He said all the right things — that he was a consensus-builder, not a confrontational leader; that his government would not tamper with the country's social programs; that he would restore fiscal prudence to the government, making it leaner but not meaner; that he would improve strained relations with the United States; that a Conservative government would let business flourish by eliminating red tape and other annoying barriers to progress. Coached by canny advisers from the Republican Party in the United States, he decided to position himself as a statesman, above the fray of brass-knuckle politics. He would be an issues man while his deputies, experienced parliamentary veterans like Yukoner Erik Nielsen and Don Mazankowski from Alberta, could handle the down and dirty political dealmaking. It hardly mattered what Mulroney said. The Liberals had no new ideas, and Canadians watched the new Tory leader with growing excitement and curiosity.

In 1983 Brian Mulroney was an unknown quantity. In 1976 he had run for his party's leadership and been defeated by Joe Clark, an Albertan he'd known since their university days in student politics. Although he failed to win, Mulroney captured the media's attention — he was handsome, smart, and outgoing, and he looked like a winner. They didn't forget him, even after he went back to his Montreal law firm for a year and then, in 1977, joined the Iron Ore Company of Canada, an American-owned branch plant of the Hanna Mining Company of Cleveland, Ohio. Within a year he replaced the retiring president of Iron Ore, Bill Bennett, and he and Mila moved their growing family into a picturesque stone house on Belvedere Road in tony Westmount. For the next several years Mulroney gathered directorships on several corporate boards, the most important being that of the Canadian Imperial Bank of Commerce. His nomination was sponsored by broadcasting mogul Doug Bassett and by Conrad Black, whose vast array of business interests included a significant stake in Hanna Mining. Mulroney was also known for his charitable and community work, especially his efforts on behalf of his alma mater, St. Francis Xavier University, for which he raised $11 million, exceeding the university's target by $4 million.

This was the public face of Brian Mulroney, the personality

Canadians heard about from time to time as reporters and colum-
nists continued to keep an eye on a man many believed would have
a great future in politics. The private side was a different matter.
John Sawatsky's 1991 biography, *Mulroney: The Politics of Ambition*, revealed that Mulroney had been so embittered by his loss to
Joe Clark that he had slipped into a dark world of depression and
despair. During his early years as president of Iron Ore he spent a
great deal of time seeking consolation with his buddies in Montreal
bars, and he squandered time and money investing in various business enterprises, some of which ended in utter failure.

Mulroney emerged from this black hole only after an ultimatum
from his wife. He sought help for his drinking, turning to Maurice
Mayer, a Montreal developer and Tory bagman, for private counselling. And he decided to take another run at the Tory leadership.

From 1979, he and his closest friends devoted their energies to
wresting the leadership from Joe Clark, another fact that was not
known to most Canadians at the time. Some — a few journalists and
the key people around Clark — were suspicious, but Mulroney was
successful at keeping his public image intact: he was a prominent
Montreal businessman, a happy family man, a strong Progressive
Conservative loyal to Clark. And when Mulroney finally did succeed
in winning the leadership in 1983, most observers thought he
deserved it. Clark had been an inept leader who blew away his 1979
minority government in a stupid act of bravado, allowing the
Liberals to outnumber him in the House of Commons and defeat his
budget on December 13, 1979. The episode showed Clark to be a
poor strategist who seriously underestimated his opponents; his
party never forgave him.

The Conservatives' electoral victory in 1984 crowned Mulroney's
leadership and seemed almost preordained: John Turner's creaky performance, a Liberal election team that dissolved into chaos, a scandal
over hundreds of patronage appointments of departing Grits, and an

almost faultless campaign by the Conservatives ensured a majority. But no one had predicted the largest majority in Canadian history. The voters were clearly smitten with Mulroney: he lacked Trudeau's snobby arrogance, Clark's dopey awkwardness. People were charmed by his beautiful wife and children. They even believed him when he said he would clean up government and reform the pork-barrel politics of the Liberals. Journalists were delighted to have an energetic new team of players to write about, and many took a secret pleasure in watching humbled Grits, from former ministers to once-mighty aides, trawling the Sparks Street Mall with empty briefcases, in search of elusive connections and consulting contracts.

Mulroney brought real change to Ottawa, including a roster of trusted advisers, many of whom were virtual strangers to the capital. His new principal secretary was Bernard Roy, a Laval law school chum, the best man at his wedding, and his law partner at Ogilvy Renault in Montreal. Handsome and reserved, Roy seemed to offer a cautious counterweight to his ebullient boss. Mulroney's policy adviser was Fred Doucet, a short, fair-haired fireplug of a man from Cape Breton who had been a buddy since Mulroney's undergraduate years at St. Francis Xavier. Doucet had served as chief of staff during Mulroney's year as opposition leader, a period long enough to teach the city's mandarins to beware of him; not only was he ferociously loyal to "the Boss," as they all called Mulroney, but he had a large ego and an inflated sense of his own importance. Doucet held a doctorate in educational administration and insisted that underlings call him "Dr. Doucet," not realizing the city was full of polite, self-effacing men and women with PhDs, including a number of his PMO colleagues who would never dream of calling themselves "Doctor." People ridiculed his pretensions, the worst insult in the deadly serious game of politics.

Another staff member with a strong personality was Bill Fox, the press secretary. Chunky and rumpled, a rough diamond from Timmins, Fox had been a newspaper journalist for seventeen years before joining Mulroney's office. But that common bond got him nowhere with his former colleagues in the press gallery, especially when his gruff affability switched to temper tantrums and a bullying vindictiveness. Peter White, a classmate from Laval law school and a former senior executive with Conrad Black's holding company, Hollinger Inc., who was nominally in charge of patronage appointments, was a complete newcomer, as was another old Mulroney chum, policy adviser Charles McMillan, a York University economics professor whose brother, Tom, had been elected as a Conservative MP from Prince Edward Island. Keith Morgan arrived from a job with Bell Canada in Montreal to handle Mulroney's constituency affairs.

Bonnie Brownlee, Mila's new assistant, would stay with her boss for nearly nine years. They worked out of freshly renovated and furnished offices on the ground floor of the Langevin Building, the first office for a prime minister's wife on the Hill. Two young men, former Sears executive Bill Pristanski and lawyer Hubert Pichet, were hired as executive assistants; Keith Hamilton and Peter Ohrt came in as senior aides; and another member of the St. FX crowd, Patrick MacAdam, who had been working as a legislative assistant for Alberta Tory MP Gordon Towers, moved over to help Mulroney with caucus liaison. This was a curious assignment; looking after the caucus was one of Deputy Prime Minister Erik Nielsen's formal responsibilities.

Nielsen, the MP for Yukon for twenty-eight years, was technically on board too, simply because he was the number two man in the government. But he soon discovered that the new prime minister's staff regarded him as the skunk at the garden party. A former backer of Joe Clark, Nielsen was there as a result of historical circumstance. When Clark stepped down after the January 1983 Winnipeg leadership review to put a campaign team together, Nielsen had been appointed interim leader of the opposition. He held the position for over seven months, from February 2 to September 6, 1983, the period that included Mulroney's leadership victory on June 11 and his by-election triumph on August 29.

Once elected to Parliament Mulroney was able to assume command of the caucus, and Nielsen stepped aside to become deputy leader with an office right next door. Giving Nielsen deputy status was designed to bring the still-bitter Clark loyalists on side, but the shotgun marriage never took. Within hours of becoming the leader of the opposition, Mulroney created a distance between them that Nielsen found not only inefficient but downright offensive.

During the months that Nielsen was interim leader, he believed it was important to have immediate access to the Tory House leader and to the whip. He installed direct phone lines between their offices; when he picked up the designated phone it rang immediately in the House leader's office or the whip's office. The system was reciprocal. When Nielsen moved out of the leader's office to make way for Mulroney, he left the system in place. One day Nielsen called Mulroney on the hot line and Mulroney answered. "The next time I tried to do it, it was blocked," said Nielsen, "although he still had the direct line to me."

To add insult to injury Erik Nielsen discovered he had to make an appointment with Mulroney's secretary to see the leader. If there was ever a chance for Mulroney to win over this proud and rather stiff-necked parliamentarian, he blew it. Not that Nielsen would ever betray his dismay with a whisper to anyone. To Nielsen, "Old Velcro-Lips," as he was dubbed on the Hill, loyalty was everything.

It was during that same year in opposition that Mulroney sent his shadow cabinet into the halls of bureaucracy to study the machinery of government, an effort directed by Nielsen. They visited high-ranking bureaucrats to discuss how their ministries functioned and then returned to their own offices to study organization charts and ways to change the system to suit themselves. Once again, Nielsen hid his disquiet when he discovered that Mulroney had a second task force duplicating his own study, a "sub rosa" group as he called it, under the direction of Don Mazankowski. For the first time a flicker of doubt about Mulroney ran through Nielsen's mind.

After the Conservatives won power, Mulroney's hand-picked

staff rushed eagerly into their new quarters in the Langevin Building, the splendid old office block facing the Centre Block that is home to the Privy Council Office and senior officials of the Prime Minister's Office.[1] The next few weeks were among the most extraordinary in Canadian history as a determined group of politicians and their aides turned old systems and hidebound traditions upside down.

The new forty-member cabinet was the largest ever named by a prime minister. With such a big caucus, one representing every part of Canada for the first time in years (Trudeau had had no MPs west of Manitoba in his last government), Mulroney was determined to give every region its own cabinet minister. Deeply suspicious of what they saw as a rigid and Liberal public service, the Tories invented a new rank of highly paid political bureaucrat, the chief of staff for each department, whose influence was supposed to counterbalance that of the deputy minister. The system might have worked but for serious personnel problems. For the most part, the new ministers were unable to attract experienced senior people to serve in these positions. Many chiefs of staff were young political aides who more properly should have served as executive assistants. Few had any institutional memory, any understanding of the complexity of their departments, or any knowledge of the legislation that governed their operations — especially with respect to the awarding of contracts. They often hid their ignorance behind blustering bravado. When a bureaucrat would explain why something could not be done, the chiefs of staff resorted to "make it happen" orders, complaining of bureaucratic red tape or misplaced loyalties, reasoning that if the public servant weren't still under the sway of the Liberals he or she would stop throwing up roadblocks and start showing results. The fallout was predictable: within months nearly forty chiefs of staff were in conflict with the top levels of the bureaucracy, and any good will that might have existed in the beginning quickly evaporated. (There were some exceptions, among them Jodi White, an old Ottawa hand who had worked for Joe Clark for many years. She moved to External Affairs when he became the minister, and she was well liked by this stuffy, rather inbred group of public servants. Another who commanded respect and affection was Bill Musgrove, Flora MacDonald's chief of staff at Communications; he was an experienced public servant who had been seconded to the job.)

Don Mazankowski's new chief of staff, Jamie Burns, made his mark in a different fashion. While the Tories were still in opposition, Burns and a few other aides, helped by a number of friendly bureaucrats, had assembled hit lists of public servants considered to be closet Liberals. After the Conservatives' victory, Burns went on organized search-and-destroy missions to root them out. Ministers and their senior staff combed through lists of upper-level public servants looking for names of old Liberal aides or related hacks. At one meeting in late 1984, Secretary of State Walter McLean, a Presbyterian minister from Kitchener, and his junior minister, Jack Murta, a farmer from Carman, Manitoba, pored over a list of their senior bureaucrats and spied the name of one assistant deputy minister who had been named in an Ottawa *Citizen* column the day before. The column identified him as a former colleague of another public servant who had left the bureaucracy to serve as a senior Liberal policy adviser. Ergo, their bureaucrat was suspect. In fact, the only political party this bureaucrat had ever worked for, before he went into the public service, was the Progressive Conservative Party. Tipped off that he was under suspicion, the disgusted public servant left the government for a university job.

All over town dedicated public servants fell under a cloud because someone once saw them eating lunch with this Liberal cabinet minister or that former Trudeau aide. And the people who actually were Liberals found themselves in real trouble — many were fired, demoted, or permanently sidelined. Among the first high-profile bureaucrats to be terminated was Joel Bell, head of the Canada Development Investment Corporation; another was Canada Council director Tim Porteous, once an aide to Trudeau. Many others followed them.

Another new development in that fall of 1984 was the sudden

emergence of powerful lobbyists. Until the Mulroney government came to office, lobbying was a discreet profession in the city, practised by a few well-connected Ottawa hands. Men like Bill Neville, who had worked for Liberal cabinet minister Judy LaMarsh before joining the Tories as an aide to Clark, and Bill Lee, who had worked with the Liberals for years and had been John Turner's 1984 campaign director, were part of the capital scene. They had lived and worked there for years, knew the players, understood what was permissible and what was beyond the bounds of ethical conduct. They concentrated on briefing their clients about ministry organization, legislation, and the government agenda. Their fees were paid in the form of monthly or quarterly retainers.

When Mulroney came to Ottawa, he was followed by a flock of cronies who were brazen in their determination to cash in on the friendship. They opened "consulting" or "government relations" offices, bragged openly about their access to the Boss, and devised billing systems based on retainers and — a new wrinkle — contingency fees, or percentages of the action should their efforts be successful. Some, the minnows in the Ottawa pond, opened modest one-man bucket shops in shabby office buildings; others, the barracudas, confident of raking in significant revenues, leased suites in the most expensive towers in Ottawa and filled them with teak tables, leather chairs, expensive art, and eager-beaver support staff. The barracudas were easy to spot. Until they wangled their way into the private Rideau Club, they made Hy's Restaurant their lunchtime watering hole.

It was here one could find former Newfoundland premier Frank Moores, one of the most powerful new players in Ottawa.[2] Moores had left his family's food business after it was sold to the frozen-food giant Birdseye to enter politics, and in 1968 he won election as the federal MP for Bonavista-Trinity-Conception. During his years in Ottawa, he shared an apartment with another rookie MP, Don Mazankowski, and the two have been close ever since. In 1969 Moores also took on the presidency of the national Progressive Conservative

Party, but he left the post and his federal seat in 1970 to run for the leadership of the Newfoundland Progressive Conservative Party. He won, and by 1972 he was the premier of the province. It was in the late 1970s that he met Mulroney, who was then president of Iron Ore, Newfoundland's single largest employer.

Moores remained in office, undefeated, until 1979, when he resigned and moved to Montreal, leaving behind his first wife, Dorothy, seven children, and a very expensive divorce settlement. With a new wife, Manitoba Tory Janis Johnson (his executive assistant during the years when he was the national president of the party), and their son Stefan, he settled in Montreal and went about the business of making his friend Brian Mulroney the next leader of the party. How he supported himself in these years is something of a mystery, but he was helped by a generous retainer from Iron Ore. During this period his second marriage failed, but there seemed to be no hard feelings.

It was after Mulroney won the leadership in 1983 that Moores moved to Ottawa with his third wife, advertising executive Beth Champion, and bought a small lobbying company called Alta Nova from Jamie Burns, Pat Walsh, Peter Thomson, and Fred von Veh, all of whom had been close to Mazankowski and who found work with him as senior aides after the 1984 victory. Moores moved Alta Nova from its no-frills quarters at 130 Albert Street into the imposing new Metropolitan Life Building at 50 O'Connor Street; Hy's was just downstairs. He was a frequent lunchtime patron, along with his partners, Gary Ouellet and Gerry Doucet. Ouellet, a Quebec City lawyer and world-class magician who had originally come to Ottawa to work as chief of staff to junior Transport Minister Benoit Bouchard, was close to Mulroney; so was Doucet, a former Tory provincial cabinet minister from Halifax. He'd been a classmate of Mulroney's at St. FX, and his brother, Fred, was just around the corner in the PMO. Greg Alford, Moores's former aide in Newfoundland politics, was named president, and new directors — among them former

Liberal cabinet minister Francis Fox, former Imperial Oil chairman Jack Armstrong, former U.S. ambassador to Canada Paul Robinson, and Robert Shea, Mulroney's old pal from Boston — were added to the team. After a year in business under the new name of Government Consultants International, Moores and his partners had thirty-five employees, billings of $4.6 million, and a client list that had the city's other lobbyists grinding their teeth in envy. It included such firms as American Express Canada, Bombardier, Saint John Shipbuilding Ltd., Gulf + Western, Mercedes-Benz, Iron Ore Company of Canada, Nabisco Brands Canada, Honeywell Ltd., and the Pharmaceutical Manufacturers Association of Canada.

The clout wielded by Moores, Ouellet, and Doucet was evident to everyone in the city. Indeed, in the months and years to come, Moores would have the power to overturn cabinet decisions — and did just that. "No question," confirmed Erik Nielsen, the only ex-minister willing to go on the record about Moores's power. "He could get virtually anything he wanted done."

There was unease about the growing influence of the new lobbyists, who made no pretense of quiet discretion. There were other power brokers, however, who kept a resolutely low profile. The city's more observant mandarins noted the clout of Guy Charbonneau, the newly appointed Speaker of the Senate. In return for his public support of Joe Clark, Mulroney had extracted a Senate seat for Charbonneau, a Montreal insurance broker, in 1979; now he was able to give him the Speaker's job. Charbonneau was a close and long-time counsellor to the prime minister; he had been his chief financial strategist since the 1976 leadership battle and had led the fundraising effort in the 1983 campaign. From Mulroney's first days in power Charbonneau was a force to be reckoned with, but he remained almost invisible for the next nine years despite his public role in Parliament.

Another major player was David Angus, the new chairman of the party's fundraising arm, the PC Canada Fund. One of the leader's privileges is the appointment of the party's chief money man, and Mulroney removed Terry Yates, the man who had run the party's wildly successful direct-mail fundraising system, to make way for Angus, a lawyer at Stikeman Elliott in Montreal. Angus had been a fundraiser for Mulroney's 1976 run at the leadership and had enjoyed some notoriety when *The Gazette* published a story saying he had successfully canvassed Montreal financier and Mulroney patron Paul Desmarais for $10,000 for the campaign. In 1975 Angus had set up a registered holding company he called Le Fond de Février 1976 (the February 1976 Fund) to handle the money he raised for Mulroney's leadership bid. He did not participate in the 1983 campaign because he was vice-chairman of the regulations committee for the convention and had to remain neutral. The day after Mulroney won, he asked Angus to take on the chairmanship of the PC Canada Fund. Balding, hot-tempered, and fiercely partisan, Angus was the one who signed the cheques from PC Canada Fund bank accounts, many of them to cover the Mulroneys' expenses.

A regular out-of-town visitor was Sam Wakim. A Toronto lawyer who was part of the St. Francis Xavier crowd, Wakim had served briefly as an MP in the Clark government. His role was to keep Mulroney briefed on how the government was playing to the folks in Toronto. What were the papers saying? What were the television pundits predicting? What was the reaction to Mulroney among Toronto movers and shakers? Wakim called almost every day from Toronto to keep him posted.

The circle around Mulroney was remarkably small, in fact. Its members were invariably loyalists and close personal friends. There was no more complete list of these trusted insiders than the one provided to staff at 24 Sussex Drive. Instead of being directed through the PMO, these individuals — fewer than forty colleagues, relatives, and chums — were allowed direct access to the residences, along with their spouses, companions, or guests. Their calls went through, their mail was delivered, they could visit unescorted by PMO aides. The list included some — but not all — of the PMO staff. One or two names were to fall off in later years (among them, Erik Nielsen's) and others were added, but when the new government swung into action, this roster was a reliable guide to the true insiders.

Aside from junior aides like Pichet and Pristanski, Bonnie Brownlee, and Ginette Pilotte, Mulroney's personal secretary who had been with him since his days at Iron Ore, the in-group included the new senior PMO officials and their spouses, people such as Bernard and Madeleine Roy, Fred Doucet and his companion, Alina Kawecki, Bill Fox, Pat and Janet MacAdam, and Keith and Gisèle Morgan.

Among Mulroney's closest cronies from Montreal were Frank and Beth Moores, Guy and Yolande Charbonneau, and David Angus. Others in this group were Laval law school classmate Jean Bazin, a lawyer and partner at Byers Casgrain, and his companion, Denise Trudeau. Michel Cogger, another Montreal lawyer, had been one of the prime minister's closest friends since their days together at Laval; in 1976, Cogger and his wife, Erica, had invited the Mulroneys to their Eastern Townships farm to discuss his running for the leadership and had encouraged him to do it. Jonathan and Diane Deitcher made the list; Deitcher handled Mulroney's stock portfolio. Paul and Jacqueline Desmarais were another pair of insiders; Desmarais, chairman of Power Corporation and among the wealthiest men in Canada, was one of Mulroney's earliest mentors in Montreal. Jacqueline Desmarais and Mila had also become close. Paul Desmarais, Jr., and his wife, Helen, were on the list as well. So were Michelle and Roger Nantel. Nantel, a dapper Montreal advertising and public relations executive, had been in charge of communications strategy in Quebec during the 1984 election campaign and was one of Mulroney's most trusted advisers.

A second group of Montrealers coalesced around Mila more than her husband. It included Roger and Andrée Beaulieu; Andrée was one of Mila's best friends in Montreal. They were members of what they called the "ballet group," women who started attending the ballet together in 1974 and remained close, supporting each other in times of trouble as well as shopping, lunching, and playing together. Cathy Campeau was another member of the Montreal ballet group; her former husband, Arthur, was a law partner of Mulroney's when the women met. Westmount neighbours Harvey and Shirley Corn were included; Harvey Corn was the Mulroneys' notary. Shirley Ann Mass and Sylvia Renusa, more ballet group girlfriends, were on the list with their husbands, lawyers Israel (Sonny) Mass and Rajko Renusa. Nancy Southam, a freelance journalist and Southam heiress based in Montreal, had been a friend of both Mulroneys for years; she too was on the roster.

The last category of Montrealers who had entrée to the residences was family: Mulroney's sister Olive Elliott and her husband, Richard; his mother, Irene, and his brother, Gary. Mila's family list included her father, Dr. Dimitrije Pivnicki, a well-known Montreal psychiatrist; her mother, Bogdana, the family matriarch (who worked for many years for Montreal antique dealer Phyllis Friedman), and her younger sister, Ivana, and brother, John.

Very few Ottawans made it into the inner circle. Despite being a Clark supporter, Bill Neville and his wife were two who did. Another was Michael McSweeney, who had served as the Mulroneys' driver during the 1983 leadership campaign, stayed with them in Pictou County during the 1983 Nova Scotia by-election, and even babysat their children. There were almost no Torontonians except Sam and Marty Wakim and Norman and Anna Ruth Atkins. Atkins had been co-chairman of the Tories' 1984 federal election campaign; at the time he ran Camp Advertising, which won the lion's share of federal advertising contracts once the party was in power. Also worth noting were Robert and Trudy Shea; Bob Shea, a confidant of Mulroney since their days together at St. FX, was a Boston insurance broker who had raised a great deal of money for the 1983 leadership run in the United States.

Other than staff and spouses, there were very few women in this charmed circle. An exception was Janis Johnson, the second wife of

Frank Moores. Manitoba-born Johnson was close to both Mulroneys even after her divorce from Moores, and she had worked hard on the 1983 leadership bid. She was, for a brief time, the national director of the Tory party.

The Mulroneys were sociable people who promised to open up 24 Sussex Drive to Canadians, a refreshing change for a city with lingering memories of a prime minister who had grown more and more reclusive. They planned to do a lot of entertaining, and they wanted everything to be perfect. Within a day or two of taking office, Mulroney had arranged a contract for designer Giovanni Mowinckel, initiating extensive redecorating at the two official residences, Mila's new office, and his own suites in the Langevin Building and in the House of Commons. David Angus used PC Canada Fund money to pay the bills for the extras, sometimes corresponding directly with Mowinckel. Mila's assistant Bonnie Brownlee usually routed the bills from the decorator and other suppliers to Fred Doucet, who in turn sent them to Angus for payment.

The Mulroneys then needed household staff and in particular, a good chef. Mila's good friend Pierrette Lucas, who had once run unsuccessfully for the Tories in Montreal and was now working as a public servant in Ottawa, introduced them to Kurt Waldele, the talented young chef who ran the kitchen at the National Arts Centre. Here was just the fellow, she said, to orchestrate the dinner parties, cocktail receptions, business lunches, and other events at 24 Sussex Drive. The Mulroneys auditioned Waldele by hiring him to cater some of their early parties, assignments he took on with the blessing of Don MacSween, then the director general of the NAC. MacSween wasn't naive; the last thing he'd do was offend the new prime minister or his wife. Despite his accommodation, it happened anyway.

One day he received a call from Fred Doucet.

"Doucet wanted Kurt to work for the Mulroneys as their chef," MacSween said. "The deal was that he'd work for them half-time and for the NAC half-time. The Prime Minister's Office would split his salary with the NAC." No dice, MacSween told Doucet. "Mrs. Mulroney is welcome to offer him a full-time job if she likes, and he's perfectly free to accept. I'll find another chef. But you know as well as I do that if the prime minister is having a dinner party and we need Kurt here at the Arts Centre, the prime minister is going to win. Every time." MacSween said he also knew that if Waldele went to 24 Sussex Drive half-time, no matter what the understanding about sharing, he'd be gone full-time and the NAC would be paying half his salary. So, no thanks.

Doucet was not happy with MacSween's decision, but eventually he worked out another arrangement. Waldele was asked to help select a new chef, a full-time person to work at the house all day, and to assist in his training. When a major event or state dinner was planned, Waldele would be brought in to help. After a competition among eleven chefs, the Mulroneys hired a tall, freckle-faced redhead, François Martin, as their new chef and household coordinator at $28,000 a year. A graduate of Montreal's highly regarded hotel school, the Institut de Tourisme et d'Hôtellerie de Québec, he was as talented as Waldele, he loved difficult assignments involving tricky protocol, and he was excited by the prestige of the position. At age twenty-eight, he also had the constitution of an ox, an important attribute for a man who was expected to arrive at 6 a.m. to prepare breakfast and who rarely left before midnight, seven days a week. "It was exciting," he recalled. "Everything was fun and within two weeks I saw that I was making a difference. And my parents were so proud of me."

The new staff were under the gun as soon as they were hired. The Mulroneys had a series of cocktail parties planned for December; everything had to be ready by then. When the holiday season arrived, the house looked splendid and the food was memorable. And there was so much to celebrate: many of those who attended the Christmas parties at 24 Sussex Drive that year were toasting their recently bestowed honours, contracts, diplomatic and judicial appointments, or positions on government boards, agencies, and commissions. New

Queen's Counsellors Bernard Roy, David Angus, Gary Ouellet, Jean Sirois, and Stanley Hartt rubbed shoulders with new board members at the Canada Development Investment Corporation such as Lucien Bouchard. Pierrette Lucas found to her delight that she was off to a new job as consul general in Philadelphia. Roger Nantel was enjoying the benefits of dozens of advertising and public relations contracts and, with an Ontario Tory, Peter Simpson, was sharing control of the government's annual $60-million advertising budget. For Mulroney's close Tory associates, this was life at its sunny best.

But soon enough it would start to rain on the Tories' parade. Rumours of unsavoury practices, patronage windfalls, and links with organized crime began to drift across the city. Curiosity about the new power brokers gave way to more critical scrutiny and some startling discoveries. The prime minister himself did not escape this examination. Many people, especially die-hard Joe Clark loyalists, continued to ask uncomfortable questions about where Mulroney had found the money to finance his 1983 leadership campaign. While a few of these rumours might have posed serious threats to Mulroney and a number of his closest associates, the matter of his 1983 fundraising should have melted away. What kept the issue alive was an extraordinary series of burglaries in Montreal.

THE BREAK-INS

O
N THE NIGHT OF SEPTEMBER 26, 1984, NINE DAYS AFTER
Brian Mulroney was sworn in as Canada's eighteenth
prime minister, three men broke into the basement of a
heritage building at 50 Rue des Brésoles in Old Montreal
and thereby begat a mystery that is still quietly discussed in the Tory
party. "It's our Watergate," cackled Michel Cogger to one Parliament
Hill aide.

Using a pair of specially designed giant pliers to twist the door
lock until its cartridge snapped, the burglars found it easy to gain
entry and then make their way to the main-floor suite of Nantel et
Associés, the advertising company headed by one of Brian
Mulroney's closest friends. Within minutes the burglars were inside
Nantel's office and the adjoining office of the firm's vice-president,
Rodrigue Pageau. They looked around quickly, listened carefully,
and then relaxed. They had not triggered the alarm and no one was
in the building; there was plenty of time. First they worked their way
through Nantel's filing cabinets, setting aside the documents they
wanted. Then they loaded the Canon photocopier with extra paper
and copied the files they'd chosen, stopping only to add more paper
and then more toner. It took at least four hours to complete Nantel's
files. While they laboured, Nantel himself was a happy guest at a
reception aboard the royal yacht *Britannia* berthed in Toronto's harbour, hosted by Her Majesty the Queen.

The burglars gathered their photocopies, replaced the files, and picked up Nantel's Apple Macintosh computer, several diskettes, and the Canon copier. They took as well Nantel's income tax returns going back to 1970, his company's financial statements for the previous seventeen years, and his collection of 500 business cards.

A search of Pageau's office next door proved less fruitful. Pageau had died of cancer three weeks earlier, and the executors of his estate had already removed his files and personal papers. The burglars could add to their stash only a case of Coca-Cola, a box of coffee, and a 100-kilogram steel safe they found in the basement, which contained about $500 in cash. Then they left the building as quietly as they came. It was only when Nantel's staff saw that the copier was missing the next morning that they realized they'd been robbed; it was only after they'd gone through their files that they knew why.

Roger Nantel and Rodrigue Pageau were among Mulroney's most valued lieutenants. Nantel had been Mulroney's French-language speechwriter and was in charge of communications for the party's Quebec wing, while Pageau had served as Mulroney's top political strategist in the province during the 1983 leadership campaign. The burglars who broke into their offices hoped their files and diskettes would contain highly confidential information about the contributors to Mulroney's leadership campaign, the size of their donations, and the strategies employed in both the 1983 leadership drive and the 1984 election.

On September 28, two nights after the break-in at Nantel's offices, there was a second burglary, this one at the Conservative Party's Quebec headquarters at 625 Rue du Président Kennedy. The thieves got in and out of the eighth-floor office so tidily that no one noticed anything was amiss until three days later. But the office staff was uneasy during those days; the place felt different, they said to one another. Jean Guilbeault, the director of legal services for the party, picked up on the mood, recalled the break-in at Nantel's office, and knew that the burglars at Rue des Brésoles had taken everything they could find on donors to Mulroney's 1983 leadership campaign. Guilbeault walked into the offices of the PC Canada Fund, which took up a section of the party's suite, and carefully examined the filing cabinets. He saw immediately that the drawers had been pried open.

Anxiously, Guilbeault checked the other rooms. Doors that were usually kept secured were unlocked, and traces of wood dust on the floor showed the burglars had used crowbars to pull them open. Once again it became clear the theft was of information. "We saw they had searched everywhere," Guilbeault said after the break-in was discovered. "They shook through many files, because we could see things had not been put back in their place. I imagine they got a pack of information, but I can't say what they stole. They opened the lists of contributors."

The burglars were after the names of all the people who had given the Tories money in 1984 and the size of their donations. They wanted the identities of the party's bagmen, whom they canvassed, and how much they collected. Once again, they were looking for the names of individuals who contributed to Mulroney's leadership campaign and the amounts each gave. This time the thieves found some of the material they'd searched for unsuccessfully in Rodrigue Pageau's office. They found the files he'd kept on the leadership.

A few days after the second break-in, Montreal police received an anonymous tip that the safe from Nantel's office could be found in a certain location near the Port of Montreal. It had been opened by experts, emptied, and wiped clean of all fingerprints. Detective Sergeant Yvon Giroux of the Montreal Urban Community Police was in charge of the case. He later told reporters that after an extensive investigation turned up no clues, he had reluctantly declared the case inactive.

These two burglaries were not the only ones in the Montreal area connected to Mulroney that year. Eight months earlier, in March 1984, a thief had stolen a copy of a cancelled cheque from the

Pointe-Claire offices of Voyageurs Marine Construction Company Limited, an underwater construction company partly owned by Walter Wolf, a millionaire entrepreneur and financier long rumoured to be a significant Mulroney backer.

Austrian by birth, Wolf came to Montreal in the 1960s where he made a fortune in the construction business. He took out Canadian citizenship, but soon discovered the tax benefits of living and working elsewhere; he relocated his business headquarters to Bermuda and his residence to Switzerland. But he maintained his ties to Canada. He kept his citizenship and a home in Montreal; he sponsored a Canadian Grand Prix auto racing team; and he married a Canadian woman, Barbara Stewart, whose grandfather had been premier of Prince Edward Island.

Within a few days of the robbery at Voyageurs Marine there was another, this one at 3491 Redpath, the Westmount townhouse of David Angus. Angus was away on holiday at the time and later told police he had lost only some cuff-links and a stamp collection. In a 1994 interview he said the burglars came in through a basement window, ransacked the house, and stole candlesticks, Scotch, and champagne as well as all his jewellery. The RCMP never interviewed him about the break-in.

Four robberies, each one related in some way to Tories and to Brian Mulroney. Even though Angus was quick to dismiss any suggestion that the one at his home was politically motivated, the Montreal police concluded, soon after the last burglary, that the goal in each case was the same: the precise details concerning donations to the prime minister's campaign to win the leadership of his party.

Although the police were never able to solve these crimes, Montreal *Gazette* reporter William Marsden did track down one of the burglars in early December 1984. The man, an ex-convict who had worked as an undercover agent for both the RCMP and various United States police forces on several important drug investigations, agreed to tell his story to Marsden on condition he wasn't identified. The story he told, which turned out to be not quite complete, was that he had broken into Walter Wolf's Pointe-Claire offices to look for information about the financing of Mulroney's leadership campaign. One of the things he stole was a copy of a cheque for $80,231.78 signed by Wolf and made out to Voyageurs Marine president Sandor Kocsis on January 17, 1983, just a week before the Tory party's convention in Winnipeg. It was in Winnipeg that the issue of leadership was fought fiercely and behind the scenes by pro-Clark and pro-Mulroney factions. Clark won support from 66.9 per cent of the convention's delegates in the leadership review vote, but he deemed it not high enough to continue. He announced his decision to recommend that a leadership convention be held in June in Ottawa.

Detective Robert Fuller, an officer with the Montreal police who investigated the theft with Detective Sergeant Giroux, told Marsden that the cheque, written on the Bank of Butterfield in Bermuda — a bank that was to figure in a number of stories about the federal Tories over the next few years — was cashed in Bermuda and the money brought into Canada in a briefcase. "[Fuller] said he has learned that at least some of the money was used in Mulroney's bid for the Tory leadership in June, 1983," Marsden reported.

The ex-convict told Marsden the RCMP had interviewed him twice about the break-in, but he had told the police only half of what he knew. "Some of the stuff I have refused to divulge," he confided to Marsden. "Some things I have admitted or not admitted." But he did tell Marsden he'd taken the cheque and other documents after being instructed by persons he would not name to look for anything related to Mulroney's leadership financing. It was part of a "private investigation," he explained, adding that he had not taken part in the burglaries at Nantel's office nor at Tory party headquarters. The burglaries were nevertheless connected, he claimed; they were all designed to get information linking Walter Wolf and Mulroney.

The Globe and Mail's Richard Cléroux, who covered the break-ins extensively, reported that the Montreal police who investigated the theft at Voyageurs Marine "came back convinced there had never been a break-in." They believed that the man who had talked to Marsden was actually a disgruntled ex-employee who had stolen the copy of the cheque and then sent it to a Toronto journalist, saying he'd been told the money had been used to help finance the dump-Clark movement at the January 1983 convention. The thief pointed to the date on the cheque — January 17 — as proof. Michel Cogger, who had helped organize Mulroney's forces at that convention, and who happened to be Walter Wolf's lawyer, shrugged it off as a coincidence.

If there were suspicions abroad about Mulroney's 1983 fundraising and his donor list, most of the blame could be laid squarely at Mulroney's door. His conduct in the 1976 leadership race had hardly been reassuring. In that campaign all twelve candidates pledged to make their finances public; only eleven candidates did so. The odd man out was Mulroney.

"I was the party's national director at the time," explained John Laschinger, now a professional campaign manager and co-author, with journalist Geoffrey Stevens, of *Leaders and Lesser Mortals*, a book on the back rooms of politics. "I got a letter halfway through the campaign from Michael Meighen, who was working for Mulroney, saying they hadn't known they had to divulge and they weren't going to be able to."

The winner, Joe Clark, declared that he had spent $168,000, far less than almost-forgotten candidates Sinclair Stevens, who said he spent $294,000, Paul Hellyer, who declared costs of $287,000, and Claude Wagner, who revealed expenses of $266,000. Mulroney's campaign had clearly been the most lavish; there were estimates that he'd spent at least $500,000. Whatever he spent, one fact leaked out soon after the convention: he had a $250,000 campaign debt. It took years to pay it off, and even when he could have had some help in reducing the debt, he turned the offer down.

"The truth was," Laschinger chuckled, "that they all spent

twice what they raised. Seven or eight of the candidates were members of Parliament and the party was in pretty good shape financially, so I suggested we give each of the candidates thirty grand to help with their bills if they had filed their expenses with us. Brian never filed so he never got the thirty grand."

Mulroney would not disclose his contributors or his expenditures, not to the party nor to the public.

The Tory party put no limits on spending for the 1983 convention, and in its wisdom it also decided disclosure was not necessary this time. Still smarting over his 1976 image of extravagance and secret big-money financing, Mulroney's organizers were careful to construct an appearance of greater frugality. The candidate and his wife flew by regular aircraft, not private jets, and travelled in a plain station wagon driven by aide Michael McSweeney, instead of arriving in a limousine. Even so, some of Mulroney's past problems came back to haunt him. When his friend John Thompson came in to manage the last three weeks of the leadership campaign and tried to set up headquarters in the Ottawa Convention Centre, Bell Canada refused to hook up the phone lines. They'd never been paid for the equipment and charges of seven years earlier. "We've been waiting for him since 1976," sniped a Bell executive to another candidate's campaign manager. The money men quickly saw to it that the bill was paid and Mulroney carried on.

Mulroney's leadership bid was certainly the most expensive in 1983. Officially Joe Clark spent nearly $1.9 million, but in fact both he and John Crosbie doled out over $3 million each. Estimates of Mulroney's campaign soared well beyond that. Not surprisingly, Mulroney's spending caused plenty of comment, especially from those who had supported Clark. Their suspicions had been fuelled by a stunning comment from party elder Dalton Camp, a former national president of the Conservative Party. A few days before the January 1983 convention, Camp said on CTV's *Question Period* that Walter Wolf was one of several sources of "offshore" money for the campaign to dump Joe Clark as party leader. Camp's remarks were followed by more rumours about Wolf having given as much as $250,000 to the effort. The stories alleged that the Wolf money was used to cover the expenses of anti-Clark delegates at the Winnipeg convention. What lent these stories credibility was that Wolf had met Mulroney in 1978 through their mutual friend Michael Meighen, a former Laval classmate of Mulroney's who was then Wolf's lawyer. When Michel Cogger replaced Meighen as Wolf's lawyer, both Meighen and Cogger became directors of Voyageurs Marine, each earning $12,000 a year.

Mulroney dismissed the stories about Wolf's support as "rumours and innuendoes and half-truths." Wolf himself had various responses; at one time he said that he hadn't donated "a cent" to the dump-Clark movement. Another time, he admitted to donating $25,000 to Mulroney's leadership campaign. As for the $80,231.78 cheque made out to Sandor Kocsis, Wolf's explanation was that it was to pay for his one-third interest in Voyageurs Marine, not for Mulroney's campaign.

Michel Cogger is a clever man, but he cannot resist an opportunity to impress people, to drop names in an effort to win a little respect. And one name he liked to drop a lot was that of his good friend Brian Mulroney. Another was that of his flamboyant client Walter Wolf. On one occasion, he told a story that completely contradicted the official explanation of the Wolf money. Toronto writer Paul Palango describes the scene in *Above the Law*, his 1994 book about the way the RCMP has protected political elites in Canada.

RCMP Assistant Commissioner Rod Stamler was returning to Canada from London in 1984 and found himself seated next to a short, chubby man who introduced himself as Michel Cogger. Stamler told him he was simply a government employee. For the next several hours Cogger talked about his involvement in banking affairs in the Channel Islands, "a place which immediately brought one thing to Stamler's mind — money-laundering," wrote Palango.

Cogger boasted about his friendships with Mulroney and Wolf; he even told Stamler how he and Wolf had established a $50,000 fund in a Bermuda bank to help finance Mulroney's political ambitions. Stamler was intrigued by a character who could so casually discuss his banking arrangements in two tax havens beloved by money-launderers. Cogger even pulled out a copy of *Maclean's* magazine to show Stamler its story on the Montreal break-ins and said he was bracing himself for a tough interview about them on CTV's *W5* program. When their plane finally touched down in Montreal, Cogger offered Stamler a lift in the helicopter he used to commute between Ottawa and his home in the Eastern Townships. Stamler declined. Later, he wrote his superiors a memo describing the conversation.

When Stamler tuned in to *W5* a few weeks later, wrote Palango, he was astounded by the performances of Cogger and Wolf. Both told *W5* interviewer Jim Reed that Wolf had only a passing acquaintance with Mulroney. Wolf did not admit to donating money to Mulroney's campaign, only to giving $25,000 in directors' fees to "people that had been associated with Mr. Mulroney" — Meighen and Cogger. And these people, he insisted, worked for him as directors of his company, Voyageurs Marine. When Reed asked Wolf if his company wasn't just a money-laundering operation and if the stolen photocopy of the $80,231 cheque from Wolf wasn't the evidence of this, Wolf produced Sandor Kocsis, the president of Voyageurs Marine, to say the cheque was Wolf's down-payment for a one-third ownership in the company.

When the show was over, both Cogger and Wolf declared they had been vindicated. Stamler was so appalled by the difference between Cogger's story on the plane and his remarks on television that he wrote a second memo on the subject to the deputy commissioner of the RCMP. After that, he dismissed the story from his mind. He was head of the RCMP's drug enforcement unit and, wrote Palango, "investigating politicians wasn't his job in 1984."

Were the Montreal break-ins coordinated? Most police officers close to the investigations agree they were. One thing is certain: several people went to a great deal of trouble, expense, and risk to look for information about the financing of Brian Mulroney's 1983 leadership campaign. Why would they do so? Blackmail is one obvious answer. Perhaps someone thought the information would be so damaging — either to a donor or to the recipient — that it could be used as leverage for future favours.

A second possibility was suggested quite openly and on the record by Mulroney supporters, among them Roger Nantel. They said they believed the RCMP had staged the break-ins to gather potentially damaging information on the new Tory leader. Almost three years after the events, Nantel was still pointing the finger at the Mounties. In a long interview in June 1987, Nantel told Richard Cléroux that the theft of his collection of 500 business cards was proof of police interest in his associates. "They wanted to know if I might be linked to unmentionable people," he told Cléroux. Unmentionable people? An odd phrase, yet in the context of events involving Montreal Tories in the mid-1980s, it proved not such a strange choice of words. Many Quebec party members were deeply involved with unsavoury characters, from small-time hoods to out-and-out mobsters.

Nantel admitted he didn't have any proof of his allegations, but he claimed to have friendly sources within the force. "The Mounties led him to believe the break-ins, which he said 'were camouflaged to look like ordinary burglaries', were the work of a group within the RCMP working on the assumption 'there was dirty money behind Brian,'" Cléroux reported. To search his office legally, Nantel said, the RCMP would have to obtain a search warrant, and to do that they needed more concrete proof of wrongdoing. A neat little break-in would solve that problem. But, Nantel told Cléroux, "they found nothing because there was nothing." Nantel floated the far-fetched notion that the police could have been looking for evidence that Walter Wolf was an international arms dealer who had "largely financed Mulroney's operations." Spokesmen for the RCMP and the federal solicitor general, James

Kelleher, vehemently denied Nantel's allegations.

It was in 1987 as well that RCMP Detective Sergeant Denis Lapointe talked to Cléroux about the break-ins. He told Cléroux that he and Sergeant Walter Wafer had been assigned to the case "after the Prime Minister's Office or somebody close to the party in Ottawa asked us to keep an eye on it and see if we could help out." This was puzzling; the burglaries were clearly a case for the Montreal police, not for the Mounties, so Cléroux wondered why Lapointe — an expert on stock fraud, not break-and-enter — was involved. Cléroux decided Lapointe was on a fishing expedition, attempting to discover how much Cléroux knew and who he'd talked to.

"It's true," Lapointe admitted cheerfully in early 1994. "We were just nosing around. But someone in Ottawa was pulling our strings." Although Lapointe said he did not know who that "someone" was, he understood the orders to investigate the break-ins came from high up in the force. "The ultimate aim of the burglars," said Lapointe, "was to get the list of Mulroney donors. There was an official list and an unofficial list. Pageau kept the unofficial list." Lapointe's guess as to the player behind the burglaries? A Tory organizer who helped to marshal the Mulroney forces during the 1983 leadership race.

Still another theory, the one most favoured today, is that someone in the Mulroney camp staged the robberies, with the real motivation being the destruction of the financial records, including all the details of donors and expenditures that Mulroney himself steadfastly refused to make public.

Ten years have passed since the break-ins in Montreal; no arrests were ever made, no convictions, no explanations. Everyone — Mulroney's associates and two police forces — agrees the burglars were after financial records of his 1983 leadership campaign. But the questions remain. Who broke into those offices and what information was so valuable that at least three and possibly four burglaries were committed to find it?

CHAPTER THREE

THE MONEY MEN

I F THERE WAS ONE MAN WHO COULD HAVE GIVEN THE BURGLARS A complete list of Mulroney's financial backers for the Conservative Party leadership race, it was Guy Charbonneau. Not only had he been an important Tory bagman in Quebec for decades, he had been Mulroney's man since 1976 and the fundraising strategist of Mulroney's 1983 leadership campaign. Few senior officials in the party had a lower public profile than Charbonneau, but none had more influence on the new prime minister. Indeed, from the day of the electoral victory until Mulroney's last weeks in office, Charbonneau and the money men under his command were the most powerful individuals in the party.

On Thursday, October 4, 1984, seventeen days after being sworn in as prime minister and eight days after the break-in at Nantel's office, Mulroney nominated Charbonneau as Speaker of the Senate. The nomination was simply theatre: although the Senate had to vote its approval, the upper house has always accepted a prime minister's choice. The Speaker's job, which pays $84,000 a year in pay and allowances, is one many senators covet. Its perks include handsome offices complete with an ornate private dining room, a limousine and driver, generous entertainment budgets, and plenty of first-class travel. Like the Commons Speaker, the Senate Speaker enjoys a quasi-diplomatic status in Ottawa, receiving foreign dignitaries, hosting government receptions, lunches, and dinners, and the same privileges as a senior Canadian diplomat when travelling abroad.

All of this suited Charbonneau, but he never lost sight of his primary concerns — raising money for the Conservatives, smoothing the way to federal government deals for contract-hungry business-men, and fostering his own financial interests. There is no question that he has done well. He now lives in a penthouse ("rented," he points out crisply) at 2 Westmount Square in Montreal, right across the street from the office he shares with his old friend André Gingras. He owns a condominium on John's Island in Vero Beach, an area where a number of wealthy Canadians have winter homes. The Florida retreat, which he bought in 1985, a year after the Tories took power, is worth about $500,000 by Florida property estimates and is owned by Charbourg Holdings, a Nova Scotia–based personal holding company whose directors are Charbonneau and his wife, Yolande. Yolande Charbonneau is a painter who counts a number of her husband's business connections among her clients. Bernard Lamarre, the former chairman and CEO of Lavalin, is a patron and a generous one; Guy Charbonneau's insurance brokerage handled a great deal of Lavalin business over the years.[1] "I hear Bernard Lamarre bought at least one of her paintings for $30,000," says nov-elist Mordecai Richler, who carefully sifts all the Montreal gossip he hears from Tory friends at Grumpy's Bar on Bishop Street and other watering-holes. When Yolande Charbonneau held a show in Montreal in 1992, the highest price tag visible was $3,000.

Born in Trois-Rivières in 1922, Guy Charbonneau was sent by his parents to Collège Jean-de-Brébeuf in Montreal, the Jesuit school preferred by well-to-do francophone families. (Pierre Trudeau attended Brébeuf and sent his own sons there.) By 1941 Char-bonneau had a BA from the Université de Montréal and was taking some classes at McGill, but in 1942, he quit to join the army. He signed on with the Mont-Royal Fusiliers; by 1944 he was a captain in the army's intelligence corps, working in Normandy with the air liaison officers of Charles de Gaulle's Free French.

After the war, the insurance business seemed like a promising career, but he also became interested in politics. His family were Liberals and his godfather was Jacques Bureau, a cabinet minister in Mackenzie King's government. But when Mark Drouin, a prominent Conservative lawyer and Speaker of the Senate, approached him to run for the Tories in 1956, Charbonneau was intrigued. "It wasn't good for the country to have only one party from Quebec," he says, so he agreed to help. But he didn't want to run himself; the back rooms were where he felt most comfortable. The challenge was to build the Conservative Party from the ground up in Quebec, and that required money. Charbonneau volunteered to raise the money to establish a financial structure for the federal Tories in the province, one that evolved into the provincial wing of the PC Canada Fund. At that time, he says, there were only four other men working to organize the federal party in Quebec, and they couldn't find candidates.

When Mulroney arrived in Montreal in the spring of 1964 to take a job with the law firm of Howard, Cate, Ogilvy, Bishop, Cope, Porteous and Hansard (now called Ogilvy Renault), he and Charbonneau gravitated to each other as members of the city's tiny Tory fraternity. They became very close, but today Charbonneau laughingly denies he was ever Mulroney's mentor. "He doesn't need a mentor," Charbonneau snorts. "He's smart enough to do it all on his own."

Mulroney secured Charbonneau's appointment to the Senate in 1979, one of a number of favours wrested from Joe Clark for a show of Mulroney's support. Reluctantly, Clark agreed, knowing full well where the crafty Charbonneau's loyalties lay.

The new senator was rather more preoccupied with his own flourishing insurance interests than with Senate duties. Soon after his appointment he set up a cross-Canada insurance network to handle the special needs of the Canadian Egg Marketing Association (CEMA). Charbonneau called the company CLLRS, after the final initials of its five partners (the C stood for Charbonneau), and he found licensed brokers for the network in each province. When he built a new company out of the framework of CLLRS in the early 1980s, he invited one of the associated CLLRS brokers in as a shareholder, but the man declined. "They moved too fast for a country boy like me," he chuckled, adding that he admired the senator's style. "Charbonneau did everything first-class, with meetings at the Ritz-Carlton and so on." The new company planned to use its existing network of key contacts across the country to take advantage of what he hoped would be a steady flow of federal government insurance business. "As it happened," said a lawyer familiar with the company, "he never needed this network. He did just fine without it."

It was at this time that Charbonneau took on the job of national chairman of the Mulroney leadership fundraising committee. He set up the fundraising headquarters in the fourth-floor office at 4150 Sainte-Catherine in Westmount that he still shares with André Gingras, another important Tory bagman. Theirs is a modern, six-storey building sheathed in dark brown glass, looking like nothing so much as a giant Caramilk bar. Inside the building the lobby is panelled in dark brown marble; the upper floors, filled with lawyers, insurance brokers, notaries, and other professionals, are decorated in pale green and tangerine. Thick fabrics on the walls absorb noise, and the halls are lit with pinpoints of halogen light. The building sits in the heart of Westmount, a stone's throw from the fashionable shops and boutiques of Greene Avenue where Mila Mulroney enjoys shopping and just around the corner from the RCMP's austere Quebec headquarters on Dorchester.

Although Charbonneau was most heavily involved in insurance interests, he and another friend, Guy Dulude, had also set up a consulting business they called Charbonneau-Dulude, Inc. They later changed the name to Chardul, Inc. Helping Charbonneau with all of these enterprises in the Sainte-Catherine office was his secretary, Louise Raymond, one of two Raymond sisters who were to work closely with Charbonneau and the Tory party over the next few years. Louise and Denyse Raymond were the daughters of a wealthy Quebec

food packager, and their own careers were built on their political connections. Denyse worked at the PC Canada Fund headquarters on
Rue du Président Kennedy, the scene of the 1984 break-in. At his recommendation, both sisters were later appointed to permanent jobs on
the federal Immigration Appeal Board in Montreal, jobs worth about
$86,000 a year.

If Charbonneau was the brain of Mulroney's fundraising team
for the leadership fight, the chief legman — the brawn — was
Mulroney's closest friend, Fred Doucet. Mulroney had friends who
were more fun than Fred, richer than Fred, more cunning than Fred.
But he didn't trust anyone as much as he trusted Fred. It was Gerry
Doucet who had first befriended Mulroney at St. FX, and Gerry who
had become so successful; when he was appointed Nova Scotia's
minister of education in Robert Stanfield's 1967 Conservative government, he became at twenty-six the youngest cabinet minister in
the province's history. After John Buchanan beat him for the party's
leadership in 1971, Gerry left politics to work as a lobbyist and
lawyer in Halifax. But it was his younger brother Fred, an administrator at St. FX, who drew closer to Mulroney over the years.

Doucet and Charbonneau were two of the small inner circle that
helped design the national fundraising team for Mulroney's run for
the leadership. By February 1983 Fred Doucet was tacking back and
forth from one small Nova Scotia town to another, scrambling to
raise money and recruit delegates to the June convention. It was not
a happy time for Doucet, and in some ways the work must have been
a relief; it took his mind off his own troubles. He and Gerry were
watching helplessly as their public company, East Coast Energy
Ltd., which they had set up just a year earlier, was floundering into
a messy, scandal-ridden receivership.[2] But there was no time to
worry about it; Fred Doucet hit the road alone in a rented car, barely taking time to stop for a hamburger and a chocolate shake when
he got hungry. He spent the next six months on the road from Truro
to Antigonish to Halifax to Sydney, and then back and forth to

Ottawa and Montreal, working flat out to wring commitments from key supporters. It was part of a carefully orchestrated plan, one designed in secret meetings held in Montreal over the previous two years by a core group of Mulroney's confidants.

The group had expanded and contracted by a member or two from time to time, but when it began to meet in early 1981 it consisted of Charbonneau and Doucet, Frank Moores, Michel Cogger, Bernard Roy, Jean Bazin, Rodrigue Pageau, Ritz-Carlton manager Fern Roberge, Toronto lawyer Fred von Veh, and Regina businessman Ken Waschuk. Most had been on board for Mulroney's 1976 leadership run; Moores had placed Mulroney's name in nomination.

Von Veh and Waschuk were the only two who were not longtime Mulroney cronies. Von Veh was there partly through his friendship with Elmer MacKay, who had been recruited by Moores. MacKay was not always able to join the gatherings and sent von Veh in his place. But von Veh had his own ties to Mulroney; they had met when both were involved in the Cliche commission hearings in Montreal in the 1960s. Ken Waschuk, a former aide to Clark, became known to the group after he joined PC headquarters in Ottawa as a staff member. Like von Veh, Waschuk was soon trusted enough to become a member of the inner circle.

This group was to become known as the Ritz Hotel gang, taking the name from the Ritz-Carlton Hotel where they met secretly in a suite provided at no charge by Roberge. (Thanks to Roberge, Mulroney was a member of the board of the Ritz-Carlton.) But as John Sawatsky discovered, they also held regular monthly meetings chaired by Mulroney in a private room at the top of the stairs in the Mount Royal Club. Their own name for themselves was the Mount Royal Club group.

The Ritz clique developed a second tier of associates, men not at the very core but important Mulroney loyalists and workers. This group included Montreal bailiff Jean-Yves Lortie (nicknamed "the Poodle" for his frizzy hair, flashy clothes, and gold jewellery); lawyer

Pierre Claude Nolin; professional political organizer Claude Dumont, who was also part-owner of the security firm that guarded the PC headquarters; marketing expert Jean Dugré; Pierre-Paul Bourdon, another political organizer; and lawyers Robert and Luc Brunet (Robert Brunet was a law partner of Marcel Danis, an active Clark supporter). Of this second tier, the most aggressive were Lortie, Bourdon, and Dumont. Their specialty that year, during the heated battles for leadership convention delegates at local nomination meetings, was to bring in goon squads of a dozen or so hired thugs "dressed in jeans, checkered shirts and steel-toed boots," as one observer later told the *Gazette*, to prevent the election of pro-Clark delegates. One April evening, after a Clark supporter raised an objection about a minor issue at a riding association meeting, Dumont lost his temper, called the man "a swine," and spat in his face.

The inner circle's first priority was to develop a national fundraising team, and the criteria for membership were straightforward: the money men had to have clout in their communities, but more important was their ability to be trustworthy and discreet. Virtually every member of the team pulled a fine patronage plum once Mulroney took power; in some cases a Senate seat, in others a top-level board position. For a few others the rewards consisted of government contracts.

To keep the books, Mulroney chose Montreal businessman John Lynch-Staunton, president of John de Kuyper (Canada) Limited, a liquor importer, as the campaign's national comptroller. After serving on the Official Residences Council Lynch-Staunton went to the Senate in September 1990. Benoît Lemay, a director of de Kuyper, was brought in as Lynch-Staunton's assistant. In Newfoundland, Peter Walsh, a former provincial politician from St. John's, was in charge; he later won a full-time job on the Canadian Pension Commission. In Nova Scotia Fred Doucet and McLeod Young Weir broker Ross Montgomery ran the campaign, working out of McLeod's Barrington Street offices. Soon after the Tories took office, Ross

Montgomery was appointed to the investment committee of the Canada Council, a nice perch for an investment dealer, and McLeod Young Weir won significant government business. Another Nova Scotian who worked for the Mulroney leadership campaign was Halifax lawyer Stewart McInnes; he ran for Parliament in 1984, joined the cabinet in August 1985 as minister of supply and services, and replaced Roch LaSalle in 1986 as public works minister.

Mulroney did not have a prominent New Brunswicker on his committee, but there was an embarrassment of riches in Quebec. Charbonneau took on the lead role provincially, in addition to his job as national manager; he was assisted by Jean-Louis Le Saux in Laval and by Sainte-Foy brewery consultant Georges Labrecque, a former Union Nationale sympathizer and then a Liberal before defecting to the Tories in 1980. (He ran unsuccessfully under Joe Clark for the Montmorency riding in the 1980 federal election.) Labrecque, well known as the developer of the Mont Sainte-Anne ski complex, was put in charge of the Quebec City region.

It took the Mulroney team some time to find able loyalists in Ontario. Lawyer Sam Wakim was his only trusted crony in Toronto, and raising money was not one of Wakim's strong points; besides, he was busy pulling together a collection of Mulroney's speeches for a book called *Where I Stand* and negotiating its publication with Toronto publisher McClelland & Stewart. His reward came in the form of generous legal contracts from the Export Development Corporation, contracts he used to get himself a job with the Toronto law firm Weir & Foulds.

Old-line Toronto Tories like broadcasting baron John Bassett and lawyer Edwin Goodman were not close to Mulroney and were as wary of him as he was of them; they were not people he could call on for something as delicate as money to knock off Joe Clark. Years later Mulroney came to depend on Toronto businessmen John Bitove, a wealthy caterer, and Trevor Eyton, a senior man in the Bronfmans' Hees-Edper holding company, to raise millions of dollars for the party as well as for the 1988 free-trade election campaign and for the Yes side of the 1992 referendum on the constitution. Bitove won huge federal catering contracts and an Order of Canada, and Eyton joined Lynch-Staunton in the Senate in 1990. However, in 1983 Mulroney did not know these men well enough to bring them on board. Donald Matthews, a contractor in London, Ontario, became the co-chairman of his 1983 leadership bid — and he was rewarded with a federal land purchase of property he owned as well as a piece of the 1993 contract to privatize Toronto's Pearson Airport. But Ontario bagmen were in short supply.

This lack of lieutenants in Ontario was to become a recurring handicap. Mulroney worked around his initial lack of fundraising strength in the province by drawing on his power bases in Quebec, Nova Scotia, and western Canada. One result was that he essentially ignored Ontario as prime minister, even when the province was reeling in the early 1990s with hundreds of thousands of job losses. The Tories were to pay a high price for their neglect in the 1993 election, when they lost ninety-eight of ninety-nine Ontario seats to the Liberals and the ninety-ninth seat to the upstart Reform Party.

There was one important Toronto businessman Mulroney could call on back in 1983, a man he became close to over the next few years. This was investment dealer Peter Eby, then vice-chairman of Burns Fry Limited. Eby was brought on board to run the Toronto campaign, and he proved to be an invaluable addition. Ralph Fisher, an accountant and senior partner in the consulting firm of Laventhol & Horwath, took on the role of Ontario comptroller. Mulroney later asked Fisher to investigate allegations of corruption at Canada Post; his firm, now bankrupt, also won substantial government contracts. Among their helpers was Phil Evershed, who went on to work as a senior adviser to Sinclair Stevens in 1984.

In Ottawa, the team recruited lawyer Stuart Hendin; he and his wife, Judith, another lawyer, were to rise in party circles when he became close to several members of the Ritz Hotel gang and she was elected president of the national PC Women's Caucus. Mulroney arranged a National Parole Board job for Judith Hendin, and on his last day in office, June 24, 1993, he appointed Stuart Hendin to the board of VIA Rail. In St. Catharines, the team brought in Harry Tomarin, the founder of a company called Niagara Structural Steel Company, Limited (later TecSyn International Incorporated). Sault Ste. Marie lawyer James Kelleher helped out in northwestern Ontario; he won a federal seat in 1984 and, after a stint as a junior trade minister, was appointed solicitor general in 1986. And in Hamilton, Mulroney enlisted the help of chartered accountant Bruno Bragoli, past president of the local chamber of commerce.

Manitoba produced two fundraisers for the Mulroney team, real estate businessman Arni Thorsteinson, rewarded with an appointment to the board of Petro-Canada, and long-time party fundraiser William Gardner. Saskatchewan may have been a poor province, but it was a motherlode of well-connected Tories, beginning with Ken Waschuk, who headed Mulroney's leadership campaign in the province. In 1985, Mulroney appointed him to the board of Air Canada. William Elliott, a Regina lawyer at McPherson Elliott and Tyreman (and brother of Richard Elliott, Mulroney's brother-in-law), was in charge of fundraising in Regina; he too went on the Petro-Canada board. Helping him was local lawyer Ronald Barclay. Saskatoon lawyer Harold Lane was on the team and later won a ten-year term on the Bank of Canada board. He was assisted by Estevan lawyer George Hill, a former head of the provincial Conservative Party and president of Souris Basin Development Corporation, which was to build the Rafferty-Alameda dams in the province. And behind the scenes was another important player, Premier Grant Devine, a Mulroney loyalist who encouraged this powerful provincial network.

In Alberta, the team recruited Allan Olson, then a senior executive at the Edmonton-based construction company Banister Incorporated. Olson, a Tory party bagman, later ran Donald Getty's successful 1985 campaign to replace retiring Tory premier Peter

Lougheed. And finally, in British Columbia, Mulroney was able to call on two men: Walter Maughan, the president of Hastings West Investments, who took on the job from his Granville Street office; and insurance adjuster Jake Brouwer, who worked out of his Dunsmuir Street offices and wound up with a CNR board appointment.

This, then, was the finance team whose names appeared on a closely guarded and confidential organization chart for the Mulroney leadership campaign. However, they were not the only individuals who raised serious money for the candidate. Among the names that did not appear on any org chart was that of Robert E. Shea, the old St. FX classmate from Watertown, Massachusetts, who was still known around Antigonish as "Mel" Shea. Shea had become an insurance broker and financial consultant in Boston; it was his job to raise money from corporations in the United States. "If Bob Shea weren't an American, he would have been Mulroney's chief of staff," said one insider confidently in 1993, illustrating how close the two men were — and still are.[3] Shea did not work alone south of the border; helping him was former Winnipegger Ross Johnson, then at the helm of RJR Nabisco in New York as its flamboyant chief executive officer. They were able to persuade several major corporations with Canadian branch plants that an investment in Mulroney's campaign was an investment in the future.

Another money man was important in Mulroney's life in the early 1980s, even though he was not part of the 1983 fundraising team nor a member of the Ritz Hotel gang, a St. FX chum, or a drinking companion during Mulroney's bachelor days. Bagmen were all very well to put together the cash to pay for an expensive leadership campaign, but Montreal stockbroker Jonathan Deitcher was also a personal fundraiser. He was the man who was going to make Mulroney rich.

For several years Deitcher, a millionaire himself with a large house at 111 Summit Circle in Westmount and a holiday home in New England, has managed a small group of seven or eight high-powered brokers at the Westmount office of Dominion Securities. A lover of fast cars, $1,500 suits, and a high-rolling lifestyle, Deitcher has long been the biggest producer at Dominion Securities, working with money managers in New York who handle funds in the tens of billions of dollars. Deitcher's father, Moses, had been a generous contributor to Mulroney's 1983 leadership race and made his luxurious King's Road house in Palm Beach and his Bentley available to the Mulroneys for their frequent Florida holidays.

Jonathan Deitcher was Mulroney's broker in the early 1980s. In 1981, for example, he invested $50,000 of Mulroney's money in an Alberta oil company that served as a tax shelter for wealthy Montrealers. The money was invested in drilling funds sold by Pillar Petroleums Ltd., a Calgary oil company; Deitcher was the powerhouse behind Pillar. He arranged for Mulroney to join Pillar's board of directors, and he brought in investment from the Birks jewellery interests in Montreal and from the Papachristidis shipping family. Pillar financed its operations by selling four drilling funds, under a Deitcher subsidiary called J.D. Shelter Investments Ltd., to Montrealers looking for a way to reduce their tax exposure. The funds allowed investors to own a share of an oil well and take part of its profits, but they could write off the cost of their investment against their taxes. Deitcher shrugged off Mulroney's investment as minor compared with the $200,000 to $300,000 that many of his clients had invested. Unfortunately for all of them, by 1983 Pillar was in a cash crunch caused by plunging oil prices and soaring interest rates. While the Montreal investors wanted to bail out because the company's value was dropping, Deitcher searched desperately for more investors and wound up merging Pillar with Renaissance Energy Ltd.

Mulroney's investment became public after a July 1984 election campaign debate with Liberal leader John Turner during which Mulroney said he supported tax reform that would stop millionaires from avoiding taxes in Canada. When reporters asked the Tory leader about his own participation in a tax shelter, Mulroney refused to respond. Bill Fox, his press secretary, said Mulroney's investments were in a blind trust and that he had no idea if his boss still had money in tax shelters. In March of the following year, Deitcher received an appointment to the board of the Export Development Corporation.

In March 1986, Jonathan and Diane Deitcher, along with his parents, Moses and Phyllis, were among a small group of guests Mulroney took to a White House banquet hosted by Ronald Reagan in Washington (others included David Angus and Power Corporation chairman Paul Desmarais). Deitcher organized an annual dinner for his key American contacts to discuss business opportunities in Canada, a dinner whose star attraction was Brian Mulroney. He also became well known to many of Mulroney's Montreal cronies; at his fortieth birthday party, held in 1986, 250 guests — including the Mulroneys — celebrated with him.

The two men were close throughout the nine years of Mulroney's prime-ministership; on one occasion he boasted that he spoke frequently to Mulroney by telephone. Deitcher is careful to point out, however, that he did not handle Mulroney's investments while he was prime minister.

In 1989, Deitcher suffered some serious aggravation from the Ontario Securities Commission in connection with a long investigation it had been conducting into allegations of front-running by Michael Biscotti. Front-running is a practice in which professional stock traders use advance knowledge of large purchase orders in order to profit from resulting stock price increases. The investigation, the largest in OSC history, centred on Biscotti, Dominion Securities' former chief stock trader in Toronto, who had taken early retirement in 1988. The OSC ordered him to appear with documents relating to transactions in 1985, 1986, and 1987, transactions that were made through several companies, including two Deitcher family holding companies, Argosy Holdings SA, based in Freeport, the Bahamas, and the All Star Trading Investment Club. Court records showed that there was a suggestion Biscotti had directed trading on

Bombardier shares in the Argosy name through an account at Deitcher's Montreal office; the transactions had netted a profit of $1.8 million. Biscotti and a nephew engaged with him in the trading exhausted all their legal avenues of delay and were finally banned from trading on the Toronto Stock Exchange for life in 1993.

When Dominion Securities was chosen as the lead underwriter for the syndicates assembled to make the share offerings for two large privatizations by the federal government, Air Canada and Petro-Canada, Deitcher bragged to close friends that he had brought the business to his firm. During the second stage of the privatization of Air Canada (the government sold its equity in Air Canada in two stages, in 1988 and 1989), the federal department responsible for privatizing Crown corporations wanted to reduce Dominion Securities' position in the syndicate. The Prime Minister's Office refused to let them do it, and a senior federal official involved in the discussions considered resigning over the issue. "Deitcher's fingers were everywhere on this," said one source who worked on the privatization and who eventually persuaded the official not to resign.

Dominion Securities was not ungrateful; the company was among the most generous of all the brokerage firms who donated to the Tories, giving the PC Canada Fund about $50,000 every year during the last five years the Conservatives held power.

Informed estimates by Tory party insiders say that Guy Charbonneau and the money men raised well over $3 million between 1981 and 1983, and they bought Brian Mulroney a successful bid for the leadership of his party. A few of their names were to become familiar to Canadians over the next nine years, but most of them remained obscure, which was unfortunate: their influence on the prime minister was greater than that of most cabinet ministers.

THE NOVA SCOTIA CONNECTION

T HE MONEY MEN WORKED HARD TO PROTECT THE DETAILS OF their candidate's finances in 1983; there was no disclosure of funding sources or of expenditures. Mulroney had been badly damaged by publicity surrounding his free-spending 1976 campaign: David Angus liked to brag that the motto then was "MINO — Money Is No Object." In 1983, the image was to be one of probity; but in fact, the campaign was anything but modest. The spending was lavish and, despite the hard work of the fundraising lieutenants, only the fact that Mulroney won the leadership saved him from a humiliating financial fiasco. Information has been carefully guarded over the years, but documents for the 1983 leadership campaign in Nova Scotia tell much of the story for the rest of campaign.

Nova Scotia was second only to Montreal as a power base for Mulroney. Here he formed his first political friendships and attracted many of his closest advisers and strongest supporters, men such as the Doucet brothers, Patrick MacAdam, New Glasgow businessman Joe Stewart, Tory MPs Elmer MacKay and Robert Coates, Premier John Buchanan, lawyer Stewart McInnes, and stockbroker Donald Ripley. Like Mulroney, most of them came from humble roots and shared the status of outsiders, accustomed to watching those from established, moneyed families enjoy the spoils of politics.

Brian Mulroney was not born to wealth. His father, Benedict Martin

Mulroney, earned an hourly wage as the chief electrician at the Quebec North Shore Paper Company in Baie-Comeau, a small mill town on the north shore of the St. Lawrence River. The Mulroneys wanted a better education for their son than the local high schools could provide and found St. Thomas High School, a Catholic boys' boarding school in Chatham, New Brunswick, which would house, feed, and educate him for $418.50 a year. In 1955, after two years at St. Thomas, Mulroney moved to Antigonish, Nova Scotia, to attend St. Francis Xavier University, a small and strict Catholic institution for men. Like St. Thomas, St. FX was a place for kids whose parents didn't have much money. It was then and is today a small university in a cosy town. Having merged with its sister college, Mount St. Bernard, it boasts only 3,000 undergraduates, and most of them still come from the old Scottish and Acadian towns in Nova Scotia and New Brunswick.

The campus, at the western edge of downtown Antigonish, is part of an old residential neighbourhood of large clapboard houses, shady maple trees, and deep back yards. But St. FX is not an ivy-covered college. While everything is neat and tidy, there has never been money to waste on perennial borders, Georgian doorways, or graceful balconies, the stuff of a Dalhousie or a Queen's or a Trinity College in Toronto. The only decorative features of the college are the white statues of saints stationed here and there in thoughtful repose on the lawns. In Mulroney's day, most of the professors were priests or nuns; St. FX did not attract the country's leading scholars.

It was at St. FX that Mulroney met Patrick MacAdam, editor of the student newspaper and a son of the Cape Breton coal mining town of Glace Bay. MacAdam roomed with Lowell Murray, like himself a Cape Bretoner, who led the student Tory party. And there was Sam Wakim, a young man from a Lebanese family in Saint John, New Brunswick; another New Brunswick friend was Paul Creaghan, a student politician from a well-to-do Moncton family. There were Gerry and Fred Doucet, Acadians from Grand Étang, Cape Breton;

Terry McCann from Pembroke, Ontario; Bert Lavoie, a francophone from Quebec; and Mel Shea, the young American from Boston. Every one of them threw themselves into student politics, all of them as young Progressive Conservatives. And all were later to become major players in Brian Mulroney's world.

In the fall of 1959 Mulroney started law school at Dalhousie University in Halifax and spent his first year having fun, partying, and playing politics. His involvement in student politics at St. FX had given him frequent contact with several prominent federal politicians, including Prime Minister John Diefenbaker and Davie Fulton, then justice minister. But in Halifax he came to know and work for Dalton Camp, the senior organizer for Robert Stanfield, then premier of Nova Scotia. And, through Camp, he met Finlay MacDonald and Norman Atkins, both powerful backroom organizers for the federal party. It was in Nova Scotia that young Mulroney made invaluable connections, where he learned the arts of grassroots politics, and where the dream of leading his party and his country was born. Nova Scotia would help make that dream a reality.

Mulroney's leadership aspirations were given a significant boost in the early 1980s by a prominent citizen of the province, Elmer MacKay, veteran member of Parliament from Central Nova. MacKay had first been elected to Parliament in 1971. In 1976 he had supported Joe Clark's leadership bid, not Mulroney's. By 1980, however, he was fed up with Clark. Clark had blown his fragile minority government, but even before that débâcle, MacKay resented the fact that Clark had not given him the cabinet portfolio he desired. MacKay had always seen himself as a passionate advocate for the underdog, one possessed of a healthy suspicion of the RCMP and other high-handed authorities. He was no dreamy idealist; he had inherited the largest private timber holdings in Nova Scotia (only the provincial government and the Nova Scotia Power Corporation held more forest land than he did), and he had made another fortune by bringing cable television into Pictou County. But business success was not his goal; he wanted to be the country's top law enforcement official, the solicitor general of Canada. When Joe Clark gave the solicitor general's job to Ontario MP Allan Lawrence, MacKay never forgave him. By 1982 he was an ardent Mulroney supporter and was eagerly embraced by the Mount Royal Club group, who welcomed the endorsement of the one-time Tory caucus chairman.

Working closely with MacKay was Bob Coates, the Tory MP from Amherst and a former party president whose open contempt for Joe Clark stemmed in part from being shut out of the 1979 cabinet. A third member of the Nova Scotia coterie was Premier John Buchanan. MacKay, Coates, and Buchanan were all Masonic Lodge brothers, and Buchanan and Coates had attended Mount Allison University together. The men were close and Mulroney could not have found a more powerful triumvirate of backers in the province.

It was in February 1983 that the Nova Scotia fundraising apparatus was established in Halifax at the Barrington Street offices of McLeod Young Weir. Donald Ripley, a vice-president of McLeod and manager of the Halifax office, was put in charge of "Nova Scotia for Brian Mulroney." Ripley had an extraordinary track record as a bagman for the provincial Tories, so good, in fact, that he'd helped Grant Devine's fundraisers in Saskatchewan with advice, names, and strategies. He had done much the same for the Tories in Newfoundland and New Brunswick, and McLeod had been the beneficiary of significant provincial bond business from all four provinces. His role in the Mulroney campaign pleased his bosses back in Toronto; McLeod president Tom Kierans and chairman Austin Taylor smelled a Mulroney victory.

Another McLeod broker, Ross Montgomery, supervised the fundraising team and reported to Ripley. A number of young party organizers were brought in to help Fred Doucet set up the networks across the province to ensure that pro-Mulroney delegates were chosen for the June 1983 leadership convention. Two of the key players at this level were Antigonish nursing home operator Brian MacLeod and David MacKeen of Halifax. MacKeen came from a prominent Halifax family; his father, Justice Harry MacKeen, was the founder of Nova Scotia Power.

As with all of the provincial fundraising efforts, overall direction and control came from the suite on Sainte-Catherine in Montreal where Guy Charbonneau was in command. On March 11, 1983, Charbonneau dashed off a note to Ross Montgomery: "Dear Ross," he wrote. "I am sending you the 1976 lists of donors to the Brian Mulroney campaign with the hope they will prove useful. Kindest regards, Guy." The list contained a few dozen names and the amounts they gave. Four days later, Mulroney followed up with a handwritten note to Montgomery thanking him for his help.

On March 24, Charbonneau assistant Denyse Raymond sent a note to members of the finance committee across Canada to let them know that Mulroney had an account at a downtown Montreal branch of Montreal Trust, a company still owned by Mulroney's close friend and patron Paul Desmarais. All donations to the leadership campaign were to go into this account, she ordered, unless people specifically asked for receipts: "All cheques are to be made payable to the MONTREAL TRUST — ACCOUNT #830," she wrote in her confidential instructions.

If donors wanted a receipt for tax purposes, the procedure was different. In that case, wrote Raymond, "cheques should be made payable to PC CANADA FUND — BRIAN MULRONEY." She warned them of the disadvantage of receipted contributions. "Please take note that all contributions sent to the P.C. Canada Fund will be split as follows: 25% to the P.C. Canada Fund and 75% to the Mulroney Campaign." Naturally, Charbonneau and the money men were encouraging donors to make their cheques payable directly to Mulroney's Montreal Trust account — a legitimate option — to avoid having to share revenue with the federal party. There was a practical advantage too: the funds were easily accessible. Mulroney could withdraw money directly because it was his own account.

In Nova Scotia, Mulroney's bagmen offered donors a third option. Two years earlier, three provincial fundraisers had set up a company called C.D.M. Investments. The C stood for Halifax lawyer David Chipman (now a Nova Scotia Supreme Court judge); D for Fred Dickson, another Halifax lawyer and one of Premier Buchanan's closest advisers; and M for Joseph Macdonald, chairman of Nova Scotia Power Corporation and another Buchanan intimate. "C.D.M. was formed in 1981 to hide donations to the party," explained Ripley. "If anyone felt secretive, it was there, available to be used. And lots of people wanted to use it." Lots of people wanted to use C.D.M. Investments to mask their donations to Mulroney as well. In 1982, soliciting for Mulroney, Ross Montgomery had sent out "personal and confidential" letters to a number of well-heeled contributors. "Political donations in Canada and particularly in Nova Scotia," he wrote, "have no limits, no disclosure and are held entirely legal and confidential. Should you be desirous there is a degree of tax relief in Nova Scotia." Those wishing a tax receipt were asked to make cheques out to the PC Party of Nova Scotia; those who didn't could choose the PC Association of Nova Scotia or C.D.M. Investments. And in 1983, as directed by Denyse Raymond, Montgomery also offered the Montreal Trust account option, but only to those he knew personally and trusted.

The team worked energetically in Nova Scotia, but the bills were high. The money raised paid for all of Brian and Mila's expenses in the province, Fred Doucet's travel and accommodation, and the expenses of full-time helpers like Brian MacLeod and David MacKeen. It paid for Room 546 at the Lord Nelson Hotel, rented for five months from March 28, 1983, until August, to serve as the Mulroney headquarters for both the leadership campaign and the subsequent federal by-election campaign. It was where Brian and Mila stayed when they were in Halifax and where the bills were sent for the intimate breakfast meetings and chowder luncheons Mulroney hosted for prospective supporters. The invoices were impressive, especially those for long-distance telephone charges; from March 28 to August 9 the phone bills added up to $5,000. The receipts show he was on the phone for hours when he was in the suite.

Other documents show that "Nova Scotia for Brian Mulroney" was paying for some campaign expenses outside of the province, in particular courier and telephone costs. That was to be expected; the Mulroney team spent more time in Nova Scotia during the spring 1983 leadership period than almost anywhere else. They would be gearing up for a by-election if their man won. Elmer MacKay had offered Mulroney his safe seat in Central Nova until the next election, when Mulroney would run in his native Quebec. In the meantime, the Nova Scotia riding was a natural choice for a man with solid ties to Pictou County and Antigonish.

Hard as the finance committee worked, however, the mounting expenses were a serious concern, and in Ottawa it was particularly grim. Just a few weeks before the June leadership convention, Rodrigue Pageau confided to a senior Tory official that the Ottawa Mulroney headquarters was in danger of being out on the street if they couldn't get their hands on funds to cover the rent. Bell Telephone hadn't been paid in five months. In Toronto, the Mulroney team working out of 11 Adelaide West was having difficulty paying its bills too. One tab racked up at the Westin Hotel in Toronto was never paid by the Mulroney campaign, despite much hounding by the hotel. Instead, the management of the Ottawa Westin decided their hotel should cover the bill in hopes of winning favour as the Tories' preferred hotel in the capital when Mulroney became prime minister. The favour did the trick.

In Halifax, expenses were also worrying Ross Montgomery, who watched the overdraft on the trust account, for which he was personally responsible, climb from $5,000 to $6,000 and steadily upwards each week. Across Canada, the money men redoubled their efforts. It all paid off on June 9, 1983, in a steaming hot hockey arena in Ottawa, when Mulroney finally won the prize he'd been chasing so long, the leadership of the Progressive Conservative Party.

There was an ironic footnote to the Nova Scotia effort. It was well financed and backed by the party's major local power brokers, who felt Mulroney's links to Pictou County and Nova Scotia generally would guarantee the votes of the province's delegates. At the leadership convention, however, Joe Clark, who had no real links to the province and no network of cronies, won 60 per cent of the Nova Scotia votes on the last ballot while Mulroney took only 40 per cent.

Three weeks later Prime Minister Trudeau called a by-election in Central Nova for August 29. The Nova Scotia team barely had time to catch their breath. Room 546 hummed with activity as Mila and Brian Mulroney returned to Nova Scotia to fight the by-election, and once again expenses were high. The Lord Nelson Hotel's bills show two cash advances of $600 each charged to Mulroney's room, once on June 13 and again on June 30; these were in addition to other charges such as room service and laundry. One advance was written in by hand; the second was entered as "rent and parking." Nowhere does the bill indicate what the "rent and parking" was for.

On Saturday, June 25, Maple Leaf Catering provided smoked salmon, devilled eggs, jumbo shrimps, steaks, salads, German tortes, and chocolate cheesecakes — along with beer, liquor, and wine — for a barbecue at Stewart McInnes's house to celebrate the leadership victory and cheer the candidate and his team on their way to by-election glory. Ross Montgomery wrote a cheque for $5,144.77 to cover the party. In mid-July, the Mulroneys moved into the riding and stayed at Pictou Lodge with Michael McSweeney in attendance.

On August 18, Mulroney was back in Halifax for an intimate dinner with his closest advisers at the Henry House; the $311.66 tab included dinner, drinks, and four cigars. Montgomery again paid the bill from the Bank of Nova Scotia account. (Oddly enough, no one thought to invite Donald Ripley to the McInnes barbecue or to the dinner at the Henry House, even though Ripley had been the fundraising mastermind. Ripley was a Micmac and a bit of a loudmouth and had never attended Dalhousie or joined the Masons; he was not quite one of the boys. Ripley soon lost his enthusiasm for the Mulroney campaign, although he remained Buchanan's chief fundraiser.)

Because a candidate is limited in the amount he or she can spend once the writ is dropped — and here, Trudeau dropped the writ almost immediately — Mulroney's Central Nova organizers disguised their lavish spending by running many of the expenses through Bob Coates's neighbouring riding of Cumberland-Colchester. Coates was not coping with an election and so did not have to disclose his spending.

Not surprisingly, the money well dried up in Nova Scotia. For all their enthusiasm, Tories grew weary of giving to Mulroney campaigns, be they leadership or by-election. Testy letters arrived from suppliers. The overdraft for the leadership fund being managed by Ross Montgomery grew larger. On October 18, 1983, Montgomery wrote a sharp letter to Guy Charbonneau to bring to his attention "the unpleasant reality that the Nova Scotia for Brian Mulroney Campaign is in an overdraft position of $10,565.65. I have discussed this situation with Stuart [sic] McInnes and Fred Doucet and the consensus of opinion is that it would do the party irreparable damage if we solicited additional funds from within the province to clear up this deficit. The Province has been solicited continuously for eight months and going to the well one more time will do more harm than good.

"As you are no doubt aware, Donald Ripley and myself raised funds after the Leadership Convention for Central Nova (Elmer McKay [sic]). John Crosby [sic; John Crosbie ran third behind Clark and Mulroney] has also been here seeking assistance in reducing his deficit.

"The overdraft is with the Bank of Nova Scotia, Scotia Square Branch, Halifax, Nova Scotia and the account is in my name personally for which I am under some pressure."

Instead of contacting Lynch-Staunton, the comptroller of the Mulroney leadership funds, Charbonneau sent the letter to David Angus attached to a "personal and confidential" note of his own, asking Angus to pay Montgomery. "As you know," he wrote, "these overdraft positions are usually the responsibility of the constituency and/or the PC Canada Fund." A relieved Montgomery soon received a cheque to pay off his overdraft. Donald Ripley states that Angus sent the cheque as Charbonneau requested.

Overdraft positions for leadership campaigns were not, in fact, constituency or PC Canada Fund responsibilities; they were the candidate's problem, and if the PC Canada Fund paid off Mulroney's debts, it didn't do the same for others. Joe Clark wound up with an $80,000 debt after his leadership run; three friends, Vancouver MP Bill Clarke, Ottawa lawyer Pierre Fortier, and Nova Scotia businessman Finlay MacDonald, held a fundraiser and the money was collected in one fell swoop. John Crosbie travelled from one begging banquet to another for months to pay off his debt. David Angus says that during the fall of 1983 Mulroney often spoke at fundraisers for his leadership rivals to help them pay off their debts, but he insisted the PC Canada Fund did not assist any of them, including Mulroney himself. "I felt, given the state of the party's finances, that the party could not be paying any debts off for any leadership candidates — including [Mulroney]," said Angus.

Perhaps Angus, who did not assume management of the PC Canada Fund until after the Central Nova by-election in late August, was partly correct in offering this assessment of the party's financial health. In mid-June 1983 the PC Canada Fund had a $500,000 surplus, the happy legacy of its moneymaking leadership convention. Run carefully, a party convention can be a financial godsend; for the Tories, the income was manna from heaven because there had been no effective federal fundraising since the late fall of 1982 when most Tories were gearing up for the party's convention in Winnipeg the following January. The money was surplus to the regular budget for staff and operations and could be added to the war chest for the coming federal election. Three months after the June convention, however, the money was gone.

"A bill came in for a new car for the leader," said one well-placed Tory sourly. "They bought it from one of his old friends who had a car dealership someplace and told us from now on all the cars were going to be bought there. There was such an expenditure of money from the time he was elected as leader until the by-election, you would not believe. Michel Cogger became legal counsel and they were blowing their brains out with the money."

Not to worry. After September 1, 1983, the PC Canada Fund was firmly in the hands of David Angus who, building on the work of his predecessors and borrowing from the practices of the U.S. Republican Party, took the Tories' fundraising to unprecedented success.

CHAPTER FIVE

THE BAGMEN AND THE BOSS

D URING THEIR YEARS IN POWER, THE PROGRESSIVE Conservatives showed themselves to be masters of the art and science of political fundraising, hauling in record donations from both individuals and corporations, and far outpacing the efforts of the Liberals and New Democrats. Most of the credit can be claimed by their computerized direct-mail fundraising system, a system that had been in development since the mid-1970s, when Malcolm Wickson was the party's federal campaign chairman. He brought in Republican fundraising guru Robert Odell from Washington to advise the party on a computerized system that would become the envy of other federal parties.

Odell had helped the Republican National Committee raise money through direct mail since the 1960s. As John Laschinger and Geoffrey Stevens report in *Leaders and Lesser Mortals*, "Wickson regularly sent staff members to meet Republican backroomers in Washington, Detroit and Columbus, Ohio, and to find out m re about fund-raising techniques that could be adapted to Canadian needs." The key, they discovered, was to have reliable mailing lists. The Americans had uncovered some real gems, the best being the customer list of Ruby Red Grapefruit Co., a Florida-based firm that sold citrus fruit by mail. "Ralph Goettler, a Republican fund-raising consultant, explained the elements of soliciting funds by mail," Laschinger and Stevens tell us. "'You have to write to people who have money and who trust the mails. The best list in the U.S.A. for both percentage response and size of donation is the Ruby Red Grapefruit list. This is a list of people who put $40 in the mail and trust the postal system to deliver them a case of quality grapefruit.'"

In 1974 Laschinger, a former national director of the Tory Party and now a professional campaign manager for political candidates across Canada, persuaded the Tories, bankrupt though they were after the hammering they'd taken from the Liberals, to give him $50,000 to start buying mailing lists. Within a few years, the investment had paid off in spades. By 1981, even though Pierre Trudeau's Liberals were still in power, the Tories were outperforming their rivals financially, raising nearly $2 million more than the Grits. In 1982, with the possibility of a new Tory leader and the retirement of Trudeau imminent, the Tories raised $8.2 million to the Liberals' $6.1 million.

In 1983, as the Tories prepared for an election that the polls said they would win, they raised a record $14.1 million, compared with the Grits' $7.3 million. By 1984, the Tories had 80,000 names in their donor files, and that election year saw the real triumph of the mailing lists and David Angus's machine: $21.1 million poured in, compared with $10 million raised by the Liberals.[1] Of that $21.1 million, $7 million was raised by direct mail, far exceeding even Odell's predictions of what could be achieved by this method. "Direct mail alone produced more than enough money to cover all the Conservatives' reportable expenses during the official eight-week election period," reported Stevens and Laschinger. In 1988 the PC Canada Fund brought in $24.5 million to fight the election, almost three times what the Grits were able to raise.

Besides direct mail, the Republicans gave the Tories other useful ideas. The most successful was the "membership" or "club" approach, a technique that exploits the universal desire to "belong." As Laschinger and Stevens point out, American Express ("Membership has its privileges") and Diners Club built their success on that desire. Like their American counterparts, the Tories introduced a PC Canada Fund membership card that contributors of even small amounts could carry in their wallets. They also sent out letters of appreciation for the donors' "magnificent contribution to democracy" along with gold-edged certificates that many people actually framed and hung on their walls. "I started to vomit," Finlay MacDonald, the chairman of the PC Canada Fund at the time, told Laschinger and Stevens. But it worked.

Another idea was borrowed from Republicans in Ohio who had established the Early Bird Club, an "exclusive" organization of donors who'd given more than $1,000 to the party during the first quarter of each year, a period when political parties were traditionally low in cash. Every year each Early Bird would receive a limited-edition print of a specially commissioned painting by a well-known American artist. If it worked in Ohio, why not Canada? Here the organization became the 500 Club, originally designed for just 500 members. Like the Ohio group, the 500 Club also commissioned paintings; Terry Yates, then chairman of the PC Canada Fund, personally paid for the first two that were reproduced and distributed. Before long, the fundraisers scrapped the idea of gathering cash early in the year and turned the 500 Club into a general fundraising arm of the party, open to anyone who gave more than $1,000. People happily scrambled aboard.

In their book, Laschinger and Stevens identify the dark side of the 500 Club. "The Tories have added a few bells and whistles that reek of selling privileged access — access to the top people in the party and (since 1984) in the government. Members of the 500 Club are routinely invited to receptions whenever the prime minister and other prominent Tories come to their community. Twice a year, on average, members are invited to Ottawa (at their own expense) for a day-long briefing by key cabinet ministers on the government's plans for dealing with the issues of the day. They also get to hear and to question the prime minister. And when they get home, they can tell friends and associates that they have been to the capital, heard the real lowdown, met the prime minister, and given him a piece of their mind." By 1986 the club was a huge success, with 3,000 members paying a total of $3 million a year for the privilege of being insiders. In 1988, the 500 Club raised $6 million.

By 1985 there were twenty-one 500 Club presidents across Canada, many of whom had helped raise money for Mulroney's 1983 leadership bid. Burns Fry vice-chairman Peter Eby, for example, ran the Toronto club out of his fiftieth-floor office at First Canadian Place. Lawyer Terry McCann, a close chum from St. FX days, was the president in Pembroke. And Denyse Angé, a public relations spokeswoman for the Fur Fashion Council of Canada, was president of the Montreal club. When it came to the national president of the club, Mulroney took no chances; this individual had to be one of his inner circle. In 1983 he saw to it that the job went to his friend Brian Gallery. Gallery, another outgoing, fun-loving Irishman like Mulroney, lived in Westmount, not far from David Angus. Gallery ran a small company that published trade magazines for the shipping industry and he knew Angus well. (Angus's legal specialty was marine law, and he had extensive business interests in shipping companies himself.) The money raised from the sale of 500 Club memberships at $1,000 a crack went straight into PC Canada Fund coffers. With two of Mulroney's closest associates running the party's formal fundraising machines and other cronies diligently collecting dollars for him through their personal networks, Mulroney had his friends controlling a lot of the Tory cash flow.

The Canadian Imperial Bank of Commerce has been the Tory party's bank for many years and it too has had especially close ties with Brian Mulroney, who served on its board before entering politics. (Today the CIBC holds the mortgage on the Mulroney house in Montreal.) Stikeman Elliott, the law firm of which David Angus is a partner, has several floors of the CIBC tower on Montreal's Boulevard René-Lévesque. When he was PC Canada Fund chairman, Angus had sole signing authority for a special account drawing on PCCF funds at the CIBC branch in his building, but the fund's main office is part of the party's headquarters in Ottawa, which is where the main banking office is as well. The cheques from Angus's special account did not have the fund's logo printed on them.

The members of the 1984 PC Canada Fund board were hand-picked Mulroney stalwarts. "I selected the board of directors myself," Angus said. In addition to Gallery and chairman Angus, the nineteen-member board included construction millionaire Don Matthews (the fund's vice-chairman); Toronto lawyer Donald Guthrie, a partner at Cassels, Brock and Blackwell (secretary); Nicholas Locke, the fund's full-time executive director; Louise Raymond-Leduc, the director of the PC Canada Fund's Montreal office and Locke's assistant; Toronto lawyer and construction magnate Rudy Bratty; Jake Brouwer, a Vancouver real estate developer; Irving Gerstein, the president of Peoples Jewellers in Toronto; Winnipeg lawyer Duncan Jessiman; Laval businessman Jean-Louis Le Saux; Saskatoon businessman Harold Lane; Quebec City lawyer Camille Lacroix; Toronto millionaire Hal Jackman, whose family controlled the National Trust Company and the Empire Life Insurance Company; Edmonton MP Peter Elzinga, winner of the 1983 party presidency, with Mulroney's backing; Scarborough businessman Phil Granovsky; Toronto lawyer Robert Hicks; and Scott Fennell, a member of Parliament from Toronto. One board member who was not a Mulroney crony but had to be included to satisfy the Clark wing of the party was Calgary lawyer Peter Clark, Joe's brother.

One of the valued assets of the fund is a little-known trust account called the Bracken House Trust, which has grown to $3.5 million since it was created in 1974 from the sale of the party headquarters in downtown Ottawa. As *Globe and Mail* reporter Ross Howard discovered in 1993, "the trust does not show up on public accounts of party financing and is used for collateral on occasional loans the party takes out." The Bracken House Trust, according to

Howard, was tightly controlled by Angus, Charbonneau, and one other undisclosed Tory; when the party found itself nearly $10 million in debt after the 1993 election and new members of the fund board wanted to liquidate the Bracken Trust to pay down the debt, Charbonneau and the other trustees said no. In the summer of 1993 Mulroney told reporters that he had left the party financially healthy with $5 million in the bank. He was including the Bracken House Trust money, Howard reported. Without the trust, he wrote, the party had millions less in the kitty.

No one ever underestimated the fundraising potential of the 500 Club, but it was essentially a club that anyone with $1,000 could join. Not very exclusive. For the very few big players who gave thousands of dollars to the party — whether they were personal donations or contributions made by their companies — the Conservatives had another scheme altogether.

However sophisticated the donor to the PC Canada Fund, or however well-heeled the prospect, few were immune to the allure of a black-tie dinner party at 24 Sussex Drive. Along with the prime minister and his wife, there was always a collection of wealthy and powerful people, beautifully dressed, comparing holiday notes, talking politics, sharing insider gossip. You could find yourself sitting beside department-store tycoon John Craig Eaton or media baron Conrad Black. Prominent journalists in attendance might include CBC anchorman Peter Mansbridge, *Globe and Mail* editor William Thorsell, or *Maclean's* columnist Allan Fotheringham. Over a glass of champagne you might have chatted about the upcoming budget with Finance Minister Michael Wilson, or as you sipped your after-dinner coffee, you could have tut-tutted with Guy Charbonneau about the sorry antics of the Liberals in the Senate. Nothing was left to chance at 24 Sussex Drive: these dinners were choreographed with callipers. The mix of guests was calculated more carefully than anything else. Potential party benefactors, even those who only showed promise, were carefully, even lovingly, dropped into the pool of bag-men, buddies, cabinet ministers, and influential journalists.

The evening would have begun with the guests' arrival at the front door at 7 p.m. sharp where Ashraf Khan, the butler, and Mila's personal assistant, Bonnie Brownlee, would welcome them. If Brown-lee was not available, Rick Morgan, Mulroney's executive assistant (and the son of his constituency aide, Keith Morgan), would be there in her place. Bonnie or Rick would escort the guests into the living room where the prime minister waited to greet them; Mila was often upstairs, still getting ready. Waiters in dinner jackets stood by, ready to take orders for a glass of wine or a cocktail, and while people enjoyed their drinks they could admire the spectacular north view from the living-room window. Directly below the house, which is set high on a cliff, is the rushing confluence of three rivers, the Ottawa, the Gatineau, and the Rideau, and beyond them lie the Gatineau Hills. On cool evenings the fire crackled, and scented Rigaud can-dles, brought in by the dozens at $3,000 a case, perfumed the rooms. Guests drank it all in, storing up memories to share with the folks back home.

Waiters would begin to circulate with silver trays of canapés and hors d'oeuvres, often tiny buckwheat blini served with caviar and sour cream or smoked salmon. Sometimes it would be Mila's favourite, a hot round of Brie baked in puff pastry; as one waiter passed among the guests, a second waiter followed to pick up the used spoons.

At 7:30 the party moved into the dining room. The staff would probably have removed the large mahogany dining-room table, which seats twenty-four people, as well as a smaller one for twelve that stood in the bay window. In their place would be five round rented tables and chairs, all covered in matching fabrics, "à la Maison blanche," as the household called it. This was Nancy Reagan's preferred style when she and President Ronald Reagan entertained at the White House, and it had the advantage of creating space for fifty guests, rather than the maximum thirty-six allowed by the mahogany tables. Mila had purchased several sets of china through the National Arts Centre, and one of her favourites, a Japanese Fitz and Floyd Starburst pattern, frequently graced the tables.

Flowers, of course, were everywhere, and the more exotic the better. Earlier in the day François Martin, the chef and household coordinator, would drive the 24 Sussex van across the road to Government House and pull up at the government greenhouses where Ed Lawrence, the governor general's gardener, would have plenty of fresh flowers on hand in his cold room. (When Jeanne Sauvé was governor general, there was a little stuffiness about allowing the Mulroneys to take the vast quantity and variety of flowers they demanded for their parties, but a quiet word was said to someone and soon there were no more objections.) Martin would race into the cold room, choose white Casablanca lilies, long-stemmed French tulips from Holland, or some other expensive blooms, then rush back to 24 Sussex to spend a frantic hour or two arranging them in the halls, the reception rooms, the dining room, Mulroney's study, and even in the master bedroom, before he turned to the dinner preparations.

Guests sat according to a plan prepared by Brownlee, often with the prime minister's help. Mulroney was very particular about where his guests were placed; a spot near him or near Mila was a signal that this guest was particularly honoured. When it was a dinner for friends, as opposed to a state function, each setting displayed an embossed menu card describing the meal; more elaborate dinners called for formal booklets with gold tassels.

The menu was a carefully planned event in itself. Take, for example, a dinner for friends held on March 22, 1988. The first course was scallops served in a mousseline sauce of champagne based on a dish from one of Émile Zola's novels ("Coquilles St. Jacques Compostelle Champagnoise Mousseline dit 'Zola'"). It was followed by a witty conceit: a loin of veal served with potatoes that had been mashed with almonds, shaped to look like whole potatoes once again, sautéed, and then decorated with bean sprouts to look like potatoes that had sprouted in their paper bag. Asparagus tips with baby vegetables accompanied the main course, which was followed by a fresh salad of rare greens with a simple "sans souci" ("no trouble") dressing. The wines were chosen with great care. That evening the Mulroneys served an Italian white Erbaluce di Caluso 1986 with the first course, followed by a Burgundy Pinot Noir Louis Roche 1983. Mulroney himself drank no wine; Mila would have very little.

After the salad course was served, Mulroney might stand in the alcove of the bay window to make a short speech, while François Martin watched carefully through the window of the door between the dining room and the pantry. The speech was his signal to ready the desserts. That March evening, the finale was a *bast'illa*, a Greek pastry of buttery filo wrapped around a mascarpone cheese and pistachio filling and served on a coulis of crushed berries.

After dinner, guests usually drifted back to the living room for coffee and cognac and by 10 or 10:30, Brownlee was gently signalling that it was time to go by starting to collect the coats. By the end of the evening you would feel like a bona fide member of the country's power elite. You would have met interesting people whose names you could drop later on; you had been inside one of the nation's most famous residences. And the Mulroneys were such wonderful hosts: funny, warm, sincerely interested in their guests, their guests' children, their working lives, their ideas for the country.

The next time a personal letter arrived from the prime minister asking for money for the Tory party, it would be hard to say no. In fact, it would be hard not to play the big spender and give more than you had planned to, perhaps more than you could comfortably afford. Clearly, the prime minister valued your friendship, and a dinner at Sussex Drive wasn't such a bad thing for business, once colleagues found out about it. In fact, thinking of business, the government had plenty of business to throw your way, and a donation to the party was probably as smart an investment as you could make these days. Given the extraordinarily generous tax credits allowed for political donations, it makes better financial sense to give money to a political party than to a church or charity.

What only a few of the PC Party's insiders knew was that many of these invitations to 24 Sussex Drive were dictated by a cold-hearted computer. A significant donation to the party was the ticket to dinner, the highest reward in a carefully structured fundraising scheme that worked like an airline's frequent flier point system. Or, if you weren't already a big donor, perhaps you were a hot prospect: a wealthy Canadian or the CEO of a major corporation.

These dinners were a stroke of genius, another idea borrowed from Republican bagmen in the United States, and part of a larger scheme designed to woo the country's business leaders. The PC Canada Fund's corporate strategy committee once again called on fundraising guru Bob Odell, who became a working member of the group for several years after 1983. The committee's chairman was Peter Clark; other members included Nicholas Locke; David Read, a Halifax restaurateur and Petro-Canada board member; and Duncan Jessiman, the prominent Winnipeg lawyer who served on Mulroney's 1983 finance team and was appointed to the board of Air Canada in 1985.

A confidential PC Canada Fund document prepared by the corporate strategy committee after consultation with the fund's banking officers across Canada shows just how sophisticated the process was by 1986 when the party was looking ahead to the 1988 election. The report recommended that the bagmen concentrate on specific targets: "chartered and other banks, insurance companies, trust companies, CA firms, lobbyist firms, major oil companies, automobile manufacturers, most wealthy Canadians (individuals), breweries, transportation, steel companies, mining and resources, pulp and paper and major American corporations."

The document emphasized the need to pamper the 220 "blue-chip" donors, most of them the CEOs of corporations, who provided as much as two-thirds of all contributions to the party. "It is also this group that receives the most valuable rewards such as private receptions with the PM and top ministers," the report stated. "Even within this elite, it might be necessary to discriminate on the basis of donation importance for the scarcest of rewards." For example, the top fifty corporate donors were to enjoy dinner with the prime minister at least once a year.

The report cautioned that there was a difference between donors in central Canada and in the Maritimes, and that benchmarks for the top donor group would vary accordingly. "In Toronto and Montreal this will be at about $5,000 but in the Maritimes it might be $2,000 or $3,000." Romancing the corporate elite, especially the major American corporations identified in the memo, would require considerable finesse. Top donors should be invited to one or two private dinners of about twenty couples each with the prime minister and his wife at their residence. Mindful of the dogsbodies who had to perform the delicate financial extractions, the memo acknowledged that they too should be rewarded. The handful of senior party fundraisers — such as David Angus — who provided the crucial "personal links to major donors" deserved the same special treatment, the document recommended.

Furthermore, top-level donors should be invited to private dinners in other parts of the country with key cabinet ministers as well as with the powerful "regional" ministers who are responsible for patronage in their own provinces. "Each regional chairman will be responsible for organizing an annual regional finance dinner to which 'blue-chip' donors will be invited for an intimate dinner with a senior cabinet minister," the report advised. These ministers' parties, the paper stated later on, not mincing any words, would be designed "to provide access for donors to cabinet."

Information was another reward recommended for the elite. The strategy committee proposed to send this group "insider newsletters providing them with useful, topical information (e.g. cabinet changes). These would be targeted primarily at explaining evolving issues (e.g. budget, free trade) or putting forward the government record. This letter could be called 'Briefing Notes' and would be printed on a discreet, quality letterhead." Such insider information would of course be of a higher quality than that found in the quarterly party newsletter that would go to ordinary fundraisers and donors "to keep them informed in a general way about the party and the fund." Blue-chip donors should be spared this newsletter, the report advised, because they would probably view it as junk mail. Informing them in a general way would be an insult; they wanted the real dope.

What the blue-chip donors also wanted was excellent connections to Ottawa, the paper said, and it emphasized the importance of having highly visible, well-connected Tories to do the soliciting. These fundraisers should be kept informed and in touch with the party and the government. "And it is important that these links be visible to ensure their stature in the political community and therefore make their jobs as fundraisers easier, since having 'connections' to Ottawa is one of the primary motivations of donors."

To help the bagmen with their task, the party had developed what it called an information management system. "The computer program for this system has been designed and is mostly operational," said the report. "It includes all capabilities discussed in earlier reports, most significantly linking prospects and donors to regional campaigns and individual canvassers as well as identifying members of 'corporate families.'"

The paper divides donors into four distinct categories: the 220 blue-chip donors, most of which are corporations; a second tier of 500 donors who contribute more than $1,000; a third tier of 300 people who give more than $500; and a final group of 1,000 or so who give less than $500. This final category is referred to as the "low-yield" group.

Committee members were brutally frank about the value of each group. Their plan stated bluntly that it was necessary to create "a subtle hierarchy" among the groups in which the most extensive "rewards and recognition" are reserved for the top echelon of donors and fundraisers. Recognition, however, should be doled out sparingly, "so as not to debase the value of the rewards. It is necessary and valuable to focus our efforts on the highest-yield areas; 'skimming the market,'" the report goes on. "That is not to say the lower-yield donors and canvassers should be ignored, only that less attention and fewer resources should be spent in maintaining them. This is not only cost-effective but also creates a subtle hierarchy that can motivate those at one level to attempt to move up, and reward those who contribute most."

A less lavish scheme that ran in Ottawa for three years showed how the lower-tier donors were taken care of. For $250 a couple, Ottawa Tories could participate in "Capital Encounters" — an evening sponsored by thirty couples who loaned their homes for dinner parties with cabinet ministers. Caterer Vic Jones of Capital Foods provided all the meals for about $65 a couple, and the rest was pure profit for the PC Party. Each host would invite between twenty-five and thirty couples for dinner, guaranteeing the presence of one cabinet minister, one parliamentary secretary, and one chief of staff in Ottawa. For their part, the politicians on display promised to stay at least two hours. Once again, the idea came from Washington, "and it was done with class and dignity," said one of the organizers proudly. "We raised tons of money." Similar events were staged in other cities. In Montreal they became rather more ambitious: on one occasion Montreal bagman and Mulroney crony Jean-Louis Le Saux hosted a dinner with senior Tory ministers for $5,000 a person.

In its detailed document, the strategy committee proposed that, in certain circumstances, Tory fundraisers remind potential corporate donors of federal government contracts they had received. The PC Canada Fund was directed to set up a system in which the file on each corporate donor would include a list of the number of government contracts, grants, or policies that had benefitted the corporation.

The fund's executive director, Nick Locke, said in a 1989 interview that the party kept computerized files on each corporate donor, and that the files were updated in 1986 after an internal review. But Locke denied that the files contained information about government contracts, grants, or policies beneficial to the donors. He also denied that party fundraisers ever mentioned government contracts or grants when they discussed a donation with a prospective donor. "They're clearly directed not to do that," he said. "Some people in this world have gotten into trouble doing things like that, but they have not been associated with the PC Canada Fund. There's no quid pro quo in this thing." Locke said that he suspected that soliciting donations by reminding donors of government business they have received would be not only improper but possibly illegal. "Our canvassers are told in no uncertain terms not to get involved in that sort of thing. If anybody started soliciting that way, they'd be drummed out."

The party's documents themselves contradict Locke's statement. One paper, titled "Implementation of Corporate Fundraising Strategy," described, among other things, the information that makes up a "corporate donor profile." Most of the twenty-four categories contain details on such matters as the size, nature, and structure of the company and the history of its donations to the party. But they also include a category called "Government Relations." An appendix to the document defines it: "Government Relations: identifies government contracts, grants or policy issues that profit the firm." The appendix goes on to suggest that this category could possibly "be suppressed unless specifically asked for."

Locke also denied that there was an "Invoicing" category. He said that invoicing — that is, securing agreement from a company to accept invoices for promised future donations — had been under consideration by the party, but had not been implemented. He said that in some cases it had been done informally but it was not officially sanctioned.

Once again, the documents do not bear out Locke's comments. The 1989 corporate donor profile for the Royal Bank of Canada showed both Government Relations and Invoicing; both categories were still on the party's computerized coding system.

A The PCCF account number: 416544

B The contact: Mr. A. R. Taylor — President

    Phone (514) 874-2132

    P.O. Box 6001

    3rd Floor, Place Ville Marie

    Montreal, Quebec

    Postal Code: H3C 3A9

C The CEO: Mr. Rowland C. Frazee

D The Donor type: 2 Corporate

E The solicitation code: 10 Corporate Canvass

F The canvasser: J. A. Tory

G The regional chairman: David Angus

H The reference number: [blank]

I The campaign: NAG- Chartered Banks

J Sales, profits, employees   Last Year — Sales: $9,549,322,000

    Profits: $450,085,000

    Prior Year — Sales: $9,132,467,00

    Profits: $479,993,000

    Employees: 38,189

K Area of operations: National

L The company fiscal year end: October 31

M Ownership: Royal Bank 113

N Government Relations: [blank]

O Type of Business: Bank

P Donor history   1 year ago: $35,000

    2 years ago: $45,000

    3 years ago: $30,000

    4 years ago: $30,000

    +4 years ago: $130,000

    Totals: $270,000

Q	Target:	$40,000	
R	Contacts	David Angus	J.A. Tory
	Date	13/05/86	15/02/86
	Result	agrees to	will invoice/
		increase	won't increase
S	Invoicing	Yes	
		01/02/87: $40,000	
		01/02/88: $40,000	
		Election: $80,000	
		01/02/89: $40,000	
T	Communications:	Xmas: yes	
		PM Letter: Yes	
		Minister: Yes	
		Budget: No	
U	Comments	all invitations go to both	
		CEO and contact	
V	Donation Detail	[blank]	
W	Corporate Family	[blank]	
X	Special Instructions	[blank]	

The Royal Bank profile revealed that the party fundraiser who solicited funds from the bank was Toronto businessman John A. Tory, who also sat on the bank's board. Mr. Tory's "contact" at the bank was its president, Allan Taylor, while the CEO was listed as Rowland Frazee.

The file showed that when Tory approached the bank on February 15, 1986, Taylor agreed to be invoiced for future donations, but he would not increase the total amount beyond the $35,000 that the bank had given in 1985. However, when a second approach was made three months later, this time by David Angus, the bank did agree to an increase. The fund had set a target of $40,000 for the Royal, and Angus persuaded the bank to give that much in 1987. The Royal Bank's contributions over the previous four years ($35,000 in 1985, $45,000 in 1984, $30,000 in 1983, $30,000 in 1982) were listed and the total of contributions collected from the bank since 1979 ($270,000) was also shown. In a section reserved for comments, the file noted that "all invitations go to both CEO and contact" — although the file does not say what the invitations are for.

Another example of a donor profile was that of Moosehead Breweries. The information in the computer printout shows that its donor number was 2474207, the contact — and company CEO — was Derek Oland, the canvasser was John Kavanaugh, the chairman of the campaign was David Read, and the target for 1986 was $2,000. "Do not solicit," the profile ordered fundraisers. A five-year donor history showed Oland had given a total of $2,101.36, but the computer had no record as yet of business information such as fiscal year-end or number of employees. It did indicate that Oland had agreed to invoicing and that he donated money to the party from his office in Saint John, New Brunswick, where a "D. Smith" was responsible for canvassing. A family history shows a total of $4,000 in donations for 1986 with previous donations adding up to $6,000.

Toronto businessman Hal Jackman, later appointed lieutenant-governor of Ontario, was both party bagman and target, because of his significant personal wealth. His donor profile lists the seven obscure companies in his corporate family, the Jackman Group, and how much each had given in current and past years. The total came to a modest $5,400. It also showed how much Jackman had given personally from 1981 through 1983 — $3,700. Although the life insurance company that he controlled, Empire Life, had given very little over the years, he made his mark with another family concern, National Trust. It gave generously: $11,000 in 1985, $6,800 in 1986, a whopping $25,000 in 1987, and a respectable $3,100 in 1988.

Profiles like these were indispensable to the strategy set out by the committee in 1986. And it would appear that the rewards system for those valued blue-chip donors was embraced enthusiastically by everyone in the chain. An examination of guest lists for the black-tie dinners at 24 Sussex Drive shows that many of the invitees were indeed the chief executive officers of the party's most generous corporate contributors. And their fellow guests were the power brokers of the Mulroney years in Ottawa: long-time cronies, party bagmen, lobbyists, politicians, and a few carefully chosen journalists.

On December 5, 1985, for example, not long after decorator Giovanni Mowinckel had finished his renovation work at the residence, thirty people arrived for dinner. As usual, the Mulroneys were careful to sprinkle non-partisan figures among the out-and-out Tories. The bagmen included Guy Charbonneau and PC Canada Fund board member Irving Gerstein, with their wives. Influential guests included Chief Justice Brian Dickson and his wife, Barbara; Paddy Sherman, the publisher of the Ottawa *Citizen* and his wife, Maureen; and *Globe and Mail* columnist Jeffrey Simpson and his wife, Wendy, a lawyer at the Department of Justice. Important donors in attendance were Loblaws heir Galen Weston and his wife, Hillary, and broadcasting executive Douglas Bassett and his wife, Susan.

Four nights later twenty-eight people arrived for another dinner. They included David Angus, whose date that evening was journalist Nancy Southam; Brian Gallery, national president of the 500 Club, with his wife, Nancy; construction magnate Donald Matthews, with his wife, Phyllis; Alain Paris, the Mulroneys' personal accountant, with his wife, Rachelle; Finance Minister Michael Wilson with his wife, Margie; Solicitor General Elmer MacKay with his date, one of Mila's aides, Lynn Belsey; Bruce Verchère, one of Mulroney's most trusted lawyers from Montreal, with his wife, Lynne; and Peter Eby, vice-chairman of Burns Fry and a member of the 1983 fundraising team for the leadership, with his wife, Jane. (Burns Fry had an interesting pattern of donations to the Tories; in 1985 the firm gave just over $1,000 to the PCs, but by 1986 the amount had soared to more than $35,000. In 1988, the amount rose even higher; perhaps because it was an election year, the donation was up to more than $56,000.) Another major donor was Denison Mines president Stephen Roman, who was at the dinner with his wife, Betty. Roman, who had once been an unsuccessful Tory candidate, was the head of Lake Ontario Cement Co. In 1987 Lake Ontario Cement donated $46,000 to the federal Tories.

Who paid for these evenings, the PC Party or the public? Not every guest was a donor or a bagman; some were influential citizens in their own right. According to François Martin, who paid all the grocery bills for the house, the costs were simply absorbed into the household expenses that were handled by the Privy Council Office. In other words, the taxpayer was actually the host when guests were greeted at 24 Sussex Drive.

CHAPTER SIX

THE TOLLGATERS' PICNIC

THE ROLY-POLY LITTLE MAN BUSTLED INTO THE OFFICE IN Cap-de-la-Madeleine, Quebec, greeted the proprietor warmly, and asked after his health. He glanced around the office and noticed a kettle on a camp stove.

"So you always keep a kettle on the stove?" he asked.

"No, no," the businessman replied. "That's for my flowers, my plants."

The niceties observed, the visitor turned to business.

"Okay," he said, briskly. "The honorarium . . . 5 per cent of the amount."

The businessman was stunned. "I can't," he stammered.

"You're not serious."

"I had $20,000. I didn't foresee giving 5 per cent."

"There are two."

"I had $20,000 for Charlevoix."

"Yes."

"Then I had $20,000 for the other, also."

"Ah . . ."

"I didn't foresee this."

The phone rang and the businessman answered, but cut the conversation short before returning to his visitor in distress.

"No, like I said before," explained the businessman, "I paid for a fundraising dinner and that was by cheque and that was deductible, but 5 per cent is money . . . If I had it, I sure don't have it now."

His visitor pressed hard. "I need this," he insisted. "If you want to continue working . . ."

"They want $2,000 in black money?" asked the businessman.

"Yes. You arrange it any way you want, okay? In any event, I'll call you back. The money will go directly to the party. But make the cheque out to the Imprimeries les Récollets."[1]

It was October 8, 1985, and Claude Levasseur, a former pharmaceutical salesman turned Conservative Party organizer, was out hustling for a kickback. He wanted $2,500 and his victim was Jean-Marie Chastenay, a land surveyor. Chastenay Gagnée et Associés Inc. had won two federal government contracts worth $50,160 — Chastenay was trying to make the amount sound smaller — for work at airports in Quebec and in the Northwest Territories.

Like so many small-time bullies, Levasseur used the mere threat of a powerful connection. Rightly or wrongly, Chastenay believed Levasseur had some clout because of Levasseur's ties to Pierre H. Vincent, a lawyer and the new Tory MP in the neighbouring riding of Trois-Rivières. Not only had Levasseur managed Vincent's 1984 campaign, but the two men were partners in a real estate development company called Les Immeubles Levin Ltée. (The "Le" in the name stands for Levasseur and the "vin" for Vincent.)

The kickback demand was not a complete surprise. Two days earlier, Levasseur had phoned Chastenay to ask for a percentage on the contract, telling him he would use his influence to secure Chastenay more contracts — as long as the surveyor cooperated by kicking back 5 per cent of their value to the party. Chastenay was furious. He called his MP, Michel Champagne, the Conservative member for Champlain riding. Champagne calmed him down, assuring him that he was not part of this extortion bid and that this was not party policy. Tape the meeting with Levasseur, he advised. When Levasseur arrived at Chastenay's office on October 8, a hidden tape machine recorded their entire conversation. Chastenay had told Levasseur he thought the $2,500 figure was too steep, and Levasseur seemed willing to accept $2,000. Although Levasseur assured Chastenay that the money was to go to the Tory party, he was to make his cheque out to a printing company in Trois-Rivières. This would launder the donation, obscuring its ultimate destination. Chastenay dug in his heels and refused to write the cheque, and an angry Levasseur stormed out of the office.

Once Levasseur was gone, Chastenay took the tape to Michel Champagne. What happened to it next became a mystery. The RCMP did not get their hands on it until 1987, more than two years after the incident took place. Where was it in the meantime? Champagne has always refused to say what he did with it, but in 1987 Chastenay, who was fed up with waiting for Levasseur to be charged, told Andrew McIntosh at *The Globe and Mail* that after he gave the tape to Champagne he'd received calls from unnamed individuals who told him they worked in the PMO. He told McIntosh that his callers asked if he had copies of the tape. He said no. Marc Lortie, Mulroney's press secretary at the time, said later that no one at the PMO had ever called Chastenay and they did not have the tape.

But in November 1987, shortly after Chastenay went public with his story, the RCMP had a copy of the tape from sources unknown; apparently they had known nothing of the incident until then. Three months later, on February 5, 1988, Levasseur was finally charged with influence-peddling. But his case did not follow the expected course. In a surprise move, Levasseur chose not to go through a preliminary hearing, opting instead for a guilty plea. With this process no testimony would be heard, and the tape would not be played. In this election year, the case could be settled without further embarrassment to the Mulroney government. The tape was never made public. On March 22, 1989, Levasseur pleaded guilty but was spared a jail sentence. He was fined $2,000, given three months to pay it, and put on probation for a year.

Pierre Vincent was successful in distancing himself from Levasseur in the Chastenay affair. Dark-haired, slimmed down from an earlier pudginess, and blessed with boyish good looks, the thirty-four-year-old Vincent was on his way up in the government. He'd come to Ottawa with a background of community service: he'd raised money for the cancer society and was involved with the local law society. During the 1984 election campaign he and Levasseur had gone out of their way to establish themselves as paragons of political virtue. In an interview with Lawrence Martin, then a *Globe and Mail* reporter, Vincent remarked that people in his riding often asked what he would do for them if they voted Conservative. "It's stunning," Vincent declared. "They are so conditioned here to getting something in return for working for Liberals or voting for Liberals that they automatically think it's a regular part of the process."

Levasseur couldn't resist chiming in. "I've got people calling me all the damned time. Give me some money and I'll do this for your candidate, they say." Vincent and Levasseur expressed their shock at such behaviour. Just imagine, they told Martin.

A few months later, while his partner was out tollgating, the former tax lawyer was making his name in Ottawa as a parliamentary secretary, first to Revenue Minister Elmer MacKay and then to Finance Ministers Michael Wilson and Don Mazankowski. A mess like this was the last thing Vincent needed. He wasted no time in expressing his shock and outrage to reporters, adding that he had long ago severed his partnership with Levasseur. In December 1985, to be exact.

Vincent was stretching the truth. He had sold his 50-per-cent interest in Les Immeubles Levin to Levasseur at that time, but they remained in business together for years afterwards as joint owners of a large parcel of rural land they planned to develop. In 1993 he and Levasseur filed suit against some foresters who'd been cutting trees on their property.

If Levasseur's had been the only case of tollgating during the Mulroney years, it would be unremarkable. But it was not. Montreal businessman Pierre Blouin was another small-time operator hustling kickbacks in 1985. A year earlier, he'd been a low-level advance man for Mulroney in the election campaign, travelling through Quebec to help local party organizers prepare for the leader's whistle-stop visits. Blouin bragged openly about his influence with Mulroney and offered to arrange a federal lease renewal for André Hamel, a Drummondville Liberal, in exchange for $70,000 — 6 per cent of the value of the lease. Public Works rented space from Hamel for Employment and Immigration offices but the lease was due to expire in 1985. When the Mounties investigated, they found two of Hamel's cancelled cheques made out to the Tory party for $25,000 each, and Hamel admitted he'd paid "to stay in the race," as he put it.

Despite his lower bid he didn't win; the contract went to Les Immeubles Brodilaf, a firm with solid Tory connections. In a fury, Hamel sued the government for the financial harm he believed had been done to him and stormed off to the police to lay a complaint against Blouin. During their investigation they turned up an extraordinary document, a legal bill from Ogilvy Renault, Mulroney's old law firm, to Hamel. The invoice showed that the firm had been in touch with Mulroney aides in the PMO over the lease, including principal secretary Bernard Roy and aide Benoît Roberge (brother of Ritz-Carlton Hotel manager Fern Roberge). Another aide who was kept briefed on the file was Roch LaSalle's chief of staff, Pierre Claude Nolin.

In the end Hamel had the last laugh: the roof of the new Brodilaf building collapsed under a heavy layer of snow before the government employees could move in. Blouin pleaded guilty to trying to obtain a kickback, was fined $3,000, and died soon afterwards of a heart attack while cross-country skiing.

Guy Racine was another entrepreneur and Tory advance man, one who thought he should have a $25,000 bite of a $425,000

Canadian International Development Agency contract that went to Wajax, an Ottawa-based heavy machinery maker. Racine asked for the money during a private meeting with Wajax president Bernard Scobie, telling him part of it would go into the federal party coffers. At the time he made his move on the astonished Scobie, Racine was employed by a company called Co-Genar Ltée, which had a CIDA contract to manage a development project in Senegal. Wajax was hoping to win a contract to provide forest-fighting equipment to the same project. The Wajax people were not inclined to take any non-sense from Racine and reported his extortion attempt to the police, but no action was ever taken against him.

Racine had excellent connections to some powerful players in the party. Co-Genar owned a third of a holding company called Consortium CRS Ltée, another third of which was owned by Marc LeFrançois, a wealthy developer and the president of Rocois Construction. LeFrançois was among a small group of men backing Quebec City MP Michel Côté, who entered the cabinet in 1984 as minister of consumer and corporate affairs. Within a few years Côté would be fired from his cabinet job for favours he took from the Quebec City group that included LeFrançois.

For the most part, the scandals that broke around men like Racine and Blouin were one-day wonders that the Mulroney government toughed out with gritted teeth, pretending they were just the occasional bad apples buried in a bushel basket of winners. Unfortunately, that was not the case. There was a prevailing ethic among many members of the party that after 1984 it was their turn. They'd been waiting outside the palace so long, noses pressed to the windows, watching the Grits feasting at the trough. The Racines and the Blouins and the Levasseurs were small fry, really, only trying to catch their piece of the action.

The Tories hadn't been in power more than three or four months before stories started to surface about outrageous kickback schemes. There was nothing subtle, for example, about the headline in *The Edmonton Journal* on January 8, 1985: "Kickbacks in the Tory camp." What had shocked the editors at the Alberta paper was that Mulroney had awarded control of the federal government's multimillion-dollar advertising contracts to Roger Nantel and Toronto filmmaker Peter Simpson, another Tory. The contract was worth $2 million a year to the men, who had set up a new company to handle the business. Rather disarmingly, Nantel told reporters the contract was not quite as sweet as it seemed: he would have to turn over some of his fee to the Conservative Party.

The PMO hastily tried to limit the damage Nantel had done by explaining that what the loose-lipped ad man meant to say was that some of the money would be channelled to "educational seminars." But Nantel remained unrepentant and did not complain about being misquoted. Yes, it's patronage, he admitted, when asked about his contract. But so what? Tories deserved it, he blustered; they had been locked out of government contracts for years. Clearly Nantel also believed that if some of the money was passed along to the party, it was only fair. This attitude towards the spoils of power infected so many of Nantel's fellow party members that Ottawa was soon seething with rumours of kickbacks being demanded everywhere and suspicions that members of Parliament were involved.

The MP who was to become famous as the king of kickbacks was Michel Gravel. Until his election in 1984, the tall, silver-haired accountant from Rivières-des-Prairies, a Montreal suburb, had been working for Henri Paquin, a childhood friend from the working-class district of Rosemont. Paquin, a multimillionaire, began his business career in 1955 with a garbage collection firm but built up an $85-million empire under a holding company, Société de Gestion DHP Inc., which owned quarries, shopping centres, commercial real estate, office buildings, and a construction company. His home base was the Montreal suburb of Saint-Laurent, where he had become the largest single commercial landlord.

One of Paquin's enterprises was Les Industries de Lavage

Dentex, a company that bleached denim fabric for clothing manufacturers. Gravel had managed Dentex since the late 1970s and assisted
Paquin with his other investments. It was at Dentex that he met his
wife, Louise, then Paquin's secretary. Louise Gravel had few illusions
about elected officials: one of her routine tasks was to count the stacks
of cash Paquin regularly set aside for municipal, provincial, and federal politicians and slip them into brown envelopes for delivery.

Michel Gravel also helped Paquin set up offshore companies and
bank accounts in the Cayman Islands, the Isle of Jersey, and
Lichtenstein. Lugging suitcases full of cash, Gravel often travelled to
these tax havens to deposit money. "I've probably been to the Cayman
Islands more times than you've been to the countryside," Gravel
bragged to reporter Richard Cléroux. Sometimes, he confided, he carried money destined for the numbered accounts of Liberal senators
and cabinet ministers, although he refused to say who they were.

Party affiliation meant little to Henri Paquin. He needed politicians for their votes on zoning and the leases, grants, and contracts
they could steer his way. His interest was simply in whoever was in
power, and Paquin could smell the Mulroney victory in 1984. He was
friendly with Rodrigue Pageau and Roger Nantel, who were recruiting
candidates for the Tories, and he was able to recommend his trusted
employee Michel Gravel.[2] The fact that Gravel had always supported
the Liberals didn't bother any of them; Gravel became the designated
Tory candidate for Montréal-Gamelin, an East End, working-class
Montreal riding. Paquin told the PC Party he would bankroll Gravel's
campaign, which he did generously, spending more than $200,000 on
rallies, parties, and souvenirs before the writ was dropped. The gamble paid off. Gravel won and Paquin had his own man in Ottawa.

A footnote to this event was the lawsuit Paquin launched against
Gravel just six weeks after Gravel scampered off to Ottawa in triumph. Paquin sued his former employee in Superior Court, alleging
that Gravel and three other people, including Louise Gravel, had
swindled him out of $562,636 between 1982 and 1984. Statements

of claim often take a shotgun approach, including allegations that cannot be supported. Nevertheless, Paquin's allegations were interesting. According to Paquin's statement of claim (denied by Gravel), he had to take over Dentex when Gravel left. When he and his sons, Marc and Denis, looked at the books they realized that Gravel was paying twice the usual price for the pumice stones to wash the denim. The extra cash, alleged Paquin, was pouring into a company Gravel had set up called Pierre Ponce Suprême Inc. It didn't take long for Paquin's rage to cool, however; he realized Gravel was more useful to him without the lawsuit hanging over everyone's heads. The men settled in mid-December.

Once he got to Ottawa, Gravel set up house in an apartment in Hull with a new Tory cabinet minister, Pierre Cadieux, a lawyer from another Montreal suburb, and was informally appointed by Public Works Minister Roch LaSalle as the "godfather" of Hull. Conservative supporters in the few "orphan ridings" won by Liberals — Hull was one of these — were deemed to need someone to keep an eye on their interests. Several Tory MPs, among them Gravel, had to serve two ridings — their own and a riding that had elected a Liberal.

Gravel was soon in touch with dozens of eager contractors, engineers, architects, and other businessmen hungry for public works contracts. One of these was Émilien Maillé, a Hull baker and a long-time Liberal organizer who looked to new opportunities with the Tories. Maillé took care to befriend Gravel, paying $4,000 to furnish and redecorate the MP's Montreal riding office. His payoff, he hoped, would be a food supply contract with the Canadian military. He wanted to begin with a Defence Department order to supply meat to the Longue Pointe military base in Gravel's riding. In March 1985 Maillé, who by now was acting as a sort of unpaid aide to Gravel, helped the MP organize a dinner at the officers' mess at Longue Pointe, a $100-a-plate event for hand-picked businessmen in the riding to hear speakers from the government's Supply and Services Department talk about opportunities for business with the new

Mulroney government. Business was certainly good for Gravel; the mess charged him $20 a head, and even though many of the guests were allowed in free, he made a profit of a few thousand dollars.

Successes like this gave Gravel grander ideas. The most notorious fundraising event he held was a lobster and Dom Pérignon party at his waterfront home in Rivières-des-Prairies on July 10, 1985; the tickets were $5,000 per person and the main attraction was a chance to hobnob with the public works minister, Roch LaSalle. The others in attendance were vying for space on the minister's fabled "short list" of companies favoured for government contracts. Gravel collected the money from his guests (not all paid the full amount and a couple of them never paid more than half), and he later testified that after keeping back $5,000 for expenses, he turned over the balance — about $35,000 — to LaSalle. The lobster party led to other events, and soon Gravel was organizing lucrative summer golf tournaments with LaSalle as the featured headliner.

About this same time, Gravel got his hands on the federal government's leasing book, a confidential list of 5,000 leases for all federal offices across Canada. The list included the value of the lease, the holder, the expiry date, and other terms. While the information in the book would be pure gold to developers who wanted to bid on federal contracts, some Tories saw the possibility of using the information to extract hefty kickbacks from eager bidders. How Gravel came to have the book is still not entirely clear; he later testified he got it from LaSalle's chief of staff, Pierre Claude Nolin. LaSalle's senior political adviser at this time was Frank Majeau; Majeau said one of his jobs in LaSalle's office was to put the leasing information together for Nolin and LaSalle. As Majeau and Gravel were to become close friends, it is also possible that Majeau gave Gravel the book.

By the summer of 1985, Gravel and Maillé were a busy team, arranging deals for everything from federal leases to construction contracts for the new Museum of Civilization in Hull. Maillé, however, was growing uneasy. He wasn't any closer to his meat contract for Longue

Pointe, or for any military base for that matter. Several other contractors who'd paid Gravel money on the understanding that they would be taken care of were also grumbling. One contractor had installed an extra bathroom at no charge in the apartment Gravel shared with Cadieux because Cadieux complained he needed his own bathroom for his morning shower; later that bathroom, valued at $6,000, was dubbed "le douche à Cadieux" by the Mounties who investigated the benefits Gravel received. When the contractor didn't get a rich contract in return he protested, as many others were starting to do.

Gravel knew he had to produce to keep the contractors happy; he began throwing his weight around with the civil service. One former public servant has vivid memories of the MP. "I was told an MP was making a lot of noise about how we weren't treating suppliers in his riding well. I met with Gravel and he said to me, 'You'd better fix that.'" The bureaucrat assured Gravel that his department would do its best. He arranged a meeting for the MP with five public servants who were all experts in procurement. Gravel became impatient with what he saw as their long-winded advice on how his constituents could win contracts. Cut to the chase, he told them. "What's the recipe?" The bureaucrats knew exactly what he meant: whom do you have to pay off to win.

"Bid lower," one said.

"What?" asked Gravel in disbelief.

"Bid lower," the unsmiling official said again.

Such impertinence was not appreciated, and Gravel took his complaints to the minister. A ministerial aide returned to the bureaucrat who had organized the meeting and reprimanded him. "That's not the answer we want," he told him. Within weeks the bureaucrat was out of a job.

By December 1985, the contractors who had showered so many benefits on him were sufficiently angered at their failure to win contracts that three of them met secretly over dinner at Café Henry Burger in Hull with Pierre Claude Nolin and Pierre-Paul Bourdon, the chief of staff to Supply and Services Minister André Bissonnette. The three men poured out their grievances to the two aides, who soon understood that Gravel had become a dangerous liability.

Gravel's freelancing was out of control. Bernard Roy was briefed and by January 1986, Gravel was under RCMP investigation. The Mounties asked Maillé to work with them as an undercover informant on Gravel's schemes; frightened by the knowledge the police had and disappointed at the absence of the much-desired defence contracts, Maillé agreed. For the next few months he wore a body pack to his meetings with Gravel, and the police eavesdropped on their conversations.

In March 1986 the RCMP raided Gravel's apartment and offices. Cadieux encouraged him to hire his good friend Montreal lawyer Daniel Rock. Rock was a well-connected Tory who had run unsuccessfully for the party in the Nicolet riding and had worked in the same law office with Boucherville MP Marcel Danis, who had become deputy Speaker of the House of Commons. Rock was best known for defending mobsters in Montreal's thriving drug and prostitution rings, but he took on the politician's case, and after Gravel was charged on May 15, 1986, with fifty counts of bribery and corruption, Rock represented him with great skill. Insisting on his client's innocence, he launched one imaginative defence tactic after another. The case did not come to court until the 1988 federal election had passed. Gravel did not run again and Rock promptly plea-bargained the charges down from fifty to fifteen. He also got the same deal as Claude Levasseur — no preliminary hearing, just a straight guilty plea and sentencing.

The RCMP had been conducting a parallel investigation triggered by their findings in the Gravel case. The MP and some of his accomplices had admitted to the RCMP that a second 5-per-cent kickback ring existed on federal leases. When the police began digging into this ring, they discovered that benefits had been paid, but at the time they could not connect these payments to criminal activities.

In preparation for Gravel's trial, twenty-seven witnesses had been subpoenaed, and the police and prosecutors hoped their testimony would shed light on the second kickback ring. Without the trial, these witnesses were effectively silenced.

On December 7, 1988, just three weeks after the federal election in which the Tories won a second majority, Gravel pleaded guilty to accepting $97,000 in bribes from contractors and other businessmen. Opposition MPs Don Boudria, Derek Lee, and Gilles Rocheleau held a news conference to object to the deal, saying the absence of testimony and the dropping of some charges kept the details of Gravel's activities secret. They were convinced that a Tory kickback system existed, the MPs told reporters, and that Gravel was just one small part of it.

Gravel was fined $50,000 and sentenced to a year in jail. He served two months. In June 1991 Gravel, furious that he'd had to do any jail time at all, revealed what had gone on behind the scenes. As soon as he'd been charged, he said, he received a call from Benoît Roberge in Mulroney's office, who promised that he'd be taken care of, that he would receive a suspended sentence, that he wouldn't have to go to jail. Benoît Roberge was the liaison between the Quebec caucus and the PMO. "He was in the party and close to his brother," the hotelier, Gravel said. "I knew Fernand and assumed he had that kind of power."

Roch LaSalle, he said, had also promised that his legal bills would be covered. Near the end of the three-year legal battle, Montreal lawyer Gabriel Lapointe was retained to help Daniel Rock; Gravel says he paid Rock's bills, which added up to about $40,000, but he didn't pay a cent to Lapointe. Gravel also says he has no idea who paid Lapointe. And when Lapointe paid Gravel's $50,000 fine in two installments in August 1989, he did not tell his client where he got the money. Gravel says he still doesn't know.

Another politician charged with taking kickbacks was Richard Grisé, a former insurance broker who rode the Mulroney wave into

Ottawa in 1984 as MP for the South Shore riding of Chambly. Like Gravel, Grisé had been a Liberal — he had tried unsuccessfully for the Liberal nomination in the 1979 federal election — and like Gravel, he did well in the federal caucus. Within two years Grisé not only had been named parliamentary secretary to Transport Minister Don Mazankowski, he was also appointed chairman of the Quebec caucus, an honour that usually goes to more senior members. The signals were clear to everyone: the next assignment would be a cabinet position.

And like Gravel, he wasted no time putting together a kickback scheme on federal contracts. It was disarmingly simple, a classic model for others that followed. He began with his own company, one he called Les Consultants Sorig Intl., to serve as the repository of the money. Then he concentrated on how to start the tap running, and a solution presented itself very quickly. In 1985 he was able to win a $245,000 grant for a community centre in Saint-Bruno, a town in his riding; all he had to do after that was hit on the contractors who were building the place. The general contractor coughed up $2,300, the firm that installed air conditioning paid $300, the plumber paid $300, and the electrician came up with $500. Another supplier kicked in $300. It added up to $3,700, and it all went into Les Consultants Sorig.

But this was chicken feed, and Grisé got a little greedier. Some MPs were discovering other ways to take home a little extra at the end of the month. Each MP had a generous office budget, about $165,000 a year to cover the cost of staff, supplies, travel, some furniture, rent for a constituency office, and so on. All the member had to do was send his or her bills to the Commons administrators and they'd be paid. There were the real costs to cover, but with some care, there was also plenty left over.

Grisé came up with a fake contract caper. He needed an accomplice and found one in his friend Joseph Hamelin, a South Shore building contractor, president of the Tory riding association in Saint-Hubert and before that, riding president in Chambly. Hamelin tapped three women he was close to, Jacqueline Marcil, a former girlfriend and employee; his wife, Ginette Jodin; and his sister, Jacinthe Hamelin. Grisé awarded each woman a contract for $800 worth of secretarial or research work they did not have to do. When the Commons administration sent their cheques for the work, the women cashed them and kicked back most of the money to Grisé, who let them keep $100 each for their trouble.

Another scam he ran with Hamelin involved a grant from the federal Department of Employment and Immigration. The money went to Hamelin's construction company, Les Entreprises Mirabel, to subsidize new workers' salaries, but those workers were actually used to help with Grisé's 1988 election campaign. Back in Ottawa, Grisé and Gilles Bernier, his Tory colleague from the Beauce region of the Gaspé, put each other's kids on their office payrolls, a practice that appealed to a few of their Commons colleagues. Two who were caught were Ontario Tory MPs Terry Clifford and Robert Hicks.

And Grisé was eventually caught too, thanks to an episode that was pure farce. Shortly before the November 1988 federal election, one of the women who had received a fake contract got into a fight with Hamelin and stormed out of his office, leaving behind her fur coat. When Hamelin refused to return it, the feud escalated. She went to the police and to the local NDP candidate in the riding, Phil Edmonston, a well-known consumer advocate. The polls showed that Edmonston, a formidable campaigner, had every hope of winning the riding and if he did, the NDP would have its first toehold in Quebec. Once Edmonston and his campaign organizer, Raymond Guardia, heard the woman's story, they went to the RCMP.

The real scandal of the Grisé affair was the way it was handled. Thanks to their own sources, RCMP Inspectors Raymond Bérubé and Jean Pierre Witty had information about Grisé's corrupt practices well before the 1988 election; they had been investigating him since the summer of 1987. The new tips convinced Bérubé and Witty that they had a strong case against the MP, a case further strengthened when they discovered that in early November Grisé had become frightened and confessed the whole story to Peter White, one of Mulroney's top advisers in the PMO.

To their shock, Bérubé and Witty could not persuade their boss to move against Grisé before the election. RCMP Chief Superintendent Brian McConnell, the head of RCMP criminal investigations in Quebec, told them to wait until after the election so the police wouldn't be accused of interfering in the political process. Bérubé and Witty were upset and the NDP, understandably, was outraged. So were the Liberals, who knew what was afoot and who hoped their candidate could slide up the middle between Edmonston and Grisé if Grisé were charged just before the election.

Four days after Grisé won his Chambly riding for the second time, beating Edmonston by 8,500 votes, the RCMP finally raided his home and offices as well as the offices of Joseph Hamelin. A day later, Grisé resigned as a member of the Tory caucus and vanished from Ottawa. He did not resign as an MP. Taxpayers spent hundreds of thousands of dollars on Grisé's salary and offices, even though his constituents were effectively without an MP while his case wound its way through the justice system. Eventually, in 1989, Grisé was brought to court, pleaded guilty, and was fined $20,000. He spent a morning in jail, had lunch at public expense, and was released on three years' probation. After his conviction, the government had to run a by-election in the riding.

A macabre sidebar to the Grisé mess was the story of one Gérard Fortier, whose sorry end passed unnoticed in the larger scheme of things. Fortier, an insurance agent in the Chambly area, was the boyfriend of Lise Barbier, Grisé's secretary. Fortier knew about the scams and just before the 1988 election, he threatened to expose the scheme. A few days later firemen were called to Fortier's house when neighbours spotted smoke and flames coming out of the building. By the time firemen found Fortier's body lying on the floor near the back door, it was, reported the coroner, "90 per cent carbonized." An autopsy showed that Fortier had died of smoke inhalation. Although firemen and police officers suspected arson, no perpetrator was ever found.

There is a dreary sameness to the kind of penny-ante shenanigans some of these MPs dreamed up, but a third Tory MP is worth mentioning just because he was so colourful. This was Édouard Desrosiers, elected from the riding of Hochelaga-Maisonneuve in 1984. Desrosiers was a former provincial policeman and convicted bank robber who had been pardoned for the crime he had committed in 1958. Within weeks of his election he was complaining to a reporter about being hard up. "The biggest problem for me," he told the *Gazette*'s Claude Arpin in October 1984, "are those $800-a-month rents for a tiny one-bedroom apartment." He explained that he was also paying rent for his family home back in the riding.

So he busied himself with ways to supplement his income. The fake contract scam had captured the imaginations of many MPs, and Eddie Desrosiers saw it as one answer to his problems. He gave $5,400 worth of contracts to two women, Monique Bazinet Legare and Evelyn Girard, to do research for his office, then submitted invoices on their behalf to the Commons administration. When the cheques came in, the women endorsed them and he cashed them for himself. Then he spotted another opportunity with a businessman who ran a manufacturing plant in his riding. The company, Les Industries Henry Mitchell, Inc., was after a federal government grant and paid $2,000 to Desrosiers for his help. Even though all this happened in 1985, it took until 1990 to sentence the MP who eventually decided, after a conversation with Mulroney, to plead guilty in return for having some of the charges dropped. Judge André Chaloux fined him $2,000 for taking the Commons money and $1,000 for the kickback.

Desrosiers left politics to start his own Montreal restaurant, Le Dauphin, on Rue Crémazie, where he entertained patrons with his singing; people who heard him said he wasn't too bad. But crooning wasn't enough in the gloomy economic climate of Montreal; his company was forced into receivership in June 1990 by its major creditor,

Société de Gestion DHP Inc., the holding company established by Gravel's old patron, Henri Paquin. When last heard from, Desrosiers was painting houses for his friend Michel Gravel and declaiming the perfidy of the prime minister. Mulroney, he told friends, had personally promised him he'd be taken care of — and now look at him.

Another Conservative MP is still awaiting trial on charges of accepting kickbacks; her case could be one of the most sensational and complicated involving former Tory politicians. Glamorous, beautiful, and blonde, Carole Jacques is a lawyer from Mercier riding who named her baby daughter Mila out of admiration for the prime minister's wife. She and her campaign manager, Jean-Yves Pantaloni, were charged in 1993 with breach of trust and influence-peddling involving an East End Montreal company that had received an $855,000 grant from the federal Office of Regional Industrial Development in 1991. The company? None other than Les Industries de Lavage Dentex, the company owned by the Paquin family. Under questioning by the RCMP, Jacques and Pantaloni admitted they had discussed a payment with Dentex president Marc Paquin; it was simply a contribution to the party to help defray the costs of sending delegates to the 1991 Tory convention.

Dentex may not have been the only firm to experience the Jacques method of fundraising. In a sworn statement, RCMP officers said that Jacques and Pantaloni had asked for money from other Montreal-area firms, some of which were seeking government contracts. One was Almac Industries, whose president, Alexander Rack, claims that Pantaloni told him the company should pay $50,000 for Jacques's continued support for a grant the firm had requested. Pantaloni is said to have told Rack he "should not expect that the service would be provided free." Rack refused to produce the money, and his firm is now bankrupt.

The RCMP maintains that Canadian General Electric sought Jacques's assistance in 1991 in a transaction with the federal Export Development Corporation. The transaction involved obtaining authorization to transfer a $35-million government-guaranteed contract from Nigeria to Brazil. After their discussion of the transfer, CGE received a letter from Jacques asking for a $9,000 contribution to help, once again, send delegates to the 1991 Tory convention. The firm contributed only $500. Ottawa refused CGE's request for a contract transfer.

Despite the serious charges against her, Jacques expected to have Kim Campbell's endorsement of her candidacy in the 1993 election. Campbell's response was swift and succinct: she threw Jacques out of the party. Jacques ran anyway as an independent and lost.

Jacques and Pantaloni found themselves back in the headlines in May 1994 when the RCMP issued search warrants in an investigation into a corruption ring that claimed to arrange early parole for convicts in exchange for money. The leader of the ring, according to the RCMP, is a parole officer with the Correctional Services of Canada; he was suspended without pay in April pending the outcome of the investigation. Documents found in the parole officer's 1994 black Saab included a letter to Jacques concerning the request for a transfer of a convicted heroin trafficker from a U.S. to a Canadian prison. When a *Gazette* reporter telephoned Jacques's lawyer to ask if his client wished to comment on why, as an MP, she was involved in the prisoner's request for a transfer to Canada, the former MP did not respond.

Jacques and Pantaloni are awaiting their preliminary hearing on the 1993 charges, scheduled to begin in the fall of 1994.

Again and again, MPs, party bagmen, and other backroom organizers were caught demanding kickbacks on contracts during the Mulroney years. MP Michel Gravel said of his own activities as a convicted kickback artist extraordinaire, "No, I didn't think it was wrong. I thought it was politics."

It hardly mattered how big or how small the deal was: it could be a highway contract or a speechwriting assignment. Some of the tollgating was highly organized, some was done by freewheeling free-lancers who bluffed their way into people's pockets.

Former Tory environment minister Suzanne Blais-Grenier complained personally to Mulroney on September 21, 1987, that the party was being blemished by kickback scandals, and she urged him to clean house. When he did nothing, she blew the whistle early in 1988, saying publicly that a kickback network existed. She based her statement to reporters on several complaints made to her by businessmen in the Montreal area. On January 19, 1988, Peter White called to ask her to say she had been misquoted. "No, I was well quoted and I cannot retract any part of what I said," she told him.

When Mulroney ejected her from the Tory caucus for her remarks, she went further, giving the *Journal de Montréal* a formal statement published on August 31, 1988. Referring to a patronage and kickback scheme, Blais-Grenier said, "I am convinced that this exists in a very organized fashion here and could be brought to light with an adequate inquiry." MPs themselves do not handle negotiations for government contracts, Blais-Grenier said in her statement; they were in the hands of backroom power brokers. "This is done elsewhere, at another level. Certain government contracts involve tens, indeed hundreds of millions of dollars . . . None of us, including myself, have been a direct witness to such schemes. What I know of it, for my part, has been communicated to me by third parties. They are generally credible persons, free from interconnections." Only a royal commission could get to the bottom of the scheme, she said.

Blais-Grenier gave lengthy background briefings to Montreal RCMP Sergeant Pierre Lange and to one or two reporters, but refused to name her sources or provide any specific details. "I cannot blame them for shielding themselves," Blais-Grenier said. "They are afraid of a scandal, afraid of losing their work . . . I understand these people's fears." The police dropped their investigation into her allegations, and her party wrote her off as a crank. When she ran as an independent in her riding of Rosemont, she was defeated and disappeared from sight, but many people — including some RCMP officers — believed what she had been saying. In a 1988 internal memo, one officer stated, "From our inquiries, it appears to be generally understood in the business community that the only way to obtain government contracts is to cultivate the necessary political connections and to contribute a portion of the profits to these government connections."

There is ample evidence that Tory party officials and organizers operated efficient kickbacks-for-government-contracts networks during the nine years of Mulroney's government. Political organizers, several members of Parliament, a parliamentary aide, and even cabinet ministers asked businesses for payments in exchange for such prizes as lucrative, long-term federal office leases, industry grants, CIDA foreign aid contracts, engineering and architecture contracts from the Department of Public Works, even help with immigration and parole cases.

And these were not the whole story. Yet another group of Tories were involved in demanding kickbacks on contracts. They were led by the peerless Frank Majeau, a classic shakedown artist, a business partner of a Mafia hit man, and the senior political adviser to Roch LaSalle.

CHAPTER SEVEN

ENTER THE MOB

UILT LIKE A FORTRESS, WITH MASSIVE BLOCKS OF QUARRIED stone blackened by a hundred years of the city's soot, Toronto's Don Jail squats above a ravine overlooking the Don Valley Parkway. Rusty bars protect the filthy windows and razor wire still circles the flat roof where prisoners used to stroll for exercise. The oldest part of the building is empty now, but back in 1984, it was an overcrowded holding pen for convicted prisoners awaiting transfer to other penitentiaries. Almost every day Frank Majeau, trim and natty in an expensive suit, would drop by the Don to visit his business partner, Réal Simard.

Simard remembers their conversations. "Frank would say, 'When you get out, what about opening an office in Ottawa for lobbying?' I said I don't know anything about lobbying. He said, 'Well, you don't have to know anything. I've got big contacts in the Conservative Party.' So I said, 'Okay, why not?'"

Majeau wasn't kidding. His political influence was considerable: not only was he one of the closest associates of the new minister of public works, Roch LaSalle, but he was friendly with a number of other senior Quebec Tories, including Marcel Danis, the lawyer who had come to Ottawa in the 1984 election and was now deputy Speaker of the House of Commons. In fact his connections were so good, bragged Majeau, that he was sure he could get Simard out of jail.

Unfortunately for Simard, it would take more than Majeau's

clout to spring him from the Don Jail. Simard, the hit man for the Cotroni family — a Mafia gang that had for years controlled most of the drug, loan-sharking, and prostitution business in Montreal — was serving a life sentence for second-degree murder. He knew that before he would be a free man again he would have to wait while the Ontario and Quebec authorities wrangled over jurisdiction, and then he would have to cut a deal with the police to become an informant.

Simard's previous residence in Toronto was a pink-broadloomed luxury apartment at the top of the Sutton Place Hotel on Bay Street. Few of his fellow guests in the hotel would ever have suspected that the man who looked like a movie star was a killer. Nearly six feet tall, dark and handsome, he was blessed with a straight nose, firm chin, warm brown eyes, and a wide smile. Simard's habitual outfit was a well-cut double-breasted navy blazer with brass buttons, a perfectly ironed white shirt with faint red and navy stripes, a navy silk tie, grey flannels, and highly polished black loafers. His only jewellery was a watch and a heavy gold ring on his left hand.

When Simard was growing up at the foot of Rue de la Visitation in Montreal's dockland area, French Canadians weren't generally welcomed in the Italian Mob. But his mother was Simone Courville and her brother, Armand Courville, a famous champion wrestler, had been in the restaurant and gambling business with Vincent Cotroni, one of the city's most notorious gangsters, for nearly fifty years. Two other uncles, Paul and Roger Courville, were also close to the Cotronis, and all young Simard wanted as a boy was to be part of the "family." He served an appropriate apprenticeship: after two years in prison for extorting money from restaurateurs, he started working for Frank Cotroni, who had taken over the family business from his father, Vincent. Simard became Cotroni's driver, ran his errands, and helped launder his money. On January 18, 1980, Simard passed a final test of loyalty to the Cotronis by stalking Michel Marion, one of Cotroni's enemies, and fatally shooting him while he ate breakfast at a restaurant in Sainte-Adèle, a resort town in the Laurentians. Over the next three years, three more hits made him one of Cotroni's most trusted henchmen.

By 1981 Simard and a few other partners, including Claude Faber and Johnny Marra, another pair of hoodlums, owned Déjà Vue, a nightclub in Montreal. It was here that he met Frank Majeau. One night a brawl broke out and Simard phoned a small-time hood and drug dealer from Longueuil, Richard Clement, for help; Clement brought his chum, Frank. "Frank came with a gun in his belt," Simard recalled. "I liked Majeau the first time I met him." The troublemakers cleared out fast.

In 1983 Frank Cotroni decided to relocate Simard to Toronto, which was still an untapped market for their drug business. The Cotronis were expanding their operations and Simard needed help; through Richard Clement, he contacted Majeau, who had moved to Toronto a year earlier. Majeau had operated at the fringes of organized crime for years, but he possessed the intelligence and imagination to go for big capers. He had once owned a small nightclub in Joliette called Le Klub Karibu, the first club in Quebec to feature nude table dancers. Within a few months, Majeau and Simard were business partners.

Roch LaSalle, another Joliette native, and Frank Majeau had known each other most of their lives. They played golf together, gambled together at the card tables, hatched get-rich-quick schemes together. Frank and his brothers were well known around Joliette as good-looking, athletic boys from a nice family; the Majeaus had been farmers and small businessmen in the area for generations. The *Parliamentary Guide* described LaSalle's earlier career as "sales manager." In fact, a Grade Seven dropout who had trained as a butcher's apprentice, he was working as a travelling cigarette salesman with regular clients like Majeau's Le Klub Karibu before he entered politics. He ran unsuccessfully for the Tories in 1965, won in 1968, and was returned for the riding of Joliette in the next four federal elections. In 1979, as one of only two Tory MPs from Quebec, he went straight to Joe Clark's cabinet table as minister of supply and services, a highly desirable portfolio that would allow him to dispense a lot of patronage to the folks who'd supported him all those years on the opposition backbench.

It was perfectly natural that Majeau would be a beneficiary of his friend Roch's good fortune. Frank was hired as an assistant to the minister and was soon applying his imagination and intelligence to an extraordinary caper. The story Majeau tells about his attempt to get a piece of the largest government contract then on the table reads like pulp fiction, but the story is true.[1]

The Clark government was about to award a Department of National Defence contract worth $5.5 billion for the purchase of 138 new fighter jets. The choice was between McDonnell Douglas's CF-18s and General Dynamics' CF-16s. There was money to be made in a deal of this size, and Majeau saw the opportunity for a lucrative kickback. But it wasn't his idea, he insists. "That was a personal project that Roch asked me to do for himself, and somebody else in the parliament," Majeau says in his less-than-perfect English. "And there was a team on that; they made me president of it, and I did organize all this project." Majeau wasn't saying who the "somebody else" was.

Majeau put together a small group of friends from the Joliette area. One member of the team, Majeau claimed, was an RCMP officer whom he had met on a fishing weekend a year earlier. The Mountie's job was to provide security advice and sophisticated electronic equipment to sweep meeting rooms for bugs. In two separate interviews, four years apart, the officer denied his involvement in the affair. The RCMP issued a statement clearing him of any involvement in 1991.

Another member of the group was Jean-Claude Salvail, who, the last anyone heard of him, was flogging health foods and vitamins for a pyramid sales chain in Quebec City. A fourth member was a Joliette lawyer who shared an office building with Roch LaSalle from 1980 to 1983 and who had acted for him on occasion.

The plan was to approach the aircraft manufacturers with a

demand for a 15-per-cent kickback on the value of the aircraft contract in exchange for Majeau's guarantee that he could deliver the order. With any luck they might extort as much as $100 million from the winning company. The intention was to keep 10 per cent for themselves and kick back the remaining 5 per cent to the company's executives. Realistically, Majeau admits, all the Joliette boys really hoped for was about $1 million each to start, $10 million for LaSalle, and then an extra chunk of cash — amounting to perhaps 5 per cent — from the aircraft manufacturer each time the Canadian government paid out for maintenance and repair.

After contacting senior executives at one of the companies, McDonnell Douglas, the group hired a private jet from Marsolais Aviation in Saint-Hubert, Quebec, to take them to St. Louis in late November 1979 for the final negotiations.

Just as they were about to leave for St. Louis, Majeau heard that the cabinet had chosen the McDonnell Douglas bid, but the announcement would not be made for a few days. Although the original plan had been to drop in on executives at General Dynamics as well, Majeau scrapped that leg of the trip once he knew McDonnell Douglas had won. He had just a few days to convince the officials at McDonnell Douglas that he could influence the decision. When the team gathered at the Saint-Hubert airport on the appointed day, no one had enough money to pay the charter fees so they divided up the cost and put it on their credit cards.

The meeting with the aircraft company went well. According to Majeau, McDonnell Douglas executives offered $10 million to secure the contract and agreed to pay an extra 5 per cent to the group on all cost overruns and extras on the project. But McDonnell Douglas wasn't about to cough up that kind of money without being sure its investment was a sure bet; the executives needed proof that the visitors had come with the authority of LaSalle. A dinner meeting was arranged between a top McDonnell Douglas representative and LaSalle at the Château Laurier in Ottawa for a date shortly after their return. Then the group flew back to Canada.

Panic set in on their arrival at Ottawa International Airport, where they saw several RCMP cars with flashing lights waiting for them on the tarmac. Police officers climbed on board the chartered craft and ordered the terrified men to leave the plane immediately. "They made us stand with our hands up against the plane and our legs apart," Salvail said, "and then they frisked us." The Mounties thought they had caught a gang of drug smugglers, but Majeau persuaded them that the group was returning from a routine business meeting. When the police found no drugs in the plane, they let the men go.

The next day the team prepared for the crucial meeting with the McDonnell Douglas official. The plan called for Majeau and others on the team to meet LaSalle at the Château Laurier and escort him to a private dinner with the aircraft company executive. Before LaSalle showed up, Majeau saw one of the team members approaching him hurriedly across the lobby of the hotel. As the man rushed past, Majeau heard a whispered codeword, a prearranged signal that meant "Abandon the project. Run." Majeau tore out of the hotel. Within seconds a Mountie was pounding after him. "I ran all over downtown, in and out of stores and restaurant kitchens, and I finally got away."[2] A few days later, on December 13, the Clark government was defeated on a budget vote in the House of Commons, LaSalle returned to the obscurity of the opposition backbenches, and Majeau returned to Joliette. McDonnell Douglas was awarded the fighter plane contract.

What went awry with the kickback scheme? The McDonnell Douglas executives had tipped off the FBI, which in turn had contacted the RCMP. Alex Marshall was the senior executive at McDonnell Douglas responsible for the bid for the fighter planes. Then the company's vice-president of international marketing for aircraft but now its ombudsman, he said he vividly remembered the affair and the visit from the Canadians. Lee Witney, a spokesman for McDonnell Douglas, added that he believed the company was first contacted by Majeau, and "when we found out what they wanted, we decided not to pursue any further business with them. We contacted the FBI."

The extortionists were never charged with conspiring to defraud the government, or with conspiring to extort kickbacks. Police officers who looked into the matter said they did not believe they had enough evidence. "We looked at it in 1987," said Inspector Jean Pierre Witty, head of the RCMP's Commercial Crime Section in Ottawa. "If we had had any evidence we would have pressed charges, but we couldn't build a case." In 1987 the RCMP sent a picture of Majeau to the FBI, who showed it to executives at McDonnell Douglas; they said they couldn't remember clearly the face of the Canadian they had met. "We had a very hard look at the affair," Inspector Witty said, "but people were very evasive."

Jean-Claude Salvail has described his role in the caper in minute detail, confirming Majeau's account. Richard Leduc, a former Hudson's Bay Company advertising manager, acknowledged he went to St. Louis with the others, but claimed he was along only to raise money for investment in a restaurant franchise. Majeau maintains to this day that he and LaSalle dreamed up the daring escapade together. LaSalle denies it. "Pure speculation," he said in an interview. "It's totally false."

After the Clark government's defeat, LaSalle struggled to make ends meet. He readily admitted he was never very good with money. In late 1979, before going into Clark's cabinet, he had to be rescued by a senior party bagman. According to *The Toronto Star*, Jean Sirois, a Quebec City lawyer, came into Joliette with a thick bankroll and settled his debts, one by one. LaSalle's creditors lined up in the office of a local notary in Joliette and dickered with Sirois over the amounts. He tried to talk them into taking so much on the dollar; most refused. Sirois denies the story.

By 1981 LaSalle was once again heavily in debt, though some of it was nickel-and-dime stuff — like the $3,000 he owed the doorman at L'Excellence Night Club in Joliette. His situation grew worse when he quit federal politics in 1981 for an unsuccessful run at the leadership of the provincial Union Nationale party. Luckily for him, he was able to win back his old seat later that year — in the by-election that had been called because he had resigned the seat. Brian Mulroney was the one who rescued him this time; Mulroney and some other friends organized a $200-a-plate dinner that raised $20,000. Back he went to Ottawa.

Majeau was able to keep busy after leaving LaSalle's employ, working at a variety of jobs in Montreal and Joliette. On one occasion in 1981 after a fight with another man in Joliette, he was charged with assault. He hired Marcel Danis, then still practising law in Montreal, to defend him, but on the day of his court appearance Danis arrived too late. Majeau brought in another lawyer at the last minute and the judge handed down a small fine. When Danis puffed in, he was upset that Majeau had hired someone else and had the case heard again; this time, to Majeau's chagrin, the penalty was increased to include two years' probation.

Soon afterwards Majeau moved to Montreal to work for strip joint owner Peter Belmont, proprietor of a place called the Apollo. Belmont was close to Danis and from time to time, when Danis and his brother, Jean-Claude, another Clark organizer in Quebec, needed help with crowd control at political rallies, they'd call on Majeau. Majeau says he was used as muscle during the shoving matches between Clark and Mulroney supporters.

During his time with Belmont, Majeau learned more about running strip clubs. When an offer was made to him to launch a nude table-dancing business in Toronto, he decided it was too promising an opportunity to miss. Going into partnership with Réal Simard a few months later, he decided, made sound business sense; he had excellent connections with French-Canadian crime gangs, while Simard's loyalties were to the Italian Mob. With the help of the Cotronis, they became partners in Prestige Entertainment, a booking agency for nude table dancers in Toronto that operated out of a small office above a tavern at 329 St. George Street. Before Simard's arrival, Majeau was booking about fifty women a week into bars. "We were the first to bring professional table dancers to Toronto," Majeau boasted. "Up to then, the clubs just used strippers." Simard felt the Toronto clubs were run by rank amateurs who were missing the truly lucrative part of this business: the opportunity to run cocaine into the city through the network of dancers. After Simard joined, the company increased its bookings to 125 performers a week, all young French-Canadian women who streamed in from Montreal, directed to Prestige by the Cotronis.

Clubs were crazy for the "hot Frenchies," as the customers called them, and Prestige found itself with more clients than it could handle. Simard pared the list down to the top fifteen clubs, places like Filmore's on Dundas and the Zanzi Bar on Yonge in Toronto, and the Beef Baron in London, Ontario. Majeau was able to rent an expensive apartment in a new low-rise building at Wellesley and Church with his girlfriend, Gisèlle Bardeau; Simard settled into his apartment on the thirtieth floor of Sutton Place, his Mercedes parked in the garage below.

But they didn't operate in Toronto without powerful protection, nor could they consider expansion into Hamilton and other south-western Ontario cities without the permission of Hamilton crime boss Johnny Papalia. With the decline of the Commisso family, for years Toronto's most powerful Mob family, Papalia was now the man in charge. For his part, Papalia did not want to offend the powerful Cotronis. He knew they were backed by Mob families in Buffalo and Detroit, cities close enough to Hamilton to warrant serious respect from Papalia.

In the summer of 1983, Simard set up a meeting, a kind of mobster's courtesy call, with Papalia in Hanrahan's bar on Barton Street in Hamilton, next door to the Stelco plant. He was accompanied by Majeau. A phone call to the Cotronis in Montreal proved to

Papalia that Simard enjoyed their blessing; afterwards, he never stood in their way. What none of the men knew was that a police surveillance team had photographed the encounter. One shot shows Majeau, Simard, and Papalia standing together at a phone booth while Simard calls Frank Cotroni's private number in Montreal.

"I didn't know who Papalia was," Majeau said years later in Montreal. "Réal just told me he wanted me to come along to meet a guy."

"He's lying," says Simard flatly. Majeau knew exactly who Johnny Papalia was, and the two continued to meet after Simard went to jail. A police officer who kept Majeau and Simard under surveillance for much of their time in Toronto said the three men planned to set up a franchise business together called Billy Rose; the idea was to buy up taverns and put topless dancers in them.

For his part, Majeau has always stuck to his story that he moved to Toronto only to bring nude dancers into bars and clubs. He also denies that he had anything to do with pushing cocaine in Toronto, but his former partner tells a different story. "We started taking cocaine into the clubs every week with the girls," said Simard. Cocaine was an important part of the Cotroni expansion into Ontario; an old friend of Simard's from Montreal was importing enough from Colombia to supply Cotroni dealers in both Quebec and Ontario. Police officers in both Toronto and Montreal support Simard's version; they say that Majeau was involved in the drug business for years.

The new business flourished — but only briefly. In late 1983, two small-time Montreal cocaine dealers, Robert Hétu and Mario Héroux, approached Simard with an interest in supplying Prestige with cocaine. Sources told Simard that what they really wanted to do was kill his old friend Richard Clement over an unpaid debt. Simard and Clement decided to strike first. Using three guns Simard had hidden in the ceiling at Prestige, Simard and Clement made an attempt to shoot Héroux and Hétu at the Heritage Inn, a small Toronto hotel, on November 12 but aborted the attempt when they saw Héroux's girlfriend, Marie-Josée Gagnon, in his room. (Gagnon worked for Prestige as one of its table dancers.) Majeau was with Simard.

A week and a half later, on November 23, Simard and Clement made another attempt. This time Majeau was out of town. Héroux and Hétu were staying at the Seaway Motor Hotel on Toronto's lakeshore motel strip. Late that night Simard knocked on the door of the room the men were sharing, killed Héroux, and shot Hétu three times in the head. Clement immediately left the country and flew to Lebanon, but Simard, confident and unworried, returned to Sutton Place. Listening to the radio the next morning he heard to his shock that Hétu had survived. Simard didn't have time to get out of town. Hétu was able to identify the killers, and within hours Toronto police had arrived at Sutton Place to arrest Simard. He spent a year in the Don Jail until police finally moved him to Montreal's Archambault Prison. Encouraged by the promise of a new identity and an early parole, Simard decided to turn informant and tell the cops everything he knew about Frank Cotroni and the family.

One well-wisher who called Simard in 1984 to see if he needed help was Daniel Rock, Marcel Danis's former law partner. According to Simard, Rock told him that his Tory contacts were good enough to help him win an early parole.[3] But Simard said no thanks; he had already made up his mind to inform. He would take his chances with the police.

Majeau stayed put in Toronto. He had his own worries. The police, he knew, were keeping a close eye on him; it was a miracle he had escaped being charged himself. While Simard was in jail, he continued to give him his share of the Prestige profits, but by mid-1984 the business was in trouble. Toronto police were keeping him under surveillance, and many of the clubs that had once been happy to see the two dapper French Canadians were now uneasy about doing business with him. But deliverance was at hand. In September 1984 his old friend LaSalle was once again in the federal cabinet.

One of the federal government's crown jewels in Toronto was a Crown corporation called Harbourfront, which owned priceless federal lands and buildings in the most valuable core area of the city's Lake Ontario shoreline. After the 1984 victory, LaSalle was the new boss. When LaSalle's chief of staff, Pierre Claude Nolin, called Howard Cohen, Harbourfront's general manager, to see if there was a spot for Frank Majeau, there was no way Cohen could refuse. Nolin's reason for Majeau's appointment was that LaSalle wanted a French-speaking aide at Harbourfront. "He needed someone who could cope with requests from the minister's office," Nolin said. "I recall meeting with Mr. Majeau and Mr. LaSalle, and Mr. LaSalle told me he thought Mr. Majeau could be very helpful on the marketing side."

But Réal Simard had another explanation for what Majeau was doing in Toronto. He was there, he suggested, to help sell Crown land. "Look at it from this point of view," he said during an interview in the Rue Bonsecours offices of the Montreal police force's anti-gang squad. "The Conservatives say they had to sell their Crown land. All the lands and buildings are too expensive. And Johnny Papalia was seeing a lot of Frank Majeau because organized crime [figures] are always interested in putting their money into legitimate things and investing in land. Majeau was a very good prospect for them because he was connected to LaSalle so that he could always know what bids the government will accept for this land or this building. That I know."

The Tories were hungrily eyeing Harbourfront's extensive land holdings near the foot of Bay Street. Harbourfront not only owned much of the waterfront land, it ran a flourishing cultural centre that sponsored theatre, dance, children's programs, authors' readings, and other events. The expectation was that some of the profits from developing the federally owned waterfront could be ploughed back into cultural programs. The place was tailor-made for Majeau's grand ambitions.

At first Harbourfront officials had balked at hiring him, saying there wasn't any money in their budget to pay Majeau's salary. The minister's office found a way: they would subsidize a major conference padded with enough extra cash to cover Majeau's one-year contract. A two-day symposium, titled "Public-Private Partnerships: New Strategies in Urban Development," was scheduled for October 1985. It was the first and last time Harbourfront has ever organized a gathering of this type. LaSalle was to be the keynote speaker, but there were twenty-three others on the program, including Toronto mayor Arthur Eggleton and Magna International president Frank Stronach. Hundreds of private-sector architects, engineers, and contractors from across Canada were invited to attend; each was to pay $500 for the privilege. The invitation lists came from several sources, but one was confidential and highly political. It contained the names of dozens of Conservative supporters, companies and individuals who had worked for the Tories and given them financial contributions. For example, of the nearly 100 Quebec companies on this list, Elections Canada party returns show that almost all were donors to the federal Conservative Party and most received federal public works contracts in the years following.

The political list of invited companies, claims Majeau, was put together by Liliane Poiré, LaSalle's associate chief of staff. (Poiré had been a secretary at Jean Sirois's law firm in Sillery, near Quebec City.) Letters from Poiré to Majeau, which accompanied the list, including one dated July 11, 1985, show he is telling the truth about the source of the list. Did Poiré assemble the names on it herself? No, said Majeau. "She got them from Guy Charbonneau."

This was the infamous "short list," the one contractors, engineers, and architects were trying to get on when they paid Michel Gravel $5,000 each to attend his lobster party to meet Roch LaSalle in that same month, July 1985. They couldn't even bid on a government contract unless their names appeared on the short list. Some of the names, said Majeau, were added by LaSalle himself: one was that of Inter Gestion GD Ltée, a company owned by his close friend

Gervais Desrochers. Another name was that of Desjardins Sauriol et Associés Ltée, a major Quebec construction company controlled by Pierre Desjardins, whose son-in-law was Pierre Claude Nolin. But the short list also carried the names of firms in every Canadian province, many of them large and well-known companies.

While Harbourfront staff journeyed to other Canadian cities to promote the conference, Majeau travelled to Ottawa and to several cities in Quebec, concentrating on the chief executive officers named on the short list. He did his homework: beside each name he noted any pertinent information that would help him sell the conference to an executive as well as any connections to Tory party power brokers. Each personal visit was a stroking exercise, assuring the CEO of the minister's friendship and the party's interest in seeing that he was happy with the new government. Majeau would also stress the opportunities for mutual profit and the advantages of the executive having a pipeline — Majeau himself — into LaSalle's office.

After each appointment, Majeau would record in his diary the results of the conversation. Annotating a call to one engineering company executive, Majeau wrote that the firm would "need political support to get the bureaucracy [to] move." Another man, who told Majeau he wanted to acquire federal land in East End Montreal, "waits for news from Pierre Claude." Another was described as having worked on the Mulroney leadership: "Brian — Advance." Another agreed to come to the conference, but wanted his cleaning contract with the Department of Labour renewed for three years. Jean-Pierre Sauriol, a construction company executive in partnership with Pierre Claude Nolin's father-in-law, was described as "très important." Guy Racine, the Quebec City bagman who had asked the president of Wajax for a kickback, was also on Majeau's appointments list. "See Michel Côté [the minister of supply and services, from Quebec City] for a reference," Majeau noted, adding Racine's concerns about too many committees looking at public works contracts, and his desire that no decisions should be taken without input from the party's Quebec City executive committee.

Majeau was an effective salesman: 70 per cent of the executives who came to Toronto were from Quebec. The hapless Harbourfront staff who were recruiting conference members from other parts of the country were not able to offer the minister's personal assurances with the same confidence displayed by Majeau. Still, 90 per cent of the people on the secret political list came to Harbourfront, and Majeau built personal relationships with each of the company presidents and officials who attended. The Harbourfront conference was a convenient vehicle that allowed LaSalle, master of the government department that traditionally does a great volume of contracting to the private sector, to become acquainted with engineers, contractors, and architects from Tory-friendly companies and raise the possibility of lucrative contracts with them. Majeau's visits hammered home the message very clearly: You stay in touch with us and we'll remember you.

Once the event was over, there wasn't anything left for Majeau to do at Harbourfront. Now it was time to exploit the contacts he'd made. Majeau went on to work in LaSalle's Ottawa office in late 1985 as a senior policy adviser, and when old acquaintances called him to arrange meetings with the minister, LaSalle was happy to oblige. Majeau flourished in Ottawa. One former aide to a cabinet minister remembers him well. "I was sitting in my office when the director of operations for my minister brought this guy in and said, 'This is Frank Majeau. Can you show him what you do?'" The aide had already heard some wild rumours about Majeau, and he didn't believe he had anything to teach him. "So Majeau asks me, 'Where do you keep the contracts?'" Many Tories were blatant about such things, the aide said, but Majeau was off the scale.

Soon Majeau was chairing Wednesday-morning sessions of policy advisers to other ministers and throwing his weight around. And he had plenty of old chums from Joliette to keep him company. LaSalle had also hired Majeau's girlfriend, Gisèle Bardeau, formerly of Prestige Entertainment. Majeau's brother, Roger, was on the staff as LaSalle's driver and errand runner, and so was a man named Gilles Ferland who, like Majeau, had a criminal record and was working as a policy adviser. Another old friend was Roger Perrault, a convicted embezzler, hired by LaSalle to work at a Crown corporation called the Canada Lands Company (Mirabel), which administered the lands expropriated by the government around the Mirabel Airport.

For Majeau, the new job of senior policy adviser had its own creative opportunities. He claims he assembled fake consortiums to bid on public works contracts. Using the short list, he would assemble a consortium comprising an architectural firm, an engineering company, and a contracting firm and tell the principals of each company that they were to submit a bid for a certain contract. He would supply them with all the details they needed to make the bid. He would warn them they would not win — "this time." The winner would be a different consortium, specially created for that contract. Later, Majeau worked with the losers to shoehorn them into winning consortiums. Majeau did not design these teams himself; all he did was follow orders from unelected party officials. Majeau was in the Department of Public Works, but sources have said the same kind of system was at work in other ministries, especially for contracts for advertising and public relations. Ad agencies were told they could bid, but "we were also told when not to bid too hard," as one company executive in Montreal put it.

Majeau kept careful records, which he uses today to back up his claims. He meticulously recorded each meeting, each lunch, each telephone call in thick three-ring TimeText binders and kept extensive notes on what action was taken. These notes illustrate how many files he worked on: there were dozens. Not all were public works contracts; some covered more sensitive issues such as information on a Joliette candidate for a federal judicial appointment. Majeau's files included matters relating to the Toronto harbour, a carpet replacement in Ottawa, post offices around the country, an elevator inspection contract in Montreal, a parkway beside the Welland Canal, a harbour breakwater in Nova Scotia, an unnamed project in Mount Pearl, Newfoundland, and something at the Halifax airport that required consultation with Stewart McInnes, the senior minister from Nova Scotia. He handled a contract for the insurance at Harbourfront, one for a proposed Health and Welfare building in Montreal, a cleaning contract in Orillia that needed input from Tory MP Doug Lewis's office, another insurance contract in Sault Ste. Marie where Nancy Stableforth, an aide in Jim Kelleher's office, was consulted. The lists go on and on. In each case Majeau worked with aides from cabinet ministers' offices or with local MPs. These diaries demonstrate how a political aide to a minister dealing with a major patronage portfolio like Public Works spends his time; they also show how many demands from so many quarters — high and low — are made on such a portfolio.

If there is one recurring item running through the bulk of the files Majeau handled, it is leasing. His TimeText diaries show that work on federal government leases took up most of his days, especially after he was asked to assemble a leasing book that would show his bosses the details of every federal lease in the country. Such a document would allow the government to shop its leases to political friends. But there were other duties for Majeau besides looking after public works contracts. One was accompanying LaSalle as he made his daily rounds, beginning with breakfast at Nate's Deli on Rideau Street. This is where LaSalle did his deals, the freelancing that so worried other Tories like Pierre Claude Nolin. LaSalle's wheeling and dealing on government contracts endangered arrangements in which other people had interests; LaSalle was seen as a dangerous meddler. And Majeau, who was being paid a relatively modest $40,000 a year, had his own agenda. When he was asked if he was there to represent interests other than LaSalle's, he smiled. When asked if those interests could be connected to organized crime, he smiled again. "What's the Mafia, the Mob?" he asked derisively. "Everything connects. There are crooked cops and crooked politicians as well as the crooks and they all connect. How can you say where one stops and another begins?"

Majeau's career as a political aide skidded to an abrupt halt in January 1987, just before *Maclean's* magazine published an article by Montreal writer Dan Burke. Not only did Burke find out Majeau's background and that he had been the business partner of a Mafia hit man, he also discovered that he had not passed a required RCMP security check before he began working in LaSalle's office. His investigative calls alerted Nolin, who talked to Bernard Roy. Just before the *Maclean's* story hit the stands, Majeau said, LaSalle called him into his office and told him that Roy had ordered him fired. Gisèlle Bardeau was out as well.

"He said, 'Frank, you will have to leave,'" Majeau recalls. "I said, 'Roch, you knew everything about me. I will not accept being fired like that.'

"He said, 'Frank, I'm not firing you. This is Bernard Roy who told me to do it. Don't worry. Take a few weeks off and I'll take care of this.'"

When he left, Majeau took with him four warm letters of reference from LaSalle and his aides, three of them written on parliamentary stationery. LaSalle's recommendation, written on February 18, 1987, on his letterhead as minister of state, was especially effusive, praising Majeau's efficiency and quickness. "His professional attitude, his bilingualism and his ability to work well with a team is much appreciated by his colleagues," gushed LaSalle. "Therefore it is without hesitation that I recommend him to all employers wanting to acquire his services."

But nice words butter no parsnips. Majeau hired Montreal lawyer Claudine Murphy to sue the government for wrongful dismissal and *Maclean's* for libel. The lawsuits dragged on for years: the wrongful dismissal suit was thrown out of court by a judge in 1991; the libel suit is ongoing to this day. For a long time, however, Majeau didn't hold any grudges against LaSalle himself: When the minister retired, Frank pulled out the stack of well-thumbed business cards he'd collected on his good-will tour for Harbourfront. He called one CEO after another, reminding them of LaSalle's friendship and influence, and invited them to buy a table for a farewell benefit dinner in Joliette in the summer of 1987. "We'd like you to buy a table," he told each man bluntly, "but we don't want you to come. We'll give the places to local people." Perhaps people were amused by the bald effrontery of his approach, but they bought tickets and stayed away in droves. A happy crowd of Joliette natives gathered in a local hall to wish LaSalle well. There had been a proposal to buy him a white Cadillac with the money they'd collected, but someone argued successfully that this was a mite flashy, so they decided to do the discreet thing and just give him the cash directly. All $50,000 of it.

But that was 1987. Today the men are bitter enemies; LaSalle carried on in comfortable retirement and Majeau went through hard times, times he blames on LaSalle and not on his own follies. As the years went on, he and Michel Gravel became close and started to compare notes on their experiences under LaSalle.

"Majeau et al. were just the remnants of the old Union Nationale view: this was how government worked," said one Conservative who had watched Majeau in action and was not amused by his activities. "Duplessis did it, and this was their sense of reality. They were stunned to find out anyone would think it was wrong."

CHAPTER EIGHT

BREAKFAST AT NATE'S

NATE'S DELI, JUST SOUTH OF OTTAWA'S BYWARD MARKET, HAS always been a popular spot with politicians; even Pierre Trudeau, a man with a taste for fine dining, was known to drop in with a few aides for a late-night supper at one of the worn Formica tables.

Breakfast was Roch LaSalle's favourite meal at Nate's. His business day began with eggs and bacon and meetings with people with deals to propose. Frank Majeau often tagged along and when they'd arrive, he claims, there would be three or four individuals waiting at separate tables for the ten- or fifteen-minute meeting the minister had promised them. Majeau had other matters to attend to on the morning of June 17, 1986, so he wasn't there when Hull businessman Glen Kealey kept his appointment with LaSalle. That day the minister had only two breakfast meetings on his schedule; while he dealt with Kealey, Ottawa developer Pierre Bourque waited a few tables away.

Kealey was happy to meet the minister. This breakfast, he hoped, would tie a ribbon around a project he had managed with loving care for almost four years. He would later be called a dreamer, a kook, and a fool, but the reality was that Kealey, a bilingual Ottawa businessman, had always been a bottom-line realist. He knew how the game was played.

In 1982 Kealey had taken over Advertising Products House, Ltd., or APH, a struggling graphics and typesetting company with forty employees. He cut the staff by half and doubled the sales; within months, the business was in the black. But he knew that his job was only half done: the future of the business would depend on bringing in new computerized equipment. His fascination with computers led him to dream about a "smart" office building, one designed, built, and wired to support sophisticated computers and communications systems. He found three partners who shared his vision; together they formed a new company called APH-MICOT. By 1985 they had hired architects, made a deal with a construction company, put together a parcel of land in Hull, and budgeted the project at $160 million.

It was not difficult to find investors. Quebec's powerful Caisse de Dépôt and the Quebec government agreed to support it; the city of Hull pledged $9 million. An umbrella organization called the Société Immobilière Trans-Québec, Inc., which had financing from such diverse sources as the CBC pension fund, the Montreal police pension fund, and union funds from the Fédération des Travailleurs du Québec, had also come on board.

What Kealey was after this morning was LaSalle's promise of a federal government lease to complete the package. In particular, he wanted to win the lease for the new space agency the government had recently announced. As he saw it, no other building in the National Capital Region could compete with MICOT's high-tech wired universe. Another selling point: the project would create, he said, 5,000 jobs.

Kealey had every reason to believe the government would back him. Finance Minister Michael Wilson had written him in December 1984 to cheer him on: the MICOT Centre, Wilson wrote, "has the potential to provide a much-needed focal point to the Canadian office technology industry . . . [It] would attract foreign visitors to view Canadian-made office technology in a live work environment and will play a significant role in developing an awareness of Canadian products in other countries." William McGowan, director of the National Museum of Science and Technology, wrote to suggest a high-level lunch meeting with such people as Larkin Kerwin, head of the National Research Council. The senior public servants followed up with more ideas and advice. Although they weren't keen on a space agency in Hull, they liked the "smart" building plan and some of them suggested another idea — a space museum.

There was even support in the Prime Minister's Office; Raynald Dorion, an aide to Fred Doucet, wrote Doucet to praise the idea. After describing the practical merits of the project, Dorion told Doucet that politically, in Quebec, "the advantages will be very important." He recommended a lavish opening ceremony hosted by the prime minister.

It was now 1986 and Kealey was eager to settle the deal and get started. Although he didn't know LaSalle personally, he figured he had all the bases covered. He was not only a member in good standing of the Tories' Hull-Aylmer riding association, he had given $1,000 in 1985 and another $1,000 to the PC Canada Fund in 1986. He belonged to the 500 Club. He had even accepted the new reality and hired lobbyists. He paid Public Affairs International, one of the city's top lobby firms, $60,000 to help him win government financing; and just to be on the safe side, he also engaged Keith Hamilton to lobby for him personally. Hamilton had formally left his staff job in the Prime Minister's Office in 1985 to set up his own lobby firm, KAT Consultants, but he served the PMO on contract for another year or two. And it was while he was on contract that he accepted $80,000 from Kealey to help him win the lease. Under government regulations, this was strictly forbidden, of course; no one working in a minister's office — much less the Prime Minister's Office — was allowed to accept a private contract and especially not one for lobbying, but Hamilton saw nothing wrong with what he was doing and apparently no one else did either.

So who could blame Glen Kealey for striding into Nate's on a lovely June morning with a spring in his step? He describes what happened next, reconstructing his conversation with LaSalle.

"When I got there the first thing that seemed to be funny was that there was another developer in the restaurant. I knew Pierre Bourque — he owned a few buildings leased to the federal government, mostly National Defence. And I knew that Mr. Bourque was building a major complex in Hull. And there he was, sitting in one corner. Roch LaSalle entered, they exchanged greetings, and then he came over and sat down at my table.

"After a couple of pleasantries, LaSalle turned to me and said, 'You know, Mr. Kealey, the time has come for the federal government to support your project and that is going to take some money.' I looked at him and said, 'But Mr. LaSalle, is $160 million not enough?'

"Mr. LaSalle said, 'No, no, no, Mr. Kealey, it's not money to build the project; it's money for our support.' For a second I was confused. I'm not naive, but I never expected a cabinet minister to be asking me directly for money. I said, 'Mr. LaSalle, I don't understand.' And he said something to the effect of, 'Do I have to draw you a picture? The money is 5 per cent, and it begins with a 5-per-cent down-payment. Have you got it on you?'

"I said, 'I hear you, but I still don't understand,' because I wanted him to repeat it. And he said, 'Well, Mr. Kealey, if you don't have it on you . . . I'm sure out of a $160-million project you can find the money, and when you do, call my secretary and we'll meet again like this under similar circumstances and your project can go ahead.'

"I got up, said goodbye, and walked out. As I'm walking out, I can see LaSalle go over and sit down at the table with the other developer, Pierre Bourque."

Kealey decided to ignore the episode with LaSalle and concentrate on construction of the building. It was only later that he recalled a column published in *Le Devoir* on Saturday, May 24, three weeks before the breakfast. Journalist Pierre O'Neill had not minced his words, reporting that an organized 5-per-cent kickback scheme existed in the Tory party. Liberal MP Don Boudria raised the story in the House on Monday, May 26, asking the acting solicitor general, John Crosbie, to request an immediate RCMP investigation into the allegations. Crosbie's response was predictable: "I would ask the Honourable Member to reconsider the wild, spurious, general, vague, and vicious charges which he is constantly spewing in this House without care, caution, or circumspection."

But Kealey did nothing. He kept up his membership in the Tory party and was elected to the board of the Hull-Aylmer riding association. At the same time he and his partners carried on, trying to raise the necessary financing for MICOT.

"What do you do when a cabinet minister asks you for a bribe?" Kealey asked. "Call the RCMP? These are the guys that appoint the RCMP. While I'm thinking about what to do next — because for me there was no question, I would never pay the bribe — news comes out that a leasing contract had been signed between the Department of Public Works and Pierre Bourque to lease Place Louis St. Laurent in Hull for $775,000 a month. The space was to be used by the Department of National Defence, but nobody there knew a contract was under negotiation or that there was even a need for one. It took National Defence over a year to move into that building and they paid rent during that whole time."

Unknown to Kealey, Pierre Bourque, a well-known Liberal, had been negotiating with the government to lease his new building to DND as early as 1983. The lease was still under discussion when the Tories came into power in 1984. At that time Frank Moores was just establishing his new lobbying company, but he was also interested in becoming involved in commercial real estate and in securing government leases. Along with Newfoundland businessman Craig Dobbin, a fundraiser for John Crosbie, and Tory businessman Jean-Paul Tessier, he tried to persuade Bourque to sell them Place Louis St. Laurent. Bourque wasn't interested in selling; instead, as Kealey discovered, he was able to win a ten-year lease from the Defence Department at $9.2 million a year.

This lease later came under attack from Kenneth Dye, the auditor general at the time. In his 1987 annual report, Dye said the government had signed the deal long before the building was ready, and taxpayers had paid more than $7 million to rent an empty building. The government, Dye explained, paid the full rent of $760,000 a month (Kealey's estimate of $775,000 was a little high) from September 1, 1985, to February 1, 1986. By June 1, the building was only 20-per-cent full. It was not fully occupied until September 1986.

Don Boudria attacked the deal in the Commons public accounts committee, forcing Public Works officials to admit there had been a dispute between Bourque and their department about the lease date. Public Works bureaucrats protested against paying Bourque for the empty building, but LaSalle, the minister at the time, hired independent consultant Maurice Mayer to look at the deal in 1985. Mayer determined that Bourque should be paid from September 1, 1985.

And who was Mayer? The Montreal real estate broker and Tory fundraiser. Brian Mulroney's confidant and counsellor. A business partner of Jean-Paul Tessier's in an office building in Trois-Rivières that won another controversial federal lease from the Tories. And a recent Mulroney appointee to the board of the Old Port of Montreal.

The revelation of his role in the Bourque building dispute was not good news for LaSalle, coming as it did in the midst of other bad publicity. It became known that one of LaSalle's closest Joliette friends, Gervais Desrochers, had set up his consulting business, Inter Gestion GD Ltée, immediately after the 1984 election. LaSalle gave his friend the job of negotiating a lease with the Metropolitan Life Insurance Company for the offices of the Free Trade Agreement negotiators at Met Life's new Ottawa headquarters at 50 O'Connor. How much Desrochers netted from that deal is not officially known, but his fee was $51,000.

(He wasn't the only one trying to cash in on that lease. An official in Mulroney's office was also involved, and Met Life filed a complaint with the FBI in Washington. The RCMP started its own investigation and was counting on a report prepared by the FBI, which had access to Met Life documents in the United States. The FBI had promised to deliver its findings to the Mounties but, as Paul Palango reports in his book *Above the Law*, the FBI document on the unnamed official's extortion attempt was lost by the FBI on the eve of the signing of the free trade deal.)

LaSalle arranged another piece of business for Desrochers in May 1985: a $75,000 contract from the Transport Department to study the feasibility of a new airport in Joliette, a town of 17,000 people. In June 1986 a second feasibility study was given to Desrochers, this time to examine the idea of using surplus Mirabel Airport lands for greenhouses, even though an identical feasibility study by federal officials was already under way. LaSalle helped Desrochers and his partner, Henri Paquin — Michel Gravel's former employer — buy a parcel of the Mirabel land, then arranged for a $750,000 federal grant to help the partners build a greenhouse.

All this was possible because, as minister of public works, LaSalle's empire included the Canada Lands Company (Mirabel), the Crown corporation set up to sell surplus Mirabel Airport lands back to the farmers from whom they were expropriated. He appointed the corporation's seven-member board and named his nephew, Pierre Hardy, as president.

Under LaSalle's administration, this tiny Crown corporation with a staff of thirty people turned into a festering sore for the government. There were so many stories swirling around about Canada Lands Company that LaSalle's successor, Stewart McInnes, was forced to set up an internal investigation and report its findings to the public.[1] Even with all the damage control a minister can summon, the findings were damning: there "could be the appearance" that a firm owned by Desrochers had privileged insider information when it was allowed to build a greenhouse at Mirabel, the report said, adding that Desrochers had information "not generally made available to the public."

The report also criticized the corporation for giving an untendered $24,000 contract to a local bar, Le Receveur, to be in charge of security checks on empty Mirabel-area farmhouses. In fact, the investigators found, the bar had received $42,000, almost twice the value of the contract. Gilbert Desjardins, the bar's owner, told the *Globe and Mail*'s Richard Cléroux that the contract wasn't worth the work involved. He did the surveillance work personally, he told Cléroux, driving around the area during the day in his car, checking empty farmhouses and barns on Mirabel properties. "Hey, it was a job, somebody had to do it," said Desjardins.

One could almost hear the report's authors clearing their throats over this as they mentioned that the bar "was not specialized in security services." Desjardins objected to this criticism, pointing to the eight years he had spent on the Montreal police force. And just as stoutly, the board defended its decision to hire the bar. Desjardins "was from the region and knew it well," the directors told the investigators. Because he owned a bar, they maintained, Desjardins "would have better access to information on things happening in the region." The investigators were not persuaded. Their report cited improper accounting of funds, improper use of sole-source contracts, splitting of contracts, the appearance of insider information, and unexplained expense accounts.

For LaSalle, the hits just kept on coming. Not all the stories were about grants, leases, and sweetheart contracts. When heroin kingpin Conrad Bouchard, who had been jailed in 1981, was paroled in June 1986, the *Journal de Montréal* reported that Bouchard had boasted to a fellow prisoner that political influence would soon lead to his release. And the paper said that Bouchard's parole request, handled by his lawyer, Daniel Rock, came just thirteen days after the appointment to the Parole Board of Joliette Conservative and LaSalle supporter Louis Laporte — who had supported early parole for Bouchard. LaSalle's insouciant response was typical. He readily admitted he had got the job for Laporte. "It was a great pleasure for

133

me to recommend Mr. Laporte be put on the list for the Parole Board after the election in '84, and I was very happy to see Mr. Laporte have the chance to sit on that board. Mr. Laporte is a very respectable man from a very respectable family in Joliette and he has been, like so many others in Joliette, a supporter."

Fortuitously, Daniel Rock also owned an employment agency and was reported to have promised the Parole Board that Bouchard would have a job with the agency if he were freed. The board always looks more favourably on candidates who have job prospects, and Rock told them he wanted to benefit from Bouchard's talents in public relations. Unfortunately, Rock did not have an opportunity to use the ex-convict's PR skills; Bouchard was arrested just four months after his parole release and charged with importing $13 million worth of cocaine into Montreal.

All these stories badly tarnished the image of Roch LaSalle. Still, Mulroney stuck by him. Although he was demoted to minister without portfolio in the spring of 1986, after all the bad press about Frank Majeau, he remained in cabinet with the attendant perks and powers. It took the Gravel scandal, which blew up in 1987, to convince Mulroney that LaSalle was too loose a cannon to keep on deck.

While the PMO was mulling over the LaSalle problem, Kealey wrote to Mulroney personally, pressuring him to think once more about putting the new space agency in the MICOT building. Within days of sending that letter, Kealey received a visit from a Quebec City lawyer claiming to be related to Guy Charbonneau, telling him to back off his lobbying for the space agency or he would lose his chance of winning any federal lease in the building. Kealey ignored the warning. A few weeks after that his partners, fearful that they would be tainted by his persistent and increasingly public complaints, decided he was a liability. They changed the locks on his office door and told him they were cancelling the project.

Kealey sued them and won his case in court but went broke in the process. It was the beginning of Kealey's long, noisy crusade against Mulroney and his cronies, one that would run until Mulroney left office. Kealey's tactics were crude and simple: call them all crooks, again and again, as loud as possible.

CHAPTER NINE

MISS GUATEMALA ET AL.

G LEN KEALEY WASN'T THE ONLY PERSON EAGER TO EXPOSE THE crooks and kickback artists operating so freely around the Tory government. Many RCMP officers were very concerned about the corrupt activities reported to them by angry business people who alleged they had been approached for money, by opposition members of Parliament who were being tipped off by their constituents, and by public servants who quietly passed on information about questionable conduct in their ministries. Ottawa was seething with rumours of politicians on the take, stories of demands for 5-per-cent kickbacks on federal leasing contracts, and speculation surrounding the staggering list of patronage appointments Mulroney had made.

The RCMP heard that lobbying was the way many well-connected Tories were cutting themselves a piece of the action in Ottawa — peddling their influence to hapless business people who were convinced they hadn't a hope of winning federal contracts or assistance without a lobbyist's intervention. The word on the street was that many of the best contracts "belonged" to the most powerful lobbyists, who would look for a client willing to pay enough to get them. The Mounties simply did not have the officers or the resources to investigate every politician and backroom operator they heard was on the take.

One group of RCMP officers in Montreal decided to do something about it. An unlikely informant had dropped into their laps, an ex-con with the connections they needed to snare their quarry. The Mounties came up with an audacious plan, a sting so risky, so expensive, and so bizarre that it has become one of the most tightly held secrets in RCMP history. And maybe the most extraordinary element of the whole operation was the man they used to front it.

Michael Mitton is a little guy, just five foot three, with curly brown hair, bright blue eyes, an engaging grin, and plenty of energy. He can charm anyone, sell anything, talk his way in or out of any situation. Now thirty-five, Mitton grew up in Pierrefonds, a pleasant suburb on the West Island of Montreal. His father, Phillip, was a Christian fundamentalist, a pillar of the Brethren Church, and a hard-working salesman for the 3M Company. Young Michael couldn't wait to escape Sunday school; he wanted lots of money and he wanted it fast. By the time he was eighteen, he'd gravitated to the Main, around Saint-Laurent and Saint-Urbain, a neighbourhood of kosher butcher shops, wholesale fabric outlets, and shabby *dépanneurs*.

Mitton was soon drawn into some of the scams run by the Jewish gangs and junk dealers who flourished in the area, people who specialized in importing goods without paying Customs. By the time he was twenty, he was keeping company with the gangs of young French-Canadian hoods who worked for Raymond Séguin, an elderly East End loan shark with an impressive rap sheet. Séguin's criminal career began in 1939 with a conviction for theft, then escalated to breaking and entering, armed robbery, and attempted murder. He was associated with one of Montreal's most violent and notorious gangs, the West End Gang, an Irish mob led by Alan Ross. By the late 1970s, as one of the city's most powerful loan sharks, he had millions of dollars on the street. Even when Séguin was charged by the police, his lawyer — none other than Daniel Rock — was almost always able to get him a short sentence and a small fine. Séguin became Michael Mitton's mentor.

Not surprisingly, Mitton was arrested by the Montreal city police in 1977 while he was acting for Séguin. In no time he'd built up a tidy record of fraud convictions and jail sentences for writing bad cheques. A Montreal police officer, noting that he was wanted by police forces in Ottawa, Toronto, Quebec City, and Sydney, Nova Scotia, described his occupation simply as "fraud artist." Finally, in 1983, after yet another conviction, a judge sentenced Mitton to six years at Collins Bay, a federal penitentiary in Kingston. But Mitton was lucky. He was a cocky, smart-ass kid of about twenty-three when he went to Collins Bay; one or two of the police officers who had dealt with him thought he was a young man who might be saved. Six months into his sentence, he was visited by a family friend, a cop who had a proposition to make. The local RCMP office in Kingston could use an informant within the prison. He would hear about drug deals going down; he would hear plans for break-ins . . . how about it?

Mitton jumped at the chance. After a brief training session with the RCMP's National Criminal Intelligence Section (NCIS), he started passing on information, intelligence solid enough to result in arrests. On one occasion he fingered a fellow convict who had murdered another inmate, and after a successful conviction, the police wondered if Mitton might be of more use outside the pen. They moved him to a halfway house in Kingston and then again to Ottawa to work as an informant among drug dealers in the city's Lebanese community. When the drug traffickers mounted a counter-surveillance on a group of undercover cops and spotted Mitton with them, his usefulness to the Ottawa police was finished. The RCMP relocated him once more, this time back to Montreal and into a far more dangerous game.

His assignment was to work his way back into Ray Séguin's good graces and report on the really big deals going down — drug trafficking, loan-sharking, truck hijackings — all the usual business of the criminals swimming in and out of Séguin's orbit. Participating in any of these activities was not in the job description. "I was just supposed to do intelligence work," Mitton says. And what was in it for him? A new identity and relocation to another part of Canada when his work was finished. When that time came, the Mounties promised, he'd have a long leash to run on, being required to phone in to a parole officer only once a year.

At first the police were worried that Séguin would question Mitton's speedy return to Montreal from a six-year prison sentence, but as far as Séguin was concerned, Mitton had done time and had not squealed. He could be trusted. Séguin eschewed his normal caution in his eagerness to groom a successor, and Mitton was soon back in the inner circle. His day often began with Séguin over breakfast. "Ray used to hold court in the Christophe Colombe, a dirty diner on Jean-Talon," remembers Mitton. "All the East End loan sharks used to have breakfast there." Sometimes they'd meet for lunch or dinner at Ruby Foo's on Décarie, where, Mitton says, many of Séguin's cronies liked to eat. The next morning, Mitton would cross the street from his apartment on de Maisonneuve for another diner breakfast, this time with RCMP officers who took down every word he said about the plans Séguin was hatching — or the gossip he passed on about what other hoods were up to.

The intelligence Mitton collected enabled the RCMP to bring down several notorious gangsters. There were the Mingo brothers, a pair of hoods who stole several million dollars worth of bonds from Merrill Lynch. The brothers tried to fence some of the bonds through Mitton and he turned them in. Another case was a series of truck hijackings, masterminded by a thug called Duval. The RCMP arranged for Mitton to use police money to rent a garage for Duval, a facility in which they had installed video and audio surveillance equipment.

It was in 1984 that Mitton told his RCMP handlers that Séguin, nobody's fool, was looking for business opportunities with the new Tory government. The idea first came to the old crook when a friend in the shoe business, to whom he had loaned a great deal of money, was looking for an increase in shoe quotas and needed a contact in the new government to help him. Quotas were important to many Canadian shoe, textile, and garment businesses, and in Montreal, Séguin specialized in loan-sharking money to people in these very lines of trade. In the late 1970s, the Canadian government had set quotas on shoe and textile imports to protect Canadian manufacturers for a set period of time while they restructured their companies to compete with a flood of cheap products coming in from Asia, especially from Taiwan, Hong Kong, and Korea. Each country controlled the quota it had been allotted, and that quota was divided and brokered in those countries by middlemen. When a Canadian shoe, textile, or apparel wholesaler received an order for so many shoes, so much fabric, or so many jackets, for example, and didn't have enough product to meet the order, he would try to buy a piece of the quota. It was perfectly legal to do so; the trouble came when the quota could not meet the demand. That's when arm-twisting, favours, and even bribes could make the difference. Naturally, the middlemen in the exporting countries attempted to sell pieces of the quota to the highest bidders, either Canadian wholesalers or Canadian brokers who acted as go-betweens connecting them with foreign middlemen.

Séguin's plan was to become a broker in a few key commodities such as shoe and textile quotas, quotas that were important to his clients in Montreal. "I was having breakfast with Ray one morning," Mitton recalls, "and he gives me a letter from a shoe manufacturer he was loan-sharking to and says, 'Go see Daniel Rock. He's got some political contacts and we need the shoe quota.'"

Séguin knew Rock had at least one political contact: Marcel Danis, the new deputy Speaker of the House of Commons. If Danis was not yet in the cabinet, it was because he was still paying the price for his support of Joe Clark, but as the years passed Mulroney grew to trust him. Danis was well known to Montreal's leading crime figures; he was among a small group of lawyers who defended them, a group that included his former law partner Daniel Rock, Sidney Leithman, Jack Waissman, and Gabriel Lapointe, who represented Michel Gravel. For his part, Danis said some years later that Séguin's name meant nothing to him.

Nonetheless Séguin reasoned that, with Rock's help, Danis and his brother, Jean-Claude, could become his conduit into the Tory party, giving him access to some of the gravy the government would be handing out. Danis, as it happened, was an excellent choice; he was interested in Korea and had good connections at the Korean Embassy, where some of the precious shoe quotas were parcelled out. Before Mitton visited Rock, he had breakfast with his RCMP handlers at the diner on de Maisonneuve to get instructions. "I'm supposed to see Daniel Rock," he told them, "and take him this letter and see what he can do with it." The officers didn't waste any time. Within a day they were in Mitton's apartment with an armload of recording equipment. Set up another meeting with Séguin, they ordered, and get clearer instructions — on tape.

Thanks to Mitton, Mounties from the NCIS were watching the development of Séguin's plan, keeping the loan shark and his men under surveillance. They observed a delivery made by one of Séguin's runners, a thug called Dave Schuster. NCIS officers watched Schuster deliver an envelope to a house in suburban Montreal. Séguin hoped a bribe would help him secure a favour for a friend. But there was a hitch in the delivery, and it provided the opening Mitton and the RCMP needed. Mitton found out from an angry Séguin that he had put $3,000 in the envelope, but that Schuster had helped himself to $500 of it. After he discovered what had happened, Séguin hit the roof and berated Schuster in front of gang members. Schuster dropped to the bottom of Séguin's list of favourites and Mitton quickly slipped into his place.[1]

Séguin's young protégé soon became close to Daniel Rock as well, and the two decided the best way to take advantage of Rock's Tory ties was to follow the example of many other well-connected friends of the party and set up a lobbying company. Séguin was to be Rock and Mitton's silent partner, financing the enterprise and directing business clients who wanted favours from the government their way. According to Mitton, Rock's job was to cement the company's relationship with the Danis brothers and to encourage them to introduce Mitton to other politicians. Mitton was the front man for Séguin, carrying his instructions and cash.

On August 13, 1985, Mitton and Rock filed documents to incorporate 144838 Canada Inc. Each was listed as a director. They called their firm Rockton Consulting, and, with Séguin's help, they identified their lobbying specialties: shoe quotas, textile quotas, contracts to dispose of military surplus, CIDA grants for Montreal companies, federal government marketing grants for Montreal companies, Canada Post contracts for goods and services, and early paroles for convicts.

When Mitton revealed the plans for the new lobbying business to his Mountie friends, the police saw their opportunity. An RCMP officer who was working with Mitton explained what happened next. "Mitton reports to the force and it goes up [the chain of command] and comes back down, very fast: 'Work this, milk this for all it's worth.' Mitton had been used by the NCIS for dope, truck hijackings, bond thefts, and so on. Now they wanted to use him on corruption." Mounties at headquarters in Montreal and in Ottawa were excited; here was a gutsy con artist, unafraid of his organized crime bosses, able to burrow into the heart of a corrupt network of political kick-back artists, bid-riggers, and influence-peddlers. Their diminutive stool pigeon was proving more valuable than they'd dreamed.

This is how one of the most sensitive sting operations in Canadian police history — RCMP file number 84 MCOM-13307 — began, an operation that cost hundreds of thousands of dollars and ran for nearly two years early in the Mulroney mandate. It was nothing less than an elaborate, expensive, and completely undercover plan to trap as many corrupt politicians as possible. To this day, the operation remains top secret. Several people who were involved will say only that the operation existed and they cannot discuss it. But with the help of some key players and with pages of confidential documents, it is possible to reconstruct the operation almost in its entirety.

The operation was moved from the NCIS to the RCMP's Commercial Crime Section, where the Mounties assembled their four-man team with care. The officer with overall responsibility was Inspector Réjean Fafard, although he never met Mitton personally. Leading the team that worked directly with Mitton was Detective Sergeant Denis Lapointe, a ten-year veteran of the Commercial Crime Section at RCMP headquarters in Westmount, where he spent most of his time investigating fraudulent bankruptcies and where he had developed an expertise in stocks, bonds, and commodities.[2] Two other commercial crime officers, Walter Wafer and Craig Richards, were also team members.

Mitton needed more than the front of a lobbying business with Daniel Rock to build his credibility with government insiders. It was decided that he should become very knowledgeable about the stock market, in particular commodity trading, involving such things as sulphur and petroleum products. Lapointe became Mitton's handler, training the young informant in the art of moving stocks and bonds. Fortunately, Mitton was a quick study; the stock market aroused all his natural flair for dealmaking.

To complete the façade, Mitton was provided with an office, a car, and an apartment. The seemingly successful young broker took an apartment at 425 Claremont Street in Westmount, a part of town that was home to most of the city's major players. The suite was small and cheaply furnished, but the address was right, and that's what mattered. His office also had to impress potential clients, so the Mounties rented him pleasant facilities for $400 a month in a well-appointed tenth-floor suite at 2055 Peel Street, on the corner of Peel and Sherbrooke. His car was a silver-grey Buick leased on a month-to-month basis for $965 a month. And every square inch of the apartment and the office and the car was wired directly to RCMP headquarters in Montreal.

Technicians installed the most sophisticated audio equipment available. At 2055 Peel they installed hidden cameras as well. Worried that their transmission of television signals from the cameras might interfere with television reception in, say, a sports bar down the street, they mounted a satellite dish on the roof of the building so they could broadcast directly to RCMP headquarters.

The car was essential to the whole operation. The technicians couldn't solve the problem of how to put cameras in the Buick and had to content themselves with wiring it for sound only. They installed a state-of-the-art German tape system that would run off the car's battery and could record for five or six hours at a time. No tell-tale click at the end of a tape would give away the car's eavesdropping capabilities. When Mitton slipped behind the wheel, he simply flicked a switch under the dash to start the tape rolling. "And when we'd get out for lunch or something," he explained, "the Mounties would go into the car, take the tape out, and put a new one in."

To ensure they didn't miss a minute of Mitton's chats with any of his companions, the Mounties gave him a false-bottomed tan briefcase fitted with a transmitter and tape recorder; the recorder was activated by a switch in the handle. Now and then he carried a man's purse, seven inches long by four inches wide, equipped with a thin transmitter — a device that was, unknown to Mitton, the Mounties' method of tracking him, in case he ever went AWOL.

The RCMP even had special jackets tailored for him, a navy blazer and a brown tweed, roomy enough to hide both recorders and transmitters in the jacket lining under the armpit. Fabric attached by a Velcro strip hid the opening so Mitton could take the jacket off and sling it over a chair back without worrying that the pocket would show. The transmitter broadcast directly to his handlers, who followed him in a van. If he was in a building or a room wired to pick up such transmissions — certain offices on Parliament Hill, for example — he would turn off the transmitter and rely on the hidden tape recorders.

Once in a while there was a close call. The worst happened one day in Montreal when Séguin and a friend picked up Mitton in the friend's car. To Mitton's horror, he saw that the car was equipped with a fuzzbuster, built into the rear-view mirror, which sounded when a police car, picking up the police radio transmissions, was near by. Sure enough, the radar detector received the transmissions from Mitton's jacket. "We kept driving around trying to escape the police," recalled Mitton. "Ray kept saying, 'That's odd — there seems to be a lot of radar out here today.' It went on for hours. I was sweating like a pig but he never figured it out."

Daniel Rock was sure the RCMP had wired his office and he was careful not to hold sensitive conversations there. "Let's go outside," he would say to Mitton whenever they met at his office and something tricky came up for discussion. The two men would leave the building and stand outside on the sidewalk. The surveillance crew's eavesdropping chores were made easier when Rock and Mitton were out of the building, especially if they were close to the van. "Once Daniel even leaned on it. You could almost see the van shaking," Mitton said, "because the guys inside were laughing so hard." Rock wasn't the only one who tried to be careful. Ray Séguin correctly surmised that his office was bugged, so he would stroll to a pay phone at the corner to make his potentially incriminating calls. Of course, the cops had also bugged the pay phone.

When the Mounties decided Mitton needed a place to entertain in Ottawa, one that could be wired for sound and video, they chose a suite at the Delta Inn of the Provinces; Mitton's cousin was the manager and agreed to cooperate with their plan, arranging for Mitton to occupy the same suite every time he came to Ottawa. He would host dinners in the hotel dining room and invite politicians and their aides back to the suite for drinks.

All of this took a lot of dollars and a lot of people, explained Lapointe. "You need security, you need the wiring plans of each building, you need protection, you need surveillance units." It cost $11,000 an hour to run a surveillance team, not including the purchase of elaborate equipment. "I wasn't home for a year and a half," said Lapointe. "I worked fourteen hours a day. My responsibility was to keep Mitton happy; I became his confessor, mentor, doctor, psychiatrist, and briefer." And there was the cost of running Michael Mitton. Along with the apartment, the office, the car, and the bespoke suits with the roomy pockets, Mitton was paid $750 a week plus expenses. The RCMP operates like any bureaucracy, and Mitton had to keep receipts for his expenses and file them regularly, signing his claim with a new pseudonym, "Jean Coutu," the name of a large drugstore chain in Quebec.

The police had legal worries as they moved the operation into gear. One was their reliance on one-party consent to the audio and video surveillance. In Canada it is legal to tape a two-party conversation if one of the parties knows it is happening. In order to introduce such evidence in court, however, Mitton would have to take the stand, which meant revealing his identity. They knew they would have problems with Mitton's credibility. The second issue was more serious. The justice system frowns on the RCMP using taxpayers' money to bribe or pay off politicians. In other words, Mitton's lobbying firm had nothing but hospitality with which to tempt the targeted individuals. A lot of hemming and hawing went on while some of these individuals waited for more substantial recognition of the friendship. As the lobbying company got rolling, though, the police expected there would be plenty of business and cash for everyone.

The game was set to begin: Mitton was trained, the equipment was in place. Rockton Consulting made introductory contacts with politicians and their aides in Ottawa and built up a client list from Séguin's business associates. The new company charged these clients retainers and fees and the revenues were divided between Séguin, Rock, and Mitton. Mitton dutifully turned over his share to the RCMP. Another portion of the earnings was set aside for operating expenses — to grease the wheels in Ottawa.

A shoe or textile quota would cost a Canadian manufacturer $25,000 to $30,000, so Rockton charged 10 per cent as its fee, earning the company $2,500 to $3,000 for its lobbying effort. Within a few months Mitton and Rock had fifteen to twenty deals under way, including one for a quota on jackets from Asia and another for a grant for the Quebec City airport runway. The partners expected to clear several thousand dollars on each deal. In the meantime, Rock and Mitton lobbied for one company to receive $350,000 in federal money for a tire-recycling plant (no one remembers what fee was promised).

Help in obtaining an early parole was extremely pricey, worked out on a case-by-case basis, but valued at several thousand dollars per parole. The firm identified one highly placed career officer on the Parole Board as the key contact, but there were others — political appointees on the board — who could help as well. This aspect of Rockton's business was not as far-fetched as one might think. Rock had bragged of his success in springing his client Conrad Bouchard, and had offered his help to Réal Simard. Carole Jacques would later run into trouble for her involvement in an early parole bid. For a lobbying firm backed by an organized crime boss, the Parole Board was an obvious target. How successful was Rockton at obtaining early paroles? "We got one or two done," said Mitton.

All of these deals took time and required perseverance and patience; fortunately, Mitton and Séguin developed a lucrative side-line that made money from the beginning. Séguin proposed that they set up a money-laundering operation; it would serve his own interests and those of other organized crime bosses in Montreal who had hundreds of thousands of dollars in cash from illicit operations that had to be filtered through legitimate businesses. And it would help in other ways too: Mitton's Ottawa friends had to be paid in cash because cheques and most other benefits left paper trails. Mitton, Séguin's trusted lieutenant, would make the perfect middleman. With the assistance of his Mountie handlers, Mitton established a separate firm in his own name as the vehicle; the new company, Pelton Petroleum Products, was registered on December 10, 1985, with the Peel Street office as its headquarters. As a federally registered company offering a service to clients, it incurred expenses, issued invoices, and received payments. The mechanics of washing dirty money were simple. Séguin, or other organized crime clients, would issue an invoice to Pelton for "services rendered." Accompanying the invoice was an amount of cash equal to the value of the invoice, plus 10 per cent. Mitton would return a cheque to the client for the amount of the invoice, a cheque that could then be deposited in a bank account and used to run organized crime's legitimate business operations. Pelton's 10-per-cent fee — paid in cash — went into a safety deposit box at a nearby bank. When entertainment or pay-off funds were required, they were taken from the deposit box.

Mobsters and shady businessmen in Montreal were lining up for their service, and a lot of laundering went on at 2055 Peel Street. "We were laundering for anyone who asked," explained Mitton. Some RCMP sources say they didn't know much about the money-laundering side of Pelton, but they must have known more than they are willing to admit today; every minute of every transaction in the Peel Street office was recorded.

An example of Pelton's money-laundering combined with Rockton's lobbying service was the case of a Montreal wholesaler who was bringing in jackets from Korea. Séguin loaned the wholesaler the money to pay for the jackets, including the payment for a piece of quota the company needed. He also had the political contacts, through Mitton and Rock, to secure the quota. Their job was to drive to Ottawa, meet the fixer, and make the payment with Séguin's cash. The fixers — whom neither the RCMP nor Mitton will identify —

used Séguin's money to buy the quota from the Korean middlemen, keeping a cut for themselves. Séguin took a series of postdated cheques from the jacket importer, who, in addition to repaying the loan, paid him generously for his trouble. Mitton took its customary 10 per cent from Séguin and 10 per cent, invoiced separately, from the manufacturer. "Ray would then have legitimate funds to put in his bank," Mitton explained. According to Mitton, one businessman wanting a major piece of federal assistance for his company laundered between $500,000 and $700,000 in a number of transactions; Pelton kept its share in cash and there was no paper trail.[3]

As the months passed, Mitton met regularly in Montreal and Ottawa with Tory politicians and their aides. Rock was often too busy to accompany him; among other things, he'd been retained by Michel Gravel to defend him during the extensive RCMP investigation into his activities. Mitton's appointments were with people like Robert Letendre, chief of staff to the junior minister for external relations, Monique Vézina, and with Senator Guy Charbonneau in Marcel Danis's office. There was a meeting with Jean Bazin at the Queen Elizabeth Hotel (where, to the Mounties' frustration, the noise of people eating, drinking, and talking drowned out the voices on the tape), during which a sulphur deal was discussed. "I flew out to Calgary to meet Petro-Canada officials," said Mitton, adding that his introduction had been arranged by Bazin. Nothing came of the Petro-Canada meetings, nor of a meeting with Michel Cogger at his Sherbrooke Street office. According to Mitton, Cogger wanted a substantial retainer, which the lobbying firm could not afford to pay.

Almost every week Mitton would drive Jean-Claude Danis to Ottawa. Jean-Claude, "the stupid brother," as some Tories called him behind his back, didn't have his own car but commuted to Ottawa regularly, first to Joe Clark's office in 1982 and 1983 and then as his brother's unofficial aide when Marcel became deputy Speaker of the House of Commons. (Jean-Claude told Mitton he was his brother's chief of staff. But the deputy Speaker doesn't have a chief of staff, and House of Commons records show that the only time Jean-Claude Danis was on the Commons payroll was when he worked for Joe Clark in 1982-83.) In 1984 Jean-Claude made his headquarters in his brother's office and from time to time he needed a lift to Ottawa from Montreal. Mitton made it his business to give it to him.

Every few weeks Rock and Mitton would host get-togethers at the Delta Inn for their new friends in the Tory party. And all this time the reels wound slowly in the van lurking nearby, or in the next hotel room, or over at RCMP headquarters in Montreal. The Mounties were recording it all, including Mitton's conversations in the very halls of Parliament, and every day they would Telex a report to their superiors in Ottawa. The response was prompt and positive. "The corruption file was priority one," said Mitton.

On occasion Mitton would hear about deals going down among Montreal mobsters — drug deals, robberies, even murders. One day, while Mitton was driving Séguin around the city in the Buick, the old hood told him about a contract killer from Vancouver who'd come to Montreal to murder another man. He had carried out the assignment and was driving the body down Fleury Street to dump it in the river when another car rear-ended his in an accident. Alarmed, the Vancouver killer leapt out of his car and fled. When the other driver came over to the hit man's car to speak to the "passenger," he discovered the passenger had a hole in his head. While Séguin was regaling Mitton with this latest bit of mobster gossip, the conversation was being transmitted to RCMP headquarters in Westmount. The Mounties, said Mitton, were not interested in the contract killer from Vancouver. The corruption file was all they cared about. (The information was, however, passed on to the Montreal police, who carried out their own investigation.)

Mitton gradually worked his way into Tory circles, slowly building trust. He became a familiar figure on the Hill, and security guards rarely questioned him as he made his rounds. Through Marcel Danis's office, he even had a parking pass for the Hill. It wasn't surprising that the Tories looked to him for a little fundraising in Montreal — specifically, to sell tables to the Prime Minister's Dinner, an annual affair that was the major PC Canada Fund event in the city. The 1986 dinner was to be held at the Palais de Congrès. Mitton bustled around, arranging for his mobster friends to buy tables. "The dinner looked like the Who's Who of the Mob," Mitton cackled later. Séguin bought a table, as did the notorious Johnson brothers, a family as feared as the Cotronis. Organized crime paid for at least five tables that year. Mitton attended with his wife, Janet, and they were accompanied by a recent acquaintance, an American entrepreneur called Kenneth Pirtle who was in Montreal to put together a sulphur commodities deal. By now Mitton's reputation as a politically connected commodities expert brought such people into his orbit.

Like Mulroney, Pirtle was staying at the Ritz-Carlton, and like Mulroney, he had a dark limousine waiting for him outside the front door. He had sent it to Boucherville to fetch Marcel Danis, whom he'd met through Mitton, for the Mulroney dinner. The day after the fundraiser, Janet Mitton walked over to the Ritz-Carlton to pick up Pirtle's girlfriend, a tough-looking blonde (Pirtle told Janet she was a schoolteacher), to go shopping. When they left the hotel, they opened the back door of an idling limo and settled themselves comfortably, only to find two astonished men in dark suits staring at them from the front seat. "What are you doing?" the men asked. "We're going shopping," the women said. "Don't you know whose car this is?" one man asked. "It's Brian Mulroney's." Oh. The women hopped out and hunted down Pirtle's limousine.

It was Pirtle who dreamed up the most audacious of all the adventures Mitton was to have while involved in the RCMP operation. Pirtle, who was in his mid-fifties, was a sight to behold. Skinny and tall, at least six foot six, with dyed blond hair and a thick coat of foundation makeup on his face, he wore tight, French-cut suits with open shirts, accessorized with cowboy boots and a purse. He could drink Black Russians — a mix of vodka and Kahlua — all night and stay sober; he carried with him a pharmacy of interesting drugs. Mitton and Rock wondered if Pirtle might be with the Central Intelligence Agency in the U.S.; another security expert scoffs at the idea. "He was probably Mob," he says.

"Well, he was a mystery man," Mitton conceded. "Plenty of money, flashing a platinum American Express card, keeping three rooms at the Ritz-Carlton, no visible means of support." And a wide network of political contacts in Central America, including Jorge Carpio Nicolle, the right-wing candidate for the presidency of Guatemala, a man who had the support of the Guatemalan military.

Mitton's RCMP handlers, through FBI contacts in the United States, learned that Pirtle was a kingpin in the pornographic movie and video business in California. In addition, "he was into commodities like oil and gas but he was also suspected of being into dope," one Mountie said. Through Pirtle, Rock and Mitton met a man called Umberto Effio, another interesting businessman of no visible means whose father was a South American cabinet minister. Peru or Colombia, they couldn't remember which. Effio, who had connections throughout Latin America, was only in his twenties. He spoke no French, but to the envy of the other men, his lack of the language didn't prevent him from being able to pick up beautiful Québécoises in any bar he chose. He claimed to be in the coffee business but the rumour was that he too was in the drug trade. And he too bought a table for the Mulroney fundraiser.

Pirtle's plan, developed with the help of Effio, was breathtaking: Canadian politicians would help Carpio Nicolle get elected in Guatemala in the December 8, 1985, election, and in return there would be big payoffs for everyone. Pirtle proposed to introduce Marcel Danis to Jorge Carpio Nicolle. Pirtle's hope was that Canada would offer millions of dollars in CIDA money to build a new fertilizer plant in Guatemala, giving the presidential candidate evidence of his clout with a democratic country. Once elected, the candidate would see to it that the Canadians who helped would be paid out of the royalties for all oil and gas imports into Guatemala for the next five years.

But Danis says he was told by Pirtle that he and his brother were wanted down there to organize a rally in Guatemala City for a presidential candidate, a losing candidate, whose name he does not remember. Pirtle's request was not unusual, according to Danis; he said that after checking out the candidates, he had assisted in elections in the United States, the United Kingdom, France, and Africa during the previous fifteen years. "I enjoy that," he declared. "I've done that before in other countries." He added that in the case of the Guatemala trip, "expenses were paid but there was no fee."

Canadian security experts have suggested that Pirtle's real objective was to establish a transfer point for the Colombian cocaine cartel. The fertilizer plant deal, even if legitimate, would have shocked most Canadians: Canada had stopped sending aid to Guatemala in 1981 as a protest against the country's appalling human rights violations. Furthermore, the Guatemalans had not repaid any of the $7.5 million loaned to them by the Canadian government to buy railroad cars from Bombardier.

The election was just days away and Pirtle wanted the Danis brothers in Guatemala in a hurry. He also wanted Mitton there. Mitton's RCMP handlers hesitated: first of all, Mitton and his group would have no diplomatic cover, and second, the Canadian government frowned on unauthorized visits by Canadian politicians to a country that was virtually shunned by Western democracies. When Mitton told Pirtle he didn't have a passport — which was true; no convict out on parole has a passport — Pirtle brushed the problem aside, saying members of the Guatemalan army would meet him at the airport. In the end, the Mounties agreed he could go. It would be the first time he was out of communication with them in a year.

Having decided to risk it, the Mounties were at Mitton's apartment within three hours of his call with a passport. "Then I called

Daniel Rock and said, Phone Marcel and Jean-Claude and tell them we need them in Guatemala. We'll pay for the trip, we'll give them money, the whole nine yards. Two hours later, and this is now two o'clock in the morning, I get a call from Daniel Rock. 'Everything's set now, Mike; get the tickets.'"

Pirtle had tickets waiting for the Danis brothers at the airport, but they did not travel together: Marcel had two days left of House of Commons duty in his role as deputy Speaker. Danis informed the Speaker's office of his travel plans, but he told no other senior government official nor anyone in the cabinet.

Mitton and Jean-Claude Danis flew together two days ahead; when they arrived in Guatemala, they were met by military drivers who sped them to a luxury hotel. At the bar that evening, their Guatemalan hosts introduced Jean-Claude to a suntanned blonde in her mid-twenties, a beauty queen who had just won the country's Miss Guatemala contest. In his spare moments during the rest of the week, Miss Guatemala showed Jean-Claude the sights as they toured around in a car driven by a colonel in the Guatemalan army. Two days later Marcel arrived. With plenty of spending money provided by Pirtle, pleasant companions, and a free hotel, the brothers enjoyed their stay, but it came to an abrupt end on election night. Carpio Nicolle was defeated by Vinicio Carezo Areuelo, a moderate civilian candidate. "We got out that night," said Mitton. "Fast." The dream of CIDA money disappeared as quickly as the promised fertilizer plant.

Pirtle had more schemes up his sleeve and he arranged for Mitton to make other trips abroad. To maintain his cover, the RCMP agreed to let Mitton travel, but intense discussions went on in their offices in Westmount and Ottawa about the direction the investigation was taking.

Senior Mounties were pleased with what was happening, and the operation's findings were becoming known to security officials in Ottawa. But the lid was kept on tight; whether any politicians were aware of it at this stage is not known, but their ignorance did not last much longer.

Intelligence from the operation was first-class. The Mitton team had 3,000 hours of videotape, 6,000 hours of audio tape, and mountains of documents and financial records, all of which pointed to the party members, organizers, aides and bagmen who were interested in laundering money, accepting kickbacks, and peddling influence. What was even more sobering to the RCMP was to see how easily organized crime figures like Séguin could operate in political circles. And Séguin was not alone; during the same period, Frank Majeau had the run of Roch LaSalle's office.

But as yet there were no charges or arrests, no "collars," as the police would say. It was time to take stock and decide what course the investigation should take in order to reach that stage. A lengthy report drafted by the team, under Inspector Réjean Fafard's supervision, spelled out the charges that could be laid at that point against some politicians and their aides and associates. The charges included conspiracy to commit fraud; conspiracy to commit breach of trust; and aiding and abetting the conspiracies. Crimes had been committed, and the officers were confident they could win convictions.

"But the Crown prosecutors wanted a little more before laying charges," said one officer. They wanted to know that these crimes had been carried through — beyond the conspiracy stage — so that the charges could include the *commission* of those offences.

Fafard's report spelled out three very clear options. The first was to shut down the operation altogether. The second was to fold the sting operation but continue to follow up, adding to the files on the politicians already approached by Mitton. This option proposed the laying of conspiracy charges based on the evidence already gathered by the team.

The third choice, and the one favoured by the team, was to crank up the investigation several notches.

"To use the fishing analogy," explained the officer, "they, the politicians, are nibbling. So we need some different equipment, different bait and lines to continue." The third option said, Give us the money and give us the tools.

What usually happens in an RCMP operation of this kind, explained a former assistant deputy commissioner of the force, is that the police will introduce a couple of undercover officers into the sting at this point. The informant — in this case, Mitton — may or may not remain involved, but the undercover officers take over, develop his contacts, and proceed with his deals. As police officers, they are gathering evidence, and when the time is ripe, they can make the arrests. This stage of the operation would be costly in man-hours alone, not to mention the thousands of dollars required to maintain Mitton's cover.

Ottawa had to authorize its Montreal officers to seek the court's permission to carry out wiretaps on telephone lines, something RCMP headquarters had so far refused to do. But the Mounties needed the wiretaps to corroborate evidence. Mitton would probably not be called on to testify himself, and that could make the evidence gathered through Mitton's recordings inadmissible. Then their glitzy investigation and the long-awaited charges would be blown away.

It was a nerve-wracking time for everyone. The officers handling Mitton were concerned that the RCMP's political masters would find out about the operation and crush the careers of senior Mounties who had allowed it to happen. There was also fear that their investigative methods would cause a political and public furore. Some civil libertarians, for example, might find grave fault with setting up a man like Mitton to run around wired for sound, cooking up deals and attempting to entrap politicians. Many believed that the police should come in *after* a crime had been committed and try to solve it, not participate in a crime in progress in order to catch the perpetrators. There were others in the force who dreaded the possibility of an aroused public demanding to know why the hundreds of thousands of dollars involved in the operation had not been spent on fighting traditional crimes such as drug trafficking.

All of these factors — the restraint of budgets, the anticipation of political reprisals, the possibility of public disapproval and careers in jeopardy — were weighed at RCMP headquarters. In the end, they decided the matter. They often do in a bureaucracy. The decision from headquarters arrived in June 1986: Shut it down.[4]

The team was not told why. All they were told was, "They're tired of it, it's too dangerous." Headquarters was not even interested in option two, the plan to keep investigations going into those politicians who had already shown a willingness to bite the bait. Instead, several officers, including some of the Montreal team and others brought in from Ottawa, were dispatched to "interview" the targets of the operation. The premise of the interviews was bizarre in the extreme.

The targets were told that the Mounties had reason to believe that some dishonest and corrupt persons were planning and perhaps even trying to buy favours from politicians. They were given friendly advice to be on their guards against such crooked individuals. It was an unsubtle way of telling these men that they were being watched, but it also meant the end of the entire operation. "It's called crime prevention," said one of the officers sarcastically. "That's also the job of the police."

The orders were firm and the sting was shut down. No more investigation of MPs and their friends, no more work on the links between organized crime and the politicians. Close the apartment and the Peel Street office and return the car. Pull the wires and the taps and return the equipment to headquarters. And give Mike Mitton $2,000 and tell him to get out of town, but remind him to keep in touch with his parole officer.

The Mounties in Montreal pleaded with their superiors about the way the force proposed to handle Mike and Janet Mitton. There had been an initial budget of $175,000 to relocate them to another part of the country under a witness protection program. You can't just turn Mike loose like that, argued Denis Lapointe. He'll be killed by the Mob. But senior RCMP brass refused to allow Mitton to return to his original role as an RCMP informant on other crimes. They wanted him gone, and $2,000 was their final offer. Mitton's handlers had squirrelled away $8,000 from earnings Mitton had made through the lobbying company; they dug out the money and passed it on. With $10,000 in their pockets the couple moved to Vancouver, and Mitton went to work in the one industry he now knew well — stocks, bonds, and commodities.[5]

Police officers, civilian sources, and Michael Mitton have very clear memories of the details of the operation and they point to all the audio and video recordings made during the surveillance of meetings and conversations.

Some time later Daniel Rock learned of Mitton's true identity and in response to questions concerning Mitton and Rockton Consulting, said, "Ask the RCMP . . . Mr. Mitton is an employee of the RCMP, so ask the RCMP what their employee did and they will tell you." He called the Mounties' attempts to trap him "disgraceful," but he was philosophical. When it was suggested that the name of the RCMP operation was "Daniel Rock et al.," Rock was unperturbed. "Well, that's possible. When you practise law the way I do, you don't make friends with the police. I have always thought it was part of the game for me to be attacked by them."

Rock would not confirm that he and Mitton were business partners, and he could not remember any meetings, social gatherings, or lobbying efforts. "You are talking to me about things that happened seven, eight, ten years ago . . . I see people every day. Did I see MPs or not? I don't remember at all." As for Ray Séguin, solicitor-client privilege prevented Rock from making any comment about him.

Marcel Danis said that he was questioned by the RCMP about Pirtle, but he denied there were discussions concerning a fertilizer plant, Canadian government funding, or oil and gas rights.

His brother, Jean-Claude Danis, refused to respond to questions about his role unless they were sent to him in writing. Questions were submitted, but the only response was silence.

CHAPTER TEN

CONFLICTS AND OTHER INTERESTS

ONFLICT OF INTEREST IS NOT A SIMPLE MISDEMEANOUR. IT'S A
far broader issue than one of politicians accepting personal benefits. Fairness, equality, and social justice are at
stake; when an individual receives a patronage position,
an honour, or a title simply because he or she has a powerful political ally, most Canadians' sense of propriety is sorely offended. As
York University professor Ian Greene points out, in thirty-five incidents of conflict of interest he has identified among federal and
provincial governments between 1986 and 1988, sixteen "involved
violations of the appearance of impartiality." Not all Canadians,
Greene says, define social justice or equality the same way, but they
do want a standard of conduct that recognizes merit, not connections, and that demands public servants put the country's welfare
above personal gain. And they want clear rules for their politicians.[1]

Until the 1960s, there were no written rules for Canadian cabinet ministers. In 1964 Prime Minister Lester Pearson wrote to his
ministers about the ethical standards expected of them. Abiding by
the law was not enough, he warned; his ministers "must act in a manner so scrupulous that it will bear the closest public scrutiny."
Following a number of conflict allegations involving federal and
provincial ministers in the early 1970s, Privy Council President Allan
MacEachen drafted legislation to deal with the issue, but it was never
passed; instead Prime Minister Pierre Trudeau presented his ministers

with a set of guidelines requiring them to disclose non-personal assets — essentially stock portfolios or shares in a company — and to either sell such assets or place them in a blind trust. In 1974 Trudeau created the Office of the Assistant Deputy Registrar General to deal with his guidelines.

Joe Clark broadened the guidelines in 1979 to include spouses and dependent children, a decision that was so unpopular with elected representatives that Trudeau reversed it in 1980. After a 1983 conflict scandal involving Alastair Gillespie, one of his ministers, Trudeau set up a task force chaired by two former cabinet ministers, Tory Michael Starr and Liberal Mitchell Sharp, who proposed the most comprehensive set of rules yet for holders of public office as well as legislation to enforce a code of ethics. Mulroney's government dropped the task force's recommendations when it came to power, but after only six months in office and a spate of scandals that pointed to corruption in his government, he was forced to keep a campaign promise of new guidelines.

In March 1985, Mulroney assigned Erik Nielsen and former Tory MP William Jarvis to the task. The pair beavered away for the next six months — a period, ironically, that saw three fresh conflict-of-interest incidents unfold. Given what was to come, they were minor affairs, but each caused an uproar in the House. The opposition went after Justice Minister John Crosbie when both of his sons were appointed as federal legal agents in St. John's; Finance Minister Michael Wilson was embarrassed when his department awarded a lucrative contract to one of his relatives; and External Affairs Minister Joe Clark's brother, Peter, was named lawyer to the 1988 Olympic Games committee in Calgary.

Mulroney released a lengthy list of new conflict-of-interest guidelines on September 9, 1985. Among its recommendations were several concerning the hiring of family members: ministers were not allowed to hire immediate family members nor members of a colleague's family unless the hiring process could be proved to have been impartial. (Mulroney himself raised eyebrows when he hired his brother, Gary, to run his Manicouagan constituency office. In his defence, it was said that Gary wasn't being paid, but as a former schoolteacher it seems unlikely he could afford to do the job without some kind of remuneration. This was never explained.)

The guidelines also specified that ministers could not do business with their former departments for at least two years after leaving office; bureaucrats would have to wait one year.[2] Few paid any attention to this rule, as an unseemly bustle of senior Defence Department bureaucrats and PMO aides into jobs at the new Oerlikon Aerospace offices in Saint-Jean-sur-Richelieu, Quebec, was to prove. There are still things to be worked out, the prime minister's statement said. "The important point is that for the first time a government has placed before Parliament a comprehensive program of initiatives on public service ethics. It provides tangible evidence to the people of Canada of the determination of this government to ensure that its actions will be governed by the highest standards of conduct."

Aside from employment rules, Mulroney's 1985 guidelines stated that the government would allow parliamentary scrutiny "on an experimental basis" (the words are the prime minister's) of senior patronage appointments in much the same way that the U.S. Congress examines presidential nominees for the Supreme Court and other high offices. "Some constitutional experts," said Mulroney, "have warned me that I am wrong to take this step, that it is foreign to our system of government and incompatible with it. These gentlemen and I have agreed to differ, but I am not unconscious of the risks involved. That is why I am fully prepared to end this experiment and to re-think the approach if it seems to be taking a wrong turn." It turned out that Mulroney did not like having parliamentarians raise questions about his chosen appointees. Only a handful of his patronage appointments ever endured parliamentary scrutiny by an all-party Commons committee, and the initiative was quietly dropped.

The widespread grumbling about aggressive lobbying practices prompted the government to include a promise to register lobbyists. This was a promise Mulroney kept when he introduced the act creating the Lobbyists' Registration Branch in 1987, but the legislation was weak, full of loopholes, and devoid of any real penalties for transgressors.

The 1985 guidelines stated that Crown corporations were not allowed to hire lobbyists. In other words, government agencies should not be paying people to lobby their own government, as Air Canada and Canadian National Railways would do in 1986 when they hired Frank Moores to lobby the government. This rule, too, was eventually ignored. In Mulroney's second term in office, for example, Defence Minister Marcel Masse hired a close friend, Tory lobbyist Paul Curley, to help him sell the unpopular $4.5-billion purchase of the EH-101 helicopters to a grouchy Canadian public, although no one would admit he was lobbying. He was there to offer advice, said Masse. Today, Air Canada — now privatized but still sporting many of the Mulroney appointees of 1985, including David Angus — has hired several lobbyists.

Initially, Nielsen had high hopes for the new guidelines, but he came to the conclusion that Mulroney had no intention of worrying about them. "I had a lot to say about conflict to Brian," Nielsen shrugs. "I spoke to him and I wrote to him ad nauseam. I gave him advice with respect to what to do. He did nothing and he . . . ignored the specific recommendations Bill Jarvis and I had put together." Even when Nielsen warned him in the winter of 1985 that there could be conflict-of-interest problems with Industry Minister Sinclair Stevens, Mulroney paid no attention. Nielsen watched with dismay as Stevens, a lawyer, stomped right through the rules. "If any professional person should recognize a conflict it's a lawyer," snaps Nielsen angrily.

Mulroney must have regretted not listening to Nielsen on the subject of Sinc Stevens. While the Mulroneys were off on their first official trip to Asia, in May 1985, *The Globe and Mail* published a series of reports that the combative industry minister had secured a

$2.6-million loan for his own company from a businessman who was a partner in a firm receiving grants from the minister's department. On May 11 Mulroney had a brief long-distance conversation with Stevens but hung up before he'd done the dirty work of firing him from the cabinet. That job was left to Nielsen, who had also been given the task of firing Bob Coates when Mulroney refused to do it. (Coates was cashiered as defence minister after he visited a sex club during an official visit in Germany.) The next day Stevens went before the House to tender his resignation.

Globe reporters Michael Harris and David Stewart-Patterson had uncovered a complicated tale. Stevens's Toronto-based holding company, York Centre, was in serious financial difficulties and had received help from some questionable sources. The stories described how Stevens's wife, Noreen, herself a lawyer and a partner in the business, had sought help from brokerage firms and wealthy individuals who were at the same time dealing with Stevens as industry minister, trying to win substantial government support for their projects. Other reporters jumped on the bandwagon, and within weeks Canadians were engrossed in the story. At the heart of it was the $2.6-million loan to York Centre from a wealthy Toronto businessman, Anton Czapka, who turned out to be an investor in Frank Stronach's manufacturing company, Magna International. Noreen Stevens was negotiating the loan just as the auto parts company was receiving $64.2 million in federal grants from Stevens's department for a new plant in Cape Breton. It was as clear a case of mutual back-scratching as Canadians had ever witnessed and the worst scandal to hit the Tory government so far.

At the time, some cabinet ministers knew of more unpleasantness: Stevens had pushed through a $5-million grant to the wealthy Ghermezian family of Edmonton to develop Fantasyland, an addition to their shopping centre, the West Edmonton Mall. Stevens's fellow cabinet minister, Don Mazankowski, had lobbied hard for the grant: the mall was an important contributor to the economic health of

Edmonton, and the Ghermezians had been generous donors to the federal Tories. Most members of the cabinet committee on industry were appalled to see taxpayers' money spent on what one called a "theme park," and they refused to approve the deal. Stevens continued to push it and the issue returned to the committee a second time. Again, the committee rejected it. After Stevens's departure, it was discovered that he had actually authorized a cheque months earlier. "There was only one solution," said a cabinet minister. "We had to approve it. But this was an offence against the Financial Administration Act." Only a handful of cabinet ministers realized the seriousness of the offence, and they weren't planning to go public with it.

During nine days of opposition attack on Stevens, it was not Mulroney who took the hit — he was in Asia. It was Nielsen who was accused of stonewalling as day after day he rose in the Commons, grim-faced, to answer questions. While the opposition bayed for Stevens's blood, senior bureaucrats and at least one cabinet colleague were berating themselves, not only for failing to make Stevens adhere to conflict-of-interest guidelines but for failing to impress their importance on Mulroney.

Within a very short time, Nielsen was indelibly stained by the affair himself. His effectiveness as deputy prime minister was over, he told close friends. When he announced his intention to resign in June, Mulroney and his other cabinet colleagues were aghast. They were then trying to cope with the stench arising from the charges laid against MP Michel Gravel on May 15, just four days after Stevens was fired. Mulroney was not sorry to lose his prickly deputy prime minister, but he did not need another ministerial resignation at that moment. Nielsen agreed to wait until January 1987 to make his leave-taking formal.

To deal with the Stevens affair, the government appointed a royal commission under Ontario Chief Justice Robert Parker. It began its hearings in a Toronto office building in August 1986, about three months after Stevens was fired. As more and more devastating testimony was heard, the story became the lead item on the news, a page-one story in most newspapers. Stevens's behaviour was at fault in almost every allegation that was made against him. He never honoured the cabinet guidelines on ministers' blind trusts, taking an active role in decisions about his personal business affairs. In October 1984 he appointed Trevor Eyton, president of Brascan Ltd., to the board of the Canada Development Investment Corporation, and within weeks of the appointment he was asking for Eyton's help in refinancing York Centre. It was the same with his March 1985 appointment of two brokerage houses, Burns Fry and Dominion Securities, to advise the CDIC at the same time that York Centre was looking for help from the two firms. A few weeks later he also brought Gordon Capital Corporation on board for financial advice to CDIC, despite the fact that the company was involved with York Centre.

In February 1987 Justice Parker listened to the final oral arguments on both sides of the Stevens case; he then spent the next ten months writing his report. On December 3, 1987, his report was tabled in the House of Commons. It was not good news. He had found Stevens in conflict of interest on fourteen occasions. With regard to Magna International, the judge ruled that Stevens was in conflict at least six times, although Magna itself never benefitted from preferential treatment. Stevens's visit to the Seoul offices of Hanil Bank of Korea in August 1985, a visit that was ostensibly an official one, was another highly improper act: one of Stevens's companies was in debt to the bank. As Parker put it, he "chose to visit the Hanil Bank to impress upon the executives of the bank his own importance as a government figure." More conflicts were revealed by the testimony of the minister's long-time secretary, Shirley Walker; her meticulous diaries showed that both she and her boss were involved in helping run the affairs of York Centre. Despite the torrent of damaging information that poured out of the inquiry and Parker's subsequent findings, Stevens remained as cocky as ever. Mr. Justice Parker, he declared defiantly at an Ottawa press conference after the results were made public, was wrong and his definition of conflict of interest was wrong. So there.

No criminal charges were ever laid against Stevens because, as Parker pointed out, the government conflict rules are only guidelines. "No legal consequences flow from their violation. The sanctions, if any, are political rather than legal." The sanctions for Stevens were indeed political; his career as a politician was over. Although he continued to represent his riding, he rarely appeared in Parliament after 1986 and was not able to run as a Tory in 1988 because Mulroney would not sign his nomination papers.

Justice Parker's comments on the government's conflict-of-interest guidelines were equally damning. The rules were "flawed and inconsistent," he reported; they failed to define clearly what constitutes a conflict of interest. Any new conflict package should include consideration of spousal disclosure as well as tough penalties for violators — penalties, recommended Parker, that should be backed by the full force of the law, including imprisonment.

Despite the damage of the Stevens affair, Mulroney was still not prepared to do anything concrete about conflict of interest. Another seven cabinet ministers would resign over episodes of conflict of interest or errors in political judgment before 1988, when the prime minister finally turned his attention to the issue again.

Broader definitions of conflict of interest came to the fore in the autumn of 1986 when Canadians found out the prime minister had gone to great trouble and expense to relocate a federal prison planned for Drummondville, Quebec, to Port-Cartier, in his own riding. And during the winter of 1987, as the Parker inquiry hearings wound on with the daily revelations about Sinclair Stevens, fresh stories appeared in the media that raised similar ethical issues.

The most damaging was the cabinet's decision to award the $1.3-billion maintenance contract for its McDonnell Douglas CF-18 fighter jets to Canadair Ltd. of Montreal, rather than to Bristol

Aerospace Ltd. of Winnipeg, the lower bidder. It became clear to out-raged western Canadians that the decision was purely political and intended to favour Quebec. In its own way, it did as much to alien-ate westerners as Trudeau's National Energy Program had done in the early 1980s; in the harm done to national unity, it marked a turning point for the Mulroney government.

For the public servant who was ordered to sign the CF-18 con-tract with Canadair, the affair was a professional crisis. "Bristol won the contract fair and square, by all measures," he said. "If the gov-ernment wants to make political contracts, that's their decision. But to pretend the Canadair decision was the right one on merit . . ." His minister, Stewart McInnes, told him to sign the contract. "I refused to sign the pinks," he said, referring to the forms required to com-plete the deal. "My father was a deputy minister, and prudence and probity were the rules of his life. He drilled it into us. But with these guys — I hated it. Every little $8,000 contract for a back road some-place . . . If it went to someone they thought was a Liberal, my min-ister would go after me."

This bureaucrat refused to endorse the deal and told McInnes that he would find no civil servant who would. "I had to get legal advice from the counsel for the department, and the advice was that legally, I could not sign this. McInnes then took the contract to cabinet, and they put it through instead. That's when I decided I had to leave."

There were more scandals waiting in the wings. The first of the new year 1987 was the *Maclean's* magazine story about Frank Majeau's connection to Réal Simard, a story that signalled the begin-ning of the end of Roch LaSalle's career. Another scandal, one that had been quietly brewing throughout 1985 and 1986 but did not blow up until 1987, was the Oerlikon affair, involving André Bissonnette, the member of Parliament for Saint-Jean-sur-Richelieu.

Bissonnette, sometimes called "the chicken king" in Quebec, was already a millionaire before he became a politician. He had left school at sixteen to work in his father's bakery, and wound up as a butcher in the employ of his father-in-law, Maurice Laflamme. Quebeckers have a passion for broiled chicken, a taste Bissonnette was smart enough to cash in on; over the next twenty years he was able to corner 15 per cent of the province's lucrative broiler-chicken market. His modern abattoirs employed 250 people. In 1984 he entered Parliament and became junior minister for transport. Bissonnette knew that the government was considering a new low-level air defence system, or LLAD, and like other MPs, he lobbied hard to get the new plant in his riding.

The Liberals had initiated the process of finding a contractor in February 1984, when the Defence Department sent out a request for proposals to interested bidders. By August there were seven bidders at the table, including the Swiss arms manufacturer Oerlikon-Buehle. The firm remained on a three-company short list in March 1985, when it incorporated a Canadian subsidiary, Oerlikon Aerospace Inc., to acquire land for a manufacturing facility. Clearly, Oerlikon officials were optimistic that they would secure the contract. It took until January 28, 1986, for the government to choose Oerlikon, although the decision was kept secret until the official announcement on April 16. Unofficially, there seemed to have been little doubt about who would win or where the plant would be located. In Saint-Jean in January 1986 there had been a scramble over a 40-hectare parcel of empty farmland that had been chosen by Oerlikon for the plant. On January 13, 1986, the firm's lawyers at Lette and Associates drafted Oerlikon's offer to buy the property for nearly $3 million.

Matters were relatively quiet for several months. But Saint-Jean-sur-Richelieu is not a big city, and stories about the land bonanza started to spread. Oerlikon had transferred its legal business from Lette to Jean Bazin at Byers Casgrain, and in August Bazin received an anonymous letter outlining a series of ownership flips on the land before it was finally sold to Oerlikon, flips that had obviously cost his client a fortune. Eventually the rumours reached the ears of Montreal *Gazette* reporter Claude Arpin, who started to dig through titles at the local land registry office. Inevitably, word of his enquiries leaked out and damage control began. In mid-January 1987 Normand Ouellette resigned suddenly as president of the PC riding association in Saint-Jean.

On January 17, 1987, a year after the defence contract decision was made and the land acquired, Arpin reported that the Oerlikon site had tripled in value from $800,000 to nearly $2.9 million in an eleven-day period immediately prior to January 13, 1986, when Oerlikon bought it. The land had been flipped through a complicated series of transactions using numbered companies.

And who pocketed the $2.1-million profit from the flips? A number of people did, including André Bissonnette, his wife, Anita, and his friend and political organizer, Normand Ouellette, who was also a trustee of the minister's blind trust. Ouellette had speculated on the land, masterminded the flips, taken the $920,000 profit he made, and divided it almost equally among four numbered companies. One was Bissonnette's holding company, one belonged to his wife, and the other two were holding companies owned by Ouellette and his wife. (The balance of the profit was distributed to others who had participated in the flips.) As soon as the *Gazette* story hit the streets, Mulroney fired Bissonnette from his cabinet post although he refused to say why. He brushed off suggestions of another public inquiry — the Parker hearings going on in Toronto at that time made it clear why he wasn't keen on another exercise like that. Oerlikon filed a $2.1-million lawsuit against Normand Ouellette, demanding he repay the firm $1,036,013.10, an amount that included the $970,000 plus 12-per-cent interest since June 1986.

The Oerlikon mess touched three of Mulroney's closest allies: Jean Bazin, who had just been named to the Senate, Roger Nantel, and Peter Ohrt. Bazin's involvement seemed straightforward — he was Oerlikon's lawyer; the issue was how he was brought on board. Lette and Associates, an internationally respected law firm, acted for Oerlikon for many years but had been dropped in favour of Bazin's firm early in 1986. Raymond Lette and his son Bernard were also dropped from the Oerlikon board and replaced with Bazin and another Byers Casgrain partner, John Lemieux (who became president of Oerlikon Aerospace Inc. in 1994). Liberal MP Doug Frith said publicly that Marco Genoni, then president of Oerlikon, had told him at a meeting in January 1986 that Bissonnette had suggested he bring in Bazin. Genoni denied Frith's allegation, but Mark Resnick, a Liberal party aide who had attended the same meeting held in Liberal leader John Turner's Ottawa office, said Frith's version was correct.

And, in an indirect way, so did Raymond Lette. In a *Globe and Mail* story, Lette was reported to have said that he lost the account because Oerlikon had been instructed to deal with Bazin. "We've been lawyers for Oerlikon for many years," Lette was said to have told a friend, "and we got this call saying, 'Raymond, we're sorry about this, but the one time we've got a big deal, we've been told by the government people . . . that to keep going with this deal, we've got to go to some guy named Bazin.'" Byers Casgrain later claimed that Lette had failed to inform Oerlikon of the flips, but Lette had done a full title search on the property and had informed Oerlikon's officials before the land deal closed. Once Byers Casgrain was retained and its lawyers were on the board of directors, it lobbied hard to nail the low-level air defence contract. And it was successful.

As for the two other Mulroney pals, Roger Nantel was on contract to Oerlikon as an advertising and public relations expert, while Peter Ohrt, Mulroney's scheduling assistant and Jean Bazin's cousin, was hired as the company's project manager. Ohrt's appointment disturbed Kingston engineer Dugald Buchanan, vice-president of the Urban Transportation Development Corporation. At the end of January 1987, Buchanan weighed in with his two cents' worth on the whole affair, saying Genoni had offered the project manager's job to him on November 26, 1986, during a meeting at the Saint-Jean golf course. Later he withdrew the offer in favour of Ohrt. Buchanan told the *Globe*'s Graham Fraser that Genoni's director of personnel called him in early December to say they'd decided to hire someone with more international experience. When Fraser examined Ohrt's curriculum vitae, he saw no international experience. "I began to realize what a web it was," Buchanan told Fraser. "You don't do business that way." And he concluded that political connections were the only explanation for what had happened. Oerlikon's response was simply that they offer jobs only in writing and that Buchanan had not received any offer, either verbal or written.

In fact there was nothing about the Oerlikon deal that wasn't political: the town, the land, the lawyers, the new employees. Opposition MPs suggested the swearing in of Jean Bazin to the Senate, an appointment announced by Mulroney in the Christmas 1986 patronage handouts, should be delayed until the RCMP's investigations were complete. Mulroney disagreed and amid much controversy, Bazin joined his fellow Tories in the Senate on February 3, 1987. As for Bissonnette, he was charged in August 1987 with fraud and accepting a bribe. On February 26, 1988, he was acquitted by a Saint-Jean jury who believed his defence plea that he did not know his old friend Normand Ouellette was parking much of the profit for his benefit. Ouellette was not quite so lucky. He was found guilty of fraud, fined $100,000, and told to repay $968,857 plus interest to Oerlikon Aerospace Inc. Bissonnette did not run again in 1988 and returned to his hometown, where he developed a hotel project that went bankrupt.

More unpleasant publicity rained on the Tories in 1987. There were RCMP investigations into leases that were awarded to Tory developers even though they were not the low bidders; there were more patronage excesses, including Patrick MacAdam's appointment to a senior job at the Canadian High Commission in London; there was the revelation of the Mulroneys' furnishing and decorating extravaganzas at the official residences, which had gobbled up $1.8 million in public and party funds in the Tories' first eighteen months in office.

Another event took place in the spring of 1987 that, had it come to public attention, would have further tarnished Tory images. It centred on Deputy Prime Minister Donald Mazankowski and the honorary degree that the Technical University of Nova Scotia granted him in May of that year. Mazankowski was a high-school graduate who had been a car dealer in his hometown of Vegreville, Alberta, before he entered federal politics. If there was one thing he regretted in his past, it was that he had not attended university and did not have a degree. His close friends and cabinet colleagues knew about his sensitivity, according to Toronto lawyer Fred von Veh. Von Veh was an adviser to Mazankowski for several years, going back to the Clark government. After Clark's defeat von Veh, Jamie Burns, Peter Thomson, and Patrick Walsh set up the lobbying firm Alta Nova to wait out the years until the Conservatives returned to power. In 1984 they sold the firm to Frank Moores, and three of them went to work for Mazankowski when he was named minister of transport. Von Veh was the new "air adviser," Burns was chief of staff, and Walsh was "marine adviser." Thomson was named to a senior patronage job in Manitoba.

Mazankowski's cabinet colleagues decided it would be a good thing if they could find their friend an honorary degree, and they put the word out across Canada. Most universities were reluctant to give sitting cabinet ministers honorary degrees, said one individual involved in this affair; they preferred to wait until the person was no longer involved in active politics. Early in 1987 von Veh called Halifax stockbroker Donald Ripley, the man who had masterminded Mulroney's 1983 leadership fundraising in Nova Scotia. Von Veh understood from Elmer MacKay that Ripley was connected to the university community in Halifax, having raised money for a number of institutions. "Von Veh said to me, 'Can we get a degree for Maz from Dalhousie?'" explained Ripley. "He asked me, 'How do you go about this?'"

Ripley told von Veh he'd make some enquiries. "I went to talk to a professor I knew at Acadia, and he wasn't too keen on the idea. I asked a friend at Dal, who asked around, and they hemmed and hawed; they were very cautious but gave me broad hints and started talking a lot of money. I got invited to a fancy lunch, then a second lunch, and had another broad hint that for $100,000 it might be possible."

Ripley raised the matter with George MacDonald, a well-known Tory lawyer in Halifax with McInnes Cooper and Robertson, where Stewart McInnes had been a partner. MacDonald had served on the board of Dalhousie, but he was also the chairman of the board at the Technical University of Nova Scotia. After checking with other members of the TUNS community, MacDonald called Ripley to say it could be arranged — for a $25,000 donation. Clair Callaghan was the president of the university at the time and he was keen; Callaghan was a well-known Tory who had once run unsuccessfully as a federal candidate.

Ripley got back to von Veh, who in turn got in touch with the heads of several national transportation companies to raise the money. They claimed to be only too delighted to oblige the minister's man, but what choice did they have? Von Veh was not someone they'd want to offend, and the amount of money they were asked for was small. The companies gave von Veh cheques made payable to "George MacDonald in Trust," and MacDonald mailed them to Ripley, who photocopied them all. "They came in from most of the major transportation companies," he explained. "CP Air, CP Limited, CNR, Air Canada, and others. It didn't come out on the nose; I think Fred raised either $23,000 or $27,000."

Von Veh, who saw nothing wrong in asking for money from companies who had to do business with his ministry, said the companies were happy to contribute. "We tested the waters with three or four calls," he said, "and then the word started to get out. The calls came in from the other direction — people love Maz."

And Maz got his degree. A celebratory lobster party was held at the St. Margaret's Bay home of Hugh and Judy Smith to fête the new doctor of laws. The Doucets, Frank Moores, and Gary Ouellet paid for a bus to carry the revellers to the Smiths' house after the ceremony. They also paid for baseball hats embroidered with the words "Dr. Maz." The insider who knew nothing about this whole scheme was Mazankowski himself.

June brought yet another scandal, one that became all too public, involving Stewart McInnes, the man who had replaced Roch LaSalle as public works minister and who had been so helpful in Mulroney's fundraising efforts in Nova Scotia a few years earlier. According to documents that found their way into the hands of Liberal MP Sheila Copps, who raised the issue in the House, McInnes was ignoring conflict guidelines by receiving regular statements from his Halifax broker, Ross Montgomery. The documents also indicated that McInnes was making decisions about his stocks, many of which were in companies receiving generous federal assistance. Montgomery had been rewarded for his services on the Mulroney team in 1983 and 1984 with a coveted position on the Canada Council investment committee, which supervised $160 million worth of investments in securities and stocks from endowment funds. McInnes's response was that he had no idea his friend and chief fundraiser had been appointed to the investment committee. He also denied he had made any decisions concerning his portfolio and Montgomery concurred, although both men changed their stories during interviews.

In an effort to deflect attention from yet another minister in trouble, the spin doctors went looking for a scapegoat. They fingered Donald Ripley, Montgomery's former boss at McLeod Young Weir in Halifax, as the person who leaked the documents. Ripley was a director of Scotia McLeod and the party's best fundraiser in Atlantic Canada, but he was an outsider with the establishment, disliked for his unrestrained and strong opinions. The case against Ripley gathered speed until Scotia McLeod fired him to save the firm's reputation for security and discretion. Eventually he lost his case before the Investment Dealers' Association, despite Sheila Copps's sworn testimony that Ripley was not her source. It would be years before Ripley was able to demonstrate that he had been the victim of a set-up and could begin to restore his reputation. In the summer of 1987, however, his downfall took the McInnes story off the front pages. A conflict-of-interest scandal that might have brought down another Tory cabinet minister was successfully contained.

The Tories were less successful damping down the Michel Côté matter, another serious conflict-of-interest affair that flared up in 1988 and scalded a number of prominent Quebec City Tories. On February 2, Mulroney fired Supply and Services Minister Côté for failing to declare $250,000 in loans received during 1985 and 1986 from a prominent Quebec City businessman, René Laberge. Under the government's conflict guidelines, cabinet ministers were required to declare any benefit they'd received valued at more than $200 from a family member or close friend, and Côté had failed to declare benefits for two years in a row. *Globe* reporter Andrew McIntosh had been digging into Côté's financial relationships with prominent Quebec City developers. Word reached Mulroney, and he fired Côté before any damaging stories could be published. When Côté met his Langelier riding association at the end of February, the handsome former accountant explained that Laberge had been like a father to him for twenty years. After running into personal financial difficulties following a failed marriage, Côté went to Laberge for help. It was that simple.

Actually, it was not simple at all. Cabinet colleague Marcel Masse had warned Bernard Roy fifteen months earlier that Côté, a dandy who favoured expensive clothes and loved the high life, was living like someone earning $400,000 a year on a parliamentary income of $120,000. When asked about this by reporters on February 8, 1988, Mulroney dismissed the story with an obfuscation about the timing of the talk between Masse and Roy, but he did not deny that it had taken place.

During the period when Côté was supply and services minister, he was the area's regional or "political" minister, responsible for the patronage and contracts flowing into the area. But he was in way over his head. Attracted to the party by his close friend Rod Pageau, Côté had been a quiet backroom organizer and fundraiser until thrust on the national stage as a politician. As *The Toronto Star*'s Robert McKenzie and Joel Ruimy wrote in March 1988, "Côté had become a principal channel for the pent-up ambitions, schemes, frustrations, envy and sometimes downright greed of Tory organizers."

His mentor René Laberge had always done well under the Liberals, but his fortunes soared with the Tories, whom he'd supported generously in 1984. Laberge had two family companies: a plumbing and heating firm called Adelard Laberge Ltée and its subsidiary, a marine repair firm called Talbot Hunter Engineering and Boiler Works Ltd. After the Tory victory, the two firms received a total of $3.5 million in federal contracts, one worth $1 million from VIA Rail and others worth $2.5 million from Supply and Services, Côté's ministry, to repair Coast Guard ships.

Laberge was also one of three developers of a luxurious $15-million condominium development, Les Terrasses du Vieux-Port, built on a historic waterfront site called Pointe-à-Carcy that had been acquired from Quebec City's Old Port, a federal Crown corporation. When he and his partners purchased the site — which consisted of a parking garage and a warehouse — in September 1985, the purchase required approval both from the directors of the Old Port, now all Tory appointees, and from the cabinet. Both approvals were secured in a matter of weeks. Oddly enough, the Old Port board didn't get around to having the property valued until 1986, when it asked Quebec City engineer and PC Canada Fund director Desmond Hallissey, a close friend of Mulroney, to do it; his valuation came in at $839,000. Laberge and his partners paid $1,008,000 for the site and planned to build office condominiums, a tower with seventy-seven luxury residential condominiums, and a parking garage. The developers' offer was lower than another bid of $1,044,000 but was accepted, said a government official, because it had a better development proposal. The deal also included the government's agreement to lease back 281 parking spaces for a dollar a year in return for paying 85 per cent of the maintenance costs of the garage.

How could Laberge and his partners have lost? They had well-connected Tory friends — the Old Port board, the evaluator, the minister, the cabinet — at every critical stage. Laberge was allowed to acquire another Old Port building the same year for a development he called Les Ateliers à Voile à Québec, planned as an industrial and commercial condominium. And Laberge won a handsome federal government lease in 1987 when Public Works agreed to pay him $120,000 a year to rent offices for use by Montreal-area cabinet ministers.

One of Laberge's partners in the Old Port development was builder Marc LeFrançois, chief Conservative organizer for eastern Quebec, who owned 50 per cent of the development; another partner, with 10 per cent, was businessman Michel Rivard, president of a heating and ventilation firm and touted as a potential Tory candidate. After Côté left his wife in 1986, he and his girlfriend, Lynn Hébert, who was also a special adviser on his ministerial staff, rented a seventh-floor river-view luxury condo in Les Terrasses du Vieux-Port from Rivard for $1,200 a month, with the first three months thrown in free. Gilles Rivard, a Quebec City lawyer who was also close to Côté, bought the minister's Sillery house for $200,000 through a numbered company; Côté's wife and four children continued to live there. And when Côté and Hébert went to Florida one winter for a two-week holiday, they rented a condo owned by Laberge, Hallissey, and Quebec City lawyers Jacques Blanchard and Jean Sirois, who were also good friends. Blanchard was an important Tory bagman and eastern Quebec organizer for Mulroney, while Sirois had served as Côté's 1984 campaign chairman.

LeFrançois was one of the biggest winners among Côté's close advisers. Even though he had hosted a $1,000-a-plate party at his home to raise money for the provincial Liberal Party in 1987, federally he was a devout Tory. His family-owned construction consortium, the Macyro Group, received the contract to build the new luxury condominiums that were part of Laberge's development and two other projects in Quebec City's Old Port. In 1987 he was appointed to the board of VIA Rail; before Mulroney left office in 1993, he made LeFrançois VIA's chairman, a post he still holds today.

Jacques Blanchard also did well; Mulroney appointed him to the board of Air Canada in 1985 and a year later gave him a federal judgeship. And Mulroney did not forget Jean Sirois, a good friend since their days together at Laval law school. Sirois remained an indispensable player to the Joliette Tories around Roch LaSalle. During the early years of the Mulroney government, Sirois was a partner at Rivard Hickson Sirois, a Quebec City law firm, and Côté steered $400,000 worth of federal legal business to him, starting with a February 1985 contract to advise Côté on reforms to the Bankruptcy Act. In 1986, Mulroney appointed Sirois as the chairman of Telefilm Canada, a decision that was to cause one of the messiest patronage scandals of the Tories' first term in office. There was even a plum for Gilles Rivard, the man who bought Côté's house. Instead of the judgeship he'd wanted, Mulroney gave him the job Erik Nielsen had designed for himself. On May 3, 1993, Mulroney appointed Rivard to a five-year term as chairman of the National Transportation Agency at a salary of up to $155,000 a year.

The Côté affair touched Mulroney personally. Three days after he fired Côté, the opposition forced an admission from Jean-Pierre Kingsley, the assistant deputy registrar general and the official responsible for administering the conflict guidelines, that Mulroney had not declared his own loans of $324,000 from the PC Canada Fund for decorating the official residences. Kingsley said the loans fell under the guidelines and ought to have been declared. The opposition happily called for Mulroney's resignation. That was a Friday; by Monday, Kingsley had seen the error of his ways. Mulroney got up in the House to read a letter signed by the repentant ADRG that said his loans did not, after all, fall under the guidelines.

Côté was the last of Mulroney's ministers to leave the cabinet in the first term over scandals involving conflict of interest or serious errors in judgment. Seven others had led the way: Bob Coates, John

Fraser, Sinclair Stevens, Marcel Masse, André Bissonnette, Roch LaSalle, and Suzanne Blais-Grenier. Of the eight, two later made it back into cabinet — Fraser and Masse.

Clearly the 1985 conflict-of-interest guidelines were ineffectual. Three weeks after firing Côté, Mulroney introduced legislation for tougher guidelines with a definition of conflict that matched Parker's: "Any occasion where a member or spouse or dependent child has significant private interests that offer the member the chance to benefit directly or indirectly because of his position of power." The rules would apply to cabinet ministers, members of Parliament, and senators, all of whom would be required to list their assets (exclusive of personal residences, vehicles, cash, or retirement savings plans). These lists could be released in part to the public, the idea being that transparency discourages conflict of interest. The ADRG would be allowed to recommend the divestment of some assets if deemed necessary. Another stipulation stated that a spouse should declare any gift or benefit that the member would have to declare if he or she had received it. This was a guideline Mila Mulroney never followed; she did not declare the gifts she received during Mulroney's years in power.

Until the legislation passed, said Mulroney, he expected his MPs and cabinet ministers to obey the spirit of the law. Tucked into the new legislation was a clause that went almost unnoticed: party leaders were exempt from the need to disclose personal loans or benefits from their parties.

The legislation died when Parliament adjourned before the September 1988 election, and it was never brought back.

CHAPTER ELEVEN

LIFE AT THE TROUGH

RIAN MULRONEY LOWERED THE DOCUMENTS HE HAD BEEN
reading aloud and looked over his narrow reading glasses
at his colleagues around the cabinet table. "I don't suppose
there's any comment with respect to these appointments, is
there?" he asked.

"Certainly not."

"No, quite all right."

"Sounds fine to me, Prime Minister."

When Mulroney looked directly at him, Deputy Prime Minister
Erik Nielsen murmured his agreement with the others. Inwardly he
was seething. He was the chairman of the cabinet committee on
security and intelligence, and Mulroney had just read out the names
of the new members of SIRC, the five-person Security Intelligence
Review Committee, which acts as the watchdog of CSIS, the Canadian
Security Intelligence Service. Toronto lawyer Ron Atkey, a minister
in Joe Clark's cabinet, was to chair the committee. In keeping with
the legislative requirement that the opposition parties of the day
have members on the committee, Mulroney had chosen former
Liberal solicitor general Jean-Jacques Blais and a former Manitoba
NDP cabinet minister, Saul Cherniack. Frank McGee, once a minister in the Diefenbaker cabinet, and Quebec City lawyer Paule
Gauthier were the two other new members. All five names were news
to Nielsen; he had not been consulted about their appointments.

No one else in cabinet had Nielsen's expertise in security issues. Even in Joe Clark's 1979 government, when he was minister of public works, he sat on the security and intelligence committee because, as he puts it, "I knew something about it and I had friends in places where members of Parliament don't usually have them." One of his closest friends was Sir William Stephenson, the Canadian spymaster known by the code name Intrepid, who had run British intelligence out of New York during World War II. Nielsen and Stephenson were part of a small network of Canadians who shared an interest in international intelligence work. Given his contacts and his experience, Nielsen had expected to chair the cabinet committee on security and intelligence. What he didn't expect was that the prime minister would undercut him by appointing five members to an intelligence watchdog board without asking his advice or informing him ahead of time of the nominees.

These were not minor appointments. To be a member of SIRC, to learn its secrets, members were required to be Privy Councillors. If they weren't already Privy Councillors by virtue of having served in a federal cabinet, they were appointed to the Queen's Privy Council and given the lifetime title of "Honourable." In this case, the two new Privy Councillors were to be Cherniack and Gauthier. Granting titles to those who had not earned them irked Nielsen; even worse, they had no experience in the security and intelligence area.

"I had no input into who was to go on that board," says Nielsen, calmer now with the hindsight of ten years. "And that was very deliberate. Brian isolated me from any input."

That was the other reason for Nielsen's anger as he sat at the cabinet table reading the names in disbelief. When Brian Mulroney won the party leadership in June 1983, he had asked Nielsen to head a task force to look at the party's patronage process. Nielsen plunged into the job with zest, and it took him a year to put a system in place. The 1984 election campaign made his efforts wonderfully serendipitous. The major issue in the campaign had become Pierre Trudeau's farewell package of patronage appointments to hundreds of party faithful, few of whom seemed deserving of such rich rewards as senatorships, Air Canada board seats, judgeships, and diplomatic postings. Former cabinet minister Bryce Mackasey's appointment as the new ambassador to Portugal and junior PMO aide Colin Kenny's to the Senate were two singular examples. (Mulroney almost immediately rescinded Mackasey's appointment.)

Over the summer of 1984 Mulroney stormed the country promising to clean up a corrupt system. At a July 9 press conference he slammed Liberal patronage and firmly spelled out his intentions: "I commit myself to set up criteria for quality which will impress the Canadian people. I think what took place is completely unacceptable in an open, democratic society. We are going to reform this instrument in our national life." On July 14 he reminded Canadians "that every dollar you pay to the end of your days will go to pay for the golden retirement of tired Liberals. It's a deceit and a sham. It has to be corrected by dramatic gestures and I propose to do that." On July 16, he said it again: "The method of making appointments could be corrected by dramatic measures . . . We are going to bring in a brand-new dimension . . . of objectivity and representation and fairness for all Canadians." Three days later he promised that competence and a willingness to serve Canada would be the main criteria for his appointments. "I pledge to you here today," he said, "that our appointments shall be of the highest order. They shall represent the regions and shall bring honour to all of you and shall bring honour to our country."

Five days later, on July 25, he trounced Liberal Prime Minister John Turner in a televised debate in which Turner stammered that he had had no option but to make yet another seventeen appointments after Trudeau stepped down. Mulroney railed at him, "Well, you had an option, sir! You could have said: 'I'm not going to do it. I'm not going to ask Canadians to pay the price.' The least you should do is apologize for having made these horrible appointments." Turner collapsed, his political career in tatters from that moment.

Mulroney's message to Tory audiences had always been quite different; in front of his own, he enjoyed pointing to grinning party faithful and listing the jobs he had waiting for them. At a celebratory picnic thrown by Michel and Erica Cogger at their Knowlton, Quebec, farm two weeks after the leadership victory, he promised 200 joyful guests that they'd be going into the Senate, the judiciary, the cabinet . . . and the crowd roared its approval. When he was asked about the discrepancies in his declarations to Tory audiences and to the general public, Mulroney was frank: "I was talking to Tories then, and that's what they wanted to hear. Talking to the Canadian public during an election campaign is something else."

Mulroney's confidence was showing in a letter he wrote to Vancouver supporter William Clancy on August 7, in response to a letter from Clancy about the patronage issue. "Over the past 16 years of Liberal rule," Mulroney wrote, "Canadians have been subjected to inbred arrogance of a government which chooses to make political appointments, not on the basis of merit, but on the basis of loyalty to the Liberal Party. The recent announcement by Mr. Turner that 17 members of Parliament will be rewarded with government positions underlines the shocking vulgarity of the whole patronage practice so exemplified under this unprincipled administration." And Mulroney went on to promise that future Tory appointments would have to meet strict standards and that the men and women chosen "must represent the highest quality of men and women for all areas of public and private life."

Mulroney was successful in selling himself as a reformer, and his coup in the debate with Turner gave him the extra push he needed to sweep the country. And when the Tories rolled into Ottawa on September 4, 1984, on a surge of self-righteous joy, Nielsen and his team were ready with a revamped appointments process, one Nielsen says would have cleaned up the system. "I designed two streams of Order-in-Council appointments," he explains. "One was the regular appointment of knowledgeable, experienced people, and the other was a political process, which should have had input from the party across the country." The way Nielsen envisaged it, the first stream would fill the top jobs at Crown corporations such as Air Canada, CNR, the Export Development Corporation, the Atomic Energy Control Board, and the CBC, as well as slots in bodies like the Parole Board and the Immigration Appeal Board, which required members with genuine expertise. The party faithful who had raised money and worked as volunteers in campaigns across the country would constitute the second stream, a pool from which candidates would be drawn to fill positions in arts agencies, marketing boards, and citizenship courts. Nielsen expected Tories to be appointed to the major boards as well, but he believed the chairmanships and presidencies should be set aside for people who had more than political credentials. There was a distinction, he insisted, between what was pure patronage and what had to be a selection of highly qualified persons to run government enterprises.

There are about 3,000 patronage appointments in the government's hands. To ensure that the grass roots of the party had a say in who received these jobs, Nielsen established provincial advisory committees to identify candidates to fill the various posts; their recommendations went to a national advisory committee, which Nielsen himself chaired. Its members were long-time party official Marjory LeBreton, who had worked for five Tory leaders over the years; Bernard Roy; David Angus; Norman Atkins; British Columbia MP Gerry St. Germain; Sam Wakim; former MP and party president Bill Jarvis; Judith Hendin; Jean-Carol Pelletier, the party's national director; Ron Doering, Indian Affairs Minister David Crombie's chief of staff; and Elizabeth Roscoe, chief of staff to junior Finance Minister Barbara McDougall. They held their first meeting just hours after the election.

The provincial representatives met for the first time on September 16, the day after Mulroney was sworn in as prime minister. Each of these PACs, as they were called, included at least one cabinet minister and one MP. Most of the chairmen were well-known businessmen; not surprisingly, many were men who had worked for Mulroney's leadership campaign. They included lobbyist John Lundrigan from St. John's; New Glasgow's Joe Stewart; Fern Roberge from Montreal; Michael Meighen from Toronto; Winnipeg's Arni Thorsteinson; Mulroney's brother-in-law's brother, Bill Elliott from Regina; oil man and rancher Peter Bawden, who had been an MP and a major party donor; and insurance executive James Macaulay, the British Columbia election organizer for the Tories in 1984. Other 1983 leadership supporters on these provincial committees were Waterloo businessman Paul Mitchell, Fred Dickson and David Read from Halifax, Winnipeg's Duncan Jessiman, and Jake Brouwer from Vancouver. Of the Quebec members who were not MPs, some were Mulroney insiders: Michel Cogger, Brian Gallery, Pierre Claude Nolin, and Jean Dugré. Also in the Quebec group were Marc Dorion, who had led Mulroney's youth delegates at the Winnipeg convention, and Montreal lawyer Mario Beaulieu, who had served as a vice-president of the Tories' 1984 election committee.

Loaded as they were with old Mulroney associates, the provincial committees were being ignored and their recommendations bypassed within three months of their inauguration. The national committee? It was a joke, "a mere façade," snorts Nielsen, "for the decisions of Bernard Roy and Marjory LeBreton. So I stopped chairing. I just simply stopped going to the meetings. My presence there was totally ineffective and superfluous." The committee's executive committee faded away and the process was taken over by Marjory LeBreton, even though Peter White, another Mulroney pal from Laval, was, for just over a year, nominally in charge of the administration of appointments. The disenchanted White left the PMO quietly in 1986 to return to a senior job in Conrad Black's business empire.

Mulroney began with two high-profile appointments that fooled no one — especially as he had been indiscreet enough to brag about their cleverness to his advisers. He named former Ontario NDP leader Stephen Lewis ambassador to the United Nations, and a former

Speaker of the House of Commons, Liberal Lloyd Francis, ambassador to Portugal.

Then the rewards to Tories started to roll across the Order-in-Council desks at the Privy Council Office. The numbers of appointments were so staggering that OIC staff could barely handle the paperwork. Their objections were insignificant compared with those from the security service agents, who were doing security checks on many of the nominees. Frequently, they would find enough disturbing evidence to put a question mark against a favourite nominee and throw it back to the appointments office with a rejection; to their dismay, the same names would often pop up again in the months and years to come. The Mulroney government did not like hearing the word no.

Room had to be made for these fresh Tory faces, and the removal of hundreds of Liberal appointees was just the beginning. An example was the dismissal, six weeks after the Conservatives came into office, of 500 legal agents — lawyers used across the country to do federal government work. They were to be replaced by Tories. Mulroney's defence of the move was succinct: "It is normal for Justice Minister [John] Crosbie to hire Conservative lawyers." Within six months most of the members of several major federal boards had been sacked, among them Joel Bell, head of the Canada Development Investment Corporation, along with his board of directors and senior staff, and Nate Laurie, Canadian executive director of the World Bank. In mid-November, the government removed Sylvia Ostry as a director of the Export Development Corporation. In December the Tories fired eleven members of the Petro-Canada board, replacing them with prominent Tories; they dismissed Vancouver lawyer Gerry Robinson, a well-known Liberal who was running a royal commission on illegal immigrants, and Edmund Clark, the associate secretary of Treasury Board, at the demand of Alberta Tories who blamed him for being an architect of the detested National Energy Program. By March 1985 they'd axed and replaced most of the chairmen of the regional ports authorities, all eight members of the Old Port of Quebec, as well as the chairman of the Canada Ports Corporation.

It was at this time that Mulroney and Transport Minister Don Mazankowski personally saw to the dismissal of thirteen of the fifteen members of the Air Canada board. An Air Canada directorship was prized above all other federal appointments, except for Senate and judicial appointments, because it came with free first-class passes to wherever Air Canada flew. Mulroney filled the chairs with his 1983 money men and leadership organizers: David Angus, Fern Roberge, Frank Moores, Peter Bawden, Fred Dickson, Duncan Jessiman, James Macaulay, and Ken Waschuk, along with Fredericton developer Jim Ross, who ran Mulroney's leadership campaign in New Brunswick; Gayle Christie, a Toronto municipal politician and failed federal Conservative candidate; Toronto management consultant Ralph Fisher; and Paul Mitchell of Waterloo. "I had thought that we were going to clean up politics once and for all, but for some people it was clear that the intention was simply to clean up," Nielsen wrote in his 1989 autobiography, *The House Is Not a Home*.[1]

After six months in office, the new government had made some 400 appointments, most of them plum jobs reserved for Mulroney cronies and senior party bagmen and organizers. If anyone raised an objection, Mulroney pointed to Stephen Lewis and Lloyd Francis as stellar examples of his non-partisanship. And what of the qualifications of the new officeholders? Brooke Jeffrey, the Liberal Party's research director in Ottawa during this period, carefully studied the qualifications of the newcomers. "Fourteen of the forty-one appointees in July 1987 to the National Parole Board listed party ties as relevant work experience," she wrote in *Breaking Faith*, her 1992 book about the Mulroney regime. Jeffrey, now teaching political science at Carleton University, also pointed out that by 1989 Mulroney had appointed twenty-four non-diplomats to key foreign-service postings, more than any other prime minister had appointed. (In fifteen years,

Pierre Trudeau had chosen a total of seventeen non-diplomats; Mackenzie King had made eighteen such appointments in his twenty-two years in power.)

When it came to judicial appointments, it was clear that being a Tory helped. Using reference books, data bases, and a wide network of well-informed sources across Canada, University of Toronto political scientists Peter Russell and Jacob Ziegel examined 224 judicial appointments between 1985 and 1989 and found a full 50 per cent of new judges appointed were well-known Conservative Party members.

Although Mulroney had promised Canadians that his judicial appointments would be non-partisan, it was evident to Russell and Ziegel that this had been far from the case. Even the system of provincial judicial vetting committees that the Tories eventually established in 1988 was badly flawed; they did not interview candidates, and the minister of justice could ignore the committees' recommendations. "The new committees are essentially toothless," wrote the professors. "There is an almost irresistible inference that the wish to cling to the important political patronage power is the federal government's primary reason for refusing to allow advisory committees the right to rank candidates."

Indignant criticism greeted the report. Toronto Tory lawyer Les Vandor, the judicial appointments adviser to the ministers of justice from 1984 to 1987, insisted in a letter to *The Globe and Mail* that the screening process was thorough and independent. But he also admitted in a private conversation with a *Globe and Mail* columnist that certain political considerations did enter the process. Although he professed himself an admirer of Toronto lawyer Rosalie Abella, Vandor said the party's largely right-wing backbenchers would never accept her appointment to the bench because she was, as he put it, "a woman, left-wing, and a Jew." (Later Mulroney came to know Abella when she served on a constitutional committee in 1991, and she received an appointment to the Supreme Court of Ontario that many in the legal community believed was long overdue.)

The patronage game is far more sophisticated than the simple dispensation of board positions and judicial appointments. There have always been bagmen and party workers who prefer to remain invisible and reap their rewards by doing business for the government. And because so many of these party faithful are lawyers, what they desire most is all those billable hours at the taxpayers' expense.

During the 1984–85 fiscal year, which ended March 31, 1985, government legal business for firms with Tory connections was almost non-existent: the Liberals had parked most of the government's business with Liberal firms. That situation had swung around 180 degrees by the end of 1985–86. By 1988 several Tory firms, especially ones with close connections to Mulroney, were growing fat on federal hours. Much of the legal work that had been handled by federal Justice Department lawyers in major cities started to move to private firms with Tory ties.

While Gerry Doucet and Gary Ouellet were partners in their Ottawa lobbying firm, Government Consultants International, they remained affiliated with their respective hometown law firms, Doucet and Associates and Levasseur Ouellet. Both enjoyed government business. Senator Jean Bazin was a partner at Byers Casgrain, the Montreal firm that billed Ottawa more than $740,000 between 1985 and 1988. When he was asked in 1988 about his billing for government work while he was in the Senate, a violation of the Parliament of Canada Act, Bazin responded that it "wasn't a personal bill, it was for Byers Casgrain work." The New Democrats raised the issue in the House in 1989, and a few hours later Bazin abruptly resigned from the Senate.[2]

Montreal's Stikeman Elliott, home to David Angus and, for several years, to Mulroney's former chief of staff Stanley Hartt, billed various government departments $616,000 between 1985 and 1988. Ogilvy Renault, Mulroney's old firm, where his former principal secretary Bernard Roy is now a partner, billed nearly $500,000, of which $132,000 was for work in 1987 by his close friend Yves

Fortier, who succeeded Stephen Lewis as Canada's ambassador to the United Nations in 1988. Roger Baker, another friend of Mulroney's from Laval law school and a partner at Montreal's Baker Nudleman, billed nearly $73,000 for National Film Board work in 1986–87 and took on two sensitive assignments: one was the defence of former cabinet minister Roch LaSalle in Quebec Superior Court and of the government in Federal Court against suits brought by LaSalle's former political aide Frank Majeau, alleging wrongful dismissal. The second was defending federal anti-smoking legislation against a constitutional challenge by tobacco companies. Another firm that prospered was Quebec City's Rivard Hickson Sirois, where Conservative Party organizer Jean Sirois was a partner; he billed the Consumer and Corporate Affairs Department nearly $267,000 in 1986 while his friend Michel Côté was minister of that department. The next year his billings were $140,000.

Sirois's rewards didn't end with payment of his invoices. On July 17, 1986, Communications Minister Flora MacDonald announced the appointment of the forty-eight-year-old lawyer as the new chairman of Telefilm Canada, the agency established by the Liberals in 1967 to help foster a Canadian film industry. Sirois, say Quebec insiders, had raised an estimated $10 million in Quebec for the Conservatives' 1984 election campaign. Sirois himself denies that he raised that kind of money. "I am not Guy Charbonneau to pick up the phone and get money," he said. "If I had raised $10 million I would be a senator." Whatever he raised, a grateful new government thanked him with over $400,000 worth of legal work before adding an appointment to the board of the Port of Quebec, a corporation that was involved in many of the important real estate decisions in the heart of the Old City. For Sirois it wasn't enough. He wanted his own empire to run, and it was decided that Telefilm would serve the purpose.

But he met his match in Peter Pearson, the executive director of Telefilm. Pearson was the head of Telefilm's Broadcast Fund in Toronto when he received a call in July 1985 from Marcel Masse, asking him to come to Ottawa for a meeting. Masse, then minister of communications, had just fired Tim Porteous as the director of the Canada Council, and Pearson wondered if Masse had him in mind for the job. But there was no offer to head the Canada Council; instead, Masse invited Pearson to become executive director of Telefilm, with a staff of 120 and an annual budget of $100 million for productions. Pearson had forgotten that the Tories had also fired André Lamy, the former executive director, for his Liberal ties. Pearson accepted, moved to Montreal, and walked into a nightmare that lasted for two years.

Before Pearson's arrival Telefilm had an appalling reputation for financial mismanagement, usually running out of money well before the fiscal year-end. The situation did not turn around in Pearson's first year. As he admitted himself, his strength was not in administration, and a consultant's report in 1986 criticized Telefilm's management yet again.[3]

When Jean Sirois arrived at Telefilm in the summer of 1986, he was determined to take over the running of the agency, even though the chairmanship was not an operating position. He earned $325 a day on the few days a year he was expected to show up; the budgetary limit was $30,000 a year. His style was clear from the day his appointment was announced, when he hosted a $1,264 celebration for himself and Flora MacDonald (who had recently replaced Masse as minister of communications) at the Ritz-Carlton. The dinner was attended by Mulroney, Brian Gallery, Roger Nantel, ad man Jean Peloquin, and Fern Roberge. Earlier the same day, he spent another $603 for a trip to Toronto to share the news of his appointment with reporters. A day or two later he treated his friend Michel Côté to a dinner at Hy's Steakhouse in Ottawa for $117.05, later explaining away the meal as a discussion of film marketing. Côté's department had nothing to do with the film business.

Mulroney also named a new vice-chairman for Telefilm: a former neighbour from Montreal, notary Harvey Corn, whose wife,

Shirley, was a close friend of Mila's. This appointment created its own waves in the agency: Corn and Sirois did not get along, to say the least. Sirois was in the habit of making derogatory comments about Jews running the entertainment industry, comments that did not endear him to Corn, a Jew.

Within six months Sirois had persuaded Flora MacDonald to increase his per diem to $500, with an annual limit of $70,000. He had racked up expense accounts that suggested Telefilm was to be his avenue to the lifestyle of an international grandee. During his first eighteen months as chairman, Sirois took seventy out-of-town trips, always travelling first-class; when MacDonald accompanied him to China and Hong Kong, for example, he'd settle down to the complimentary champagne while she bustled back to business class. Sirois always stayed at the best hotels. "Instead of taking a $75 room at the Park Plaza in Toronto, he'd get a $175 suite at the Four Seasons," remembers one Telefilm staffer. In 1986 he stayed at the Beverly Wilshire Hotel in Los Angeles, where his bill for five days was $4,165; a year later he went to California for the Oscars and spent $5,780 for airfare, tickets to the awards ceremony, and a reception. Sirois was determined to have his daughter at the ceremony; a Telefilm board member "had to troll the streets outside the Academy Awards to get a ticket for her from a scalper," said a source familiar with the episode. "It cost $5,000 and he billed Telefilm for it. The board approved it." (Sirois says he paid for the ticket himself.) Sirois's predecessor, Labatt's executive Ed Prévost, had never attended more than one film festival a year, and that was Cannes; Sirois went to every one he could find, including those in New York, Martinique, West Berlin, and Havana. After a year and a half on the job, his expenses added up to $76,398; Prévost's had never been more than $3,000 to $4,000 a year.

Not surprisingly, Sirois clashed head-on with Peter Pearson, who was so infuriated by the chairman's expenses that he refused to sign any cheques for him. But Pearson was even angrier about Sirois's attempt to take over the day-to-day management of the agency and to force funding decisions on Telefilm. Former staff and board members remember it well: no contract was too small for his notice, not even snow-clearing around the building. "He went to A.E. Lepage and visited all these office buildings because we needed new offices," says one senior Telefilm member, "and he wanted to negotiate the leases. There was no area of the administration he didn't try to participate in — office supplies, computers . . . He wanted a job for Elmer MacKay's wife in Ottawa . . . He even wanted us to give him money for videos of dying people."

Dying people? It wasn't a joke. Sirois was — and still is — on the board of a company called Arbor Capital, a large publicly traded Canadian company that owns forty-four cemeteries and twenty-one crematoriums and has interests in forty-seven funeral homes. It owns twelve funeral homes in Toronto alone. In 1994, Arbor Capital had revenues of over $100 million. Sirois may have been daydreaming aloud, but he thought it would be a great idea if Arbor prepared tasteful videos of loved ones before they died so families could play back cherished memories. Peter Pearson, says a Telefilm employee familiar with the story, laughed Sirois down. Sirois himself has a good chuckle over the plan today. "That's a good one," he said in a recent interview, before denying the story. He also denies that he was interfering in Telefilm contracts, blaming such tales on jealous English Canadians at the agency.

What finally brought the simmering feud between Sirois and Pearson to a head was the financing of three controversial projects: the movie *Bethune*, starring Donald Sutherland; the television series *Mount Royal*, directed by Robert Lantos and loosely based on the life of Montreal financier Paul Desmarais; and Rendez-Vous '87, an ambitious winter celebration in Quebec City, timed for the annual *carnaval*, that would involve a fashion show and a hockey tournament between Soviet and Canadian teams. Pearson was strongly opposed to funding any of these projects but was overruled by his board of directors, led by Sirois, who began bypassing Pearson to negotiate directly with Telefilm staff for the money. Pearson does not speak publicly about Sirois; at a board meeting, however, Pearson listed four good reasons why he and his executives had unanimously agreed not to finance *Bethune*. The budget estimates were $5 to $7 million too low; the legal chain of title to the documents needed was not satisfactory; the producers' completion guarantee was not totally in order; and the producers were too inexperienced to make a picture as big as this one. After listening to Pearson's argument, Sirois merely shoved himself away from the table, left the room, and called Flora MacDonald. He was back within minutes. "Telefilm is doing *Bethune*," he announced triumphantly.

All the dire predictions came true: not only was the movie universally panned by critics, it took years to make and ran several million dollars over budget. Much the same thing happened with *Mount Royal*, which Telefilm executives believed would be another turkey and another financial horror story; again they were overruled. The Rendez-Vous '87 affair was a much smaller expenditure, but it irritated Pearson even more than the others.

In a letter he wrote later to Flora MacDonald, he explained that during a trip to Los Angeles in the fall of 1986, Sirois had ordered him to attend an after-dinner meeting at the Beverly Wilshire Hotel with Marcel Aubut, the owner of the Quebec Nordiques. Aubut wanted $600,000 from Telefilm for two television shows about Rendez-Vous '87, but Sirois had promised Pearson he would not support the project. Two weeks after the promise he was telling him to attend the meeting at the Wilshire. Pearson protested that he'd just arrived from Montreal and it was 1 a.m. his time. Sirois insisted.

When Pearson arrived, Sirois and his son were there with Aubut and another man. They were aggressive from the start, Pearson told MacDonald. "The conversation started up with questions like, 'Where is my check?'" Pearson wrote. "'Why are bureaucrats so difficult to get along with?' and other unpleasant jovial remarks that were inappropriate." Pearson told Aubut flatly that his approach was not acceptable. If he had a project to submit, Telefilm would welcome it. "I told him the details of the Broadcast licence and other parameters. He said that no wonder Telefilm has such a bad reputation. And was generally abusive. At no time, did the Chairman in any way support me or the organization in this very difficult and awkward meeting."

Later that month Sirois invited Pearson to fly to Quebec City on Aubut's private plane for another meeting; Pearson objected on several grounds, not the least of which was the impropriety of a public servant accepting a ride on a private plane. "He laughed at me and said I was too strict," Pearson wrote in his letter to MacDonald. After much argument, Telefilm finally gave Aubut $200,000 for the project, but Pearson's relationship with Sirois was finished. Sirois was accusing Pearson of mismanagement and obstreperous behaviour, and Pearson finally quit on October 12, 1987. Sirois claimed Pearson had overspent the Telefilm budget by $48 million; a subsequent investigation showed that the amount in question was $30 million and that it was not a shortfall, but a commitment for the next fiscal year. In fact, the investigation found that Telefilm was showing a $6-million surplus.

A flood of stories on Sirois's expense account follies and his interference with contracts finally persuaded Flora MacDonald that he had to go. But it wouldn't be easy given that he had Mulroney's protection. MacDonald and her willing accomplice, Jeremy Kinsman — who is now Canadian ambassador to Moscow but was then an assistant deputy minister of communications — found a window of opportunity in April 1988. Mulroney had boarded a plane for a NATO meeting in Brussels. While he was temporarily unavailable to anyone, MacDonald phoned Sirois to say she was considering not renewing his term as chairman. Unable to reach Mulroney, Sirois did what MacDonald and Kinsman expected him to do. He flew off the handle and resigned. (These were not happy days for the Sirois family; just a month earlier his uncle, Pierre Boutin, another Quebec City

Tory, had resigned as chairman of the National Arts Centre after his leadership was also put under scrutiny.)

Harvey Corn took over as chairman of Telefilm, but the Sirois affair was not over. It seemed that while at Telefilm he had set up a new federal corporation, the Canadian Film Year, to promote Canadian films through his new Montreal law firm, Sirois Rousseau Cossette. He had moved $600,000 of Telefilm money over to help it get going; he was forced to move the money back when the arrangement became public. Although he denied moving the money to the new corporation, MacDonald's press secretary flatly contradicted him, saying the money had indeed been moved and had been returned. His plans to attend the Cannes festival in May 1988 on the Film Year's budget also had to be cancelled when they were discovered; defiantly Sirois blurted that he would pay his own way.

Mulroney stuck by Jean Sirois to the bitter end. In his last round of patronage appointments in 1993, he appointed the flamboyant lawyer to the board of VIA Rail.

ON THE ROAD

ILA MULRONEY SPIED THE TALL, SLIGHTLY STOOPED MAN with the trim grey beard and hailed him from across the room. "Joe Plaskett!" she cried. The man smiled politely, waiting while she pulled her husband over to say hello. "She recognized me from a self-portrait that hung in a Toronto hotel," explained the British Columbia artist. A guest at a Canadian Embassy reception in Paris in February 1986 during the Francophone Summit, Plaskett had been chatting with Richard Hatfield, then the premier of New Brunswick, but, "feeling beyond my depth in such august company," as Plaskett put it, he was getting ready to leave. Mila stopped him; she was thrilled to meet Plaskett, for years one of her favourite painters.

Plaskett, who is now seventy-six, moved to Paris in 1949 and has lived there ever since, although he returns to Canada occasionally to teach and to show his paintings at galleries across the country. His still-lifes and urban landscapes of courtyards and balconies, reminiscent of his own neighbourhood in Paris's Marais, offer tantalizing glimpses of a private world of old friends and good talk, of fresh flowers in a jug and simple meals with a decent wine. A few years ago Plaskett bought a cottage in Suffolk, England, and there he paints the surrounding fields, the summer delphiniums, the gardens at evening. At a show in the fall of 1993 at Toronto's Bau-Xi Gallery, one crowded with faithful friends and well-wishers, red dots sprouted discreetly on the corners of almost every frame as patrons snapped up his works. A show at Walter Klinkhoff Gallerie in Montreal earlier the same year did even better.

For Mila, running into Plaskett was a happy accident. "I was naturally flattered by the attention," Plaskett said. "She spoke of seeing a double portrait I had done of Molly and Bruno Bobak [two other famous B.C. artists, now living in New Brunswick] and laughingly suggested I do one of her and her husband. I laughed in return."

The Mulroneys had started to collect Canadian art a few years earlier; any time a Tory group — the caucus or the PC Canada Fund or the 500 Club — wanted a present for the prime minister to mark his birthday or for Christmas, they knew a painting would be appreciated. To his relief, Plaskett was not asked to do a double portrait. But soon afterwards he was asked to paint a portrait of Mila herself. The commission came from her close friend Helen Vari.

Vari and her husband, George, are intimates of the Mulroneys, so close that members of their social circle describe Helen as almost like a mother to Mila, while George is something of a mentor to Brian. The couple moved to Canada from Hungary in 1957 and became Canadian citizens in 1962, but Vari's company, Sefri Construction, has been active in many cities. In Paris, it built the fifty-eight-storey Montparnasse Tower; in Moscow, the Cosmos Hotel; and in Toronto, the Novotel in North York and the Intercontinental Hotel on Bloor Street. These are just a few of the forty-three hotels George Vari has erected around the world. And the Varis own several homes: a penthouse in Granite Place in Toronto, a luxurious flat on Grosvenor Square in London, and another in Paris with a view of the Seine. There is a hillside villa near Saint-Paul-de-Vence on the Riviera and a ski retreat in Crans, Switzerland. About four years ago they purchased a country home near Cobourg, Ontario. The Varis have become major art collectors; according to writer Peter Newman, who visited their Toronto apartment in 1990 for a *Maclean's* profile, the place was "crammed with canvases by Monet, Picasso, Chagall, Dufy, Utrillo.

Most of the furniture dates back to 16th- to 18th-century France, including some Louis XV pieces. The total effect is that of a turn-of-the-century high-society salon, where the best and the brightest gather to discuss recent cultural trends and the latest political perfidies."

Helen Vari has made a name for herself in high government circles in France by helping to finance the restoration of a number of Paris monuments. She was the founding president of the French chapter of the World Monuments Fund, whose major project at the time was restoring the interior of the Hôtel des Invalides, the home of Napoleon's tomb.

Soon after the reception at the embassy, Helen Vari called Plaskett to see if he would agree to do a portrait of Mila, intended as a birthday gift from Mila to Brian. It had to be done quickly, and it had to be a surprise. Plaskett rarely does portraits, but he agreed to do this one. "I was at least happy it was not to be the double portrait," he said. But to his astonishment, Vari asked him to lower his fee. "When my price was named (I suggested $8,000), I was told this was too high, that the Mulroneys did not have much money, and I was finally persuaded to do it for $4,500." Furthermore, Vari wanted him to do the painting in a sitting room in her apartment near Mila's hotel, rather than in the studio of his salon in the old Marais *quartier*. "I accept the odd commission and I treat it as a challenge. But I prefer to do it in a relaxed setting, in my own studio. She wanted a more central place than mine — Mila had a lot of shopping to do."

Plaskett's own description of his week with Helen Vari and Mila Mulroney cannot be bettered.

I was naturally overawed by this luxurious setting, looking out over the nearby Eiffel Tower. I suggested she pose in front of a mirror above the fireplace, since my work makes frequent, even obsessive use of mirrors. On this mantelpiece there was a magnificent ancient Egyptian head carved in granite which I would love to have incorporated but it was thought a conventional bouquet of flowers would be more appropriate.

The sittings each afternoon went on for most of a week. One day there was to be a reception at the house in the evening and as the portrait was to be a secret, it had to be hidden away in a bedroom. The plastic sheeting which protected the white carpet under my easel was used to cover and hide the painting. When I returned the next day and set up my easel, somehow the plastic sheet which had been against the painting had picked up colours and that side was laid on the carpet. When I discovered the mishap I made frantic but vain efforts to remove the evidence with turpentine, then soap and water. Mila was about an hour late and I had time to try vainly to remove ultramarine and cadmium red from the precious carpet and to stew in my anguish. Several times I had long waits like this, but was able to work on the bouquet, an expensive assortment of lilies, irises, roses etc. which did not charm me.

Mila was a good model. She has an animated personality and one could not help being attracted by this and being inspired by her attractive physiognomy. However, as the portrait progressed I had the strange sensation that after a certain point I could penetrate no deeper. The face had become a mask. Perhaps I found her too pretty. Her beauty may well have had hidden depths which I was not able to penetrate. I think I produced an acceptable likeness, but cannot claim to have made a great portrait. I think this must have come from my being intimidated by the setting, as by the nature of the commission. (I had been reassured by Madame Vari that the spots on the carpet could be removed and I was not to worry.)

Mila brought the unframed portrait back to Canada rolled in a tube and spread it out before her chef, François Martin, a gifted painter himself, for his reaction and for his advice on how to frame it. "She liked it," Martin said, "but when I looked at it, I thought, this artist did not like her."

The real significance of the painting was the question of who paid for it. Martin says he remembers discussions at 24 Sussex about how it would be paid for. Only when Helen Vari stepped in and agreed to pay was an agreement reached with Plaskett. "The business side of this arrangement," said Plaskett, "was handled by Madame Vari." She paid him; whether Mila paid her back, he did not know. (When asked about these financial arrangements, Helen Vari confirmed Plaskett's comment that she had told him the Mulroneys were not well off, but George Vari interrupted her to say that they had had nothing to do with paying for the portrait. "No, we didn't make any arrangements," he snapped angrily, while his wife, at his side, looked uncomfortable. After the interview Helen Vari wrote to say they did not pay for the portrait, "directly or indirectly.")

Several years later, Mila was to acquire a second Plaskett. Obviously less poor than she was in 1986, she attended his 1993 Klinkhoff show in Montreal and bought one of the splendid paintings from his Suffolk series — the same painting, in fact, that the gallery had used on its invitation. What she paid for the painting is not known, but the asking prices for this series were between $15,000 and $16,000 each.

The Plaskett portrait ended up over the sofa in Mulroney's study at 24 Sussex Drive. It may not have been a gift, but many other items were given by Helen Vari to Mila over the years. While Martin worked for the Mulroneys in Ottawa, Vari often arrived with Louis Vuitton suitcases stuffed with new outfits for Mila. She would bring about twenty dresses or suits on every visit, a total of at least 200 outfits over a four-year period. Martin never saw Vari take the empty suitcases with her when she departed. If Mila paid her friend for the outfits, no one knew; Martin and the rest of the staff were under the impression they were gifts.

Regarding her generosity to Mila, Mrs. Vari dismissed it simply as "gifts to loving friends," remembrances they gave naturally at

Christmas, birthdays, and anniversaries. The Varis also received gifts from the Mulroneys, said Helen Vari. "Mila never forgot a birthday or an anniversary." That's quite true; along with the list of those allowed access to the house, Mila's staff kept a memorandum of the birthdays of family, close friends, and godchildren. Neither list, however, included the names of George and Helen Vari.

As Helen Vari knew better than anyone, Mila and Brian Mulroney's lifestyle cost a small fortune to maintain. When they could get help from friends in paying for their expensive clothes, jewellery, furniture, artworks, or travel, they didn't hesitate. The Varis treated François Martin to a holiday in the staff house at their villa in Nice in 1988 when he was in Düsseldorf attending a conference of chefs who worked for heads of state and government. (Helen was not happy with her guest when he turned up with his sister and then failed to show for a brief apprenticeship she'd arranged for him with the famous chef Roger Vergé, at his nearby three-star restaurant Le Moulin des Mougins. Martin admits he went into the restaurant only twice. He didn't feel comfortable, he said. "I was no more expected there than you would be," Martin told an interviewer. He believed all Mila wanted was to be able to tell her friends that her chef had done a "*stage*" at Vergé's.)

Not everyone was as eager as the Varis to help the Mulroneys keep up appearances. Marty Alsemgeest, one of Toronto's most exclusive bespoke tailors, was introduced to Brian Mulroney through a mutual friend, hockey czar Alan Eagleson. Alsemgeest declined the suggestion of a special price for a dozen suits for the prime minister. Was that because he was expected to make them for nothing? Alsemgeest, ever the gentleman's tailor, refused to do more than lift an eyebrow, shrug, and murmur, "I never made any for him. Let's just say we couldn't agree on the price."

Another clothier, a Montreal furrier, had a more disturbing experience with Mila. Soon after Mulroney was elected prime minister, Mila spoke to her friend Denyse Angé about the need for a new

fur coat. Angé, who had been an actress in Quebec, was then the
public relations officer for the Fur Fashion Council of Canada in
Montreal and the wife of John Bremner, manager of the Queen
Elizabeth Hotel. (Bremner was a friend of Brian's; his name appears
on a contact sheet of useful numbers kept by the Mulroney household staff.) "Mila had only one fur coat, a raccoon," explained Angé.
"She needed something better." So Angé set up a meeting for Mila
with Irving Camlot, a famous Montreal fur wholesaler and the owner
of Natural Furs of Canada. Camlot was the man who loaned the fur
coats to Miss Grey Cup candidates for their open-air convertible
rides in the Grey Cup parades. Mila tried on several black mink coats
at his Montreal showroom and took home a number of them — most
sources say three — on approval.

When Camlot did not hear from her, he went to Angé to enlist
her help in soliciting payment for the coats. Angé was embarrassed,
but her own situation was rather difficult. By this time, the
Mulroneys had arranged her appointment to the Immigration Appeal
Board (now called the Immigration and Refugee Board), a comfortable sinecure that paid about $85,000 a year. She holds the job to
this day. In a 1986 interview, Angé said that she could lose her job if
she talked about the incident, but she admitted there had been some
difficulty about Camlot getting paid for the coats and that the furrier was upset — although he had agreed afterwards to lend Mila a
magnificent ankle-length golden sable coat, one of about fifty he
made each year, for an overseas trip she and the prime minister were
making. Camlot agreed to an interview about the mink coats with
The Globe and Mail, but minutes before the scheduled appointment
he appeared, visibly agitated, in the foyer of his Montreal office to
say he had changed his mind. "Mrs. Mulroney is an old and valued
customer," he said, cancelling the interview. "I was happy to lend her
the sable coat. That is all I am going to say. You must leave. Now."
Angé admitted she had called the Prime Minister's Office about the
questions she was being asked.

A few months later, after *The Globe and Mail* ran stories on how the PC Canada Fund had paid for hundreds of thousands of dollars worth of antiques and other furnishings for the Mulroneys, Camlot was phoned again. This time, he was more than friendly. Yes, he said happily, Mrs. Mulroney had indeed paid for the mink coats. Yes, he said, she signed the cheques herself; they did not come from the PC Party. No, he chuckled, he would not say when she had paid. What was clear was that there had been some tidying up of old accounts after the PC Canada Fund story became public.

The Mulroneys' style was established early on. Right after the Bonn summit in the spring of 1985, Mila flew on to Rome to shop with her interior decorator, Giovanni Mowinckel; she was accompanied by an RCMP officer and Bonnie Brownlee, while Mowinckel brought his assistant Karen Large. They all stayed at the Hassler, one of Italy's most expensive hotels, perched atop the Spanish Steps and overlooking the Via Condotti, Rome's most exclusive shopping street. Canadian taxpayers paid for the group's meals and accommodation and provided a $3,500 cash advance for Mila, demanded by PMO aide Keith Hamilton in a telegram to Canadian Embassy officials. Any further details on the specifics of the hotel bills or whether the cash advance had been repaid were withheld by government officials who alleged that such information was "personal."

There are few better examples of the Mulroney style abroad than the Francophone Summit in Paris in February 1986. Just how much was spent is a story that has never been fully told, and it is presented here thanks to painstaking efforts made in 1986 by reporter Richard Cléroux, then at *The Globe and Mail*. In 1986 Ottawa journalists were writing about the sky-high travel expenses of the Mulroneys, bills run up by their demands for the most expensive accommodation, for an entourage of dozens of aides and cronies, for money to splash around like water when they reached their destination. Journalists have unearthed many examples of such trips, but the 1986 Francophone Summit trip was exceptional. Mulroney was accompanied by three cabinet ministers and ten MPs from all parties. The Order-in-Council authorizing their junket was passed a week *after* they left on the trip, and the all-party selection was a smart move. Take enough politicians with you, ensuring that some come from the opposition benches, and the blame is spread equally; no one will later question the expenses in the House.

Despite these precautions there was an uproar in the Commons the following June, when newspapers reported the costs for the summit and for a $1,200-a-night suite for the Mulroneys at the Hotel Pierre in New York in October 1985. In the six months between October 1985 and March 1986, Mulroney's travel expenses, disclosed under the Access to Information Act, added up to more than $811,000 for trips to New York, Washington, and Paris.

The Paris trip caused the biggest fuss. The *Globe*'s Cléroux, *The Toronto Star*'s Edison Stewart, and Southam News reporters discovered that the Canadian delegation comprised fifty-four people, including seventeen staff members, the three cabinet ministers, and the ten MPs. The entire delegation stayed at the Plaza Athénée, one of Paris's grandest hotels. The Mulroneys' suite, at $3,400 a day, was the most expensive, but the cabinet ministers and five Mulroney aides and their spouses stayed in rooms that cost $850 a day each. Other members of the delegation were accommodated for $370 a day each. The delegation spent $1,662 for fifty ballet tickets, $109,000 for chauffeured cars, and $583 for a dinner for the Mulroneys and two guests at the Tour d'Argent. Lucien Bouchard, then Canada's ambassador to France, blew $600 on flowers for a lunch in Mila's honour.

The invoices the journalists were able to obtain showed expenses of over $520,000 for the six-day visit, a figure that did not include airfare. When he later tried to defend the extravagance, Mulroney said it was the French government's decision to put him in such a nice hotel, and as they were paying for it, why should anyone object? What he did *not* say was that the French had paid only part of the costs — the bills for himself and his wife plus five members of his entourage. He would not say precisely how much the French government had contributed or what items it had covered. The French Embassy in Ottawa also refused to divulge this information for fear of upsetting French citizens if the true costs were to become known, an embassy spokesman told Cléroux. "Between secrecy and the public there is '*discretion*,'" Simone Poudade told him. The rest of the Plaza Athénée bills were tossed into the laps of the taxpayers back home.

The press attention caused a major flap at External Affairs, a disturbance Lucien Bouchard recently acknowledged in his memoirs. After stories appeared about the trip's cost, he wrote, "The Prime Minister's Office became very agitated and the temperature in External Affairs ran close to boiling point." So close, in fact, that External, on orders from Fred Doucet in the PMO — which needed a scapegoat — recalled a hapless diplomat from the embassy in Paris as "punishment." Bouchard threatened to return permanently on the same plane as the diplomat. The recall was cancelled.

Journalists reported on the cost of the trip and went on to other stories, but PMO officials realized they could have a public relations disaster on their hands. When Cléroux asked for all the bills under access-to-information legislation, a massive cover-up began, one that involved months of secret meetings and negotiations at both the PMO and External Affairs. What were they trying to hide? Quite simply, the names of two members of the delegation and a number of purchases charged to rooms at the Plaza Athénée. Among the guests at the hotel were Mila's younger brother, John Pivnicki, and Brian's brother-in-law, Dick Elliott. They were not along for official reasons, but they were put on the hotel register as part of the Canadian delegation.

When the officials first released the Paris hotel bills to Edison Stewart and Southam News, they saw too late that they contained the names of Pivnicki and Elliott. Luck was with the prime minister — reporters were too preoccupied to connect the two names to the Mulroneys. But Cléroux continued to press the issue, and the PMO was frantic to head off any further bad publicity.

External Affairs enlisted the help of the French foreign ministry in the summer of 1986, months after the trip, and the French leaned on the Plaza Athénée to get a completely new set of documents. These bills, on hotel letterhead and dated February 1986, were reconstructed to erase any trace of Pivnicki and Elliott. The new bills also indicated that certain amounts had been recovered by the government for personal expenses incurred by members of the delegation, the Mulroneys in particular.

Memos and telegrams obtained under access-to-information laws by Cléroux, as well as his confidential interviews, show that in September 1986, nearly eight months after the Francophone Summit, the PMO was making arrangements for the PC Party to pay the hotel bills for Pivnicki and Elliott. "I saw one of the cheques," a source at External told Cléroux. "It was PC Party of Canada — no two ways about it. They were paying for quite a few things after the fact, after the information request came in. I gathered there was a whole series of these cheques designed to basically cover up expenses that the prime minister and his entourage had incurred. Paris was the worst one because that's when things were most extravagant. We set up a bloody task force headed by the inspector general of the bloody department." The official also told Cléroux that everybody had been ordered to stonewall. "Everybody was so damn afraid of getting Fred Doucet angry at them," he explained.

Prompted by Cléroux's requests for information, the task force scrutinized the bills for each member of the delegation. Whenever a dubious charge was found, a task force member chased down the individual and asked for payment. A number of telegrams from External Affairs to Paris in September 1986 show that Bouchard had to repay $398.40 for charges on his bill, something he does not mention in his book. (Even though he lived in the Canadian Embassy on Rue de la Montaigne, he had a room at the hotel for his personal use during the summit.)

*Montreal insurance broker Guy Charbonneau, in charge of
raising the money for Mulroney's 1983 leadership bid, was appointed
Senate Speaker in 1984. (Canapress Photo Services)*

*Montreal stockbroker Jonathan Deitcher handled
Mulroney's investments and has been a close friend
of the Mulroneys for many years. (Gazette)*

Gravely ill with cancer, 1984 campaign strategist Rodrigue Pageau,
a close Mulroney chum, was flown by air ambulance to Baie-Comeau to
share in the victory celebrations but died a week later. (La Presse)

Montreal lawyer David Angus,
chairman of the PC Canada Fund
from 1983 to 1993, arranged for
monthly expense cheques from the
party for the Mulroneys. (Harold
Rosenberg/Maclean's)

Former Newfoundland premier
Frank Moores first dedicated himself
to getting Brian Mulroney elected
prime minister of Canada and then,
in 1984, introduced Ottawa to
Washington-style lobbying. (Gazette)

*German businessman Karl-Heinz Schreiber, who set up
holding companies in Alberta for wealthy Germans – including Bavarian
premier Franz Josef Strauss, chairman of Airbus Industrie – befriended
influential Canadian politicians. (Alberta Report)*

*Walter Wolf, the mysterious
Austrian entrepreneur, was said to be
one of the offshore contributors to
Mulroney's 1983 leadership fund.
(Mac Justen/Gazette)*

*For years Fernand Roberge,
manager of the Ritz-Carlton Hotel in
Montreal, was one of Mulroney's
inner circle. He was rewarded with a
Senate appointment. (Gazette)*

Caucus liaison adviser Patrick MacAdam (left) meets with Mulroney aide Bill Pristanski and the prime minister in 1985. (Murray Mosher/Maclean's)

A 1983 police surveillance photograph in Hamilton shows Mob hit man Réal Simard (left) conferring by phone with his boss, Montreal Mafia chief Frank Cotroni, while his partner Frank Majeau (centre) and Hamilton crime boss Johnny Papalia (right) listen. (Private collection)

Even after being fired in 1987, Frank Majeau (centre back)
organized retirement fundraisers in Joliette for his former boss,
Roch LaSalle (foreground). (Private collection)

Between 1984 and 1986 Montreal ex-convict Mike Mitton,
pictured here on his parole card, helped the RCMP run
one of the most secret operations in the history of the force.
(Correctional Services Canada)

Toronto filmmaker Peter Pearson (left), appointed executive director
of Telefilm Canada in 1985, clashed with Telefilm board chairman Jean Sirois
(right), a Quebec city lawyer and Tory fundraiser. Sirois became so famous
for his high travel and entertainment expenses and for his interference
in Telefilm's administration that his appointment was not renewed.
(Left: Len Sidaway/Gazette; right: Gazette)

Distinguished Canadian artist Joe Plaskett, who lives in Paris,
painted a portrait of Mila Mulroney in 1986 for half his regular fee when
told she was too poor to pay the whole amount. (Dave Sidaway/Gazette)

*Yukon MP Erik Nielsen, deputy prime minister until
1987, was forced to defend Sinclair Stevens in the Commons and
quit politics in disgust over corruption in his own party.
(Chris Schwartz/Canapress Photo Services)*

*In February 1987 Montreal lawyer Daniel Rock angrily denied that he used
his PC Party connections to obtain an early parole for one of his clients, convicted
heroin trafficker Conrad Bouchard. (Paul Chiasson/Canapress Photo Services)*

*On his way into Senate Speaker Guy Charbonneau's office
for his 1987 swearing in as a new senator, Montreal lawyer Jean Bazin
faced reporters' questions about his role in the Oerlikon affair.
(Fred Chartrand/Canapress Photo Services)*

*The RCMP delayed its raid
on the office of Chambly Tory MP
Richard Grisé until the day after
the 1988 election; he was later
convicted of fraud. (Gazette)*

*Roger Nantel, Mulroney's top
communications adviser in Quebec
until his sudden violent death in
November 1990, was raising money
for a mysterious trust. (UPC/Gazette)*

One urgent telegram from an anonymous official at External to Paris embassy staff, stating that the department needed "a full explanation to satisfy an access to information request," demanded an explanation of charges of $5,357.65 in February and $13,685.40 and $4,782.12 in March, a time when Mila was back in Paris having her portrait painted. But the prime minister and his wife were not chased for money the same way the other travellers were. "That doesn't apply to certain individuals," an official told Cléroux. "Not when you have a party fund." He was referring to the PC Canada Fund.

In the case of the Mulroneys, Cléroux learned, External would send a note over to Doucet citing expenses that could not be covered or explained away, and almost immediately a PC Party cheque would come back. None of these requests involved the access-to-information staff, as the regulations require; instead, the shots were being called by Fred Doucet and PMO staff. External's access-to-information coordinator, Simon Wade, was required to run everything past Doucet, even though under the act there should not have been any input from political staff on access requests. A September 9, 1986, memo from Wade to Doucet shows the PMO disregarded such bureaucratic niceties if the PM's reputation was at stake. "Dr. Doucet," wrote Wade stiffly, "I attach as requested a draft of my letter to Mr. Cléroux regarding Canadian participation in the Francophone Summit and Prime Minister Mulroney's bilateral visit to France. A revised summary of expenses which will be appended to the letter is also attached." Here Wade was referring to the revised invoices. But "ultimately," he warned Doucet, "Mr. Cléroux will have access to the actual records regarding the visit."

The Mulroneys' Plaza Athénée bill added up to 104,110.93 French francs, or $28,697 for six nights. This included bills for shopping in the hotel boutiques and for other expenses such as room service; those items totalled $8,297.24. In other words, they ran up "incidentals" of more than $1,300 a day. No one else in the delegation came close to this amount of "extras" — the nearest was a secretary who accepted about 9,000 francs' worth of charges on behalf of other members of the delegation. Third was Monique Vézina, with just over 7,000 francs' worth of incidental expenses. After the task force went through the bills and found some items of clothing charged to the room, they asked the Mulroneys for repayment of $3,538.40. The PC Party obliged.

Cléroux then asked for records relating to a three-day trip the Mulroneys took to New York in October 1985, when Mulroney addressed the United Nations. The trip cost taxpayers $32,000 for accommodation at the Pierre, the Mulroneys' favourite hotel in New York and, like the Plaza Athénée, one of the most expensive hotels in the world. Their suite cost $1,200 a day and hotel staff delivered twenty-nine pieces of luggage — most of it Vuitton — to the couple's rooms. Fred Doucet's room cost $826 a day, while Bill Fox managed in one for $535; other staffers made do with rooms at $330 each per day.

Once again, it was an access-to-information request that forced the PMO to go to the PC Party to cover miscellaneous expenses on the New York trip. In this case, Cléroux was asking for documents with regard to an invoice of $1,990.97 for limousine service for Mila. The limousine was one of six hired by the PMO at $30 (U.S.) an hour to shuttle Mulroney and the Canadian delegation around New York. Mila's limousine was used to take her shopping, and her bill was paid initially by External Affairs. Nine months later, but shortly after Cléroux made his enquiries, the PC Canada Fund sent along a cheque for $1,990.97. It arrived at External Affairs, said Cléroux, bearing the familiar red, white, and blue logo of the PC Canada Fund; "amused officials passed it around, chuckled, recorded it and quickly cashed it."

David Angus gave Cléroux the official story that he and the prime minister had an "absolutely clear-cut" arrangement dating back to 1983: the party would pay for some of these personal expenses when it appeared that the party benefitted in some way. The New York limousines were paid for by the party, he said, because Mila appeared on U.S. television and it made the Tory party look good. He also said that Mulroney would sometimes pay back money if the two of them decided the expenses were truly personal in nature. "There's nothing secret," Angus said. "I can tell you that whenever there are personal items, I've got a comptroller and staff that give me a list every month of anything that might be questionable. I sit down with the prime minister and we identify the things that are personal and I then prepare a billing on a regular basis and it always gets paid. I can't imagine anything more businesslike and that's the way it's always worked."

Sometimes, Angus conceded, the Mulroneys would remove things from the account that they didn't think they should have to pay and then the bills would go back to the PMO. "It goes around some process, if you will," Angus explained, "between the prime minister and his office and whatever, and the ones they want me to pay, I pay, and then I recover back the money when they are not party things — payments of personal things."

There was a third excursion, a $1.1-million jaunt to Asia in May 1986, that caused another major flap. This time the Mulroneys took an entourage of fifty-two people with them in a Hercules L-1011 jet borrowed from the Defence Department for a two-week trip to the economic summit in Japan, with official visits to Korea and China. The $1.1-million figure did not include hotel, meals, and other expenses for Mulroney himself and for several members of his delegation whose costs were paid for by the host countries. Nor did it include the $300,000 spent by the Defence Department to ferry video equipment around Asia to record the trip.

What attracted serious criticism was the news that among the fifty-two travellers were the Mulroneys' butler, Ashraf Khan, and a household maid, Linda Narcisco. Mulroney lied clumsily about this on CBC Television in October, saying, "I didn't take a butler. I didn't take anybody. I took the people who help us travel." Cléroux rooted through the documentation that proved the butler and the maid were there. Things got more complicated when Marc Lortie told the press the truth: that the butler and maid had gone along to serve meals, pour tea, and help the prime minister and his wife dress. But to the folks back home in the ridings, this didn't play so well, so the spin doctors at the PMO came up with another explanation. Solicitor General James Kelleher quickly stepped in to say that Lortie mis-spoke himself. That's not why the servants were there at all — they were there for security reasons. "They were closing the gap," he said. "There's outside security and there's inside security." The Khan-Narcisco team were inside security. When the prime minister is "out of his suite, they must remain in his suite at all times, to make sure that unauthorized people don't come in," Kelleher said.

There was a slight problem with this explanation: the RCMP were also guarding the room. The hapless solicitor general tried to elaborate. "Let me give you an example," Kelleher told reporters. "When a chambermaid comes in to deal with the bed, we want to make sure that our people are there to ensure that she is in fact a chambermaid and isn't doing something or leaving something that is unauthorized. When the prime minister is discussing some other matters of urgency with the prime minister or head of state of some other country, we don't want maids from the hotel wandering in and out serving tea or cookies or doing things of that nature because they can overhear things of a very serious nature." Kelleher added that he didn't call Khan and Narcisco "the butler" and "the maid" when they are on a foreign trip. "I call them GR-2 employees," Kelleher said.

"There is no job classification known as GR-2," reported Cléroux gleefully, "and Mr. Kelleher may have meant to call them GS-2 — general service, second level employees. That classification includes people who do domestic services such as washing and drying clothes, pressing and repairing clothes, cooking, housekeeping, tailoring and barbering." Like a butler and a maid.

And that was just the flap about the maid and the butler. The press enjoyed it so much that most didn't pay attention to the fact that some senior aides, including Bernard Roy and Charles

McMillan, took along their spouses. Marc Lortie tried to explain the presence of McMillan's wife, who is Japanese by birth, by telling reporters she went along to translate for Mila. When it was pointed out to Lortie that the bills showed that the government had also hired a Tokyo translator, Motoko Ishimura, for $2,572.80 to translate for Mila, he dismissed the question airily, saying it is normal to take translators abroad from Canada.

Despite the odd revelation or speculation in the media, nothing seriously threatened the extravagance of the Mulroneys' foreign travel or the size of their entourages. But the PMO was determined to stop these stories about wretched excess on the road, however tame. In November 1989, Auditor General Kenneth Dye complained that a request to audit $2 million in travel expenses by federal cabinet ministers had been turned down. Some details slipped out anyway. In May 1991, for example, Mulroney made another visit to Asia, this time an eleven-day trip to Hong Kong and Japan. It cost nearly $1 million for an entourage of fifty-six individuals plus fourteen police bodyguards. Daily expenses ran to $76,941. During the same year, Mulroney travelled to Ireland, England, Zimbabwe, France, Germany, Italy, New York, and California; as Canadian Press reported, these journeys cost taxpayers $2.95 million. Mulroney also filed an additional $25,402 in personal travel expenses. "A trip to the summit of leaders of the big industrial democracies in London last summer — including a side trip to Ireland where Mulroney reveled in his Irish roots — cost $606,182. A trip to California last fall for a speech cost $95,140." No one was going to stop Brian and Mila Mulroney from travelling in the manner to which they had become accustomed.

It is also worth noting that while these details came to light as a result of access-to-information requests by a few determined journalists, that avenue was not always wide open. The 1993–94 annual report from Information Commissioner John Grace, the man responsible for investigating complaints under the Access to Information Act, spelled out the Mulroney government's general attitude. "The relationship between the government of Brian Mulroney and the access law was anything but comfortable," wrote Grace. "It got off the rails almost from the start. The then Prime Minister was personally wounded when records of what appeared to some as extravagant travel costs were released. As is often the case, the ministers, too, cooled towards that which the Prime Minister saw fit to disparage, at least in private.

"The chill was made more frigid by a letter which came to be known as the 'check with Fred' letter. It was sent by the Clerk of the Privy Council [Paul Tellier] to two deputy ministers instructing them to check with the Prime Minister's Office before releasing information relating to the Prime Minister. In no time at all, it seemed, the government lost patience with the access legislation." This antagonism, explained Grace, had an unfortunate trickle-down effect that meant "openness was not the order of the day."

Mulroney's first term in office coincided with heady boom years in the stock market and real estate, a period when international conglomerates were gobbling up their weaker rivals in a frenzy of mergers and acquisitions. And during these free-spending years of conspicuous consumption, Canada's Brian and Mila Mulroney indulged their taste for foreign travel, luxury hotels, large entourages, backup planes, fleets of limousines, and personal servants. Without a personal fortune of their own, they travelled like kings, much of it justified by the excuse that security considerations demanded it.

The media observed it all and reported to an increasingly cynical public. When Ottawa journalist Claire Hoy, who had broken a damaging story that RCMP officers had been ordered to salute Mila, nicknamed her "Imelda II" after the extravagant wife of Philippines dictator Ferdinand Marcos, the name stuck, at least with the media. And when Guy Charbonneau was asked in the summer of 1994 why he had not reined in the prime minister and his wife, advising them to live more modestly when it was clear that the public was offended by their opulent style, he burst out laughing. "You don't tell Brian that!" Trying to change Mulroney, said Charbonneau, is impossible; "he goes his own way." If Guy Charbonneau could not curb the Mulroneys' behaviour, no one could.

THE POPE OF BISHOP STREET

J
UST INSIDE THE DOOR OF LE MAS DES OLIVIERS, A SMALL BASEMENT
bistro on Bishop Street in Montreal, there's a corner table for
four with a commanding view of the room. During the Tories'
years in power, this was where his friends could usually find
Senator Guy Charbonneau at noon, lunching alone or, more often,
with one or two other associates. The corner table allowed Charbonneau to conduct his affairs while keeping an eye on everyone else
in the restaurant. It was known to be his favourite haunt, and
Charbonneau was known to be the most powerful man in the
Mulroney circle. The place naturally attracted sycophants eager to
pay their respects. They would proceed, a little self-consciously, to
Charbonneau's table and shake his hand; fascinated observers wondered if these supplicants would actually bend to kiss his ring. Not for
nothing did Charbonneau earn the nickname "the Pope" among those
hungry for contracts and favours. The moniker was used by Tories on
Parliament Hill as well, an acknowledgment of his influence with
Mulroney and his role in placing senior staff in ministerial offices.

Le Mas has been a favourite lunch spot for Fred Doucet too, ever
since he left his PMO job in 1989 to set up his own lobbying firm. You
can observe the bombastic Nova Scotian busily doing his deals at his
own table, after stopping, of course, to pay obeisance to Charbonneau.
Sometimes you'll spot Mordecai Richler, in for the day from his house
in the Eastern Townships, slouched over a double Glenlivet and a

steak, watching the others from his own corner of the room, missing nothing. Nobody likes a good gossip better than Richler, and the regulars are not put off by his mournful face and drooping lids; in conversation a sweet grin spreads across his face as he takes in the latest news. You'll watch Serge Savard, former hockey great and now the manager of the Montreal Canadiens, happily manoeuvring around the tables like a genial headwaiter, working the crowd.

There are very few women at Le Mas. "Unfortunately," laments Charbonneau. (If he were to lunch with a female friend it might be Marthe Carrière, whose full-time appointment he helped to secure at the Immigration Appeal Board in 1987. The menu is not designed for women; it is old-fashioned macho bistro: steak, *frites*, pork chops, celery soup, Caesar salad. A salad offering veal sweetbreads served *"tiède"* is one of the kitchen's few nods towards a more contemporary French cuisine, but the food is cooked for businessmen who want Martinis first, then large quantities of red meat and red wine. Lunch for two will run around $85.

For most Montrealers, Le Mas is just another expense account hangout for well-fed men in expensive, slightly snug, Italian suits with perhaps a little too much silk in the silk-wool blends. For Brian Mulroney's cronies, men like Charbonneau and Doucet, the restaurant replaced the Maritime Bar at the Ritz-Carlton Hotel and the Mount Royal Club as the meeting place of choice. Those retreats, luxurious as they were, had become notorious: everyone knew they were the places where the cronies had met to plot Joe Clark's overthrow and Mulroney's ascent. Besides, Mila came to Montreal once or twice a week and usually took lunch at the Ritz-Carlton with members of the ballet group, and lunch was not a time to share with the ladies. Le Mas became the place to drink, dine, and do deals.

It was at Le Mas on March 4, 1988, that Guy Charbonneau, his fellow senator Michel Cogger, and businessman Pierre Ducros met to talk about one of the largest government contracts then available, one whose ultimate value might escalate to well over $200 million.

External Affairs had been looking for a new communications system since 1981; ideally such a system would link some 4,000 work-stations at embassies and consulates around the world, at CIDA offices, and at headquarters in Ottawa. Officials also hoped it would allow Canada's intelligence agencies to talk to one another and to transmit what are known as "funny papers" — the data collected by Ottawa's ultra-secret electronic eavesdroppers, the Communications Security Establishment.

In 1987 two External Affairs officers, Howard Balloch and Douglas Woods, put forward a proposal for COSICS, the Canadian On-line Secure Information and Communications System. It would use personal computers to connect the United States desks at External to thirteen consulates in the U.S., and then expand to include Canadian embassies worldwide. And it would handle both routine and top-secret communications. When the proposal won approval at Treasury Board, people who understood security and intelligence in Ottawa were stunned: it had been given the go-ahead without a single feasibility study. "It was a quick and dirty back-of-the-envelope submission," says one person who watched the process, "and Treasury Board, for no reason anyone could understand, gave them the money and let them proceed."

Many experts believed the proposal was not workable, that a single communications system could not transmit both routine data and top-secret information at the same time. "Seepage" between the linked PCs would prevent the intelligence system from being truly secure, the experts insisted, pointing out that even the most sophisticated encryption software couldn't repel a determined high-tech hacker. COSICS supporters at External Affairs refused to back down. A single system could do both jobs, they maintained, and they won the day.

At that early stage there were only two companies in Canada with the technical expertise to create this kind of dual-purpose system. One was Ottawa-based SHL Systemhouse Ltd., whose president,

Rod Bryden, was a loyal and active federal Liberal; the other was Montreal's Groupe DMR Ltd., and DMR's president was Pierre Ducros. At the eleventh hour, a third company had entered the ring, but it had no track record with high-tech projects like COSICS: Fenco-Lavalin was a consortium assembled expressly for the purpose of bidding on the project by the Montreal-based engineering giant Lavalin. It was assisted by well-connected lobbyists, led by GCI's Frank Moores, Gary Ouellet, and Gerry Doucet; and Lavalin itself was run by Bernard Lamarre, the best-connected CEO in Canada's engineering community at the time.

Charbonneau had been doing business with Lavalin for about thirty years, starting when the company was still called Lalonde & Valois. Bernard Lamarre joined the firm in the mid-1950s, took control a few years later, and changed the name to Lavalin. As Carole-Marie Allard noted in her book *Lavalin: The Strings of Power*, as the company's insurance broker, Charbonneau had an interest in all Lavalin's endeavours in Canada and abroad. "The Lavalin account brought him substantial income which he was able to cash in on when he sold his firm, Charbonneau Dulude and Associates, after he was named to the Senate." After he went to the Senate, wrote Allard, Charbonneau travelled to China, Italy, the Soviet Union, and Thailand on behalf of Lavalin, in most cases helping the company sell the transportation systems it was developing through the Urban Transportation Development Corporation, its subsidiary in Kingston, Ontario. In Italy, for example, Charbonneau met with Amintore Fanfani, then the prime minister, to lobby for a $230-million contract for the Milan subway; in China, he lobbied senior politicians for the contract for Beijing's subway. He often combined trips he took abroad as Speaker of the Senate with meetings to promote Lavalin's interests. "Yes, for them and for many others . . . Bombardier and God knows how many others," Charbonneau says with a small smile. "I've done a lot of hustling for Canadian companies. I loved it. It was good for Canada. It keeps you in shape." He admits Lavalin was the firm for whom he did the most. "Bernard Lamarre was a good friend of mine and he was aggressive. It was the biggest engineering firm. I'd been handling their insurance since the 1950s."

COSICS was a rich prize, and the competition for it was intense and political. The contest had begun on September 29, 1986, when the federal government sent out a letter of intent for a communications system to a number of interested companies. Twenty-two responded. Toronto-based Fenco Engineers Inc., the defence project division of Lavalin, did not receive the letter and did not express interest. But one company that did was Honeywell Ltd. That fall one of its representatives, Scott Flagan, took Rod Bryden to lunch at the Rideau Club to talk about the project. Honeywell, Flagan is said to have told Bryden, was going to win a big procurement project but needed a subcontractor to do the systems work on it. Would Systemhouse be interested? Bryden already knew about the government's plans; he had received the letter of intent and was shocked by Flagan's impudence in assuming that Honeywell's bid would be the winning one. Bryden turned the offer down. His position was that Honeywell did not have any computer hardware appropriate to External's requirements, and besides, Systemhouse was planning to bid on the project itself. Flagan calmly repeated that Honeywell had the project. If Systemhouse wanted in, Honeywell could use them; if not, fine. Perhaps he was right to be so confident; Honeywell's lobbyists included the ubiquitous GCI trio of Frank Moores, Gary Ouellet, and Gerry Doucet.

When contacted some years later by reporter Mario Possamai about his meeting with Bryden, Flagan was hostile. "I'm not at liberty to say anything," he snapped. "I'm under the Secrets Act. I can't even acknowledge that I worked on COSICS or say what COSICS is." Possamai asked Flagan how Honeywell could have been involved in COSICS when the company was out of the computer business by then. "Honeywell didn't provide computers," Flagan replied. "That wasn't our role in any of the COSICS work."

By February 1987 the computer division of Honeywell had

merged with Bull, a French company, to become Honeywell-Bull and had stopped making computer systems in North America. The remainder of the North American company, called Honeywell Ltd., continued to manufacture controls such as those used to run elevators and turn on furnaces. But that didn't mean Honeywell Ltd. was no longer interested in competing for the COSICS contract; it just meant it would look to partners for the necessary technical expertise. They found such a partner in Fenco-Lavalin. The COSICS bids were due on June 9, 1987; just three weeks before this deadline, the people at Supply and Services who were managing the bid process learned that Honeywell Ltd. wanted to substitute the name of Fenco-Lavalin on its bid for COSICS; Honeywell Ltd. would go in as the subcontractor. And Fenco-Lavalin proposed to use the same hardware as that specified by Systemhouse, hardware from Digital Equipment.

The top people at Systemhouse were stunned by news of the last-minute Fenco-Lavalin bid and wondered if there had been leaks about the Digital hardware. Such leaks, they believed, had come not from Digital but from government insiders who had access to the bid information.

The tenders were reviewed in August 1987. In October, the competing companies were told their bids were "non-compliant" and that there would be a bid recall instead of the customary bid repair. In other words, companies would send in new bids without learning what was wrong with their old ones. Around Ottawa, this was discussed as yet another example of a bidding process that had been interfered with in order to grant an advantage to one company. Veterans of the scene recognized the pattern; bid-rigging is an old game in politics and the Tories certainly didn't invent it.

In January 1988 DMR tendered its second bid but decided it needed to beef up its political efforts as well. By now Ducros was convinced that political influence would be a significant factor in the decision. He hired a lobbyist and arranged to meet with Michel Cogger, the lawyer who had helped incorporate DMR back in 1973.

Ducros made another move as well — he met with Supply and Services officials to express his concerns. After a brief three- or four-day internal inquiry, they got back to him with verbal assurances that everything was on the up and up. But Ducros wasn't taking any chances; he asked Cogger to organize the lunch with Charbonneau at Le Mas des Oliviers in March. According to Ducros, who has never discussed the affair with reporters but who did testify at a later inquiry, Charbonneau told him flatly that DMR's bid would not be considered because one of his partners in the bid was a French company that had not received NATO security clearance. Ducros said Charbonneau asked him if he would be interested in making a deal with one of the other bidders, specifically Fenco-Lavalin. Ducros did not know about the similar proposal made to Rod Bryden by Honeywell's representative, but, like Bryden, he was confident that his company could do it without help. He said no.

"I didn't know Mr. Ducros," Charbonneau said in an interview in the summer of 1994. "He thought I could help him, but as it turned out I didn't know anything about this. I don't get involved in contracts. And the contract that he thought I could help him on, it had already been granted. I checked and found it had been granted in January [1988]." But it hadn't been granted — at least not officially. Officially, it wasn't awarded until August, a full five months later, and officially it wasn't announced until October. The second bids weren't even received until January 19, 1988; there would scarcely have been enough time to evaluate them and make a decision in January. If Charbonneau was able to discover that a decision had been made that month, then Bryden and Ducros were right to be suspicious — the fix was in.

During the months that Bryden and Ducros were fretting about interference, political staff in ministers' offices in Ottawa were doing their best to gather intelligence on the project from the bureaucrats. What are the figures? they asked. Who's ahead? What's happening? It's possible to reconstruct their activities from memos, message slips, and other documents. Bureaucrats at Supply and Services and the project's managers at External Affairs complained that staff from Michel Côté's office, in particular Fred Loiselle, Bernard Côté, and Pierre-Paul Bourdon, called them repeatedly for news. A senior aide in Mulroney's office frequently called the office of Paul Dick, the junior defence minister at the time, to find out what was happening to Lavalin's bid.

It's especially interesting to follow the trail of Pierre-Paul Bourdon in this period. Bourdon had been André Bissonnette's chief of staff, but he left in 1986 to take the same position with Paul Dick in Defence, where the hot issue was the Oerlikon contract. In 1987 Bourdon became chief of staff for Supply and Services Minister Michel Côté and they bird-dogged the COSICS file intently. When Mulroney fired Côté in February 1988 for failing to disclose the loan from his friends in Quebec City, Public Works Minister Stewart McInnes was put in charge of the ministry, but he was so busy handling two portfolios that the real political boss at Supply and Services was Bourdon. Otto Jelinek took over the ministry in early April and Bourdon moved on yet again — to a job at Lavalin.

By the early summer of 1988, both Bryden and Ducros knew they weren't going to win the COSICS contract. Their own sources had discovered the Fenco-Lavalin had indeed captured the prize, and even though the formal announcement had yet to be made, Bryden asked Georgina Wyman, then the deputy minister at Supply and Services, to investigate. He also wrote to Treasury Board president Robert de Cotret on June 1, 1988, to protest the "procurement error" in the process. Among Bryden's complaints was the serious allegation that Fenco-Lavalin simply did not have the competence and experience to build the kind of system External Affairs needed. It had, wrote Bryden, "no experience or record of project design or delivery of computer systems." Such a bidder wouldn't normally pass the first screening for so complex a project. And Fenco-Lavalin had pulled together its bid in just a few weeks; both Systemhouse and DMR had spent months in preparation. Systemhouse estimated its costs at $750,000; Ducros later told police DMR's costs had run to millions. "It is a miracle that a civil engineering firm and a controls company achieved this feat," Bryden noted icily. "It is a mystery why they were asked by the Government of Canada to do so."

Bryden also pointed out to de Cotret that a 1988 government document cited the names of three leading Canadian companies in the systems integration business: Systemhouse, DMR, and Lavalin. "To our knowledge, this is the first record of Lavalin ever having been associated with this business. In 15 years we have never encountered them as a competitor nor are we aware of any such business they have done. It is curious that the report would make this reference while the COSICS supplier selection is being done." After questioning the suspicious timing of other aspects of Fenco-Lavalin's bid, Bryden said he was hearing rumours that Fenco-Lavalin's bid had come in just slightly under the Systemhouse price. His question was blunt: Had the details of his bid had been leaked to his competitors?

De Cotret never responded but Georgina Wyman did, especially after her new boss, Otto Jelinek, received a tough letter from Fruji Bull, the president of the Canadian Association of Data and Professional Service Organizations. "CADAPSO has learned that the Government of Canada is about to award the largest ever computer systems integration contract . . . to Lavalin, a consulting engineering firm with no proven experience or reputation in systems management," wrote Bull. "Two of Canada's largest systems integrators have spent considerable time, effort and money in preparing their bids for this project. It seems inconceivable that the government would give more attention to a company not even in the business."

The senior bureaucrats got the message. Jack Manion, deputy clerk of the Privy Council, arranged for an investigation on May 9, but gave senior Ottawa bureaucrat Gerry Berger only five days in which to complete an inquiry into a highly political and extremely complicated deal. Although Berger delivered a report to Manion on May 13 that concluded the bidding process had been properly conducted, he did not drop his enquiries. Over the next few weeks he continued to discuss the matter with Ducros and others, and on June 20 he briefed RCMP Inspector André Beauchemin on the case. The RCMP initiated their own investigation, which lasted less than a month. On July 22, RCMP Commissioner Norman Inkster sent a brisk letter to Georgina Wyman to say the Mounties found that "the complaints received were totally unfounded. No evidence of wrongdoing surfaced . . ." Inkster admitted that questions from ministerial aides could have given "a perception of interference" but, he added, "the investigation established that in fact no interference took place."

The COSICS controversy, which had not become public at this time, was shunted aside by the 1988 summer election campaign and the free trade debate. Liberal Leader John Turner surprised everyone with a hard-fought, passionate campaign, and the Tories were seriously worried. The business community responded with a multi-million-dollar advertising campaign in support of the government's free trade initiative, and Mulroney won the election on November 21, 1988, with another majority. Life returned to normal for the Conservatives in Ottawa.

The contract with Fenco-Lavalin had been signed in August and the announcement made quietly in the midst of the election campaign. Bryden and Ducros continued to believe the bid had been rigged. For Bryden the blow was particularly damaging; investors soon lost faith in the company and his board looked critically at his management of Systemhouse. He owned most of the shares, and when their value dropped by five dollars a share, his personal loss was almost $100 million. Within two years the company could not meet its debt obligations and was taken over by Bell Canada Enterprises. Bryden resigned; today he owns the Ottawa Senators hockey team.

In 1991, three years after the Fenco-Lavalin contract was let, the cost of COSICS had soared to some $130 million and the system wasn't working. Many sources claimed that the true costs to date had been $207 million and that it would take another $200 million to get it right. All the Conservative government would admit to was a total cost of $258 million, a healthy increase over the originally projected $53 million.

Some embassies abroad were lumbered with incredible expenses to accommodate the system; the new embassy in Beijing, for example, had to have three extra floors built for it. In the final analysis, it seems, no amount of money would have made the system function as had been promised. Instead of a sophisticated system to link Canadian diplomats all over the world, allowing them to communicate directly with one another, Fenco-Lavalin's system was so limited it could be used only to link the thirteen Canadian missions in the United States. The transmission of top-secret intelligence reports was never a possibility.

Faced with an inadequate Fenco-Lavalin design, the Mulroney government decided it would have to build a second-tier system to handle the international communications COSICS was supposed to manage. They concluded Fenco-Lavalin wasn't up to the job. By this time, Lavalin had collapsed into financial chaos, with the government of Quebec having to pick up the company's eclectic art collection — including Yolande Charbonneau's work — as part of the debt they were owed. Lavalin's remaining assets were folded into Quebec's other engineering giant, SNC. Garrett Lambert at External Affairs, project manager for COSICS and its most passionate defender, admitted in October 1991 that the system was not "as terrific as we'd like it to be. It was the best we could get then, but it's not as attractive as options available now with personal computers." So phase two, approved by Treasury Board that same October, will eventually see a move to a new system based on personal computers that will handle far more data than was ever envisioned for COSICS. COSICS itself is now part of a new system called SIGNET, Lambert said, and the $258-million total approved would cover costs up to 1996. Today, any mention of COSICS in Ottawa wins a grimace and a quick switch to another subject. Someone, somewhere, made a lot of money on this turkey.

In 1988 the RCMP's Special Federal Inquiries Unit, established in 1978 to handle political corruption cases, was headed by Rod Stamler. Stamler was not convinced that the COSICS process deserved the blessing given to it by the force and the bureaucrats at Supply and Services. His suspicions were reinforced by a parallel investigation that was under way that autumn into Michel Cogger's lobbying activities on behalf of a Senneville, Quebec, businessman called Guy Montpetit. Then, on December 29, Pierre Ducros visited Stamler's offices.

Ducros's complaint that day was that no police officer had ever interviewed him before giving a clean bill of health to the COSICS bidding procedure. Stamler and Beauchemin listened to his story very carefully. After reviewing the complaints filed by Systemhouse, DMR, and Fruji Bull, the SFIU initiated another investigation, this time concluding that the process had been badly flawed, appeared unfair, and was more than a little suspect. Whether any criminal act had occurred, they could not say.

A number of senior RCMP officers besides Stamler were concerned by the COSICS affair. They believed there was ongoing interference in bids and contracts, but they also knew that the people who could confirm it were frequently too frightened to come forward. By this time in the Mulroney period, many public servants had been fired or demoted for resisting political orders, however unethical or bizarre, and business people knew all too well how quickly contracts could evaporate if they protested against unfair treatment. Rod Bryden was initially reluctant to complain; Systemhouse had grown prosperous on government business. "Look at these people," he said to a visitor one day as he opened the door to a floor full of busy employees. "There are 300 people here who count on us to keep their jobs. If I make a public scene, they're the ones who will get hurt." Bryden was speaking for anyone in Canada who depended on business from federal departments, agencies, or Crown corporations. The RCMP needed the full cooperation of an individual close to the event and to the players. If not Bryden, what about Ducros?

On January 16, Inspector Beauchemin met Ducros in Montreal to discuss the whole affair. Ducros claimed there could be serious security problems with Fenco-Lavalin's plans for the COSICS system; he was convinced the company didn't have the expertise for the job. And why, he demanded, hadn't the police come in sooner? And didn't they know that people were concerned about political influence with the bids?

After their talk, Beauchemin invited Ducros to come to Ottawa for a meeting to hash out the whole affair with his colleague Inspector Tim Quigley.[1] Before that meeting, Beauchemin and Quigley prepared a memorandum outlining the problem they were dealing with, the suspicions that had been raised, and their belief that businesses wanting federal contracts had to pay kickbacks. In their best bureaucratic language, they made it clear they weren't going to solve these crimes by sitting back and waiting for hard evidence to fall into their laps. It was time to give the tree a good shake. They put on paper a plan for what they called Operation Sack.

Intelligence has been received by this Section to the effect that senators have been involved illegally in the process of awarding Federal Government contracts to private industry. More specifically, Senators COGGER and CHARBONNEAU have been mentioned in several investigations as having been involved in suspicious circumstances relating to various large Federal Government contracts. Traditional investigative techniques are unlikely to succeed in achieving conclusive results in some of these investigations such as the COSICS file. From our inquiries, it appears to be generally understood in the business community, that the only way to obtain government contracts is to cultivate political connections and to contribute a portion of the profits to these government connections.

OBJECTIVE
By applying a pro-active method of investigation through the introduction of a police agent, attempt to confirm or dispell that Senators COGGER and CHARBONNEAU accepted by corruption, money or non-monetary benefits for intervention or influence in decision in the process of awarding contracts for the Federal Government.

ACTION PLAN
Step 1. Cultivate the President of D.M.R. (Pierre Ducros) as a source/agent.

Step 2. Instruct agent to communicate with Senator Charbonneau and/or Cogger verbally to state his willingness to "cooperate" in future contracts.

Step 3. If the agent can arrange verbal communication, same will be monitored via "one party consent" policy.

Step 4. Monitor upcoming contracts and select the first one that fits our needs.

Step 5. Hire Paul Vidosa to lobby on behalf of source.

Step 6. Continue to openly investigate COGGER, reference his activities with [blacked out] — questionable payments etc. — Refer to Senator COGGER file.

Ducros was the ideal candidate to serve as a "source agent." Rod Bryden was an active Liberal, and even if he was willing, he would never have been able to discuss contracts at Le Mas des Oliviers with the likes of Cogger and Charbonneau. Ducros was more acceptable; despite his well-known grief over DMR's failure to land the COSICS contract, Ducros had been at the forefront of Quebec's support for Mulroney's free trade deal.

The policy of "one-party consent" was the same one relied upon in the 1984–86 Mitton sting called "Daniel Rock et al." The source —

and they hoped it would be Ducros — would have to agree to tape all his conversations with Cogger and Charbonneau. If this stage of the investigation were successful, the police would likely proceed with a more expensive operation with undercover agents and wire-taps in place.

CONSIDERATIONS

1. Source could form a new company to accommodate our specific needs.

2. Assuming the source will have incurred expenses, the RCMP should assume responsibility for these expenses (bidding expenses, etc.).

3. Further, RCMP should be willing to pay an award to the agent depending on the success of the operation.

4. Should we consider involving [blacked out] in a double-pronged approach?

5. Should we involve Government [blacked out] in our project?

6. "Entrapment" — Is this a problem? (research required).

7. What are the <u>consequences</u> of this operation? e.g.:

    (a) political sensitivity;

    (b) criticism from government, press and public;

    (c) validity of contracts and bidding process, especially as it relates to innocent parties involved.[2]

These points made it clear that Operation Sack could become an expensive undertaking and that the RCMP officers were grappling with many of the same issues that had hung over the Mitton sting: entrapment, public reaction, and political repercussions. There was a strong possibility that their investigations could lead them straight to Mulroney's office. How would the politicians react? What would the press and the public think? They were plenty of issues that needed to be thought through very carefully.

On January 26, 1989, Ducros came to Ottawa to meet Beauchemin and Quigley. Our traditional methods are not working in this case, the police told him. Would you be willing to help us in an operation to trap Cogger? Ducros was startled. You've got the wrong man, he told them. It's not Cogger you should be looking at. It's the other senator, Charbonneau. He's the one with the Lavalin connections. And then Ducros told the officers about other contracts in which he suspected political interference. But as for helping them, he wasn't sure. He'd have to think about it.

On March 2, Ducros gave them his answer: he wasn't prepared to help with Operation Sack. Quigley and Beauchemin decided to go ahead without his help. And they decided to leave Charbonneau out of the investigation; Ducros was the only person who had ever raised his role in the COSICS affair.

TO CATCH A THIEF

ITHOUT DUCROS'S PARTICIPATION IN OPERATION SACK, the SFIU officers adopted an alternative strategy: the use of an experienced undercover informant. Their choice was the somewhat volatile Paul Vidosa, a contract informant who had worked for the Mounties on international drug operations. His latest assignment had targeted a group of Ismailis based in Vancouver who were suspected of laundering profits from drug deals through a courier business, using the infamous Bank of Credit and Commerce International. Although the operation had not been successful, the RCMP Drug Enforcement Unit had seized $1.08 million (U.S.) in January 1989 from Ismaili couriers at the border and had frozen the courier company's assets. With the investigation stalled, the Mounties moved Vidosa to Operation Sack on a contract worth $1,500 a week.

The Vancouver operation was tricky and dangerous work; even so, a sting against a senator was quite another matter. This would be a sophisticated white-collar crime operation and Vidosa, to say the least, was not the solid businessman type they needed. Back in 1982 he'd gone to the press about a bad experience he'd had as an RCMP informant and Commissioner Robert Simmonds, who considered him an unreliable flake, had issued an order that he should not be used again. Inkster maintained the ban when he took over, but while Inkster was away, Stamler got a special dispensation from Deputy

Commissioner Henry Jensen to use Vidosa on the Ismaili case. Now Jensen agreed he could also be used on Operation Sack.

Vidosa's cover story was that he was assisting the Ismailis in their efforts to retrieve some of the $1.08 million that had been seized by the Mounties in January. Vidosa phoned Cogger on March 21 to enlist his aid, but Cogger wouldn't bite, saying it wasn't his kind of case. He told Vidosa to hire a lawyer instead.

Shortly after, Cogger and another man were having lunch with Pierre Ducros to discuss yet another contract, one Ducros later described to the Mounties as a "far-fetched proposal." If the deal wasn't illegal, it was at least questionable. Ducros kept his cool until the second man left; once alone with Cogger, Ducros scolded him for his brazen impropriety: "Stop doing things like that," he snapped. "You're already under investigation by the RCMP." He may have meant well, but Ducros had given the game away. Cogger had been alerted to the plan to trap him.

Further confirmation came in the fall of 1989 when Vidosa also tipped him off about the sting. Why would Vidosa do this? Because the Mounties had been unable to get the Cogger operation off the ground and after five months Stamler had cancelled his contract. In retaliation, Vidosa called Cogger and told him everything. Not content with that bit of mischief, Vidosa revealed all to the Ottawa *Citizen* in January 1990. He claimed that the Mounties suspected Cogger and other Canadian politicians of laundering money through offshore bank accounts. "I felt it was wrong what we were doing to him," Vidosa told *Citizen* reporter Stephen Bindman. "Maybe they had good reasons, I don't know. Whatever reason they had, they never told me." Inkster's reaction to the publicity was to order an internal investigation into the use of Paul Vidosa. A few days later Pierre Ducros also went public with his story of being asked to help — although he failed to mention that it was he who had made the formal complaint to the Mounties.

On February 13, 1990, a tearful Michel Cogger rose in the

Senate on a question of privilege to put his case before his peers, making allegations that he wisely refused to repeat outside the Senate, where his parliamentary immunity would not protect him. The RCMP were engaged in criminal conspiracies intended to destroy him and his family, he said, wiping his eyes. He began by talking about Paul Vidosa.

He was given the job of tying me to a money-laundering ring when the RCMP, by its own admission, had no reason to believe I was involved in any criminal activity. The RCMP was determined to destroy me, no more and no less. Entrapment, odious and repugnant as it is, remains an accepted method of police investigation which is recognized by the courts, provided there are "reasonable grounds." For lack of reasonable grounds, the above-mentioned actions are nothing more or less than criminal plots by members of the RCMP against me . . .

I am talking here about my fundamental right — not as a senator but as a Canadian citizen — to be able to live my life, to carry on with my profession, to pursue my career like everybody else, free of malicious prosecution, entrapment, undue suspicion, and police harassment. I am referring to my right not to have my telephone conversations tape recorded; my right to carry on my business or profession with other Canadians who are not paid by the police to entice me into criminal activities. Honourable senators, like most of you, I want the right to travel on an airplane and not have to worry whether my seatmate is a plant of the RCMP.

Senior Mounties told Paul Palango that the results of the internal review into the Cogger sting did not please Commissioner Inkster. Superintendent John L'Abbé found that the SFIU team had done nothing wrong, and that was not what Inkster had wanted to hear. On March 15, 1990, he ordered an independent inquiry under former Ontario judge René Marin. Marin was the chairman of the RCMP's External Review Committee, which handles disciplinary matters for the force, and he had also conducted an earlier review of the force for the commissioner.

Inkster's action stunned Stamler, who had just retired after serving with the RCMP for thirty-three years. One of the reasons he had left was his belief that politicians were far too cosy with the commissioner, a relationship that he believed had undermined the integrity and independence of the force. On the face of it, he knew, the Canadian public would regard Inkster's decision as fair, but in Stamler's mind, the inquiry would accomplish only one thing — completely derail the ongoing RCMP investigation into Cogger's activities. "It was absolutely unheard of to have an inquiry being conducted by a judge into an investigation when the investigation was still ongoing," Stamler told Palango. The more Stamler thought about it, the more he believed the inquiry was quite deliberate. The whole idea was to turn the heat on the Mounties and take it off Michel Cogger.

Certainly some Tories believed René Marin would be a compliant judge in the inquiry and would be just as outraged as they were about the Mounties' behaviour. Cogger himself was one of these. "Cogger laughed," said one person he spoke to about Marin. "He showed me the CV of René Marin. He said, 'Marin is looking for a job in government.'" Cogger went on to say he was hoping this would lead Marin to go easy on him. "If it was seen that [Marin] was being anti-Conservative, he would not get the job."

René Marin was not quite the patsy Cogger hoped for. Both Inkster and Solicitor General Pierre Cadieux refused to open the inquiry to the press, but Marin told the press he was prepared to make at least part of his findings public. In May, Southam News went to court to try to overturn the press ban, thus postponing the start of proceedings.

The month of May proved to be one long nightmare for Cogger. Just as the Marin inquiry controversy was heating up, Revenue

Quebec slapped a $68,588 lien on his 80-hectare farm near Knowlton in the Eastern Townships. The property was already burdened with $350,000 worth of mortgages and liens, and over the years Revenue Quebec had put at least three other liens on it for unpaid taxes; this fourth lien was for unpaid tax on his 1987 and 1988 income. Revenue Quebec also garnisheed his Senate salary.

Cogger was in deep financial trouble. He'd put his farm on the market in 1989 for $950,000, but the real estate market had just collapsed and there were no serious buyers at that price. His wife, Erica, had a job as a saleswoman in an upscale dress shop in Knowlton, but her salary was not enough to pull him out of his financial slough. His law practice was drying up in the face of all this bad publicity. As a result, he was having trouble paying the smallest debts, including a $400 bill he'd run up in the parliamentary dining room. He was always cadging loans from people who worked for him; his Senate secretary, for example, who earned $40,000 a year, frequently loaned him small sums — from $40 to $200 — in the uneasy belief that her job depended on his good will. Once he'd pocketed the cash, he'd hop into his Mercedes-Benz and drive home to Knowlton.

Why was he so hard up? He'd been Walter Wolf's lawyer for years. Wolf called him in Ottawa at least once a month, and the two were working on a deal to get road-building contracts in Eastern Europe. His part-time secretary in Montreal, who worked with him in the Wolf offices on Sherbrooke Street, was paid $15,000 a year, but it didn't come out of Cogger's pocket, it came from the Senate as a research grant. Cogger was also working with contacts in Quebec City on a waste treatment company, and he was in constant touch with Henri Lachapelle, the co-owner of Trans-Quebec Helicopters, the company that flew Mulroney around during the 1983 leadership campaign and the 1984 election campaign. For several years Lachapelle paid the salary of a farm-hand to work on Cogger's property, and to this day he lends Cogger an apartment for his own use in Place Alexis Nihon in downtown Montreal. Then there was all the other money he'd earned, revenues that had so interested the Mounties.

Cogger had acted for the Federal Business Development Bank, the federal agency that lends money to small and medium-sized businesses and provides management counselling services. Cogger had an agreement with Guy Lavigueur, the FBDB's president, to bill $1,000 a hour for his counsel between 1986 and 1988. During that period, he billed the FBDB $74,250 while his law firm, Lapointe Rosenstein, invoiced the bank for two further amounts, $117,750 and $50,210. By 1989 the totals for the firm, including Cogger's billing, added up to $232,210. Not only was his hourly rate wildly exorbitant, it was completely against the Parliament of Canada Act for Cogger, a senator, to be billing a government agency for anything. The law says that no person may earn income from the government when he or she is also being paid as a parliamentarian. A bank official said the FBDB had obtained a "verbal legal opinion" that it could use Cogger's services despite his Senate position. When the RCMP investigated, they found evidence that Cogger had never done any legal work for the FBDB. The Mounties examined the billing files at Lapointe Rosenstein, and their search warrant states, "There is nothing in the [law firm's] file that supports or justifies the bills sent on February 10, 1987 and July 5, 1988 to the Federal Business Development Bank by Senator Michel Cogger." But the RCMP were unable to convince Quebec Crown prosecutors to lay a charge against Cogger for this billing.

The FBDB also gave the Université de Sherbrooke a $100,000 loan to support a Cogger-controlled company called Pluri-Canaux Ltée, a firm that offered correspondence courses to adults. Other shareholders were developers Alfred and Meyer Lawee, two cousins who lived near each other in Westmount. It occurred to Cogger that he might be able to sell the courses to the government itself, but this time he consulted the Senate law clerk. The clerk told him most emphatically that selling Pluri-Canaux courses to the government would be a serious breach of the Parliament of Canada Act.

Cogger then thought about setting up a blind trust to administer Pluri-Canaux; the man he had in mind as trustee was Guy Lavigueur. (He was unable to complete this plan before he began running into problems with the Mounties.) Clearly, Cogger's friends were trying to help the little lawyer earn a healthy income. But none of it was enough.

At the end of May 1990, about twenty RCMP officers swooped down on Cogger's Parliament Hill office, his Montreal office, and his farm to search through his financial records. Inspector Tim Quigley even tried to search his Mercedes-Benz, he told reporters indignantly. "Can the Mounties really believe I would leave incriminating documents in my car?" he asked. "Seven months after [then] Solicitor General Pierre Blais confirmed I was being investigated and more than eighteen months after the beginning of the investigation? [Quigley] just wanted to intimidate me."

The Marin inquiry was delayed nine months until December 1990, when Inkster reversed his stand and declared that part of the hearings could be held in public. René Marin finally opened the proceedings on January 15, 1991. His first witness was Cogger himself, who began by pleading poverty. He couldn't afford to bring his lawyer, Bruno Pateras, and he thought it only just that the RCMP, the force that was investigating him, should pay his legal bills. "My financial situation is difficult," he told Marin. "It is impossible for me to retain a lawyer where the mandate will result in legal fees amounting to tens of thousands of dollars." Marin concurred, although his recommendation that the force pay Pateras's bills infuriated many, among them Liberal MP Sheila Copps. "I think it's outrageous that the government should be footing the legal bills of an individual who's under investigation," she protested. "For him to be crying poverty . . . Why doesn't he get a monthly payment plan? A lot of Canadians are faced with onerous legal bills and they don't get them defrayed by the government." The decision on the bills was left to Commissioner Inkster, and he agreed that the RCMP should pay them.

Cogger's testimony was overshadowed some days later by the statements of Quigley and Beauchemin. Both inspectors told Marin about Ducros's remark that they were going after the wrong senator. "Perhaps Cogger wasn't the right target," Beauchemin quoted Ducros as saying. "He felt the implication of the second senator was a lot bigger."

A second senator? The police had made copies of their plan for Operation Sack available to the press, but had inked out the second name. Even so, one could see it was eleven letters long and the last letter was "u." It was also known that the lunch meeting at Le Mas des Oliviers had been conducted in French. "It's sure not me," Tory senator Gerald Ottenheimer told the *Globe*'s Allan Freeman. "I'm from Newfoundland." When Freeman asked Saskatchewan Liberal senator Sidney Buckwold if it could be him because he had a long name, the senator replied ingenuously, "I don't speak French." Senator James Kelleher took it more seriously. "I was solicitor general at the time," he huffed. Everyone knew it was Charbonneau.

While the testimony continued, Canadians had a rare opportunity to peer into the heart of an RCMP operation. If they were listening carefully or reading between the lines, they soon learned that the force was as much a hotbed of political ambition as the Hill itself. When Deputy Commissioner Hank Jensen gave his testimony, for example, his strong dislike of Inkster was unmistakeable. Jensen, an experienced criminal investigator, believed that he, not Inkster, should have replaced Bob Simmonds as commissioner in 1986. Inkster had been an administrator — head of personnel and Simmonds's executive assistant — before being given the top job; he had little experience in criminal investigations. And both Jensen and Stamler were among those senior officers who were unhappy with the close relationships between Simmonds and Inkster and Mulroney and his cronies.

Although it was one of the RCMP's best-kept secrets and not one he shared with the Marin inquiry, Jensen was one of the few who knew of a favour Inkster had once done for Simmonds. As commissioner, Bob Simmonds had been under considerable stress. On one occasion, a couple of years before retiring, he had disappeared for a few days. No one knew where he was, and the force's brass were frantic with worry. About a week after his disappearance, a call came in from a police officer in Los Angeles. We have a guy here who says his name is Bob Simmonds, the officer said; he claims he's the commissioner of the RCMP. You folks know him? Inkster helped to retrieve the wayward commissioner and did so with the utmost secrecy and tact. When Simmonds retired, he recommended Inkster as his replacement.

A clear indication of Jensen's lack of respect for Inkster was his authorization of the use of Vidosa — the informant who had blown the whistle — despite the ban by Simmonds. "I went into it with my eyes wide open," said Jensen defiantly; the force had enjoyed "many successes" with Vidosa. "Nothing is forever. I don't believe one parliament binds a future parliament. I don't believe one commissioner of the RCMP binds another commissioner of the RCMP." And when he went on to describe the kind of informant the RCMP employs for sensitive operations, he might well have been describing Mike Mitton. "They probably do not come from the upper strata of your society. They probably have connections with undesirables. They sometimes have been involved with forms of criminal activity over their life." When an operation ends, they can feel a void in their lives, he said, and they will sometimes turn to the media for recognition.

At the end of January, Marin was scheduled to hear from Paul Vidosa, but Vidosa, who was supposed to testify in camera, cancelled at the last minute. Unless he could testify in public, he refused to say a word. An unidentified man had phoned his wife the week before, he explained, and threatened her and their three children. The only way he could protect his family was to testify in public. Lawrence Greenspon, Vidosa's lawyer, explained his client's reasoning. Vidosa, he said, had no plans to name names in his testimony, but the only way he could prove it was to testify in public. Marin offered a compromise:

he would take Vidosa's testimony in private but release censored transcripts soon afterwards. Forget it, said Vidosa.

Marin himself was deeply troubled by some unusual conversations he had had. He confided to one or two people he trusted that someone was trying to "buy" him. (Marin himself refuses to be interviewed on this subject.) He knew that the Conservative government was hoping for a report that concluded the Mounties were out of control in their Cogger investigation. Such a report would force the RCMP to abandon further investigations into Cogger's activities.

One day in 1990, while he was getting ready to begin the inquiry, Marin received a phone call during a business meeting he was attending at Montreal's Château Champlain Hotel. His caller was a top civil servant. At the time, as head of the RCMP External Review Committee, Marin had the rank and salary of a deputy minister; when he took on the inquiry, he also assumed the status of a judge. The bureaucrat was blunt. "I just met with the prime minister. He wants to appoint you to a senior position." Mulroney had instructed him to telephone Marin, the bureaucrat explained, adding that the prime minister had said that "it was about time for [Marin] to get a promotion."

The telephone conversation was brief. "It came from [someone] high," confirmed a source close to Marin. "It was a person in authority very close to the prime minister. The civil servant was very polite. He told Marin, 'You were very good to have accepted the mandate to do the commission of inquiry. You know we will not forget that you have rendered many services to the government, and now it is time for you to be given another appointment.'"

Marin's reply was equally to the point. "Look," he responded, "I am in Montreal and I am presiding over a hearing into the RCMP and I am sorry . . . but I can't talk about this now. Thank you very much."

It was more than being placed in an awkward position, it was downright dangerous to even think about accepting a promotion from the prime minister while he was presiding over an inquiry into circumstances surrounding the RCMP and the prime minister's close friend. Not wishing to offend his caller, Marin added that he would consider the offer if it were to be made later. But Marin was also too experienced not to understand the implications of the conversation, and he felt it would be prudent to mention it to the legal counsel to the inquiry — which he did.

Marin may have rebuffed the bureaucrat, but Cogger's friends did not give up. A few weeks later another approach was made, this time at a dinner in Ottawa, by a lawyer close to Mulroney, Cogger, and Charbonneau. "The government won't forget you for all the work you have done," he told the startled Marin that night. After claiming to know everything that was going on in the Tory party, the lawyer emphasized, "You will not be forgotten; I've heard that a nice appointment is on the way." Marin considered this approach even more direct than the call from the senior public servant. Soon afterwards the inquiry wrapped up its hearings — which, incidentally, cost nearly $1 million in lawyers' fees and administrative expenses — and Marin went off to write his report. It was while working on his final draft that the bureaucrat phoned him a second time. This time he asked Marin when he would be free to accept his next appointment. Once again, Marin fended off his query. "I am in the process of writing the report," he replied. "I don't know."

Marin's report finally appeared in April 1991. Cogger and his allies were hoping for a strong assault on the Mounties, but they were bitterly disappointed. The RCMP's SFIU had acted ethically, concluded Marin. They had good reasons to target Cogger and to try to get to the bottom of the COSICS affair. The force's initial investigation of the COSICS bidding process had been "somewhat cursory," but the officers in the SFIU "were overworked and understaffed at the time." A major new investigation into the COSICS affair was entirely justifiable. "Suffice it to say," wrote Marin, "questions have been raised [about COSICS] during the Inquiry which cause me great concern."

Marin defended the SFIU, saying they had been assigned "new and sensitive areas of enforcement without the appropriate resources. These resource problems seriously undermined the ability of the Unit to act responsibly and effectively." While Marin rapped the SFIU on the knuckles for using an unreliable undercover agent like Vidosa, the full force of his report was in support of the activities of Jensen, Stamler, Beauchemin, and Quigley.

Not surprisingly, René Marin did not receive the federal appointment that had been dangled before him. In January 1992, less than one year after his report was made public, the government moved to abolish the RCMP External Review Committee and Marin was out of a job. Ironically, the legislation that would have dissolved the committee was blocked by the Senate. Jennifer Lynch, president of the Progressive Conservative Women's Association, was named to replace Marin. She was still there two years later. Today Marin works in Ottawa as a security consultant.

CHAPTER FIFTEEN

GIGAMESS

B Y 1989 MICHEL COGGER HAD TURNED INTO THE TORY PARTY'S very own Pigpen, the troubled little character in the Peanuts cartoon strip who wanders about, trailed by a perpetual cloud of dust. From the day in June 1983 when he threw a Saint-Jean-Baptiste Day party at his farm to celebrate Mulroney's leadership victory and found his swimming pool filled with fresh manure, to the day when he discovered that the federal government had garnisheed his Senate salary, Cogger's miseries had been multiplying like fruit flies. Notwithstanding his troubles, Cogger was extremely well liked by his many acquaintances, friends who have remained steadfast and loyal. They are amused by his lively sense of humour, his wit, and his love of a good party; they dismiss his failings with a tolerant shrug.

Drink and fiscal extravagance are the two demons responsible for most of his problems. He has twice been convicted of drunk driving, and his loose tongue has been an endless curse for both himself and his party. The cross-Atlantic conversation with a fellow airline passenger who turned out to be Rod Stamler was just one example of Cogger's indiscretion. Cogger was known to talk openly in bars and at social events about the seamier activities of the Conservative Party, a habit, one friend says, that earned him a reprimand from Guy Charbonneau, who issued a stern warning about his excessive drinking and loose lips. Although Charbonneau says he never called Cogger on the carpet,

Cogger, during one of his drinking bouts, told others about Charbonneau's putting him on notice.

His lavish lifestyle is legendary. The farm near Knowlton, Quebec, is a large property that includes a Victorian house, a servant's cottage, a pool, and extensive stables. Cogger enjoys horseback riding in the Eastern Townships hills with companions like Laurent Beaudoin, the chairman of Bombardier. Knowlton is the summer home to many of the country's wealthiest power brokers, and their houses are a testament to the affluence that gathers around Lac Brome every June. Cogger's undoing is that he cannot resist emulating the ways of the wealthy, a weakness that has driven him deeply into debt. For years in Knowlton, the hardware stores and other small merchants have politely refused him credit, knowing his neglect of their overdue bills.

Cogger also fancies himself a dealmaker, which too often during the Tory years led him to boast about his close ties to Mulroney. Did Cogger have influence? Did he have Mulroney's ear? The answer is irrelevant because Mulroney allowed the ambiguity that enabled Cogger to exploit their relationship. He was given room to operate, and his indiscretions were always forgiven. As Mulroney told his biographer L. Ian MacDonald, Michel "will always be number one on my hit parade." Each was an usher at the other's wedding, and each is a godfather to one of the other's children. Ever since their days together at Laval, the men have been close, their friendship strained only in 1983 when Mulroney found it prudent to distance himself from Cogger because of Cogger's association with Walter Wolf. By May 1986 Mulroney felt enough time had passed that he could offer his chum a Senate seat without risking criticism. Godfather, usher, number one: no wonder no one dared call Cogger's hand.

But even Cogger could not have predicted that he would become a key player in a deal for a company called GigaText that would contribute to the downfall of Grant Devine's government in Saskatchewan. Or that his relationship with GigaText's owner, Guy Mont-petit, would bring on his own darkest hour.

That Cogger and Montpetit were in Saskatchewan at all was thanks to Cogger's friendship with Ken Waschuk, the small-time Regina pollster who was a member of Mulroney's inner circle during the run for the 1983 leadership. At that time, Waschuk was a staff member at PC Party headquarters in Ottawa, where he remained until the Mulroney victory; but soon afterwards he returned to Saskatchewan where new opportunities awaited him with Grant Devine's Conservative government, elected in 1982. In 1985 Mulroney appointed Waschuk to the Air Canada board, and in 1988 Waschuk headed the federal Tories' election campaign in the province. When Mulroney made his daily conference call to what became known as his "kitchen cabinet" Waschuk was in on it.[1]

Saskatchewan was the western province in which the Mulroney network was strongest, and Waschuk was one of several useful contacts Cogger could exploit in the province. There was Bill Elliott, the Regina lawyer and one of the most prominent Conservatives in the province, whose brother, Dick, was married to Mulroney's sister. Another pair of influential supporters were Fred Hill and his son Paul, Regina developers and media owners who had historically backed the Liberal Party. Fred Hill and Mulroney had come to know each other when both served on the board of the Canadian Imperial Bank of Commerce. In the late 1980s the Hills' company, McCallum Hill, donated to neither the federal Liberals nor the Conservatives. In 1992, however, a $5,000 donation to the Tories shows up in Elections Canada records. The Hills are among the wealthiest people in Saskatchewan, and Fred Hill and his wife were welcome guests at 24 Sussex Drive during the Mulroney years. Finally there was Mulroney's relationship with Conservative premier Grant Devine, who seems to have hero-worshipped Mulroney. Whatever Mulroney said was fine by him, whether it be on the constitution or free trade or the privatization of Crown corporations. Over the years Devine gave Mulroney less flak than any other premier except, perhaps, John Buchanan of Nova Scotia.

When Devine's Tories defeated the NDP government in 1982, they took over a province that had always been prudently managed — regardless of the party in power — by a succession of tight-fisted prairie politicians. The Tories arrived to find a tidy budgetary surplus in the bank for the current fiscal year, along with a $3.5-billion long-term debt in Crown corporations. When the Tories were thrown out of office nine years later, the annual operating deficit was $975 million and the debt had ballooned to $15 billion, an awesome figure for this prairie province of 950,000 souls. And there was no mystery about the origins of the debt: it was the result of dozens of rotten deals the Devine government had cut with private enterprise; secretive, incautious, crazy deals that drove the provincial auditors to despair and rage. When they complained about questionable business practices and unethical behaviour, Devine responded by slashing their staff and turning over half the provincial audits to private firms, most of which had management consulting contracts with the government. Conflict of interest was no more than a theoretical concept to Saskatchewan's Tory government. The public service became deeply politicized during the Devine years; his government fired 2,000 public servants in the belief that they were NDP sympathizers.

Devine's deals sparked three provincial inquiries after he and his party were defeated; some of these enterprises involved hundreds of millions of dollars. Compared with most, GigaText was small potatoes: it cost the taxpayers only about $5.5 million. Still, this was the deal that got up the voters' noses, this was the last bloody straw. Devine admitted it himself in an interview. "Sleaze . . . well, it happens with every administration. I had some people with a lot of problems. I think with all the deals, the biggest thing was GigaText . . . It didn't work and we got painted with $5 million. We lost $50 million on a paper mill and got less flak than I did trying to translate some statutes into French."

Trying to translate some statutes into French was the whole justification for the GigaText deal. In February 1988 the Supreme
Court of Saskatchewan ruled that a number of provincial statutes
had to be available in French. It seemed an ideal opportunity for
Quebec businessman Guy Montpetit; his company, GigaMos, had a
translation system at the ready and a political contact in place.
Michel Cogger had been the company's lawyer since 1985.

Montpetit was a silver-tongued, silver-haired entrepreneur who
saw a great future in the high-tech industries. He planned to make
his fortune with silicon chips. He hoped to convert the former head
office of Hoffmann-La Roche — a modern fourteen-storey facility in
Vaudreuil, Quebec, that was once dubbed "Valium Heaven" for the
sedative that was produced there — into a manufacturing plant. The
only hitch in Montpetit's plans was financing, and he and Cogger
travelled North America and Europe in search of the funds they
needed to convert the building. Various brokers and advisers were
called on for assistance. One was Toronto businessman John R.
Gamble, the head of Offshore Financial Consultants, who had tried,
unsuccessfully, to find Montpetit his financing through a
Panamanian company. He sent a $5,239.87 bill to Montpetit in 1986
with a complaint that he had worked long and hard to raise funds
and wanted his invoice paid. Gamble had been no more help than
the others in finding the money.

But in May 1986 Montpetit met his mark. Takayuki Tsuru
was a Japanese multimillionaire prepared to invest his own fortune. Montpetit convinced Tsuru that he had the political connections to win federal government support for the factory, a claim
that was neatly demonstrated when his lawyer, Cogger, went to the
Senate that same year. In December, Montpetit received encouraging letters from officials in both the federal and Quebec industry
ministries, saying he was eligible for a total of $45 million in
financial assistance. Thrilled by these promising developments,
Tsuru handed over the first installment of a $39-million loan to

Montpetit in May 1987. Montpetit then went on a spending spree. In June he bought LISP Machines Inc., a worn-out high-tech company based in Lowell, Massachusetts, for $3.2 million. Among LISP's assets were a number of old Lambda computers, equipment that would eventually find its way to Saskatchewan.

Through Cogger, Montpetit had met Dr. Douglas Young, a Manitoba scientist who worked in the field of artificial intelligence.[2] Montpetit and Young shared a pet theory: that it was possible to use computers to translate English to French. Young had developed the software to do it. Montpetit and Young incorporated a new company called Norlus Inc. to sell the software, and they were not in the least discouraged by a federal study done in 1986 that declared their translation system unusable.

Montpetit's preoccupation in 1987 was to secure the $45 million in grants from the federal and Quebec governments. Despite Cogger's political clout and the relentless pressure he exerted on senior bureaucrats in the Department of Regional Industrial Expansion, the project kept being bounced. Cogger went into overdrive on his client's behalf.[3] He phoned Gabriel Voyer, then an official at DRIE, and ordered him to "get moving" on Montpetit's request for funding. Voyer said later in sworn testimony that in the same conversation Cogger claimed that Voyer's Quebec counterpart had approved Montpetit's application. He checked with Quebec and found that no such approval had been given.

Cogger also went after Michel Côté, then the minister of industry, raising Montpetit's project with him during the regular Wednesday-morning Conservative caucus meetings. Cogger arranged for Côté to meet with Montpetit on more than one occasion and at subsequent caucus meetings would ask him, "Well, is my project progressing? Will I be getting news soon?"

Cogger regularly harassed Julian Beliveau, chief of staff to Côté, about the progress of Montpetit's grant request. Beliveau said Cogger became irritated when told that Montpetit's chances were slim.

Another chief of staff, Paul Brown, who worked for Pierre Cadieux, then the labour minister, said Cogger spoke to him on about five occasions about the grant. Was he exerting undue pressure? "Senator Cogger was involved," Brown replied, "but in Ottawa you get used to everybody being involved in projects."

Another public servant, Louis Doyle, testified about a 1986 meeting chaired by Cogger that he described as the only one of its kind in his eight years at DRIE. Doyle was responsible for projects involving aerospace electronics. The meeting was attended by Côté, Cadieux, Cogger, and other government officials. Doyle said Cogger "was demanding a decision as quickly as possible, [saying] money had already been invested, as well as time." Doyle said he told the meeting that the matter would be referred to the department official responsible for Montpetit's project, but Cogger objected, saying: "Impossible. If he takes the project we are not interested. He's an incompetent."

Tom Creary, chief of staff to Robert de Cotret, who succeeded Côté as industry minister, was another Cogger target. He said that Cogger complained to him about not having a decision on Montpetit's request. Cogger asked for a meeting with de Cotret and once again made his pitch. Then he tried to convince Bernard Roy and Charles McMillan of the project's viability. Cogger pestered everyone. He even tried to persuade a Conservative cabinet minister in the Alberta government to support the project. The federal government hemmed and hawed and shuffled its collective feet.

While they were dithering, Tsuru was becoming nervous. He had placed $39 million in Montpetit's hands and it was not being repaid. In April 1988, the federal government finally turned Montpetit down. In October, Tsuru went to the police and brought a lawsuit against Montpetit. But when Saskatchewan beckoned, Montpetit was ready to spring. Once the court had told the Saskatchewan government it would have to translate its statutes, Cogger and Montpetit started lobbying again for government support for Young's translation system, this time in a province that was willing to be seduced by Montpetit's high-tech prattle. Ken Waschuk came on board as their key man and introduced Montpetit to Deputy Premier Eric Berntson. Berntson, a florid former pig farmer from Saskatoon, became so enthralled by the plan that he agreed to consider a more ambitious proposal from Montpetit to move the whole GigaMos operation to Regina. High-tech! Silicon chips! If the feds would cough up $20 million to help finance a factory, Saskatchewan would match the dollars.

Montpetit started wooing Saskatchewan cabinet ministers in earnest, flying them to Winnipeg, Montreal, and Boston in the Cessna he had bought with the hapless Tsuru's cash. Guests on the plane included Berntson, Science and Technology Minister Joan Duncan, and Trade and Investment Minister Bob Andrew. On May 10 Berntson sent a begging letter to the federal government requesting financial assistance for Norlus, the company established by Young and Montpetit to do computer-assisted translations. The letter went to Secretary of State Lucien Bouchard, whose department was responsible for administering the government's official languages policy, including translation programs. Ten days later, a five-person team of experts in translation and artificial intelligence from Bouchard's department arrived in Regina to meet Montpetit, Young, Waschuk, Terry Leier, an adviser from Berntson's office, and Otto Cutts, head of the Saskatchewan Property Management Corporation.

The Ottawa team were mindful of the 1986 report by another group of translation experts who had evaluated the Norlus system. "The machine produced good results on a pre-defined corpus," the report said. "When random sentences were tried the machine output was rarely usable." After examining the system for a second time, the team of experts recommended that the federal government not give any money to Norlus. The system had not progressed much in the past two years, they told Bouchard: "The weaknesses of two years ago are still present." They added that the Norlus theory was interesting but not practical. If Norlus used systems that were currently available, the experts said, some of the problems could be fixed, but

Norlus claimed to be ahead of those systems. "In light of the fact that the province is seeking assistance of $20 million and the company is preparing to market the product, one might well wonder what use is being made of this money," they concluded.

Despite Cogger's personal appeals to his old law school chum, Bouchard didn't hesitate. On May 26, in a letter marked "Secret," he wrote to Deputy Prime Minister Don Mazankowski concerning Berntson's letter of May 10. Bouchard was blunt. "The Saskatchewan proposal has no direct relevance or utility with regard to the question of provincial statutes," he wrote. "There has been little if any progress since it was evaluated and rejected in November, 1986." Bouchard urged Mazankowski to call Berntson and tell him the system had no value. At the same time Bouchard was also a practical politician and knew the rules of the game. Bouchard was prepared to offer Berntson $4 million towards the restoration of the French-language Collège Matthieu in Gravelbourg, Saskatchewan, which had been destroyed in a fire. "I believe that such an early commitment would please the Fransaskois community and the provincial government which has been under considerable pressure on this matter," he added tactfully. Bouchard sent copies of his letter to the two Saskatchewan cabinet ministers in the federal cabinet, Ray Hnatyshyn and Bill McKnight, as well as to Lowell Murray, who was responsible for federal-provincial relations, and Bernard Roy, Mulroney's chief of staff. Plenty of people were in a position to know that Bouchard had turned Berntson and Montpetit down.

Bouchard's clear warning about the uselessness of the system did not appear to have reached Saskatchewan, or if it did, it came too late.[4] The day after Bouchard wrote to Mazankowski, the Devine government handed Montpetit a cheque for $4 million; shortly after, he set up a new company called GigaText Translation Systems. Under the terms of an agreement crafted by Berntson, Saskatchewan held 25 per cent of the equity in GigaText and the balance rested with Norlus, the holding company owned jointly by Montpetit and Young.

Montpetit had sole signing authority for GigaText's funds; Waschuk and Leier became members of the GigaText board. And the $4 million? It flew into a GigaText bank account and effectively disappeared, lost in an electronic web of U.S. and offshore bank accounts.

Just before the deal was signed, Young and Montpetit had a conversation about paying off their supporters in Saskatchewan. Young later wrote a memo recording the details of their exchange, beginning with Young's explanation that he had invested $600,000 of his own money in Norlus, while Montpetit had put in only $150,000, and that was government money he withdrew from the GigaText bank account.

"Some weeks before the GigaText agreement was signed, Guy Montpetit invited me to his new home at Senneville," Young wrote, "and in a discussion about the forthcoming agreement I was told it is normal, in an agreement involving several millions of dollars, to provide 'considerations' to one or more people who have helped to achieve the agreement but who themselves are not members of either party to the agreement. Not having any previous experience or knowledge of this size of transaction, and having no reason at that time to doubt what he was saying, I said that if this was the custom, then we had to try to make some provision for it.

"Later, on a flight from Regina shortly before the day of closure, Mr. Montpetit brought up the matter of those considerations, and the total figures he mentioned, for the several people he said had to receive them, seemed to amount to many hundreds of thousands of dollars, and I expressed concern at this. In mentioning that I would not be able to come up with the money myself, he said that as he would have to raise the money, I would have to dilute my 50/50 share holding with him by agreeing to some new shares for him being issued."

Montpetit's proposal would give him 67 per cent of Norlus; when Young objected, "I was told that unless I agreed to this, the agreement with Saskatchewan could not be achieved because he would not be able to honour the promises he had already made to certain individuals. He also said he would hold the shares in trust, although he may dispense some to the named persons, and that one person in particular had to receive only cash." Young said he found out later that none of the considerations Montpetit mentioned had been necessary to obtain the agreement with the Saskatchewan government.

It was at this point that Montpetit and GigaText entered into an interesting real estate deal. Bill Elliott, the Regina lawyer, was a senior partner at McPherson Elliott and Tyreman, a leading law firm in the city. The firm's offices occupied a two-storey building in a suburb. The wealthy Hill family wanted to build an office tower in downtown Regina and went to Elliott for a large loan because he was chairman of the provincially run Saskatchewan Pension Funds. Elliott helped them win approval for the loan, and as soon as the tower was up, Elliott's law firm leased two floors. Sixty per cent of the building was rented to the provincial government for offices. Then the law firm sold its old two-storey building to the Hill family for $1.75 million, an excellent price for the firm. The Hill family needed tenants for the old building, too, and fortunately GigaText appeared just in time to fill the space. The lease arrangement made everyone happy.

As for considerations, the only two that appear on the GigaText books are those Montpetit gave to Ken Waschuk and Terry Leier, the lawyer who advised Berntson. Montpetit gave Leier $5,000 for his time and trouble, and he made a generous loan to Waschuk. As they explained it later to a sceptical public, one miserable rainy day in Regina, the two men were hacking their way around a golf course and Waschuk stopped for a moment. He was having a few financial problems, he confided to Montpetit; $150,000 should see him out of his difficulty. Could Guy see his way to a modest loan?

No trouble at all. By this time most of the Saskatchewan cash was in offshore banks, one of them the Bank of Butterfield in Bermuda. Cogger knew the bank well, and he was able to help Waschuk set up his own account there. The money was paid from Montpetit's personal Bermuda holding company, Koyama Trading Ltd., to Waschuk's brand new offshore company, Libra International Ltd.

The Saskatchewan money allowed Montpetit to arrange all manner of benefits. He paid himself a salary of $60,000, which seems modest enough until one examines the accompanying perquisites — an $18,000-a-month expense account, for starters. GigaText paid $35,000 a month to lease the Cessna jet for his travel — the same aircraft he had paid for with Tsuru's money. Saskatchewan's funds covered the expense of leasing the jet from himself. He used more of the money, $2.3 million to be exact, to purchase those old Lambda computers he had acquired with LISP Machines; he bought them from himself, of course.

Things started to fall apart in October 1988 when GigaText's twenty-two employees realized they couldn't get the computers to translate the statutes. By the end of the month Devine's cabinet had to accept the bad news that the GigaText system wasn't workable and that the $4 million was gone. Grimly, the government took over the company and continued to cover its operating costs. It was too soon to admit its investment in such a boondoggle. Maintaining a brave front was the order of the day until an expert assessor could evaluate the company's prospects.

Meanwhile, back in Montreal, examination for discovery was under way in Takayuki Tsuru's lawsuit against Montpetit. The court ordered an audit of Montpetit's finances to find out what had happened to the $39-million loan from the Japanese investors. Forensic accountant Pierre St. Laurent of Thibault Marchand Peat Marwick was engaged to sift through the records; his specialty was white-collar crime and money-laundering through false companies and offshore accounts. Some details of Cogger's finances were also hitting the press in December. The *Gazette* discovered that the Lawees, Cogger's partners in Pluri-Canaux, were paying for renovations in Cogger's farm kitchen. It found that Trans-Quebec Helicopters, co-owned by Henri Lachapelle and Jacques Blouin, had once paid the salary of Cogger's farm-hand. By 1988, however, that farm-hand, a man called George Smith, was being paid by Montpetit. The *Gazette* story caused Cogger more grief with Revenue Canada; it seems he'd claimed Smith's salary as an income tax deduction.

All in all, 1988 was a tumultuous year for Cogger. If it wasn't Beauchemin and Quigley setting up a sting in Ottawa to investigate him on influence-peddling in deals like the COSICS contract, it was the eagle-eyed auditors at Revenue Canada noting the farm-hand deduction or the fraud specialist Pierre St. Laurent sifting through Montpetit's finances. And things got worse in 1989. In January, just as Beauchemin and Quigley were coaxing Pierre Ducros to help them with Operation Sack, the *Gazette* ran another damaging story, this one about how Lachapelle's helicopter company had been awarded hundreds of thousands of dollars in federal contracts.

Back in Regina, Devine's government didn't know what to do with GigaText. Officials closed their eyes and gave it a loan on March 16 for $1.5 million to cover operating costs; the government's only security on the money was a derisory $137,000 mortgage on a condominium it was leasing for the company's operations director, Jean-Pierre Paillet. The government also paid to lease him a Mercedes. The NDP opposition had a field day; they called GigaText "snake oil."

In May, Pierre St. Laurent's report was released and everyone's worst fears were confirmed. It said that Montpetit would have needed $100 million to get his Vaudreuil silicon-chip factory into operation and that he had squandered Tsuru's money on a $1.2-million house, the Cessna, two luxury boats, and a private tennis court. Early in June Saskatchewanians found out about the $150,000 loan Waschuk had arranged with Montpetit that windy day on the golf course, and the NDP hammered the government about it day after day in the legislature. Montpetit defended the loan, saying, "Waschuk had rendered us good service" in securing the Saskatchewan government money.

Backed into a tight corner, Waschuk went on the offensive,

attacking the media for their reporting and claiming that the loan had nothing to do with GigaText. "That's a matter that's got nothing to do with this. It's got to do with my private business." What about his success in attracting GigaText to the city? "You would think," he whined, "that with all this publicity there might have been one good article that suggested maybe I did a good thing." The RCMP's Regina office immediately decided to investigate Waschuk's finances.

Waschuk and the government continued to deny that his money came from the taxpayers' funds that had created GigaText until Pierre St. Laurent unfolded his flow charts. They illustrated how Montpetit had washed the money from the government's account to GigaText to LISP to a new company called Edubi International Corp. to his personal holding company, Koyama Trading Ltd. in Bermuda, and then on to Waschuk's Libra International Ltd.

There were other fascinating nuggets in St. Laurent's audit. One was that Montpetit had paid $800 to Vaudreuil's member of Parliament, Pierre Cadieux, in trust. When the auditor went back to GigaMos's Vaudreuil plant to retrieve the cancelled cheque, he found the cheque was missing. It was the only document of thousands that was unaccounted for.

There were revelations that Montpetit had used the Cessna for purposes unrelated to GigaText; a year earlier, in June 1988, he had been ferrying senior Quebec Tories involved in the Lac-Saint-Jean by-election campaign of Lucien Bouchard. On one trip were party organizer Jean-Yves Lortie, Waschuk, Cogger, and Mario Beaulieu, Quebec chairman for the November 21 federal election; the flight was billed to GigaMos Labs, the Montpetit firm that had been looking for assistance from Bouchard's department. Logs showed Cogger frequently flew on the plane and once took a flight with his family to Bermuda. Montpetit used it for holidays in San Francisco with his assistant, Grace Sim, on one memorable occasion writing himself a cheque for $300,000 in spending money from the GigaText account.

By August 1989, Devine's government knew that they had to

take some action to defuse public indignation. They appointed Regina lawyer Gerry Gerrand as an independent adviser to see if charges should be laid in connection with GigaText. Three days later, after consulting with the RCMP, he stated that no charges should be laid.

The citizens of the province were horrified by this decision; so too were many members of the province's legal community. But to get charges laid, the RCMP had to go to the Crown prosecutors. The investigation of Waschuk was closed.

In Montreal, however, Tsuru won his case against Montpetit, who was ordered to repay the $39-million loan. Within days, the Saskatchewan government quietly closed GigaText and wrote it off as another of its many failed schemes. Early in 1990 the Quebec court ordered Montpetit jailed for two months for contempt of court: he had sold a sailboat and disposed of some furniture in defiance of a court order not to sell any of his assets. But the police were unable to arrest him; Montpetit simply left the country and disappeared for the next twelve months.

Michel Cogger continued to surface in the news. On October 31, 1989, the *Gazette* reported on Cogger's bills for legal fees to the Federal Business Development Bank. In his fifty-two-page affidavit, RCMP Inspector Antoine Couture said it was his conclusion that Cogger had not done any work to justify the payments of $74,250. Couture also noted that Cogger had received a total of $275,000 from Montpetit. A year later the Toronto-Dominion Bank foreclosed on his Knowlton farm when he failed to pay $304,000 in delinquent mortgage payments. Liens registered against the farm in 1991 showed that he owed a total of $178,000 in unpaid federal income tax from 1983 to 1990 and accumulated penalties and interest. In late August 1991, the Quebec Revenue Department seized Cogger's Senate salary for non-payment of $107,000 in Quebec income taxes; unfortunately $2,000 a month was already being withheld for non-payment of the federal taxes. His take-home pay was only $1,426.08 a month.

Desperate for money at this time, Cogger made what would

prove to be yet another foolish move. When he read in the papers that two shippers at the *Journal de Montréal*, Michel Bounadère and Pierre Gauthier, had won more than $5 million in a Lotto Québec draw, he contacted them for a $15,000 loan, impressing them, they admitted later, with his powerful connections.

Once again, Cogger's friends moved in to help. After the TD Bank seized his farm, John Lynch-Staunton told Mordecai Richler that he and David Angus passed the hat among the gang in Montreal.[5] On December 5, 1991, Cogger sold the property to a numbered company, 2732611 Canada Inc., whose only officer is listed as Jean-Yves Lortie. Also registered with the deed is an undertaking by the numbered company to be a guarantor for Cogger's debts to Revenue Canada. The numbered company was sticking its neck out for Cogger; not only does it have to answer to the mortgage creditor but it is also liable for the income tax. The farm, where Cogger still resides, is now mortgaged with two lending agencies: General Trust for $300,000 and notary André Bourassa in trust for a further $330,000.

On September 13, 1991, Cogger was charged with one count of influence-peddling for allegedly receiving $212,000 from Montpetit. Four days later, Montpetit was charged with giving $212,000 to Cogger as payment for the senator's influence. The RCMP issued a warrant for his arrest, and on November 15 Montpetit gave himself up to the police.

Cogger's preliminary hearing began on May 19, 1992, but other questions were being raised elsewhere. In June, at a meeting of the Senate committee on national finance, Liberal senator Royce Frith asked FBDB president Guy Lavigueur about the bank's use of lawyers. Lavigueur explained that the bank has an in-house staff of three lawyers as well as a staff lawyer for each region of the country. When Frith pressed him to explain why he would have hired Cogger and paid him $74,250 in fees, Lavigueur ducked. "There are criminal charges pending against a senator," he hedged. "There is a ban on information that applies to the press and witnesses." There was no such ban, but the committee's chairman, Tory senator Roch Bolduc, allowed Lavigueur to seek legal counsel before answering the question.

On September 8, Cogger changed his selection from trial by judge and jury to trial by judge alone. His preliminary hearing dragged on through the winter until February 5, 1992, when, in an extraordinary move, Crown prosecutor Pierre Lévesque declared he would call no witnesses at the trial. Instead he would file the 653 pages of testimony from the preliminary hearing for the judge to read, and the judge could make up his own mind.

On June 18, 1993, Quebec Court Judge Jean Falardeau found Cogger not guilty of influence-peddling. The judge said Cogger simply did not have the "guilty mind" or "blameworthiness" required for a conviction under the charge. Cogger and his family and friends were, understandably, elated.

But the senator's troubles are not over. First of all, the Crown is launching an appeal against Falardeau's decision. (Montpetit will not go to trial himself until that appeal is heard.) In July 1993 the two Lotto Québec winners grew tired of Cogger's excuses and sued him in Quebec Superior Court for the $15,000 he'd borrowed from their winnings. Gauthier said Cogger told them he was close to Mulroney and that he had studied with him and was godfather to one of his children. Gauthier said he did not know why Cogger needed the money; just that he had an "urgent" need. Cogger admitted he'd told the men he was expecting a $50,000 tax refund and could repay out of those funds. He didn't tell them he owed back taxes to both the Quebec and federal governments.

Cogger's salary is under seizure by the Banque Nationale for $17,000 in unpaid MasterCard bills, a year after the bank sued him for defaulting on a loan of $19,465.00. In August 1993 his sons' school, Collège Jean-de-Brébeuf, obtained an $8,549 judgment against him for not paying the tuition. (He was also sued by his daughter's school in 1990 for $1,414 in unpaid tuition.) Today Cogger still makes use of Lachapelle's apartment in Place Alexis

Nihon during the week and still works out of Walter Wolf's office on Sherbrooke Street. When he fell into arrears with the TD Bank, it took action against him. Cogger failed to pay the court costs so the bank seized the furniture from the office. Cogger called a lawyer friend to have the seizure lifted, and then he failed to pay the lawyer. In 1994, the lawyer filed a claim in Small Claims Court against him. And so it goes.

CHAPTER SIXTEEN

LEASES R US

EMPIRE AUCTIONS OCCUPIES A 10,000-SQUARE-FOOT BRICK AND siding warehouse on Cyrville Road in Ottawa's East End. Once a month, it is the site of well-attended auctions of estate jewellery, antique furnishings, and important paintings, events that attract two men who have become regulars at the weekend viewings over the past few years.

They're an odd couple, these two. Patrick MacAdam, one of Brian Mulroney's oldest and most loyal friends, often brings along his Jack Russell terrier, Birkenhead. His friend is Ottawa developer Pierre Bourque. On viewing days they wander about, chunky and solid to the ground, serious. They do the rounds, muttering to each other as they pull out drawers to examine the dowels, turn over old chairs to look for splits, and peer at the paintings to confirm the signatures. If something catches their fancy they might come Monday or Tuesday; one night, for example, MacAdam bought his wife, Janet, a magnificent emerald ring. But usually they're just here Wednesday nights for the art sales. Once seated, their thick bodies don't move a lot, but their eyes do; they never stop taking in the crowd, assessing the bidders. And when they bid, it's with the merest flutter of the catalogue, a lifted finger, a curt nod. Over the years MacAdam has acquired a nice collection of canvases — a Franz Johnson here, an A.Y. Jackson there.

Aside from their interest in antiques, one might think these men had little in common, MacAdam, the die-hard Tory, the fanatic

Mulroneyite, and Bourque the hard-bitten Liberal developer. But this pair has as tight a relationship as MacAdam had with "the Boss." Bourque was MacAdam's boss too.

MacAdam had started his career on the Hill as a low-paid legislative assistant, although he also claimed later to have been a consultant to Iron Ore of Canada. Once Mulroney was prime minister, MacAdam became part of his staff. In 1988 he won a plum diplomatic posting to the Canadian High Commission in London as minister for information, but he was back in Ottawa after a couple of difficult years there. Then he did what so many of his former PMO colleagues had already done: he joined a lobbying company. In 1989 he became an employee of Government Consultants International. There were three partners in the later years: Frank Moores, Gary Ouellet, and Pierre Bourque. Bourque's part-ownership was a well-kept secret; despite the best efforts of Sean Moore and John Chenier, publishers of the city's widely read *Lobby Monitor* and *Lobby Digest*, they could not prove Bourque was an owner. But they suspected it.[1] And even though Bourque owned a third of Ottawa's best-known firm, he hired an outside lobbyist as well, Montreal bailiff Jean-Yves Lortie, AKA "the Poodle," whose firm was Consultants Mirabel. Lortie must have been a useful man; not only was he fronting the numbered company that had saved Michel Cogger's farm, he was working for Pierre Bourque.

MacAdam was at GCI to represent Bourque's interests. He was not known for his astute business sense, but he accomplished one task for his boss that more than earned his keep. In March 1991 MacAdam sweet-talked officials at Public Works into renegotiating an existing federal lease with Bourque four years early, a move that gave the cash-strapped developer $1.64 million a year more in rent than he had been receiving. The building was Place Louis St. Laurent, which Bourque rents to National Defence. The lease had been signed in 1988 and was to expire in 1995, but MacAdam had been able to have it extended for another ten years at a higher rate of $10.8 million a year, with a 5-per-cent inflation rate tacked on.

It couldn't have come at a more propitious moment for Bourque. Place Louis St. Laurent had several liens against it, including one for $335,348 in corporation taxes by Quebec's Revenue Ministry. On October 18, 1990, the Federal Court of Canada had granted the federal tax department a writ allowing the seizure of Bourque's personal property, including his huge Coltrin Road house in Rockcliffe Park, to recover $786,851 owed under the Income Tax Act. To top it off, he had been an equal partner with his son, Pierre Bourque, Jr., in an electronics repair company that had gone bankrupt in May 1990.[2] The new lease saved his bacon. He was able to refinance the office building and keep his real estate.

"From conversations I have had with officers of the Prime Minister's office, Deputy Prime Minister's office and the office of the Minister of Public Works (Elmer MacKay), I am confident that all negotiations will be concluded before the end of April and you will have a new, signed lease which will expire in 2005," MacAdam wrote to Bourque.

When Gord McIntosh at Canadian Press broke the story on September 6, 1991, a Public Works spokeswoman was defensive. "We figured it was a good deal," said Louise Proulx. "We got it for a good price and it was independently appraised before we negotiated."

In fact the deal was odd for a number of reasons. MacAdam was a professional lobbyist but he had not registered as one under the Lobbyists' Registration Act, nor had he registered Bourque as a client when he started phoning high-ranking officials. Lobbyists who do not register their clients face fines of up to $100,000 or two years' imprisonment. The explanation? According to Gary Ouellet, GCI's chairman, MacAdam didn't have to register because he was doing the work out of pure altruism, not for a fee. "We are friends of Bourque," Ouellet told McIntosh. "Pat MacAdam is a close personal friend of Pierre Bourque's. GCI was not retained and has no interest in the St. Laurent Building." Bourque was not just a friend of GCI, he owned a third of the company. Bourque didn't pay because MacAdam was his employee.

Registration aside, this was as clear a case of using influence with powerful friends to enrich someone at substantial and unnecessary extra cost to the taxpayer as one might find. And it was not the first time Bourque had benefitted. As Glen Kealey discovered, Place Louis St. Laurent had been leased by the government long before the building was ready for occupancy. Between September 1985 and February 1986, taxpayers had paid more than $7 million to rent an empty building. Following Auditor General Kenneth Dye's attack on the deal in his 1987 annual report and opposition protests in the public accounts committee, Roch LaSalle, public works minister at the time, engaged Maurice Mayer to examine the arrangement. Mayer sided with Bourque. What a cosy arrangement this all was, what a taste of the future. Mayer, the Montreal real estate broker, Tory fundraiser, and Mulroney's counsellor, was a partner of Jean-Paul Tessier, another Tory businessman, who happened to be a friend and client of Bernard Roy, Mulroney's chief of staff.

As Frank Majeau had stated so bluntly, the Tories were intent on giving rich federal leases and land deals to their friends, and Tessier and Mayer popped up repeatedly in these deals. In April 1987, for example, Public Works Minister Stewart McInnes had to admit that the RCMP were investigating a lease given to Tessier. When opposition MPs discovered that Bernard Roy had been Tessier's lawyer for twenty-five years and that in 1985 the government had broken the developer's $1.6-million-a-year lease on Place Vincent Massey in Hull, replacing it with a much richer deal, they rose angrily in the House to denounce the new lease as political favouritism. Their indignation was based on the fact that Place Vincent Massey, the home of Environment Canada, would give Tessier a windfall profit of $15 million. His bureaucrats objected, but LaSalle overruled them. The lease was renewed for twenty-five years at nearly twice the price. LaSalle's justification was that the employees would not have to move out of the building for another twenty-five years. Another bonus, he said, was that taxpayers wouldn't have to buy $4.1 million worth of fire safety improvements because Tessier would cover those costs. In 1988 the RCMP said they had closed their investigation without laying charges.

Then, in November 1988, the *Globe*'s Andrew McIntosh reported that a new company called Le Bourg de Fleuve — owned by several prominent Tories including Tessier, Montreal psychologist Jean-Pierre Hogue (who was elected an MP in 1988), and André Gingras, the Tory fundraiser and business associate of Guy Charbonneau — had won a $10-million contract to lease space to ten government departments in Trois-Rivières. Maurice Mayer had been an original member of the group but had sold his interest during the negotiations. Another partner was L.M.B.D.S. Sidam Inc., an engineering construction company whose name could be found on the notorious Tory short list. Internal government records prove that Public Works had a less expensive option than Le Bourg. The department could have renewed most of its existing leases in the city for five more years or constructed its own building and saved at least $7 million over fifteen years.

LaSalle had kicked off the negotiations for the lease contract in January 1986 when he wrote to a senior bureaucrat asking that an agreement be negotiated with Le Bourg "so it can plan the over-all project and start construction." After that, Public Works worked on the lease with Le Bourg for nearly a year. Perhaps because of LaSalle's notoriety by then, someone at Public Works decided it might look better if they actually held a competition for the Trois-Rivières lease and asked for public tenders. Even so, it had the smell and feel of a rigged bid: bidders' sites had to be within a five-square-block area in downtown Trois-Rivières and have at least 2,300 square metres of usable ground-floor space. Given these specifications, only Le Bourg could win. And it did, on April 29, 1988.

How did the minister explain away this lease? McIntosh contacted LaSalle in 1987 just as he was preparing to retire from politics. All he could remember, LaSalle replied, was that he had asked for a study of the government's future office space needs in Trois-Rivières. When told that the *Globe* had a copy of his January 1986 memorandum, he tried to shift responsibility to Treasury Board, saying it didn't matter what he proposed because "in the end, Treasury Board has to approve the project or nothing goes ahead." As cocky as ever, LaSalle added that he saw nothing wrong with his requesting that a lease agreement be negotiated directly with Le Bourg.

But the documents McIntosh dug out of Public Works through access-to-information requests show that the project was put together in the expectation of winning federal business in Trois-Rivières and nothing could have stopped it. The paper trail began on April 14, 1985, when Le Bourg was federally incorporated. About eight months later, in December, LaSalle received a letter from the new company, offering to rent up to 100,000 square feet of office space in its new Trois-Rivières complex. The city's mayor, Gilles Beaudoin, had written LaSalle in support of the same project two weeks earlier. The city had assembled the downtown land and sold it to Le Bourg, then called 141398 Canada Inc., for $750,000.

LaSalle's office sent both letters to Guy Wolfe, director general of the Quebec region for Public Works. Wolfe drafted possible replies for the minister's signature and sent them to LaSalle on January 17, 1986. Essentially the letters said thanks, but no thanks. Nice of them to think of the government, but there were no plans at that time to consolidate office space in Trois-Rivières. But don't think the government is ignoring Trois-Rivières; it will shortly spend $8.1 million redeveloping the city's Old Port. These politic answers were not quite what LaSalle had in mind. A couple of weeks later he wrote to his deputy minister, Maurice Lafontaine, to say the project would have great socioeconomic spinoffs and the impact on employment in Trois-Rivières would be "very significant." "I would appreciate if you would talk with Courbec [the project coordinators who were associated with Maurice Mayer] to discuss our needs and negotiate an agreement so that they may plan the over-all project and start construction." It was an order.

Wolfe's boss told him to rewrite his draft letters to the mayor and the developer, "taking into account the comments of the minister." On February 20, 1986, Wolfe sent the revised replies back to Ottawa. This time the chastened public servant suggested that Public Works was developing "a tactical plan" to regroup all federal employees in Trois-Rivières under one roof after its ten existing office leases in the city expired. The proposed response to the developer said Wolfe "would be pleased to meet" company officials "to explore the possibility of integrating our needs with your project." Not long after, LaSalle was demoted to minister without portfolio, but the project went full steam ahead. To be fair to LaSalle, this was not one of his deals; he was just following orders. These developers were not his cronies.

By the end of the Tories' first term, leases and land deals had become one of the biggest boondoggles Ottawa had ever seen. While Erik Nielsen was deputy prime minister, he examined ways to eliminate duplication and waste in government through an ambitious project he called Program Review. As he worked, real estate became a preoccupation, and he made several recommendations about its handling. One was to move leases out of the public works ministry. "The reason is that wherever there are large sums of money involved, the crooks will come out of the woodwork," he says. "They are out to get a piece — by whatever means possible — of that huge chunk of money, and the largest chunk of money in the federal government is in its real estate holdings. My guess, based on preliminary research I had garnered, was that it was pushing $60 billion." Nielsen had ample evidence to persuade him he was right; alas, his report was scrapped and his recommendations shelved when he resigned.

Kenneth Dye was an outspoken critic of the government's management of leases and land deals, and he went after Public Works tooth and fang. Not only did he attack them for renting Bourque's empty building in Hull, he also singled out a deal with Donald Matthews, Mulroney's 1983 leadership convention co-chairman and one-time president of the party. Just three months after the 1984 election, said Dye, the government bought twice as much land as it needed from The Matthews Group Ltd. of London, a company controlled by Matthews, for a pesticide research station. Public Works paid $839,800 for it, about $546,000 too much, in Dye's estimation.

It started when Agriculture Canada went looking for 8 hectares of land for the research station. They narrowed a list of thirty-six sites down to four and of these four, three were 10-hectare parcels that were all more or less the right size. The fourth site — the Matthews property — was 27 hectares. This was the site that was chosen. Most of the parcel lay outside London's city limits and was valued at $5,000 an acre by local real estate appraisers. The government paid $12,000 an acre, leading to an overpayment, said Dye, of $546,000.

Maurice Mayer was among those who prospered as brokers in land deals such as these, striking a rich vein of contracts with the Montreal Port Corporation, which is responsible for shipping, container terminals, wharves, and other business activities in the Port of Montreal. Like other port corporations, it controls valuable real estate. Mulroney appointed André Gingras to its board in August 1985. In October 1985 he put Mayer on the board of the Old Port, a sister Crown corporation responsible for the city's historic port area. (Other well-known Conservatives joined him. Montreal lawyer Roger Beaulieu became chairman of the Old Port board. Beaulieu was a Tory fundraiser and a 1983 leadership bid supporter. So was another new board member, Georgine Coutu. Over at the Montreal Port Corporation, Bernard Finestone, the new vice-chairman, was a former Tory candidate in Westmount. Later, Mulroney named his former aide Peter Ohrt to this board.)

When Gingras first joined the Montreal Port Corporation, he found it was looking at eleven parcels of waterfront land suitable for port expansion. On the advice of its own real estate department, the corporation asked Public Works to start the expansion process by buying 150 hectares of riverfront land at Contrecoeur, 40 kilometres east of Montreal. In December 1986 Gingras recommended to the corporation's chairman, Ronald Corey, and general manager, Dominic Taddeo, that they hire Mayer to help them acquire land in the South Shore area around Contrecoeur.

"Public Works did the first work and set up the options to purchase," one source said. "They also hired surveyors. Then another real estate agent prepared the actual options." That agent was Mayer, who moved in after all the preliminary work had been done. Hiring him was a board decision, and Gingras readily admitted he'd arranged it. Mayer said he was worth it. "I am an expert in land assembly," he said in an interview at the time, "and I was hired because it all had to be done on an anonymous basis." In 1989, the corporation paid him $94,197 for acquiring a $1.97-million parcel of land that had belonged to Stelco Inc. and $92,500 for acquiring a $1.92-million parcel from The Prenor Group Ltd. In January 1990, Mayer was paid $33,031 for three other land purchases.

Later, the corporation spent $16.75 million on an adjacent parcel of land owned by the Iron Ore Company of Canada. On this occasion, the corporation said, Mayer had no role in the acquisition. But the question here was whether the land was even needed. Tonnage in the port had been dropping steadily and so had the port's net income, but port officials defended the purchase by saying they were developing a land bank. Another issue was the condition of the wharves on the property — they needed millions of dollars in repairs. Why should the corporation buy this land? One good reason was that Iron Ore wanted to sell it. The company had shut down its Montreal office and moved its Canadian operations to head office in Cleveland. It was a happy day for Iron Ore when it found the government so eager to buy its old site. André Gingras replaced Ronald Corey as chairman of the Montreal Port Corporation in 1990; that same year Maurice Mayer was appointed to the board of CNR.

The hunt for leases heated up when the bottom dropped out of the real estate market and the recession deepened at the end of the

1980s. A solid lease with the government — whose cheques didn't bounce — became more desirable than ever. Developers and their lobbyists were clawing for contracts and some of the scraps became very unpleasant.

In 1989 there was an uproar in the House of Commons over the government's decision to renew its lease with Place de Ville in Ottawa, the asbestos-filled (and, it was found later, fungus-infested) office tower owned by Robert Campeau that was home to Transport Canada. Initially, the government had announced its intention to lease a new tower to house the department, and twenty-six developers came forward with construction plans for a building that would cost about $200 million; Public Works Minister Elmer MacKay was adamant that the project would proceed. Just before the federal budget was released, MacKay and his chief of staff were called to a meeting in the Prime Minister's Office with chief of staff Stanley Hartt and told that for "optical reasons" the project was being cancelled in the name of restraint. The government said it couldn't afford the capital cost of $200 million.

But the proposed building was a lease deal; where were these "capital costs" coming from? It's hard to embarrass officials at Public Works — they are so used to brazening out these lease deals — but even they were unwilling to explain what was meant by "capital costs," nor would they comment on why Campeau won when his bid had not met the criteria. Not only was Place de Ville too small to accommodate the department's employees, the company wouldn't agree to a number of other conditions. And the lease would cost $7 million more than some other bids. Furthermore, the building's asbestos problem would take $35 million worth of new ductwork and renovation to repair, and the government agreed to pay half the costs. All in all, it was a very expensive deal.

Shortly after the negotiations with Campeau were completed, the flamboyant entrepreneur plunged into a spectacular bankruptcy, thanks to reckless and underfinanced department-store purchases in the U.S. What remained of his empire after the dust had settled was a restructured and downsized company called CamDev. The new boss was Stanley Hartt, who replaced the ousted Campeau in 1991. Hartt worked hard to keep intact the remnant of the empire. One of his objectives was to arrange stable long-term leases with the government on its Ottawa office buildings, the Journal Towers and the asbestos palace, Place de Ville. Stable leases did for him what they did for Pierre Bourque; they allowed refinancing of heavily liened properties. But Hartt didn't manage it without plenty of controversy; following the announcement of the government's restraint policy in the budget, it didn't call a public tender for the transport department lease.

In Quebec City, another real estate deal quietly unfolded in 1989 that never made the newspapers but was just as interesting as those that did. This untendered lease fell into place so neatly that one has to admire the brains trust that pulled it together. The matter began on January 25, 1989, when a company called Groupe G.L.S. paid fees to obtain a building permit from the city. The company was jointly owned by developer and Tory organizer Marc LeFrançois and a firm called Société Immobilière Primat, owned by four business-men from the Saguenay–Lac-St.-Jean area. As yet, there was no evidence that Groupe G.L.S. had the land, a contract to build, or even a lease for a finished building.

On March 2, 1989, a construction permit was given for a $1.8-million building. Three weeks later, on March 28, city council approved a resolution to sell 5,233 square metres of vacant land on the Boulevard de la Capitale to Groupe G.L.S. for $238,692. The actual sale went through on June 18, 1989. Less than a month later, Primat signed a twenty-year lease with Canada Post Corporation for a mail-sorting plant — the $1.8-million building described in the March building permit — which was to be constructed on the vacant land. The lease does not mention LeFrançois's name nor the names of either of his companies, Macyro or Rocois. It was Rocois, however, that now started to build the plant.

The final stage in these transactions took place eighteen months later, on November 29, 1991, when LeFrançois bought Primat's share in the partnership for $133,500. The four Primat partners went their separate ways, splitting the proceeds and no doubt congratulating themselves on earning a healthy fee for fronting the deal. Macyro took over the ownership of the land and the new plant, property that was now valued at $2,210,770. What Canada Post paid Macyro to lease the building is not known, but a twenty-year federal lease would make any banker smile — not to mention the property owner.

In 1993 Liberal MP Don Boudria attacked the Mulroney government for yet another deal, this time for reneging on an agreement between Public Works and a Toronto-based development company called Martel Building Ltd. For the previous eighteen years Martel had leased space to the Atomic Energy Control Board in its Martel Building on Albert Street in downtown Ottawa; by 1993 the value of the lease, which included a floor each for two government departments, was about $3 million. The federal government spent $1.5 million that year improving the AECB's space. After nearly two years of tough bargaining during which Martel president Sid McMurray agreed to lower the rent substantially, provide extra space, and undertake another $1.6 million worth of renovations, Public Works agreed to renew the lease. Suddenly it backed off, demanding a public bidding process. Public Works officials gave Martel three days to prepare a bid that took into account 150 pages of demands. Then Public Works awarded the lease to Standard Life Assurance. Martel filed a $35-million lawsuit in the Federal Court of Canada charging that Public Works had amended Martel's offer to make it $1 million more expensive and more costly than Standard Life's bid. After all the manipulation the difference was only 50 cents a square foot; it would have cost Public Works about $60,000 to leave AECB and the other departments where they were. "We're devastated," said McMurray. "And I am so angry. They've justified this with all kind of numbers but it's nonsense." McMurray also claims it will cost taxpayers an extra $5 million to move the AECB to the Standard Life building.

Standard Life's ace up its sleeve was its leasing agent, Brendan Hanna. Not only had Hanna organized Mulroney's 1992 $500-a-plate annual fundraising dinner in the capital, he was also the chief Ottawa bagman for Jean Charest's leadership bid. Sources familiar with the deal say a standard agent's commission for clinching the lease would be as much as $800,000.

Hanna enjoyed success with other recent leases as well. He arranged for Standard Life to team up with an Ottawa builder, José Perez, after Perez and a Toronto-based developer, Bramalea, had ended their partnership. PerezBramalea had won the contract for a sixty-six-year agreement to refurbish and operate the historic Chambers Building at the corner of Sparks Street and Elgin in downtown Ottawa, a stone's throw from Parliament Hill, with a plan that included a fourteen-storey tower behind the Chambers Building itself. When Bramalea pulled out because it was in bankruptcy proceedings, Standard Life stepped in. But to make the development plan viable, Perez told the government, he had to have a major tenant. In a deal worth $58 million, the government arranged for the National Capital Commission to occupy about 85 per cent of the space. Competing Ottawa developers were incensed; they had been assured that no anchor tenant was promised to the partnership; such an arrangement, they said, was grossly unfair. Once a major federal tenant is promised to a developer, where is his risk?[3]

There wasn't much risk for Perez, who became the city's new Robert Campeau during the Tory years. In the Liberal era of Pierre Trudeau, Campeau had started modestly like Perez — both built suburban housing. But Campeau moved on to federal office buildings and became a multimillionaire; Perez had the same ambitions. His big chance came with the new Canada Post headquarters in 1991. Perez had an unusual contact at Canada Post in Georges Clermont, the vice-president of finance whose responsibilities included real estate. Clermont's son was a Formula One car racer, and Perez was his sponsor. When Perez teamed up with Bramalea, the partnership won the $170-million contract for the new headquarters.

The Canada Post headquarters and the Chambers Building development were the two richest federal construction contracts in Ottawa during the Mulroney years, and Perez had them both. People close to him say his style is extraordinary; no one but Perez himself completely understands his business. He moves his deals through a maze of at least two dozen companies, using three law firms and two accounting firms. He works with clients one on one and keeps every deal close to his chest. "I was asked to do certain things that were unacceptable to me," said one former employee. "He would tell me to go and 'fix it, offer him anything.' Do whatever it took to get the deal."

Perez overreached himself when he suggested to Elmer MacKay, just before the cabinet changed in June 1993, that he was interested in buying one of the government's crown jewels, 240 Sparks Street, a complex that houses the Bank of Canada, the Industry Department, and Holt Renfrew, among others. "He proposed to buy it if the government would give him a twenty-five-year lease at a billion dollars a year," said one political aide. "MacKay told him to fuck off." Some long-time public servants are predicting the withering of Perez's influence now that the Liberals are in power; when he sought bankruptcy protection at the end of August 1994, after racking up debts of $40 million, their predictions appeared to be coming true.

Like Hanna, Perez had powerful allies, among them Guy Charbonneau, who often entertained him at intimate dinners in the splendid private dining room he commanded as Speaker of the Senate. Perez bragged about his friendship with Charbonneau to his staff. In an interview in his Montreal office in July 1994, Charbonneau confirmed that Perez's boasts were quite true; he and Perez were friends. At first the senator demurred over questions about whether he had assisted the developer in obtaining the contracts with Canada Post and the NCC. "How could I help with leases?" he asked with a slight smile. "I was Speaker of the Senate. I had one social secretary and one secretary and my hands were full." Eventually, however, Charbonneau did admit that he made regular calls to government officials and ministers' offices about contracts and leases. "I may have asked on contracts sometimes because people have been helping us for years . . . If they are qualified, could they be on the list? Every member of Parliament does that. With Perez, I helped him be considered, but that's it. I think it's the department that decides."

When it came to leasing deals, well-placed Tories say now, Guy Charbonneau had considerable influence over the decisions. "But you rarely saw the hand of the man," said one of these Tories. There was a moment, though, just at the end of the Mulroney mandate, when he did show his hand. The lease in question was extremely valuable and it went to a Montreal-based company owned by two families, the Vocisanos and the Favrettos.

The families were closely related and had done well in Montreal in the construction and real estate industries. Angelo Favretto, one of the family's elders, was president of Favo Holding, a real estate holding company, and by some fortuitous act of fate he had attended St. Francis Xavier University. Other family members, including Maurizio Favretto and Mario and Robert Vocisano, were involved with Angelo in several construction companies — Dominic Supports and Forms Ltd., Concrete Column Clamps (CCC) Ltd., North American Granite, Plurico Investments, and Ancor Granite Tile, Inc. — as well as in several numbered companies. The families had extensive holdings in Ottawa, including apartment buildings owned through a company called Bona Building and Management Ltd.

In 1990 Bona started work on a seven-storey office tower on the Vanier Parkway and McArthur Avenue in Ottawa, not far from RCMP headquarters further south on the parkway. "Building boom starts in Vanier," read the September 1990 headline in the Ottawa *Citizen*, describing a number of projects under way in the community. It's too bad that Stanley Levine didn't look more closely at the brief story. Levine is an Ottawa developer who had the misfortune of buying, in

July 1991, the Chomley Building at 400 Cooper Street in downtown Ottawa. This building is the legendary Spy Central, the offices of the RCMP's "A" Division, an elite division that handled sensitive investigations into the activities of politicians and their friends. It included a national security investigations unit as well as the VIP protective force for politicians and diplomats. And it was home to a second federal agency, CSIS — the Canadian Security Intelligence Service. About a thousand people worked in the Chomley Building. Over the years the government had customized the building with the kind of security embellishments that would have done Ian Fleming's Q proud: high-speed secure elevators; bombproof walls, floors, and ceilings on many floors; an NCO mess and an officers' mess; three jail cells; a photo lab; a large gymnasium and locker facilities; secure access; and special wiring. The building was fit only for the tenants who were in it.

When the Chomley Building came on the market in 1991, Levine believed it was a good buy, even though the government's ten-year lease had just three more years to run. Don't worry, Public Works officials reassured him: although "A" Division wants to move into new quarters, there's no money for capital expenditures. Levine researched the building extensively and finally bought it, encouraged by the comments of RCMP officers themselves who said they expected to be there another five to eight years.

Five months after the purchase, Levine discovered that the government had no intention of keeping the RCMP in his building. Public Works officials now told him the government planned to construct a new building for "A" Division, and the best he could hope for was a two-year renewal with a one-year option at the end. And the rent offered, he believed, was derisory. For the next six months he argued fruitlessly with Public Works about the terms. His stubbornness cost him dearly: the officials started negotiating terms with the Favrettos and Vocisanos for the RCMP to move into their building when it was completed.

Levine was in an unfortunate bind. Because CSIS was staying

and keeping its offices on specially wired and designed floors that were several stories apart, security considerations would prevent the space between from being rented to an ordinary tenant.

Public Works finally put the RCMP's lease out to public tender. Again, because of the security requirements, only two companies could enter the contest — Levine's company and Bona Building Management. "The terms, requirements and conditions of the bid were tailor-made for the Bona Building," Levine later wrote in a letter to Dave Dingwall, the new Liberal minister of government services, in December 1993. The specifications demanded by the government would have required Levine to gut his tower and completely refit it. He was prepared to do that to keep his tenants, but then he found out the government was using incorrect figures in assessing his bid. Public Works, he explained to Dingwall, "was using an overblown and incorrect rental rate of $254 a square metre for the RCMP lease at the Chomley. In fact, the actual rate is . . . between $213-$215 a square metre."

Bona Building's winning bid was for $212 a square metre, but the move to new facilities would cost several million dollars over and above the lease. In May 1993, while the Tories were preoccupied with the upcoming leadership convention, Treasury Board quietly approved the Bona Building deal. When Levine threatened to sue, Government Services Minister Paul Dick listened to his tale, ordered an audit, and tried to repair the damage. But within weeks Dick was defeated in the federal election. "There is no question that there was gross interference in this contract," said one of Dave Dingwall's staff months later. Some senior bureaucrats agreed, while the ones who made the deal dug in their heels and refused to budge on their reasons.

In the meantime, "A" Division moved into the Bona Building. Pushing Bona, right from the beginning, had been Guy Charbonneau. And when the contract was secure, Charbonneau started lobbying for another deal: that the government should pick up the building tucked in snugly behind the Bona Building along with the adjacent land. The Vocisanos and Favrettos owned that building too. Charbonneau was certain that the RCMP were soon going to need even more space.

Charbonneau admitted he lobbied for the Bona Building and for the sale of the McArthur Bowling Lanes. "I remember something about that," he said, "but I can't remember putting any pressure or anything like that. I may have said, 'If it's feasible . . .' My point is, in the few phone calls I made, I said, 'Look, these people should have consideration, if everything is okay.' . . . And I think they should do it." Given his influence with the prime minister, given that he was often considered the most powerful man in the party next to Mulroney, given that everyone in Ottawa knew that the Speaker of the Senate interested himself in contracts and leases, didn't he know very well that his calls would be seen as serious interference? Charbonneau lifted an eyebrow, let a small smile cross his lips, and shrugged.

CHAPTER SEVENTEEN

SELLING SUMMERSIDE FOR A SONG

OST CANADIANS ARE SENTIMENTAL ABOUT OUR MILITARY forces and think it's a darn shame when a grand old base with a glorious military history is closed. We sympathize with the young families facing upheaval and unemployment and with the aging veterans, losing yet another link with treasured traditions. The last thing that concerns us is what's going to happen to the land and the buildings. The last thing we suspect is a real estate ploy.

Acquiring government leases and selling overpriced land is one reliable way to make a fortune, but the reverse of this procedure — *buying* land from the government — can work just as well. Especially if one buys it for a song. And a song is about all some people paid during the Mulroney years for thousands of hectares of military land and property. From 1984 to the spring of 1993, the Conservative government sold off dozens of old military establishments — everything from large bases like CFB Summerside in Prince Edward Island to equipment depots, usually without the public taking much notice. Eighteen radar bases were sold, mostly to the local governments or provinces in which they were located, and some of these sales worked out well for the communities, bringing jobs and prosperity. Senneterre and Chibougamau in Quebec were two such success stories. All too often, however, the sales resulted in prosperity for a few lucky individuals and nothing at all for the local citizenry. And there could well be more; in early 1994 the Liberal government announced another round of base closings as well as the shutdown of two military colleges, Collège Militaire in Saint-Jean, Quebec, and Royal Roads in Victoria. It now seems the provinces will take over these colleges and keep the property in public hands, but taxpayers should remain vigilant about the fate of the other, less visible institutions. We can learn from these lessons of the past.

CARTIERVILLE

The sale of Cartierville, an old military airfield owned by Canadair and used to test its planes, went almost unnoticed when the government sold Canadair to Bombardier in 1986. Until then, Bombardier was best known for making snowmobiles, but it had moved into manufacturing aircraft and railway cars.

Cartierville and the Canadair plant were located in Saint-Laurent, a suburb of Montreal; the airport was the last large parcel of open space in the city. In the deal for Canadair, Bombardier agreed to pay the government an extra $11.5 million for Cartierville, $5 million of which went back into airport improvements. The net benefit to the taxpayer was only $6.5 million. For its money, Bombardier became the owner of 152 hectares, or 22 million square feet, of urban land. Under the agreement any proceeds from sales of the land were to be put back into Canadair.

Four years later, in 1990, Bombardier announced plans to develop the land for housing. By this time, despite a real estate crash in eastern Canada, Greg Thompson, a financial analyst with Prudential-Bache Securities Canada Ltd. of Toronto, valued the land at between $114 million and $190 million. Company vice-chairman André Bombardier told *The Globe and Mail*'s Ken Romain that the company had formed a real estate division to develop the property, adding that the company had moved Canadair's assembly line to a new plant at Dorval Airport to free up the Cartierville landing strip for development.

By July 1992, Bombardier's real estate arm, now called Bom-

281

bardier Real Estate Ltd., was fully involved in a $1.5-billion project — named Bois Franc — to build 8,000 rowhouses, duplexes, and triplexes costing $86,000 to $299,000 each. As *Gazette* business columnist Hugh Anderson put it, "This means that Bombardier is starting with land that cost it chicken-feed but which is one of the last few available sites for large-scale residential development on the island of Montreal."

Curiously, Bombardier never made an announcement about Bois Franc; its shareholders found out what was going on only when the company asked the Saint-Laurent city council to rezone the land. The day after this story broke, a nervous stock exchange halted trading in Bombardier shares until the company made a statement about its plans. The company simply denied it was in the real estate business. "Bombardier is not entering the field of real estate development," said spokeswoman Hélène Crevier flatly. "The only thing we can say is that some of the land will be sold." Another employee said the profit would be only a "minimal portion" of the $1.5 billion and would come from land sales, not construction.

But by November 1993, the city council had amended the by-laws and the project was under way through a Bombardier subsidiary called Bois Franc Immobilier Inc. Bois Franc immediately started an aggressive selling campaign with a $500,000 marketing centre, complete with fireplace, wing chairs, and videos. The company made deals with an architecture firm and four builders to do the actual design and construction. Bombardier stands to become one of Canada's richest real estate developers thanks to a privatization that nobody really noticed — or understood.

FALCONBRIDGE

Like most of the other bases in Canada, the Falconbridge radar base was a self-contained community with administrative buildings, houses, and sports and recreation facilities. Situated on a hill on the outskirts of Sudbury, the base occupied 290 hectares of land and boasted 101 housing units. For the families living on the base, there was a school, a church, a library, a medical building, and garages with sixteen service bays. And there were excellent recreational facilities — a driving range, two ball fields, a downhill ski facility, a gymnasium, even a bowling alley with saunas. And finally, there were over 100 acres of industrial land.

After the government decided to sell Falconbridge, it had local appraisals done in 1986. The value of the entire package — land, buildings, and sports facilities — was set at $5.2 million. Then the appraisers looked at the value of the residential component alone. Based on estimated rental incomes, one appraisal came in at $1.58 million, another at $1.3 million. The housing units were expected to earn between $250,000 and $310,000 annually.

The government asked for bids and received two serious ones. On February 4, 1987, Public Works sold the Falconbridge base to General Leaseholds Ltd., a large property developer, for $140,000. That's *3 per cent* of its appraised value. General Leaseholds is a publicly traded company whose two principals at the time were Mitchell Seigel, a wealthy Sudbury contractor who owned a company called Acme Construction, and Edward Kernaghan, a Toronto stockbroker. The same day General Leaseholds bought the base, it flipped it to a numbered company, 676504 Ontario Ltd., a company registered to a Sudbury trailer-park owner, Henry Shepherd. He paid $190,000, using a $50,000 loan from General Leaseholds to finance the deal.

The excuse for the laughable price was that the base needed extensive work and so many upgrades that it was a white elephant. Even so, the owners have been able to keep the housing units rented so far without any major repairs. Shepherd sold the base a year later for ten times what he had paid, but no company has yet developed the property.

LAC SAINT-DENIS

Except for the fact that it was located in the Laurentians, a valuable resort area north of Montreal, the radar base at CFB Lac Saint-Denis near Saint-Adolphe-d'Howard was very much like Falconbridge, a small, close community of families and workers who enjoyed the excellent facilities even if their homes were modest. Because of its prime location, the base was valued at $8 million.

In 1986 there were three potential buyers for Lac Saint-Denis, all of whom met with Ron Lefebvre, an aide to Stewart McInnes. But the favoured bidder, one who had been backed by Roch LaSalle while he was still a cabinet minister, was a Montreal gerontologist, Dr. M. Duquette, who offered $1.1 million, jobs, and a new rehabilitation centre for the elderly. He intended to call his project Médicaville.

The only hitch for the lucky gerontologist was that while his was the winning bid, he found himself temporarily without funds. This was not an inconvenience suffered by the other bidders, but the government did not let a minor problem like lack of money interfere with the proceedings. The government let Duquette have the base anyway in October 1987 and allowed him to keep it rent-free for nine months while he raised the money he needed. A tough-minded Public Works manager in the Quebec region, Diarmid Hugh Hylands, did force him to pay $170,000 in interest for this period. Hylands's job was to find the best buyer for each property, and he was used to having his recommendations accepted. When they weren't, when he was forced to let Duquette have the base, he made sure he wrote a letter to McInnes expressing his displeasure, and later he shared the letter with a couple of reporters.

The provincial government eventually denied Duquette permission to build a seniors' rehab centre; the province already had more than it needed. So he tried a few other things; he opened a theatre, started a music camp, and began building a hotel. But he was never around much, and none of these activities provided more than a handful of jobs for the locals. Indeed, he brought construction workers in from outside the community. After he neglected to pay his local taxes of $70,000 a year for three years, from 1986 to 1990, the municipality took him to court. The case was eventually settled out of court for a payment of $100,000. At the end of 1989 Duquette sold all the houses on the base.

MOISIE

Of all the base sales, the one at Moisie caused the biggest controversy. It sparked a brief RCMP investigation, and it showed public servants what can happen when they confront a cabinet minister.

The Moisie radar base, which comprised 290 hectares of land and ninety-three houses and had once employed 170 people, was something of a hot potato because it was near Sept-Îles in Brian Mulroney's riding of Manicouagan. And it was desirable because the land fronts the Moisie River, one of the ten finest salmon rivers in the world. The other side of the property runs along the St. Lawrence River. Although fishing in the upper section of the Moisie River was leased to private concerns by the provincial government, the water beside the base was public. With fishermen coming into Quebec from all over the world to fish the Moisie, the base was a potential gold mine for anyone interested in a luxury camp.

Such a development was the dream of the local people, many of whom survived on welfare payments. The radar base had been the economic lifeblood of the community, and now the locals were desperate for something, anything, that would take its place.

In 1985 the estimated value of the base was between $4.5 million and $6 million; one estimate came in at $3.6 million for the houses, recreation facilities, and administration buildings and another $814,000 for the land. When the government put the base out for tender in February 1988, a familiar phenomenon occurred: the offers that came in were far, far below the appraised value. The two highest bids were submitted by Raymond Lefebvre et Fils Ltée, a Shawinigan company whose business agent was Conservative Party organizer Jean-Guy Côté, and by Sept-Îles hotel owner Pierre Thibeault. Thibeault was the choice of the town councils in both

Moisie and Sept-Îles as well as the Sept-Îles chamber of commerce; they believed he had the best plan to develop tourism on the base. There was a preliminary round of bidding that saw Lefebvre move ahead, but then more property was added to the package, and on the second round Thibeault came in ahead.

Just a minute, the politicians said. Both Côté and Jean-Claude Gosselin, an unsuccessful Tory candidate in the 1984 federal election and another aide to Stewart McInnes, interfered in the process at this point — something they admitted later, but without any apologies. Hylands reported that Côté and Gosselin insisted on a meeting with him. When they arrived at his Montreal office they were accompanied by Lefebvre and Lefebvre's brother-in-law, a man called Luc Olivier. "Côté came in like he owned the whole government," Hylands told *Gazette* reporters. "He said he had worked on cases like this before and that there were always ways of arranging things." The men told Hylands the purpose of the meeting was to find a way to help Lefebvre win the bid.

Hylands was summoned to another meeting in Ottawa in May. This time Gosselin was there with Raymond Lefebvre and Luc Olivier as well as Public Works officials including Liliane Poiré, the minister's chief of staff. Hylands had informed his superiors about the meeting before he went and was surprised that no one told him not to go. The purpose of the get-together was again quite clear — the base was to go to Lefebvre. Almost immediately after the meeting Gosselin was sent to a diplomatic posting in Jamaica; he denied knowing who Côté was when contacted later by reporters. Ron Lefebvre, the aide who had negotiated the Lac Saint-Denis deal, replaced him. (He is not related to Raymond Lefebvre.) After some manoeuvring Raymond Lefebvre was allowed to tack an extra $2,500 onto his bid to win with an offer of $187,500.

It soon became clear that a close friend of Mulroney's was also involved in this mess: Sept-Îles land surveyor Rodrigue Tremblay, who had been the 1984 campaign organizer in the riding and had been appointed to the board of the National Museums in December 1984. Once Lefebvre's bid was cinched, Tremblay emerged as a spokesman for the company.

Gosselin wasn't the only one transferred out of harm's way; so too was Hylands. He was pulled off the file and colleagues were told not to have any dealings with him. At a lunch with a *Gazette* reporter, Côté and Olivier defended the process, saying their man won because he was the highest bidder. "For us to win, it was like a Cinderella story. It was like winning the jackpot in the lottery."

As the *Gazette* discovered, Rodrigue Tremblay soon showed his hand; he was the individual whom people contacted to buy houses on the property. He told one prospective buyer that even though Raymond Lefebvre et Fils had bought the base, a new company was being formed and the ownership of the property would be transferred to it. Soon after the sale, the transfer did take place and a numbered company bought the property.

The story was far from over. The loser, Thibeault, was upset, and so was Moisie mayor Bernard St. Laurent. In fact it seemed everyone in the area was upset except Mulroney's office in Sept-Îles and Tory party officials. One of these, a party organizer in the riding, took St. Laurent aside during a casual street interview with a *Gazette* reporter and warned the mayor not to talk to the press.

Another unhappy man was Diarmid Hugh Hylands. He believed there had been improper political interference in the deal. He would not have recommended Lefebvre as the best purchaser. Hylands had studied the man's history and discovered that he was a salvager, not a developer. In other words, his interest was in selling off everything of value on the property to make his profit. Lefebvre had done this before at a Miron Cement quarry he'd bought; Hylands believed it would happen again, despite Lefebvre's written commitment to spend $340,000 developing the base. Thibeault's bid was different, he told a producer at the CBC's *fifth estate* when the program was considering a story on the sale; the bid complied with federal land management policy, which takes into account economics, the environment, and social benefits.

The deal was formally announced on July 26, 1988. After mulling it over for a few days, Hylands wrote Stewart McInnes a personal letter about the whole mess, telling him about the meeting with the political aides and explaining how he had been pulled off the file. McInnes did not bother to reply. By late September the *Gazette* had published details of the letter, the RCMP had started an investigation into the sale, and the Liberals were hammering McInnes in the House, demanding to know why he hadn't taken action on Hylands's serious complaints. All McInnes's answers were damaging. He figured the letter was just a bureaucrat complaining about a "personnel issue," he told the House, and he saw no reason to give the letter to the Mounties. Yes, he admitted, his aides had met with officials in charge of the sale, but there was nothing improper about this. Then Defence Minister Perrin Beatty got into the act, and the government line began to tack and shift. Beatty told the House the RCMP had already looked into the sale and concluded there were no improprieties. He also assured the House that no officials in the PMO were involved. The next day Beatty had to correct his statement in the Commons; this time he admitted the RCMP had opened a new investigation and that a junior official in the PMO had made "entirely routine" calls about the file.

Just as Dr. Duquette had done at Lac Saint-Denis, Lefebvre decided the August 1 closing date was inconvenient for him, and he refused to take possession of the base until November 1. This meant National Defence spent $20,000 a month on security, heat, and upkeep during those months, and another $10,000 draining the pipes. If these costs had been factored into the final price, Thibeault's offer, obviously, would have been far more attractive.

Hylands's predictions about Lefebvre came to pass. By 1990 the land had not been developed for tourism and all the promises of the millions to be invested in jobs and development, commitments required in the tender, blew away with the wind. Only one man was hired to work on the base. By 1990 Lefebvre's group had sold fifty-one houses for between $20,000 and $30,000 each, for a profit of over $1 million. Then they stripped the base of everything salvageable, including the equipment that had been left behind to help open a bank, a restaurant, a post office, and other small businesses. Lefebvre's group made millions from these sales. Nothing he did was of any help to the local economy.

The personal fallout on this case was also heavy. If there was a lesson learned during the Mulroney years, it was the serious consequences of standing in the way of a cabinet minister or the prime minister. Nor was it smart to speak publicly about one's concerns to the newspapers.

In St. Laurent's case, he went from being a popular mayor to a pariah in the community and he felt he had no option but to resign his office. A few weeks after the sale of Moisie was raised in the Commons, the country went to the polls, in November 1988. Mulroney's riding had changed slightly and he now represented Baie-Comeau; the new MP for Manicouagan was Charles Langlois. Langlois made it clear to St. Laurent's successor, Daniel Raymond, that it would be a good thing for the council to pass a resolution saying it did not support the old mayor. Without such a resolution the Mulroney government would not be inclined to do anything for the riding. The resolution was passed at the first meeting of the new council late in 1988. St. Laurent had always been well liked in the community; now he found people avoiding him. The best job he could find was as a jail guard.

Thibeault was a prosperous businessman before the sale, but he claimed that he had lost about $1 million, $200,000 of which he spent preparing his bid. Worse was to follow. Thibeault owned a company that did building repairs, many of them for Iron Ore of Canada, which had a big presence in the area. That work — including one $450,000 contract — dried up almost completely. Another problem surfaced at his hotel in Sept-Îles. Until he complained about the land sale he had plenty of government business, but after the story became public, he lost his federal clients.

As for Hylands, after his colleagues were ordered to ostracize him, he retired and went off to a long holiday in Europe. Shortly after his return he suffered a serious heart attack.

But Bernard St. Laurent survived to triumph another day. On October 25, 1993, he was elected as a Bloc Québécois MP for Manicouagan, Mulroney's old riding. His old constituents decided he was on their side after all.

SUMMERSIDE

In some ways, the sales of all the other military bases pale beside the case of CFB Summerside on Prince Edward Island. The beauty of the site, which is also known as Slemon Park after the late Air Vice-Marshall Roy Slemon, is unparalleled: 1,500 green and rolling hectares on Malpeque Bay in a tiny and proud province that has strict rules about land ownership and that depends on tourism as its number one industry. Most visitors are attracted for the first time by the lore of Anne of Green Gables and they come again because the Island is as gentle and lovely as they hoped it would be. The heart of Anne country is the town of Cavendish, just a few miles from the Summerside base. Japanese tourists are especially enthralled by Anne; they pour onto the Island by the thousands, and more than one canny business person has made the connection between Cavendish and an air base that can land large charter aircraft from the Far East. Furthermore, the new bridge under construction between P.E.I. and New Brunswick, the one the Tories pushed through in a final legislative fling days before the 1993 election, is also at the Anne end of the Island and also close to the base. Serendipity.

Summerside was no minor radar base with a desperate populace that could be frightened or bullied into submission, as was the case at Moisie. But the closing of the base was dreadful news for the

Island and for the town of Summerside, a community of fewer than 15,000 people. It meant the loss of 1,300 jobs in the area. To try to limit the devastation, the federal government announced it would set up a new $38-million GST processing centre in Summerside, which would employ 400 people.

But the GST centre would be in the town of Summerside itself, not on the base, which is several miles to the north. What would happen to the base's 253 houses, to the golf course, and to the Olympic-quality sports facilities with the pool and the arena? What would happen to the barracks, the administration buildings, the control tower, and the four fine, modern hangars? The government didn't have a plan for them until an idea arrived in the mail. A business-man in London, Ontario, Don McDougall, wrote to Barbara McDougall (no relation), who was then minister of employment and immigration. Don McDougall was a strong Tory who had been born and raised on the Island, the son of a CN station agent. His sister, Pat Mella, is the leader of the provincial Conservative Party, and his brother Phillip is the province's deputy minister of finance.

He was also a long-time federal fundraiser and had been a good friend of Mulroney's since 1957, when they met as Tory student organizers in Atlantic Canada. In 1972 McDougall ran unsuccessful-ly for the party's nomination in Vancouver, but was beaten by lawyer John Fraser. By 1973, after twelve years at Labatt's Breweries in London, Ontario, McDougall was made president of the company; he resigned in 1979. That same year Prime Minister Joe Clark asked him to head a task force on privatizing Petro-Canada. When the gov-ernment fell, McDougall won the party's nomination in London but was defeated in the 1980 election, so he went into business for him-self, setting up a project management firm called Rambri Inc. Rambri owns a Quebec pulp mill as well as Novatronics Inc., a Stratford company McDougall bought in 1983 that does electronic research for the aerospace industry. In 1994 Tory leader Jean Charest announced that McDougall was taking over from Toronto merchant banker Robert Foster as chairman of the PC Canada Fund, the organization that was run for ten years by David Angus.[1]

In 1989, when the government announced it was closing Summerside, McDougall wrote his letter to Barbara McDougall; her response was to ask him to write a report for her on his ideas for the base. Don McDougall hired his cousin Clair Callaghan, another prominent Atlantic Tory and the former president of the Technical University of Nova Scotia, to help him with an evaluation of future economic activity in Summerside. Their document was ready in 1990. Because of Summerside's facilities and equipment, the men recommended turning the base into a kind of private-sector aerospace shopping mall, with a couple of anchor tenants to attract other businesses. The report said the government should turn the base's assets over to a private corporation, which would then market the facilities, bring in tenants, and hire a management team.

The Mulroney government agreed to McDougall's recommendations and asked him to head up a new private corporation that would turn his plan into reality. There was no public bidding process, no tendering for the base, no public input concerning the base's future. Within months of the submission of McDougall's report, the government turned over all the assets of the base in trust to Rambri, along with $15 million to help develop the facility. In August 1991, Rambri transferred the assets to the new company, Slemon Park Development Corporation, whose chairman was Don McDougall.

The value of these assets was never formally determined. The military could only guess at an amount somewhere between $200 million and $800 million. When the government decided to close Summerside, Public Works officials were instructed not to do an evaluation. Their political masters told them they considered the base a liability, not an asset, and therefore it did not need an appraisal. The government of P.E.I. did do an appraisal for tax purposes, one that federal Public Works officials acknowledged was vastly lower than its real value. The provincial appraisal valued the base at $45 million.

The P.E.I. government under Liberal Premier Joe Ghiz was desperately worried about the fate of the community at Summerside after the base closed. The island has only 130,000 permanent residents and very little wealth beyond that created by the Anne industry and the Island's potato business, which is controlled by New Brunswick's McCain and Irving families. Even the provincial legislature building is owned by the federal government. The province could not afford to keep the base alive; it decided to cooperate with the federal government's plans, and Ghiz appointed two local businessmen to sit on the Slemon Park board. McDougall appointed the others. The board issued 100,000 shares to the new corporation, and share ownership was offered as an incentive to senior managers and investors.

The board hired a management team headed by a successful local engineer, Cliff Campbell, and began working with the P.E.I. Development Agency and the federal government's Atlantic Canada Opportunities Agency, run by Elmer MacKay. The strategy was to concentrate on a centre that could repair aircraft and train skilled workers in the industry, but there were hopes of attracting other businesses as well. It wasn't long before the corporation found its first anchor tenants. One was Craig Dobbin, the St. John's millionaire who was John Crosbie's chief fundraiser and Frank Moores's business associate in a number of endeavours, including the frustrated real estate ventures in Ottawa. Among the fifteen or so companies Dobbin owned or controlled was the world's largest helicopter company, CHC Helicopter Corporation. Dobbin agreed to open a subsidiary of CHC Helicopter at Summerside. (The CHC board was full of prominent Conservatives, including former party fundraiser Robert Foster; a newcomer to the board, since his retirement from politics, is John Crosbie.)

In 1992, the year Dobbin went into Summerside, CHC did well; it enjoyed a net income of $3 million on revenues of $84 million, according to reporter Deborah Jones in a 1993 profile of Dobbin for *The Financial Post*. It won many federal contracts for military support flights and search-and-rescue work, among them a 1992 $2.8-million federal Fisheries Department contract for surveillance and search-and-rescue along the southwestern Nova Scotia coast. A competitor who lost the contract to CHC was bitter. Wayne Kenney, director of marketing at Cougar Helicopters of Halifax and a former employee of Dobbin's, commented: "Our understanding is his mandate is to bid any contract he can, and to underbid whatever you have to take that contract."

The new Dobbin company at Summerside, Atlantic Turbines Inc., repaired aircraft engines for CHC's helicopters and for his other aircraft at the base, using hangars and equipment at the water side of the property. Today it is possible to drive almost all over the base, but one road — the road to the ocean and to the hangars — is barred. This is the road to Dobbin's part of the base. Visitors need a security pass to get through. Dobbin received a grant of $4 million from ACOA and another $1.75 million from the province, as well as 40,000 shares of Slemon Park Corporation. In return, Dobbin agreed to create 310 jobs within four years. If he maintains the jobs for ten years, until the year 2002, the 40,000 shares will be his permanently which means, effectively, that he will be the largest single shareholder in the base — and the taxpayer will have given him considerable financial support in his efforts.

McDougall himself has taken no shares, nor has he paid himself the large salary that was rumoured all over the Island. "Any perception that Don McDougall was making money on this is full of shit," said Cliff Campbell, who was the president of Slemon Park Development Corporation. "McDougall has the kind of integrity I've seen in very few people in my life."

Since the military turned the base over to McDougall's group in March 1992, the corporation has brought in another smaller anchor tenant, Bendix Avalex Inc., a subsidiary of Allied-Signal Inc. of New Jersey. So far Bendix Avalex has been promised no shares, but it did receive $1.55 million from ACOA even though it had just closed two plants in Ontario. Another company received $1 million to develop sports facilities; a restaurant got $400,000. Some of this money has come from a $6.5-million grant to upgrade facilities at Slemon Park from Canada Employment and Immigration, Barbara McDougall's former ministry. The federal government has given Slemon Park more than $25 million for development, and so far about eighty permanent jobs have been created. To entice new tenants in 1992, the federal and provincial governments offered generous twenty-year tax holidays to aerospace and aviation companies.

But by the winter of 1994 at least one senior employee began to wonder what was really going on at the base. In September 1992 the corporation hired Fred Fenton, who had thirty years of experience in the aviation industry, most of those at Pearson Airport in Toronto. Cliff Campbell brought him in to market Slemon Park, a job made easier in July 1993 when the airport was designated an international airport and aircraft on domestic and overseas routes could stop to refuel there.

Fenton believed Summerside had the best facilities in Atlantic Canada. Soon after he joined the corporation, he went to the aviation industry's largest trade show, held in Atlanta, Georgia, for 18,000 visitors and 685 exhibitors. Fenton had approval to set up a Summerside booth at the show, but just a couple of days before his departure, the management yanked his plans. He was allowed to go to Atlanta — "but all I had was a bunch of business cards and a handshake," he said. He still brought business back to Slemon Park, he said; the management thanked him and ignored his leads. "They waffled for months and months so I never pursued the business. The board was so secretive about everything."

Fenton suspected that the board did not want to market the base after all. It turned down an opportunity with Esso, the fuelling company for the airport, which had plans to build corporate aircraft for VIP clients and wanted to use Summerside as its construction facility. Then Fenton tried to interest the board in the enterprise of businessman Kevin Rofe, who hoped to start a small commuter airline in Atlantic Canada. Rofe was told there was no hangar space available for him, and when he protested, he was told he could rent bays from Dobbin at $20,000 a month. Everything possible was done to discourage Rofe, said Fenton; he and Rofe could only conclude that Dobbin did not want competition for his own commuter airline, Air Atlantic. Certainly Craig Dobbin led a charmed business life under the Mulroney government.

In September 1993 the Ottawa *Citizen* obtained copies of confidential government memos showing that the Tories wanted to turn over Canada's Coast Guard operations to a private company, despite fierce opposition from the public servants who insisted that privatizing the operations would be inefficient, could put the whole service at risk, and would cost taxpayers millions of dollars more than current budgets.

But at that time the operation utilized forty-two helicopters, so it's not surprising that Craig Dobbin wanted the business. Privatizing the Coast Guard had been his idea a year earlier. Dobbin's allies included Mulroney himself, who had been a guest at his Newfoundland fishing retreat in July 1993, along with Jean Charest and former U.S. president George Bush. Dobbin's registered lobbyist in Ottawa for his helicopter business, the *Citizen* said, was James Good, John Crosbie's former chief of staff. Referring to the privatization of the Coast Guard, Mark Dobbin, Craig's son and the company vice-president, told the paper that Good "has really been the one pushing things along in Ottawa on the helicopter deal."

When the first response came back from the bureaucrats nixing the idea, Transport Minister Jean Corbeil declared the report unacceptable, and he hired a private consulting firm to study the plan all over again. But the consultants too said it was a lousy idea, and the minister ran out of time. The 1993 fall election was upon him and the privatization scheme died. Had it lived, Summerside would have made an excellent base for the Coast Guard operation, and Dobbin would have solidified his holdings at the base.

Even before the election, matters were souring at Slemon Park. There was friction at head office and in September 1993 Cliff

Campbell quit abruptly; in February, Fenton and his small support staff were laid off. "I had five hours to clean out my office," said Fenton ruefully. "That's more than Cliff had." Campbell won't discuss his departure, but Fenton said the reason given to him was that there was no money. In the meantime, Craig Dobbin waits until 2002, when he will own 40 per cent of the former base. The Canadian taxpayer, who put up the money for all those jobs and improvements, will have no equity whatsoever.

A footnote to all this came in the spring of 1994, when the public discovered that one of Dobbin's businesses was in deep trouble. Rumours started bubbling up in March 1994 that Air Atlantic, a regional airline of which Canadian Airlines owns 45 per cent and Dobbin 55 per cent, couldn't pay its bills and was in debt to the tune of about $60 million. The Royal Bank was threatening to repossess one of its planes. In early May 1994, Dobbin filed for protection under the Bankruptcy and Insolvency Act to stop angry creditors from seizing company assets. Dobbin told the court he hoped to have a restructuring plan ready within six months. Despite this difficulty, Dobbin's other companies seem to be healthy, and no one expects to see the Newfoundlander on the bread line. If Air Atlantic fails, the rest of his massive empire is still intact. And he's still got 40 per cent of Summerside, and that's not bad.

RETURN TO NOVA SCOTIA

I T WAS 1 P.M. ON MONDAY, SEPTEMBER 19, 1988, AND MOST OF THE
overnight guests at the Wandlyn Inn in Dartmouth had checked
out of their rooms. Mr. P. Graham of Kentville, Nova Scotia, in
Room 157 should have been among them; he'd told the maid
the day before he was staying just one more night. When she tapped
on his door and heard no answer, she wasn't surprised. She inserted
her pass key, opened the door, and walked into a horror movie. Blood
everywhere, in thick pools on the rug, soaked into the sheets, spat-
tered on the furniture. And the stabbed and lacerated body of a man,
naked, kneeling on the floor, his arms outstretched on the bed.

Eleven minutes later the Dartmouth police arrived. Even hard-
ened officers drew their breaths when they saw the room. The bathroom was almost worse than the bedroom. Dried blood covered the
floor. The bathtub was half-full of blood-stained water. A serrated
blood-stained knife rested on the toilet-paper holder and another
bent knife was found in the tub. Three empty vials — two of Halcion
and one of Serax, both anti-depressants — were found in the man's
carrying bag. By 2 p.m. Dr. Roland Perry, the chief medical examin-
er for Nova Scotia, was at the motel, as the shocked staff clustered
in the hallways, kept away by the police.

The body in the room was not that of Mr. P. Graham of Kentville. It was the body of John Grant, a prominent forty-seven-year-
old Halifax lawyer and Conservative Party bagman, whose frantic

family had been searching for him since Saturday, when he had disappeared. Grant had checked into the motel later that day under a fictitious name, went out Saturday night and was seen by people who knew him, and was still alive on Sunday morning at 11 when the maid had knocked on his door. That was when he had called to her, through the door, that he was staying on another night. Sometime in the next twenty-four hours, this nightmare had happened.

A suicide, was the rumour that raced through Halifax. John's killed himself. But the room, they whispered to one another, they say it was an abattoir. No, of course it wasn't, chided close friends, frightened and alarmed, trying to stifle a scandal, trying to shield his devastated wife and children. John was just very depressed, he just . . . well, he took his own life. It's a dreadful thing, but who could blame him? Just thinking of his family, he was. Now don't be spreading any stories. A suicide it was, then, and so certified Dr. Roland Perry on January 10, 1989, nearly five months later.

But look at the report Dr. Perry filled in at the post-mortem on September 20, the day after the maid found the body: "Multiple cutting and stabbing injuries," including seventeen to the heart. His handsome face ruined with several more cuts, including one on the chin and a deep V-shaped cut in the forehead. A scrape over the nose. A clean horizontal cut to the neck, five centimetres long. At least nine cuts to the left arm at the wrist and elbow. Several more to the right arm at the wrist and elbow. A bruise at the thumb. Stabs in the chest savage enough to collapse the left lung and part of the right lung. A deep stab to the abdomen, deep enough to expose the intestines. A toxicological examination showed there was no alcohol in his blood. A liver scan detected traces of benzodiazepines — tranquillizers — in his system. A glass of straw-coloured liquid was found in the bathroom, presumably the dissolved tranquillizers, but it doesn't appear that he swallowed any of this. If he had tried to dissolve the Halcion the liquid would have been blue.

John Grant had reason to take his own life. It's just that it was a hard and crazy way to die, and he certainly wasn't high or stoned or drugged or drunk when he did it. Could it have been murder, asked some. Of course not, others snapped, silencing the impudent who dared to question. He took a knife from the kitchen drawer. A knife was missing. That's why his family was so worried. He took his own life, that's sure. All things considered, some believed, it was the brave and decent thing for Grant to have done.

Grant had toppled from grace in a most spectacular way. Born in Sydney, raised in Halifax, he'd graduated from Dalhousie Law School and moved to Ontario, where he was called to the bar in 1967. For the next four years he practised law at McMillan Binch in Toronto, the firm John Turner went to when he stormed out of Pierre Trudeau's Liberal cabinet in 1975. In those days it was a small firm, but well respected, and Grant soon became one of the lawyers to watch in the city's legal establishment. In 1971 he returned to Halifax to join the venerable firm Cox Downie and Goodfellow, and to plunge into a world of Tory politics. From 1976 to 1982, he was president of the provincial Conservative Party, and he had a foot in the federal camp as vice-president of the party for Nova Scotia. When Mulroney won the 1983 leadership, Grant joined the board of the PC Canada Fund and served as president of the local 500 Club. After the 1984 election victory, Grant was appointed to the board of the Canada Development Investment Corporation, along with high flyers like Trevor Eyton, the dour Brascan executive from Toronto.

Grant and his wife, Deborah, a Halifax city alderman, had four children. They seemed the perfect family — attractive, plenty of money, a weekend place in Chester, memberships in the right clubs and volunteer organizations, loyal friends. Deborah Grant had planned to run for mayor in Halifax. A year before his death, Grant set up a Canada–Hong Kong business association and was working actively with immigrant investor funds. If anyone in Nova Scotia seemed to have it made, this handsome, fair-haired lawyer did.

But like so many others, he got greedy. The slide began with the unlucky fluke of a magazine article in 1988. Michael Crawford, the editor of *Canadian Lawyer*, published his annual "Tally at the Trough," a list of the law firms that received the most federal government legal business during the previous year. To the astonishment of the partners at Cox Downie, their firm ranked ninth in the top ten, thanks mostly to a hefty bill from John Grant for $299,000 to the Department of Regional Industrial Expansion. The bill was news to Grant's partners; as far as they knew, it had not passed through their books. After grilling Grant about the story, the firm fired him in June 1988 and started looking a little more closely at the records. The lawyers in the firm were sworn to secrecy, but bits of gossip seeped out and no other firm would touch Grant as he looked around for a new berth. There was talk of his other business interests being investigated by the Mounties, including an immigrant investor scheme and a school in Hong Kong. Grant wasn't alone in these affairs, and sweat beaded the upper lip of more than one prominent Haligonian on the verandahs of Chester that summer.

And as that summer wore on, Grant learned that the Nova Scotia Barristers' Society was meeting to discuss his case. He grew more and more depressed. He played a lot of tennis and talked to a number of old friends; they all found him very worried. On August 19, he went to see Donald Ripley at his Halifax office, ostensibly to give him a $500 donation for the provincial Tories' upcoming election campaign, but really to ask how Ripley had coped with the disgrace of being fired from a big job and accused of impropriety. How did Ripley stand the press speculation? How had he survived? Ripley hardly knew what to say; he had fought his battle in the confidence of his innocence; Grant was here acknowledging his guilt.

Ripley described the visit in his diaries and later in his 1993 book, *Bagman: A Life in Nova Scotia Politics*. He quoted Grant as saying, "I've done some stupid things, but I've offered to undo them, and I know I'm wrong and have to pay, but some people want to put me out forever. There's even talk of jail." It got worse. Grant told Ripley that he was being blackmailed by Paul Walsh, a drunken journalist who had threatened Grant with the information that Grant had charged one of his clients, a Chinese businessman, $80,000 for a political favour and representation. The businessman's cheque was cashed outside of Canada. In both his diary and his book, Ripley writes that Grant admitted to him that day that the story was true. If the incident were to come under public scrutiny, it would obviously lead to problematic questions about Grant's offshore banking activities.

The two men talked on and on that day, Grant pouring out his heart, scared of all the shadows in his path. The scrawled pages in Ripley's diary even record Grant's revelations about a group of prominent men in the community — judges, politicians, lawyers, and businessmen — who were gay and how they were all afraid Walsh would betray their secrets. Walsh, a bisexual, was nasty enough and desperate enough for money to blackmail them too. Ripley tried to calm Grant, gave him some advice about coping with scandal and humiliation, and sent him home. Other close friends, including at least two Toronto lawyers who were old friends from Grant's days at McMillan Binch, offered counsel and comfort as well — right up to the day before he disappeared.

On Friday, September 16, Grant was called before the Barristers' Society and told he had been disbarred. He was also told that he should prepare himself for an RCMP investigation. The next day he quietly left his home in Halifax's fashionable South End and checked into the Wandlyn Inn across the harbour in Dartmouth.

At the funeral, attended by all the powerful people in Halifax, individuals gathered in quiet conversations, murmuring regrets and speculations. He saved his family from further disgrace, the discreet voices said. Probably understandable in the circumstances. "He did it to spare you and the children," soothed one mighty federal politician as he embraced Deborah Grant in the receiving line. "No, he did it to spare you and the party," she retorted angrily.

But did he do it at all? It's true he had reasons to take his life. It's true he had sought medical help for depression. But surely no torment, however desperate, could bring a human being to destroy himself with such savagery. Very few people knew the actual details of his death; no one added up the wounds and wondered aloud. But there are questions that should have been asked. First of all, his body was naked; people who commit suicide are rarely found naked. The deep cut on his chin and the abrasion on his nose were not typical of a suicide; such injuries suggest a fight. A third curiosity was the sheer number and severity of the wounds. A fourth was his medication, anti-anxiety drugs, which would tend to calm him down. And finally there was his method: male suicides almost always use guns. If the victim does not own a gun or have access to one, the second choice is usually drug overdose.

One of Canada's most experienced homicide detectives later studied the autopsy report and said investigators should have looked at the stab wounds carefully to understand their depth and angles. With a suicide, the person's fist usually holds the knife in such a way that the sharp side enters on the high side of the wound. Were photographs taken to determine these details? Did anyone check to see if some of the wounds were made after death? On the other hand, the detective pointed out, there seemed to be no defence wounds on his hands, the undersides of his forearms or between his fingers, cuts a victim usually sustains when trying to fend off an attacker. The absence of these injuries supports a suicide verdict.

But as one of Grant's close friends said in 1993, years after his death, "John had so many ways to go through the eye of the needle that he would not have killed himself over being disbarred. He was not the kind of guy who takes his own life."

That fall the Nova Scotia Tories went to the polls and squeaked to a victory while the federal Tories, in defiance of gloomy predictions, roared back to a second majority government. Bits and pieces of information about Grant continued to surface. *Canadian Lawyer's* Michael Crawford, a Maritime lawyer himself who had worked in Halifax for CTV, sobered by the role his magazine had played in exposing Grant's activities, went to Nova Scotia to talk to people about all the rumours. He got an earful about double-billing and other dubious practices that had alarmed the Cox Downie partners. Citing sources "close to police and law society investigations," Crawford wrote, "The clients affected were as far afield as Hong Kong and included both [federal] government departments and individuals. The billing discrepancies allegedly total in the high six figures. There are also allegations that Grant misrepresented his political influence to some foreign clients. In one case, he apparently told Japanese clients he could easily arrange for the issuing of offshore fishing licenses."

John Grant's tragedy should have put the brakes on some of the Tories in Nova Scotia during the Mulroney years, but few really believed that they shouldn't go on snatching every advantage they could while they had a chance. After all, this was a province built on a long tradition of patronage politics, one that made other provincial cabinets look like amateurs when it came to doling out the spoils. And federal money flowed like honey into the province that first sent Brian Mulroney to Parliament. Conservative premier John Buchanan, a Mulroney stalwart, worked closely with the federal Tories to ensure that the largesse went to the right companies and the right people.

Through two organizations — Enterprise Cape Breton, which replaced the Cape Breton Development Corporation in 1985, and the Atlantic Canada Opportunities Agency, a $2.1-billion program set up in 1988 — the federal and provincial Tories found ways to pour hundreds of millions of dollars into some of the daftest projects anyone could imagine. Between 1988 and 1992, ACOA spent $800 million in Atlantic Canada and created, the agency's officials say, 26,652 jobs in that time. The agency spent another $1.1 billion on joint ventures with the provinces. In Nova Scotia the funds were often directed by the province's powerful provincial barons, Elmer MacKay and Bob Coates, as well as by Mulroney's own backroom boys, the Doucet brothers. The prime minister appointed many old friends to the boards of these agencies: one of the runners for the 1983 fundraising campaign, Brian MacLeod of Antigonish, was appointed to the ACOA board. (Another runner, David MacKeen of Halifax, was given a full-time job on the National Parole Board.)

Lawyers, business consultants, and lobbyists grew rich on ACOA's bounty, while the political pratfalls were legion. The bulk of the $110 million spent on projects financed by Enterprise Cape Breton since 1985 has been flushed down the drain, a loss defended by the federal government as the price we have to pay for supporting "high-risk" projects. (The government never explained just how it came to pass that taxpayers *agreed* to support high-risk projects in Cape Breton.) By 1991, for example, ECB had committed $90 million to thirty projects in Cape Breton; of this amount, $72.3 million was spent on companies that failed or never opened their doors. The police were called in to look at several of these ECB collapses. And by 1992, Peter Lesaux, the president of ACOA, admitted the RCMP was investigating at least a dozen of the companies to whom ACOA grants had been given.

Here are just a few examples of the companies assisted by these government agencies.

WORLD COMNET

In 1986 ECB approved over $4.6 million worth of loans, grants, and tax credits to a fly-by-night scam operation run by a group of stock promoters operating out of Vancouver and Los Angeles. Born of a Cayman Islands tax refuge called Haven, World ComNet (or WCN as it was also called) claimed to be setting up a computerized tour reservation system in Sydney, Cape Breton; in fact, it was a sophisticated stock market scheme to run WCN stock on the Vancouver Stock Exchange. Made respectable by its federal government support, the stock soared to become the highest flyer on the VSE in the late 1980s, its value running from an original penny a share to over $60 a share at its pre-split value. When the promoters finally blew off the stock in 1991, its descent was swift and fatal, and taxpayers were looking at a $6.8-million hit. Staff who worked in both the California and Sydney offices admitted after the company collapsed that some people had made a fortune on the stock, but that no real work was done in the offices. One employee in the Sydney office spent his last year there playing computer games. ECB officials were warned repeatedly that this was a typical VSE scam operation; they persisted in supporting it.

CURRAGH RESOURCES

This Toronto-based mining company received an interest rate buy-down of $8.75 million as well as a guarantee on 85 per cent of a $100-million loan from the federal government — on top of a $12-million loan from the provincial government. The political godfathers were Mulroney, Coates, MacKay, Buchanan, and Don Cameron, all of whom worked to secure the money for the Westray Mine in the face of steadfast opposition from bureaucrats in Ottawa who asked disturbing questions about the mine's safety and viability and about Curragh's financial state. When the mine blew up on May 9, 1992, twenty-six men were killed and the biggest criminal investigation in Nova Scotia's history began. Despite incredible bungling on the part of the police and the provincial Justice Department and an immense amount of stonewalling and defensive posturing in Ottawa, criminal charges were eventually laid against the now-bankrupt company and two senior managers. None of the money was ever repaid.

TECHNITREAD MARITIMES LIMITED

A dubious company out of Brampton, Ontario, this enterprise won $2.2 million in federal funding to recap tires in an old coal mining building in Glace Bay. The company opened in 1990 after many delays but never went into production; instead it tried to squeeze even more money out of the government. Frank Elman, the lawyer who acted for ECB and ACOA, also acted for the company; he found himself under investigation by both the Barristers' Society and the RCMP, as did ACOA board member Joe Stewart, who charged the company $30,000 to help it prepare a business plan. The company's owner, Mike Dicenzo, claimed to have used the government money to buy expensive new equipment from Italy, equipment that was actually bankruptcy-sale stock from New England. A year later ACOA sold the machinery to the Chinese city of Rongcheng for $430,000.

CAPE BRETON CHEMICAL CORPORATION

This company, set up at a cost of $21 million to make plastic wrap for food producers, was supposed to employ 140 people but never had a staff of more than 30. It went under in September 1990.

UNIVERSAL METALS

In 1987 this firm received $669,000 in ECB loans after promising to turn abandoned ships into scrap metal, a business that would provide up to 200 jobs in Sydney. Its total payroll was no more than forty. The owner — who was later charged by the police for fraud — abandoned the ships, leaving ECB with a $400,000 job of cleaning out the asbestos in the wrecks. A Calgary businessman, Gordon Low, bought the remnants of the business and had another wreck brought into Sydney for salvage. In 1989 Low sold the wreck again to a company called North Atlantic Towage, which brought in a refugee from the Philippines, Virgilio Gumapac, thirty-four, married and the father of four, as a watchman. In December 1989, a company official left Gumapac alone on the unheated boat with some bags of groceries and a charcoal barbecue. A month later some curious workers, laid off from the scrap metal company, went on board and found Gumapac's frozen body. He had died of carbon monoxide poisoning after lighting the barbecue in his tiny cabin to keep warm. Nobody is blaming ACOA or ECB for his death, but he was clearly an innocent victim of a heartless company that remained unsupervised by any authority whatsoever. The RCMP conducted an investigation and laid no charges.

CAPE BRETON MOLD TECHNOLOGY COMPANY

After receiving $12.2 million from ECB and another $4.5 million from the province, this Sydney Mines company went into receivership in November 1991, laying off thirty-eight workers. The company produced steel molds for manufacturers of plastic containers.

NSC DIESEL POWER INC.

This Sheet Harbour company was set up in 1988 by Ottawa lobbyist and former Ottawa Rough Rider football player Rick Black with $8.5 million in federal money to test diesel engines for the *Louis St. Laurent*, a federal icebreaker. (The icebreaker was in the middle of an $82.3-million refit, a contract given to Halifax-Dartmouth Industries Ltd. NsC Diesel was meant to meet the Canadian content requirements of the *St. Laurent* contract with HDIL.) By January 1990 NsC Diesel was in receivership, awash in two dozen lawsuits and under investigation by auditors trying to comprehend a series of financial transactions. For example, the auditors discovered that the company had paid a $270,000 premium to Bahamas-based Swiss-American Fidelity Insurance Co. and Guarantee Ltd. for a $4-million performance bond. Swiss-American, however, had lost its insurance licence. As they unravelled a complex web of money transfers among eight other Black companies, the receivers found NsC Diesel had funnelled $3.4 million to these companies. "There are many complicated and unexplained transactions . . . for a company that has not yet begun operations," said Ernst & Young's January 1990 report on NsC Diesel. "The custodian expresses doubt about the appropriateness of these payments."

ARROW L.M. MANUFACTURING

In 1988 this Port Hawkesbury company, set up to manufacture printing equipment, received $2.7 million in grants and loans approved by the ECB board and then subcontracted the construction work to a local company owned by prominent Tory John Van Zutphen. Van Zutphen happened to be the chairman of the ECB board. Lowell Murray, who was then the minister responsible for ACOA and ECB, admitted in the Commons that Van Zutphen's firm was the only construction company in Atlantic Canada allowed to bid on the work, but he said the government had a policy of not interfering in ECB's decisions. In 1989 Arrow crashed into bankruptcy.

CELCOM
A cellular phone company, Celcom received $2 million from ECB and never started operations.

HI-TECH WOODWORKERS LTD.
This wood products manufacturer, which opened in Hammonds Plain, Cape Breton, in 1990 and lasted three months before folding, left taxpayers on the hook for $5.6 million in grants and loan guarantees. In 1991 it was sold to Marwood Ltd. of Truro, Nova Scotia, without any hope of recovering any of the money.

CAPE BRETON WALLCOVERINGS
This wallpaper company went into receivership after spending $13.9 million of federal money.

Joe Stewart — "Big Daddy" — in New Glasgow, the man who had been such an important confidant and organizer for Mulroney in 1983 and again in 1984, was one of the key people in the process of doling out ECB and ACOA money. For almost a decade he was also Mulroney's senior adviser on patronage appointments for the province, a job that would normally have fallen to Elmer MacKay. MacKay was not as interested in this chore as Stewart, who happily jumped into the breach. In 1988 Mulroney put Stewart on the board of ACOA to supervise the awarding of grants and loans, a position that allowed Stewart to become the political boss of a unique $10-million fund called the Pictou County Development Fund, set up in 1988. It was a special fund, affiliated with ACOA, to put money into projects in Pictou County — the county that first sent Mulroney to Parliament, the county that had returned Elmer MacKay so many times.

For nine years, any astute Tory who wanted a favour in Atlantic Canada made the pilgrimage to Stewart's office over the Pizza Delight on Main Street in New Glasgow. Supplicants for federal loans and grants and jobs would park in the laneway at the back, climb an outdoor staircase to the second-floor balcony and knock at a small door under a yellow plastic canopy. Inside they'd find Big Daddy working the phones. While they waited for Joe to wind up his telephone chats, they could admire his collection of framed photographs of himself with Bob Stanfield or Elmer MacKay, or hugging Mila, or beaming beside the Mulroney kids. There are plenty of pictures of Joe with his own family and aerial shots of Tory Haven, the 100-acre oceanfront property in Antigonish that he inherited from an aunt. "Hello!" booms the message on his answering machine at his cottage. "Welcome to Tory Haven! Pat and I can't come to the phone right now, but if you leave a message after the beep we'll get back to you. Have a wonderful Nova Scotia day!"

Anyone who meets Stewart is unlikely to forget him. Along with the belly of a Burl Ives, he has white hair and pink cheeks, a cheerful grin, and a pair of the shrewdest blue eyes you'll ever see. "The King of Bullshit" is what Mary Daley, the mayor of nearby Westville, calls him and the moniker fits; he spins out a fine line of patter, blarney, and bluster.

Stewart presided over considerable generosity to Mulroney's old riding. There was ACOA money to fix up Pictou Lodge, the resort that was home to the Mulroneys during the summer of 1983, before the Central Nova by-election. There was federal money for a new highway, for new railcars from the works at Trenton, and above all, for the Westray Mine at Plymouth in Pictou County. Joe Stewart watched the money pour into the province with great satisfaction, but as the years went by he couldn't believe he wasn't offered a Senate seat. One by one the Nova Scotia spots were filled by individuals he considered lesser men. With the flames of several scandals licking at his feet and the RCMP closing in with an investigation, John Buchanan was pulled out of the province at the last minute by Mulroney in August 1990, to a safe haven in the upper house. (The RCMP later cleared the former premier of any illegal behaviour, but he was damaged by subsequent stories about the way provincial Tories had funnelled hundreds of thousands of dollars to him through secret trust funds.) Michael Forrestal, a former MP who was listlessly pushing paper in his patronage job as a member of the Canadian Pension Commission in P.E.I., was also rescued by Mulroney's offer of a Senate seat. And the third spot went to Don Oliver, a Halifax lawyer who had been severely disciplined by the Barristers' Society for unethical behaviour. Still, Stewart could take comfort in his role as the power behind most of the patronage appointments and federal money doled out to the province. And Mulroney continued to call and consult, right up to his last days in office. When 200 faithful gathered at 24 Sussex Drive after the official tribute on June 9, 1993, Stewart was there.

The good times came to an end for Big Daddy in April 1994 when he was scheduled for trial on six charges of evading taxes on income of more than $500,000. Three of the charges were for filing false returns, three were for failing to pay income tax. According to documents filed with the court, Stewart reported a 1987 income of $23,412 but failed to declare additional income of $101,834. The next year, in 1988, he reported income of $41,027 and failed to declare another $203,800. In 1989, he reported income of $21,185 and failed to report $222,560. Stewart was also charged with failing to pay federal income tax of $159,014 between 1987 and 1989 on his undeclared income. Where did the extra money come from?

According to people close to Stewart, it came from businesses that had hired him as a consultant on federal grants and loans. One, as we have seen, was Technitread. As a member of the ACOA board, Stewart was clearly in a conflict of interest.

A couple of years ago Stewart sold the three Pizza Delight franchises he owned in Pictou County and in Halifax to work as a business consultant and lobbyist, but the pickings will now be slim. With the Liberals in power in Halifax and Ottawa, Tory havens are few and far between.

If Stewart was the ultimate backroom boy during these years, MacKay, the minister for ACOA, was the front-line politician. Although he didn't share Big Daddy's taste for the wheeling and dealing above the pizza parlour, he had his own dreams for himself and for his province. When Mulroney moved on to run in Manicouagan in 1984 and MacKay was returned once again as the MP from Central Nova, he finally became the solicitor general of Caanda, the job he'd always wanted.

Almost immediately MacKay made two serious mistakes. The first was to meet secretly in the fall of 1984 with Richard Hatfield at Ottawa's Château Laurier Hotel after Hatfield had been charged by the RCMP with possession of marijuana. When the opposition and the press got wind of the meeting, the accusations flew of ministerial interference, obstruction of justice, and other choice insults. MacKay was a former defence lawyer and certainly knew better. The second crisis came in 1985 when another Lodge brother and cabinet colleague, Bob Coates, then the minister of defence, found his feet firmly stuck in the glue after playing hookey at a strip club in Lahr, Germany, during an official trip. A friend of MacKay's said, "At a press conference and out of a clear blue sky, Elmer gave the press a lecture on how terrible they were to poor Bob Coates and how he was innocent. That was the last straw for Mulroney; he had to get him out of the portfolio."

Mulroney demoted MacKay, appointing him minister of revenue, but he wouldn't do the dirty work himself. As Erik Nielsen has reported, Mulroney never liked to fire anyone — he always tried to find others to do it. In MacKay's case, the messenger was Fred Doucet. "That hurt," said MacKay's associate. "That was a killer." Doucet told MacKay he was being moved over to Revenue Canada, a portfolio that held little interest for him; later he became minister of public works with responsibility for ACOA, and that was a little better.

While he was minister MacKay turned to other projects. The one that most interested him was a proposal from Thyssen AG, the huge German engineering and armaments company, to build a $58-million plant in Port Hawkesbury, just across the Canso Causeway in Cape Breton. The lead players on this project, which would operate through a Thyssen subsidiary called Bear Head Industries Ltd., included Karl-Heinz Schreiber, a Calgary-based German businessman with a long history with the Alberta Tories who was now the Thyssen man in Canada, as well as lobbyists Frank Moores, Gary Ouellet, and Gerry Doucet.

In the 1970s and 1980s Schreiber had set up several Alberta holding companies for powerful and wealthy Germans, including one he registered in 1980 for the premier of the German state of Bavaria, Franz Josef Strauss, and his family. Until his sudden death from a heart attack, Strauss was the chairman of Airbus Industrie, the consortium that sold nearly $2 billion worth of Airbus 310s to Air Canada. Schreiber has always been considered an important deal-maker on this contract as well.

Greg Alford, a former Moores aide who was briefly the president of Moores's lobby firm, was put in charge of Bear Head, which wanted to manufacture light armoured vehicles in Port Hawkesbury for buyers in the Middle East. The company had received several thousand dollars from ACOA for an engineering study, and now they were after another $20 million or so from the federal Industry Department for the plant. That wasn't all. The project would not go ahead, said the Thyssen team, unless the government promised them the contract for light armoured vehicles and tanks. In return Bear Head would provide jobs to about 400 people in an economically distressed area of Atlantic Canada, with the possibility of 800 additional spinoff jobs thanks to the new plant.

The project was controversial for a number of reasons, not the least of which was that German law prohibited German companies from selling military equipment to Middle East countries. Many observers, especially in Canada's outraged Jewish community, saw the Nova Scotia plant as a way to get around the rules in Germany. Canada too had a rule about military equipment — it was not supposed to be sold in areas of conflict. But Bear Head's supporters thought they could get around that with exemptions. Still, there was ferocious debate in cabinet and in the caucus about the money and the contract for Bear Head. The plan was eventually killed when the normally complacent Ontario ministers roused themselves to insist that the defence contract for the vehicles go to General Motors in London.

During these years of intense lobbying MacKay became very close to Schreiber, often visiting him in Munich, where the company's head offices were located. The German arranged for MacKay's son, Peter, a young lawyer, to work at Thyssen for several months in 1992, and he was more than hospitable when the MacKay kids were travelling in Europe. All this attention made some of MacKay's family members and close friends uneasy; they felt Schreiber was trying too hard to ingratiate himself. Schreiber himself visited MacKay in Pictou County as often as once every three or four weeks over the years, even after MacKay left politics in 1993, and he was said to be extremely frustrated over the government's failure to do anything for Bear Head. To this day, there is talk of a Thyssen lawsuit against the federal government for breach of promise. Thyssen invested a lot of money in the project, although no one, not even his enemies, suspects MacKay of taking anything from the company.

MacKay decided not to run again in the 1993 election. Politics had disappointed him. Mulroney had disappointed him. He had not been able to accomplish the things he'd set out to do for his riding and for his province. Bear Head and Westray had been two notable failures, and all the other ACOA and ECB disasters hadn't helped. But he did not leave politics without flourishing his power one last time, and he did it with the kind of arrogance that finally ended his popular support in the riding. First, he found a full-time ten-year appointment at the Canadian Pension Commission for his long-time assistant, Joan Fennimore. Then he engineered the appointment of a judge from his riding.

Under the Tories, the appointment of judges was always political, even though they had set up a system to make it appear otherwise. Each regional minister put together a local advisory committee in the province to give advice on judicial appointments. These were supposed to be blue-ribbon committees; in fact, they were all too often dominated by party hacks. In MacKay's case, he'd selected a committee, and on the whole they agreed on the nominations for Nova Scotia, which would then go to Mulroney in Ottawa. When he was leaving office, MacKay pushed forward one last name — that of Ted Scanlan, a New Glasgow lawyer and the president of his riding association. Scanlan had been a lawyer for only ten years when MacKay had arranged for him to be named a Queen's Counsel; at eleven years, he nominated Scanlan to the Nova Scotia Supreme Court. At this, his hand-picked judicial committee bridled. We won't support Ted Scanlan's appointment, they said. Fine, said MacKay, and dismantled the committee. He appointed a new committee that included his girl-friend, Sharon Lloy, a veteran Tory worker in the province, and the committee did what it was told. When it came time to install Scanlan, the province's chief justice, Lorne Clark, politely declined the honour of officiating. I'm tied up with some law students, he said by way of excuse, several weeks after classes had ended for the year.

In November 1993, the safest Tory riding in Canada, the one chosen to send Brian Mulroney to the House of Commons ten years earlier, voted overwhelmingly for the Liberal candidate, Roseann Skoke.

CHAPTER NINETEEN

IT PAYS TO ADVERTISE

NDRÉ VERRET COULDN'T BELIEVE HIS EYES. A FRIEND HAD TOLD HIM that if he sat in the Ritz-Carlton Hotel's Café de Paris at breakfast any weekday morning, he could watch hotel manager Fernand Roberge hold court at a corner table for a stream of interesting individuals. "Out of pure curiosity," said Verret, a senior public servant who had moved from Ottawa to Montreal in 1984 to work in the public affairs office at VIA Rail, "I went to have a look. Every morning around 7 or 7:30 people would spend about fifteen minutes with Mr. Roberge, well-known people, lawyers and the like." Sometimes a dozen people in all would meet with Roberge over coffee, each person or group of two or three taking no more than twenty minutes. "It was really like his office," said Verret, adding that Roberge's visitors would leave the table "with beautiful smiles on their faces."

Like pilgrims searching for the Holy Grail, hungry contract seekers had a number of choices during the Mulroney years. As we've seen, some were comfortable cutting their deals with Roch LaSalle over a power breakfast at Nate's in Ottawa. Many Atlantic Canada businessmen found their way up the back staircase above the New Glasgow pizza parlour to try to humour Big Daddy. A few of the more sophisticated would book a table at Le Mas des Oliviers in Montreal to lobby Guy Charbonneau. And some, as André Verret discovered, preferred the Ritz-Carlton's Café de Paris. Advising on federal advertising contracts in Quebec was among Roberge's pleasant duties, according to half a dozen well-connected advertising executives based in Montreal and Toronto. At least one senior official in the federal government's Advertising Management Group, the agency set up to handle the government's advertising, routinely received calls from Roberge — who was at this time a private citizen with no official authority of any kind.

During the Mulroney years, Montreal's advertising and public relations community made the Ritz coffee shop something of a hangout in the mornings. Perhaps they were hoping for the chance of a word with Mulroney, who always stayed in the hotel when he was in town, or maybe they were just making sure they had regular contact with Roberge. "There was a real clique there," said one of the advertising executives. One of the members was Marcel Côté, a partner in Sécor, who later worked in Mulroney's office as his communications adviser.

One morning in March 1985 Verret was just finishing his breakfast when he saw an acquaintance, then a senior manager at a Montreal advertising firm called Publicité Martin, run by Montreal ad man Yvon Martin, in an intense conversation with Roberge. A few minutes later the man rose to his feet, shook Roberge's hand, and left, grinning broadly. When he saw Verret, he came over. He spoke enthusiastically about landing the VIA Rail advertising account. Verret, who had been at VIA Rail since June 1984, was sceptical. "In that kind of contract there is always a call for a public tender," explained Verret, and as far as he knew when the Martin official spoke to him, that process was still under way. "Six or seven or eight firms are invited to tender, and we always tried in the past to be as fair as possible."

Back at VIA, several other people were just as incredulous as Verret. To begin with, although the company had been in business for fifteen years, Publicité Martin had not made the original list of potential agencies drawn up by VIA's advertising department because the firm was not considered to be equipped to handle large national accounts, certainly not one as significant as VIA's. But Mulroney had just fired the old VIA Rail board and appointed a new one packed with cronies and party bagmen. It was a crew that was feeling its oats, and one of the recently arrived board members saw to it that Martin's firm was added to the short list.

The final formal bidding process began in March 1985, just before Verret encountered his friend at the Ritz. About nine firms were invited to present their pitches over a two-day period to a committee of three new VIA board members, Gary Brazell from Winnipeg, Paul Norris from Edmonton, and Marc LeFrançois from Quebec City, and five executives from VIA's advertising and marketing departments, vice-president Michael Kieran, Jim Warrington, Christina Sirsley, Preston Beaumont, and Nicole Alyot. By the end, three firms had been dropped from the roster, and two of the nine firms needn't have bothered to show up. One was MacLaren Advertising, the firm that had enjoyed a near-monopoly on advertising under the Liberals; a second was McKim, which was known to have backed Joe Clark's failed bid to hang on to the Tory leadership the year before. "They were treated like shit by the board members," said a witness to the proceedings. "It was very embarrassing."

After the first day of presentations, the VIA board members and staff went off to dinner at Montreal's Atlantic Pavilion, courtesy of VIA, and feasted on seafood, everyone trying to guess what was in the minds of their companions concerning the day's events. Some members continued the evening's festivities at the Ritz-Carlton bar where they quaffed champagne, again at VIA's expense, until the small hours of the morning. Others retired to their hotel rooms to prepare for day two of the presentations. This would be the day on which Martin would make his presentation, and Paul Norris and Gary Brazell had already made it clear they were strong supporters of the firm.

When Martin's firm formally made its pitch, it seemed to overwhelm the board members and underwhelm the VIA staffers. "At best it was mediocre," said one staff person who was there. Another former

VIA official agreed. "The pitch was not very good, it was not strong," the official said. "If they had been innovative and understood the problems of VIA they would have done a better job, but they did not do their homework and gave a presentation that was somewhat silly, that was not up to the task. They did not understand what trains are about in Canada, they did not do the research to understand it."

The next day, a Saturday morning, the eight committee members met at the Queen Elizabeth Hotel for a final review. The board members stated their admiration for Martin's presentation but agreed that the one done by Cossette Communication–Marketing Publicité had also been excellent. The VIA staffers were of a different view. Kieran vehemently opposed Martin and said so, while his colleagues mouthed perfunctory platitudes about Martin's pitch and then stated their preferences for some of the other agencies that had competed. After hearing their remarks, Paul Norris looked surprised. "I don't think we were all at the same party," he commented. Kieran did not give up without a fight. He was relentless and persisted against the obvious will of the board members. "It was extraordinary that the board would involve itself with such matters," says Kieran today. "It was not illegal, mind you, but it was extraordinary."

About two weeks later the official decision was made at VIA's head office and the committee members were duly notified. There were two winners, Martin and Cossette. Cossette had been high on everyone's list and it won 50 per cent of the total contract, or $4.5 million. Known to spend lavish sums on its creative talent, Cossette was to handle VIA's national advertising — everything outside the Windsor–Quebec City corridor. Now an industry giant, in 1985 Cossette was still a small regional agency, explained one advertising executive, "but it was known to be extremely tight with Roberge."[1] Martin, an outfit that was reputed to place a higher value on its accounting department, was given the corridor and $4.5 million to do the job. Yvon Martin was disappointed with the results; he had hoped to land the entire package. But he didn't need to worry, especially after his firm went on to win other excellent federal contracts. To celebrate his good fortune, Martin, who had started the company in his own home and was still the sole owner, bought himself a new $70,000 Jaguar.

Another former VIA employee, a senior manager who was familiar with the contracts, agreed with Verret's version of events and remembers what happened after the first ad campaign ran. "We did reviews of his [Martin's] firm: how successful they were with our campaigns. The presentation the agency made to us was the pits. They really ignored VIA. They took the contract for granted. They never assigned the right account executive to it and their ads were shitty." This executive would complain to the VIA manager who dealt with Martin and the manager agreed but could say only, "I can't do anything. My hands are tied." Martin still has the VIA Rail account, and he has it all: Cossette no longer has half.

Hands were frequently tied when it came to advertising campaigns under the Tories, but one person who resisted the pressure was Tom Scott, the president of Toronto-based Sherwood Communications Group, a large Tory firm with many subsidiaries, including Foster Advertising. Sherwood had offices all across Canada. After becoming the leader in 1983, Mulroney asked Scott to be chairman of the advertising campaign for the upcoming election and Scott agreed, on condition that he have total control of the budget. Although he could select his own team for the rest of Canada, there was no choice in Quebec; he was told who would be working with him there. The fact that he controlled the budget soon became a bone of contention; Jean Bazin made it clear to him that he believed the budget should be split fifty-fifty between English Canada and Quebec, an arrangement Scott resisted. Bazin also wanted to meddle in the administration of the campaign. "Bazin called me three or four times a day for weeks pressuring me to accept Roger Nantel as co-chair," says Scott. "Finally he went away. But the amount of pressure I had to do this raised suspicions in my mind about Nantel."

Nantel's clout became apparent right after the election when Mulroney gave him the biggest untendered plum of all, the job of placing federal government advertising in newspapers and magazines and on radio and television. Nantel and Toronto filmmaker Peter Simpson established a company called Media Canada to place the ads, worth about $60 million a year, and they were paid handsomely for the privilege: a minimum of $125,000 a month, or 3 per cent of the total billing. "I'm trying to figure out how I can make a lot of money with this government," Nantel confided to one startled advertising executive who had the same ambition but lacked the chutzpah to declare it quite so baldly. It didn't take Nantel long, although he later complained that the expenses at Media Canada were too high to make any real money. It was a break-even proposition, he claimed; the company made only $7,200 in two years. Despite his whining, it's hard to believe the partners didn't prosper. In addition to their regular monthly percentage, they won contracts from Media Canada itself.

Given that he pops up everywhere in any account of these years, it is not surprising to find that Michel Cogger got himself into the advertising business. One of those who took him on, at $4,000 a month between 1986 and 1989, was Tom Scott. Cogger says he was on board to do Sherwood's legal work in Quebec, but that's not what Scott remembers. The company's president in Quebec, Dennis Jotcham, had retired just before the Tories took power; and while the staff was excellent, Scott explained, Sherwood was left without a senior player in Montreal's business community, someone who could mix with the likes of Royal Bank chairman Rowland Frazee or Air Canada's president Claude Taylor, as Jotcham had done. The only people of this kind that Scott knew in Montreal were Tories he'd met over his years in the party, and Michel Cogger looked as if he could fill Jotcham's social shoes. In 1986, Scott retained Cogger after checking him out with Toronto lawyer Graham Scott (no relation), a partner at McMillan Binch, who was close to Cogger. Graham Scott gave Cogger, a godfather to one of his children, a strong endorsement. "He was my eyes and ears in Quebec," says Tom Scott, adding that he didn't need Cogger's influence with Mulroney. "I could pick up the phone and call Mulroney myself any time I wanted to." Cogger was there as Scott's point man with the business community. Legal work was not in the job description.

After Mulroney appointed Cogger to the Senate in 1986, Scott worried that there might be a conflict of interest between Cogger's position with Sherwood and his Senate job; he arranged to meet Cogger and his partners at Lapointe Rosenstein to discuss the issue. Cogger was able to allay his concerns. He told Scott that the Speaker of the Senate, Guy Charbonneau, had given him the green light. "Quoting the Speaker," recalls Scott, "Cogger told us that 'if that [his arrangement with Sherwood] constitutes conflict of interest, then none of us would be in the Senate.'" (When the RCMP later came to see Charbonneau about the retainers, Charbonneau gave them a written statement to the effect that he had never given Cogger an opinion on the ad agency retainers.[2])

Scott decided to continue the retainer arrangement based on what he believed to be the Speaker's reassurance and his own intention not to use Cogger on government business. He actually came to like Cogger and stuck by him, even after Cogger fell under RCMP investigation, and even though, he admitted, Cogger had done nothing for him during all those years. "I don't believe I ever asked him to do a thing," says Scott. "Actually I did, once. I asked him to send me an annual report of a large Quebec company we were interested in doing business with. I wanted to know who was on the board of directors. I don't think he ever sent it." Was he getting his money's worth? "No. But that was my fault. I didn't have a clue what to get him to do. And it wouldn't have been the most money I've ever wasted."

Unknown to Scott, Cogger had made the same arrangement with at least three other advertising firms and was hauling in about $16,000 a month in retainers from ad agencies. Recognizing the rich vein of ad contracts to be tapped, Cogger had also helped Roger Nantel set up an advertising company called Socancom Inc., and it was this company that formed one-half the partnership with Simpson in Media Canada. "Socancom is a new shell company that we've got involving Blue Thunder," explained Nantel in January 1985 to Diane Francis, then a reporter with *The Toronto Star*.[3] "This is the communications team I put together previous to the last campaign to set up and organize a substantial communications effort on behalf of the PCs for French Canada," Nantel told her. The profits, he prattled on, "won't go to individuals but will go to special events for the sake of the party, like seminars with Quebec ministers so they can interface with the grass roots."

This cheerful admission that profits from Media Canada would be funnelled back to the party caused a furore. Tory ministers scrambled to explain that Nantel had misspoken himself. But it was confirmed by Peter Swain, a prominent Tory ad man from Toronto who headed Media Buying Services, the largest media buying company in the country. He acknowledged that the deal with Media Canada would generate cash for the Tory party. And he said that he had refused to go along with the deal when he was invited to become a part of the group with Nantel and Simpson, despite the fact that Simpson was a former partner and Swain had placed all the Tory campaign advertising since 1972. "The terms and conditions proposed were unacceptable," he told the *Globe*'s Hugh Winsor flatly. Those terms would have required him to kick back some of the money to the party.

One of Swain's concerns, aside from the kickbacks, was the fact that he did not believe Nantel and Simpson had the expertise to manage the media buying for the government. It would require forty seasoned advertising professionals, he told Winsor, but Nantel had a small public relations firm with no expertise in advertising and Simpson was essentially a filmmaker. Nevertheless, Media Canada plunged ahead and the controversy over the plum contract soon died down. But this blatant example of tollgating raised an issue with

Ontario advertising agencies that remains a grievance to this day. In Ontario, there has been a long tradition of politically affiliated advertising agencies; some, like MacLaren or Vickers and Benson, had well-established ties to the Liberals, while others like Camp or Foster were known to be Tory firms. When the federal Liberals are in power, the Tory firms are virtually shut out of federal work; the reverse is true when the Tories are in office.

"It doesn't work that way at all in Quebec," explained one agency president. "In Quebec, ad agencies are *never* political. Here the firms run a loose tollgating arrangement instead. It's a great leveller." What this means is that firms simply pay a percentage of their contract back to the party, regardless of who is in power. During the Mulroney years, the government had a policy of splitting contracts, giving half to a firm based in Ontario and half to a firm in Quebec. Many people working in the big Ontario firms complained among themselves that their Quebec associates, working out of smaller firms, did not have the expertise for these big federal contracts and were always having to be rescued by their Toronto counterparts.

Nantel and Simpson were not the only ones bird-dogging federal advertising contracts. In November 1984, the Tories also brought in Robert Byron, a vice-president with Toronto's Case Associates Advertising Inc., who had run the party's constituency services during the 1984 election campaign. Byron was put into the public service on special assignment, and that's where he stayed for the next nine years until he retired and moved to Peterborough. His job was to help vet all the advertising and polling contracts. Working with him was veteran Tory organizer Jean Peloquin, Bazin's former brother-in-law, the organizer for Mulroney's youth delegates in 1983, and the director of Tory operations in Quebec from 1985 on.

By the end of the first year in power, reported *The Globe and Mail*'s David Stewart-Patterson in February 1986, ten Tory agencies had won 80 per cent of all 1985 contracts for advertising services worth more than $50,000 for a total of $12.8 million. The biggest contract, one for $4.8 million to handle tourism ads, came from the Department of Regional Industrial Expansion and went to Camp Associates Advertising in Toronto, a company then run by the 1984 campaign chairman, Norman Atkins.

The second-largest, reported Stewart-Patterson, was another one from DRIE for $2.8 million that went to Peter Simpson's company, Simcom Ltd. of Toronto. And the third-largest went to RLS Ltée, a company owned by Richard Le Lay, a close friend of Roch LaSalle, then the minister of public works. Jean Dugré was a senior executive with the firm. Public Works gave the company a $1-million contract while Transport Canada came through with a second worth $500,000. And Bob Byron's former firm, Case Associates, won contracts worth over $1 million in that same period.

Publicité Martin's luck held with the Tories; over the next few years they became the ad agency for other federal bodies, Crown corporations, and departments including Canada Post, the Montreal Port Corporation (a Crown corporation very much under the influence of its chairman, André Gingras, Guy Charbonneau's business associate), the Canadian Space Agency, the Department of Justice (on the gun control campaign), the federal Science and Industry Department, and the Old Port of Montreal (where another Gingras associate, Maurice Mayer, was on the board). The quality of the company's work continued to draw complaints.

One example turned up at Canada Post. Bruce Calvin was in charge of customer service at Canada Post in 1988 and wrote a frank letter about the company to Gérard Séguin, the general manager of sales and service at the corporation. After Calvin had outlined all the objectives of a new customer service campaign, he said, Publicité Martin had recommended using a newspaper campaign to sell the postal code and standards, an idea that demonstrated the agency didn't understand the campaign objectives. The advantage for Martin, wrote Calvin, was that agency staff could design the campaign quickly, spend a lot of money, and then declare it had reached its target audience. "Total cost: $1-million. Results: zero," was Calvin's scathing summary. The kind of campaign required here, he said, was a massive television blitz supported by direct mail, trade publications, lobby posters, and so on, the kind of campaign Ford and Chrysler had used when customers lost confidence in the companies' cars. Publicité Martin, unfortunately, simply didn't have a clue what was needed. "They don't appreciate the scope of the challenge, and they don't have the necessary expertise and depth within their organization to develop a comprehensive campaign which will support the objectives I have identified," Calvin wrote. Canada Post had waited nine months for a simple promotional brochure and it still wasn't ready; another black mark was the agency's failure to prepare "promotional material to support the 1987 postal code directory." In the end, it didn't matter that Martin lacked the depth or that the firm kept Canada Post waiting; Martin was the political choice.

During the first three years of the Mulroney regime, no one was flying higher than Roger Nantel. Few had greater access to Mulroney; the Boss called him every Saturday morning to talk things over, and Nantel and his second wife, Michelle Lépine, were welcome guests at 24 Sussex Drive. They'd even been invited to Nicholas's 1985 christening. Nantel's string of luck ran for a long time. Not only did he share the contract to hand out government advertising, but Nantel himself prospered with other windfalls. Here is a record of them, most of which have been gathered by Richard Cléroux. These were in addition to the monthly fee of $125,000 to $129,000 he and Simpson billed at Media Canada.

Contracts from Michel Côté, the minister of consumer and corporate affairs, to Nantel et Associés (unless otherwise indicated):
• November 19, 1984: A contract of up to $10,000 to provide Côté with "an appropriate strategy" for metric conversion over the following four months. Department officials told Cléroux that no report was

produced; all that happened was that a small group met one Sunday afternoon to devise a communications strategy and Nantel advised the group verbally.

• May 1, 1985: Synchrocom Communications, a company in which Nantel had a one-fifth share and whose records showed Stuart Hendin as a director, won a $40,000 contract plus $8,000 in travel expenses to review and write a report on "the efficiency and effectiveness of the communications branch" at the ministry.

• May 20, 1985: A $25,000 contract to study "office communications procedures" in Côté's office. On November 1, another $25,000 was added to the contract because more work was involved.

• July 1, 1985: Synchrocom won a $41,000 contract to provide Côté with "communications services"; Côté personally signed the contract.

• August 22, 1985: A $24,600 contract to organize activities around "Export Month" in Quebec.

• February 3, 1986: A $50,000 contract "to develop and implement a communication plan for the province of Quebec."

• April 1, 1986: A $25,000 contract to advise Côté on the forthcoming Patent Act, giving greater patent protection to pharmaceutical companies. For a number of reasons, this contract had to be redrawn the following fall and Nantel was paid only $12,500 for this contract, but at the same time he was awarded another contract for $25,000 for the same project.

• May 15, 1986: A $25,000 contract "to develop and implement a communications strategy for the ministerial committee on the development of the Montreal region."

• November 14, 1986: The preceding contract was reopened and Nantel was paid an additional $25,000.

Contracts from other ministries:
• January 28, 1985: A $24,500 contract from Secretary of State to give Youth Minister Andrée Champagne "strategic advice on an as, when and if basis" in connection with International Youth Year.

Secretary of State David Crombie told the Commons in a written statement that Nantel was chosen without tender because it would have
cost more to familiarize another firm and since the youth year had
already begun, it was important to get a firm on board right away.

• January 30, 1985: Another $49,700 contract from Secretary of
State "to elaborate and execute the launch for International Youth
Year." Crombie told the Commons the contract was untendered
because of the "extremely limited time available for planning and
implementing the launch."

• October 9, 1985: Synchrocom won $42,000 plus $12,626.94 in
expenses "to identify themes" promoting the Department of Regional
Industrial Expansion. Nantel talked to Sinclair Stevens, the DRIE
minister, as well as a few other politicians and aides about the department's name and the effectiveness of its communications department, but he never submitted a report.

• October 1985: Synchrocom won a $250,800 contract from the
Justice Department to "plan, organize and conduct the public relations program on impaired driving on behalf of Justice Canada." The
money included $144,000 for expenses.

• October 1985: Synchrocom won another $9,000 contract from Jus-
tice to have one of its senior executives accompany Justice Minister
John Crosbie on a provincial tour.

• November 1, 1985: A $7,000 contract from Secretary of State "to
administer an organizational blitz concerning elements of interest to
the Secretary of State and the personnel in his office." Once again,
this contract was not put out for tender, Crombie told the Commons,
"because of the extremely limited time."

• May 29, 1986: A $3,000 contract to write a speech for Commu-
nications Minister Marcel Masse. He was shuffled before he could
deliver it and replaced by Flora MacDonald, who reopened the contract and gave Nantel an extra $2,000. On the same day Nantel was
paid $11,337.45 by the National Museums of Canada "for a posi-
tioning study" on the museums.

- January 6, 1986: A Transport Canada contract for $15,000 to act as an adviser to the Montreal Airport Advisory Council.
- June 26, 1986: Media Canada won an $80,000 contract from Secretary of State "to provide data necessary to prepare an official list of newspapers" for the various federal departments.
- November 7, 1986: Nantel was paid $9,250 plus $2,266.08 in expenses to write a forty-minute speech on the Transportation Act for junior Transport Minister André Bissonnette.
- December 3, 1986: Media Canada won a two-week, $20,000 contract from Supply and Services "to compile demographic information on the audiences of public affairs programs in the electronic media."
- December 4, 1986: Media Canada won a $14,500 contract from Supply and Services "to provide data on the target audiences of advertising campaigns of the federal government."
- January 19, 1987: A $1,700 contract to write a ten-minute speech on the Highway Transportation Act for Bissonnette, a surprising contract since Bissonnette had been fired from the cabinet the previous day over his role in the Oerlikon affair. Nantel was also working for Oerlikon as its public relations consultant.

There were several other contracts, including one for External Affairs under which Nantel helped draft the communications plan to announce the letter from Mulroney to Ronald Reagan asking to open negotiations on free trade. "I spent a month at External Affairs with [Derek] Burney to put together a communications plan for free trade," he said in one interview. The value of these contracts is not known, nor is the value of several Canada Employment and Immigration contracts Nantel received to do work in the provinces.

That's not all. In April 1987 *La Presse* reported that Nantel was a partner, with Jean Peloquin, in a company called Les Productions Indigo Inc., which received over $300,000 from the federal government to produce films. Nantel and Peloquin, two senior Tories who were in control of government advertising, were receiving large contracts themselves through a variety of companies — Nantel through Media Canada, Nantel et Associés, Synchrocom, Socancom, and Les Productions Indigo; Peloquin, through Les Productions Indigo.

Once again, protests were raised and this time people were not as forgiving as they had been in the Tories' early days. Supply and Services Minister Monique Vézina was forced to order an internal investigation into allegations of conflict of interest involving Peloquin. At the same time, however, she stoutly defended the government advertising system, saying that the Conservatives had killed the patronage system designed by Trudeau's Grits. Defiantly, she agreed that the system did not always award the contract to the lowest bidder. "As the government, we have the privilege to choose the companies in whom we have confidence," she said. "If you had to hire a company to promote your programs, wouldn't you hire a friend you can trust? . . . I know I would." But it wasn't long before Vézina confirmed that she'd dropped Peloquin as an adviser on who should receive government advertising contracts.

It's obvious that Nantel was a happy traveller on the government gravy train, earning a fortune in fees from his friends in cabinet. But there was one other task he performed in the early years of the Tory regime. He became the bagman for what was called the "Rodrigue Pageau Trust."

Rod Pageau was dying of cancer in the last weeks of the 1984 campaign, and arrangements were made for an air ambulance to bring him to Baie-Comeau to be at Mulroney's side for the victory celebrations on September 4. It was said after that night that Mulroney had promised his dying friend his family would never want for anything. Pageau died a few days later and Mulroney kept his word. Early that fall he arranged for Pageau's widow, Huguette Joubert, to be named a Citizenship Court judge, a non-judicial position she will hold until 1997. It appears to be the longest-running patronage appointment ever made by Mulroney, with the exception of appointments for his friends to the Senate or to the bench.

Nantel also established what he called the Pageau trust, and he was given responsibility for raising the money. His targets were companies that did business with the federal government; whether their people had been close to Pageau — or even known him — was beside the point. "I got a call from Nantel, and Nantel wanted a donation to the bag," remembers one businessman who had just won an excellent contract with the new government. "I said, 'What's the goal? What kind of a trust are you raising? What sort of standard of living has been decided is acceptable here for the prime minister's friend's widow and children?'"

Nantel's answers were vague, but he promised to be more specific when they met for a scheduled lunch a few days later. Over a meal in a Montreal restaurant, "Nantel brought it up," the businessman said, "and he made it very clear to me — with a wink — that it had a purpose much broader than simply sustaining the family.

"Then there was a period when everybody in the world had his phone ring. Anybody who could have heard that the prime minister made a promise at Pageau's deathbed got a call to contribute to this. And other people started making calls for donations to the trust. It was very clear [to me] that the trust was a Trojan horse," the businessman said. "They were raising the money for somebody else." He finally turned down Nantel's request for a donation to the Pageau trust.

Gaetan Laflamme, an accountant with the Montreal consulting firm Samson Belair Deloitte Touche, had been Nantel's personal financial adviser for many years. He too says that Nantel talked to him about doing something to ensure that Pageau's widow would never want for anything for the rest of her life. But Laflamme says that as far as he knows Nantel never set up a trust for her, although he did put Joubert on the company's payroll and she worked there five days a week until her patronage appointment began.

In 1986, Nantel's wife, Michelle Lépine, who knew her husband was the bagman for the Pageau trust, was at a political dinner and ran into Joubert. By this time Lépine and Nantel were estranged and living apart; during a friendly chat with Joubert, Lépine asked her a casual question about what Nantel was doing these days. It was completely innocent; after all, their husbands had been business partners and shared the offices on Rue des Brésoles. The next morning Nantel was on the phone to Lépine demanding that they meet right away. He'd heard something he had to discuss with her, he explained. Puzzled, she agreed, and they chose a convenient café on Avenue Laurier in Outremont, halfway between her home and his office. When she arrived, she had never seen him so angry. "Don't ask any questions about what I am doing," he hissed. "I have good insurance. You will be well taken care of." Storming out in a rage, he left her behind in the café, stunned and frightened.

Lepine realized that someone had told her husband that she'd been talking to Pageau's widow and for whatever reason it made him crazy. The subject of Pageau and especially of the Pageau trust remained out of bounds, but members of Nantel's family believed that he was collecting money and depositing it in a bank in Europe for the trust — or for some close friend in the Conservative Party.

When she was contacted in 1994 about the trust, Joubert was bewildered. No, she said, there was no trust in her late husband's name and she'd never heard of anything like it. And no, she had not received a cent from her husband's friends since his death. What she had been given was the patronage job as a Citizenship Court judge.

It wasn't long after Michelle Lépine was berated by her husband about the conversation with Huguette Pageau that the Nantels decided their marriage was over. He was openly involved with another woman, and the bickering over child support and alimony became acrimonious. If Lépine asked for too much, Nantel warned her, he would declare personal bankruptcy. With no income of her own, Lépine could not afford to hire lawyers and accountants to prove her suspicions that Nantel had plenty of money squirrelled away in offshore accounts.

A friend who was an official with the federal Liberal Party offered to help her, but there were strings attached. The Liberals, he told her bluntly, had heard that Nantel was running banking errands for a very senior Conservative, errands that involved trips to Swiss banks. Nantel, they said, was depositing money into an account in Zurich for himself and the high-ranking Tory. If she helped them get the information they wanted, they'd make sure she was taken care of. After much soul-searching, Lépine turned down the offer, tempting though it was. Not only was she terrified of Nantel's wrath if he should find out, but she decided her quarrel was with her husband, not with the Conservative Party.

Michelle Lépine, now fifty-one, is a beautiful woman. Petite and chic, with strawberry-blonde hair, fair skin, and deep blue eyes, it is easy to imagine her as the ballet dancer she once was. She had been Nantel's second wife for fifteen years, they had a son and daughter who were very dear to him, and it had been a bitter blow to discover that he planned to leave her for another woman. On September 4, 1987, Lépine swore an affidavit as part of her divorce action. In it she said that she and Nantel were married in 1974 and that her husband had left her on October 22, 1986. She'd stayed at home to look after her family, she said, and now, at forty-four, it was too late to build a new career. To live decently, in the style to which she'd become accustomed, she was asking for $5,952 a month. And, she added, it was little enough. After all, her husband was living with a mistress in comfortable circumstances: "My husband has continued to follow the same luxurious lifestyle that I knew during our marriage. A great part of this lifestyle was financed by his companies and by his expense accounts. He stays in the best hotels and eats in the best restaurants." The affidavit goes on to describe Nantel's $50,000 BMW 735 automobile, one provided by a company in which he can deduct "100% of his activities."

Since July 1986, she said, Nantel had stopped paying her any housing allowance; she was receiving just $460 a week, which was not enough to live on. "My husband," she swore, "is the owner and director of one of the most important communications companies in

Canada; my husband is considered the *éminence grise* of the Prime
Minister of Canada and he was in charge of the advertising campaign
and public relations for the Conservatives in Quebec in the last federal election." And it was because her husband was so important, she
said, that she had great difficulty finding an accounting firm that
would act on her behalf to investigate his net worth, a net worth she
said included full ownership of Nantel et Associés and Nantel Communications and 50 per cent of Media Canada.

Michelle Lépine eventually succeeded in finding Richard Wise,
a Montreal accountant, to represent her, and he did it with a
vengeance, forcing Nantel to produce all his credit card receipts to
prove her claim of his first-class lifestyle. The receipts provided a
close-up picture of Nantel's business dealings — a picture that
included frequent trips to Paris, Zurich, and other European cities
during the Tories' first three years in power. In early May 1986, he
visited the Oerlikon headquarters just outside Zurich, about the time
the company was completing its bid for the defence contract. Since
Nantel became the company's public relations spokesman, his presence at the Swiss headquarters could be explained. But what of the
other trips? Nantel was not a man who worked on the international
advertising or public relations circuit. Lépine believed he was moving cash into Swiss bank accounts.

During the divorce case, Nantel pleaded poverty, denying his
wife's statements about his affluence. He claimed it was his wife who
wanted the divorce and who told him she planned to move to Paris
with the children. Before their marriage, he noted, she had taught
ballet and worked in an art gallery. Surely, he said, she could try her
hand at these activities again. As for car expenses, he didn't have a
BMW 735, only an old 733, and he'd traded it in for a four-by-four,
which was not a company car . . . His list of grievances went on and
on. Divorces are rarely genteel affairs and this one was no exception;
the trial went on for twelve days in a Montreal court as the two sides
fought over the disposition of Nantel's assets.

Lépine and her lawyers played hardball at the trial. Not only did they subpoena her husband's passport as evidence that he'd made several trips to Switzerland, they tried to get Nantel to admit he'd travelled overseas to deposit money collected by himself and by other political organizers in a special account for the Conservative Party or for a particular Tory. Nantel vigorously denied the accusations, and because divorce proceedings are held in camera in Quebec, the public never learned of the testimony nor of the allegations.

Gaetan Laflamme served as an expert witness for Nantel at the divorce trial. Today Laflamme says that both he and Nantel believed Lépine's case was being financed by the RCMP; they knew she couldn't afford this lengthy and aggressive court procedure. They had no proof of their suspicions. Knowing that Nantel had travelled to Switzerland on a number of occasions, Gaetan Laflamme himself tried to find out from his client whether he had any assets tucked into banks there. Nantel always denied it, but Laflamme was not convinced. "I told him there were ways we could bring the money back without leaving any trace," the accountant remembers, "but he insisted there was no money abroad."

Two months after the divorce trial, just as he had threatened to do, Nantel declared personal bankruptcy. An examination of his bankruptcy records suggests he planned it carefully. On June 26, 1987, Nantel sold his condominium to his own company, Nantel et Associés, for $350,000. He used part of the money, $31,077, to pay off a loan he had taken from Henri Paquin in March 1987.[4] On November 4, Nantel filed for bankruptcy. In his bankruptcy statement he declared total assets of $45,000 and liabilities of $208,498. His other company, Nantel Communications Inc., which owned 75 per cent of Nantel et Associés, had no assets and a small debt of $26,623, while his personal debts added up to $205,000. The largest personal debt was $189,742 for unpaid federal and provincial income taxes.

Two weeks after he declared bankruptcy, Viviane Landreville, the chief executive officer of Nantel et Associés, issued a press release to say that she didn't want anyone to think the company was in trouble. Nantel et Associés was just fine, she said; the company in difficulty was Nantel Communications. Nantel's bankruptcy, she stated, was a personal one, and he was no longer a shareholder in the company. She didn't mention that Nantel Communications owned three-quarters of Nantel et Associés.

Five months later, on March 16, 1988, Nantel et Associés sold his condominium to a numbered company, 2549-4055 Quebec Inc., for $290,000, $65,000 less than they'd paid for it the year before. The numbered company is, in turn, owned by a holding company called Proficom Inc., which was established in 1987 at 50 Rue des Brésoles, Nantel's business address. On December 16, 1988, at a bankruptcy hearing in Montreal, Judge Jacques Dugas discharged Nantel from personal bankruptcy after he agreed to pay $20,000 of the $190,000 he owed on his income taxes. Revenue Canada officials had opposed Dugas's ruling; both Revenue Canada and provincial tax officials stated that they believed Nantel had staged a fraudulent bankruptcy to evade his tax obligations. Their objections were futile. The following June, Nantel et Associés was liquidated, and after all its debts were paid, there was no cash left.

While almost everyone believes Nantel went bankrupt to thwart Lépine, one or two business associates say it's quite possible he went under because he was not a good businessman. "Nantel was not a shrewd man and he had no business acumen," said an associate. "I almost felt like putting his fingers over my lips when I talked to help him understand what was going on."

And then Nantel disappeared from public sight and from all government ad work for a long while. He found contracts with Conrad Black's UniMedia, Inc., the newspaper publishing company that owns *Le Droit* in Ottawa, Quebec City's *Le Soleil*, and other publications. He worked for a physicians' association and with CAE Industries Ltd. Life was still good for the dapper bon vivant, so good that he was thinking of cutting his work week back to three or four days and operating out of his country home at Brigham in the Lac Brome district of the Eastern Townships. He had bought the house with his new wife, Lucienne Appel, for a little over $100,000.

Three years after the bankruptcy, on November 14, 1990, Nantel and Jean Peloquin met for lunch at Le Mas des Oliviers. They had a project to discuss — they were thinking of starting a newspaper in Paris. The talk turned to other subjects, and Nantel told Peloquin he planned to spend the weekend at Brigham, where he enjoyed gardening and puttering around the property. Lucienne was still at work, so after the lunch he left a message for her at their Grosvenor Street house in Westmount and drove to their country place. That evening Lucienne called him at 8 o'clock and again at 11. No answer. She wasn't overly concerned and went to bed. The next morning, she tried twice again. Still no answer. By now she was worried, so she got in her car and drove to Brigham. At 3:40 in the afternoon she found him dead, sprawled on the floor of the solarium. He was dressed in outdoor clothes, a Thermos of coffee and a leather bag carrying some hunting gear nearby. A .308 rifle lay beside the body.

There was no inquest, no police investigation. His ex-wife, Michelle Lépine, and their children were not notified for thirty-six hours, and after they were informed, no police officer ever questioned them. If the police had troubled to talk to the family, they would have discovered some interesting facts. They would have learned that Nantel disliked hunting and that in fifteen years of marriage to Michelle, he had gone hunting only once. Nevertheless, Nantel knew better than most how to handle a gun. He had been educated at a military college, Collège Militaire de Saint-Jean, and was familiar with loading and cleaning guns. "And he certainly knew enough not to load a gun in the house," said one family member.

The police would also have discovered that a few weeks before he died, he was in the country with his daughter when a stranger in a large black BMW pulled into the narrow road leading to his property. Although the driver said he'd taken the wrong turn, Nantel was disturbed by the incident. The day Nantel died, a motorist had asked people in a nearby village for directions to the cottage, something no one had told the police.

The local coroner, Jean-Charles Godreau, examined the body in the morgue at Cowansville Hospital and reported that Nantel had died as a result of a gunshot wound to the head. A pathologist, Dr. Yasmine Ayroud, then did the post-mortem. Her report showed that Nantel had been in excellent health, took no medication, had no history of drug or alcohol abuse. Nor did he have any financial or marital problems, added the coroner's report. There was no reason, he said, for Nantel to take his own life. But what was especially odd was the way he had died. Powder burns around his nose showed that the rifle had been pointed at the right nostril and then fired, blowing off the top of his head. At the very least it was an odd angle at which to hold and fire a rifle, and an unusual way to use a gun in a suicide, the police admitted.

If they'd dug a little further, they would have discovered that the gun did not even belong to Nantel. It was a light Remington .308 of the 600 Series, and Nantel had borrowed it from a friend a few years earlier. He'd been invited on a deer-hunting trip, he'd told his friend, and didn't have a suitable rifle. The friend offered to lend him the Remington, a prized gun that is no longer made; it was light to carry but still an accurate gun for hunting deer. This was the single hunting trip Lépine had remembered. His friend was irritated because Nantel had failed to return the gun despite several requests; later he was aghast to learn that this was the weapon that had killed him.

The police ran ballistics and fingerprint tests on the gun and finally concluded there was no evidence of foul play. How did they explain the death? "I have the impression it was an excess of 'buck fever,'" wrote coroner Godreau. "That is to say, a state of enthusiasm that affects hunters for two weeks every year. They become so preoccupied with a dream of a 400-pound buck with their picture in the paper and with a trophy on the wall of their living room that they are imprudent and dangerous to themselves and to anyone who may be in the woods . . . There is no reason to believe that this was a suicide, there was no good-bye letter, no particular problems [in his life]," added the coroner. He dismissed the case as an accidental death.

"I thought his death was very suspicious," Lépine said in a brief interview. "I still do." But with Nantel dead, the most flamboyant ad man of the Tory era was gone, and with him died the secrets of all those trips to Switzerland. There was no point in pushing to find the funds she believed her husband had stashed away. All he'd left their children was $25,000 each in insurance to be paid when they turned twenty-one. Mulroney rushed to the aid of Lucienne Appel and appointed her to an $85,000 job at the Immigration and Refugee Board, a refuge much favoured by Montreal Tories for wives, widows, and mistresses.

There was nothing for Michelle Lépine. Broke and in despair, always moving from one cheap apartment to another with her children, she finally swallowed her pride and called some of her husband's former friends, now all senators: Guy Charbonneau, Mario Beaulieu, and Michel Cogger. Charbonneau agreed to see her at his office but the discussion was chilly. When Lépine left, it was with the thought running through her head that the senator was trying to assess how much she knew about her ex-husband's activities and that when he was satisfied that she knew nothing important, he dismissed her with a cool suggestion that she send him her curriculum vitae. "She was in dire straits," recalls Charbonneau, "and I circulated her CV." Eventually the Tories produced a three-year appointment to the Unemployment Insurance Review Committee, an occasional low-paid job usually passed by MPs to low-level party faithful in their ridings.

Eight months later, people close to Lépine say, she called Senator Mario Beaulieu for help. He invited her to lunch at Le Petit Logis, another one of Charbonneau's favourite lunching spots. The meeting was deeply uncomfortable for Lépine. There were just three other customers in the restaurant, all men, and one of them was Charbonneau.

She believed she was there to be watched by Charbonneau; once again, she thought to herself, they were checking to see what she knew.

The only one of the three Tories she called who showed any sympathy was Cogger, but his neck turned beet red when she suggested that the RCMP was interested in Nantel's banking trips to Switzerland for a senior Tory. Cogger dismissed the notion, saying that no one would have trusted Nantel with large sums of money.

People close to Lépine say she has been warned not to talk about Nantel. One RCMP officer told her the Mob was probably behind his killing, before adding the friendly warning that no good could come of inquiries into his mysterious death.

After Nantel's death, hand-picked Tory advisers continued to give federal advertising contracts to favoured companies. If there were complaints, they were silenced or not expressed publicly. Mulroney had faced down his opponents before and no one felt that protests would have any effect. The last real fuss about advertising concerned the nature of the advertising itself, not who got the contracts. Under the energetic efforts of Toronto businessmen John Bitove and Trevor Eyton, the Tories raised millions of dollars to pay for ads in support of the free trade deal, advertising that essentially encouraged Canadians to vote Conservative in the 1988 election. Several interesting stories emerged out of this campaign, including allegations that Alcan donated $250,000 to the free trade cause and soon afterwards received federal permission to proceed with the Kemano Dam in British Columbia, a dam that is expected to kill at least 20 per cent of the salmon population in the B.C. river system. The RCMP investigated allegations of payoffs and other criminal activity but eventually dropped the matter.[5]

Thanks to Chris Cobb and Mark Kennedy, two reporters at the Ottawa *Citizen*, more information came to light on federal advertising and polling contracts in late 1992 and early 1993. Their findings revealed what was, in a way, the last mad fling. The first story

concerned lucrative polling contracts handed out during the 1992 constitutional referendum to an Ottawa firm whose partners were members of the government's national Yes Committee. The Yes Committee,
composed of leading lights from all three major parties, was assembled
to advise the government on how to win the citizens' support of the
Charlottetown agreement. Throughout the referendum campaign, the
government indulged in massive polling.

Among the Ottawa members of the committee were former Tory
election campaign director Harry Near, who was now the committee's co-chairman; Bill Fox, Mulroney's former press secretary; and
Michael Robinson, a former financial officer in the federal Liberal
Party. All three were partners, with another prominent Tory, Bruce
Anderson, in a company called Earnscliffe Strategy Group — a company that had been founded by yet another Tory veteran, Hugh
Segal. Segal sold his shares in 1991, a few months before he moved
into the PMO in 1992 as Mulroney's principal secretary.

Cobb and Kennedy discovered that an Earnscliffe subsidiary,
run by Anderson and called Anderson Strategic Research but whol-
ly owned by all the partners, had received several polling contracts
from Joe Clark's office when he was the minister of federal-provin-
cial relations. The Earnscliffe partners huffed that they had earned
the polling contracts, worth $305,000, on their own merits, although
they admitted that Anderson Research had been picked by Allan
Gregg, head of Decima Research, the Tory party's official pollster.
Anderson had worked for Gregg at Decima before moving into the
Earnscliffe partnership. (Decima won referendum contracts for
$947,000.) Equally interesting was the fact that Anderson's wife,
Nancy Jamieson, worked for Lowell Murray as a senior adviser and
de facto chief of staff; all the contracts were untendered and
approved by Murray in his role as chairman of the cabinet commit-
tee on communications.

A second story revealed the details of a $21-million advertising
contract for Canada's 125th anniversary as a confederation. These

were the famous "feel good" ads, one of which featured a young girl singing. The child bore an uncanny resemblance to Mila Mulroney, and the opposition parties protested that they were Tory propaganda. "When you're the government and you're at 16 or 17 per cent in [opinion poll] popularity, there's no doubt that anything which will make people feel better is bound to have positive repercussions on you," Liberal MP Don Boudria told Mark Kennedy in July 1992.

Once again, it was Bob Byron, chairman of the government's Advertising Management Group, who handled the contract, which was awarded, untendered, to two companies with close ties to the Tories. The bulk of the contract went to PNMD/Publitel of Montreal, while a smaller portion was given to Palmer Jarvis of Vancouver, a company that had donated generously to the Tory party and received other government contracts. (PNMD/Publitel had given $10,000 to the Tories in 1990.) The decision was made without consulting the Secretary of State's Department, which paid for the ads. Although bypassing the department was strictly against government policy, the Tories were typically defiant in their dismissal of the rules. Byron reported directly to Lowell Murray, and the public servant in charge, Nick Mulder, the deputy minister at Supply and Services, said that was fine with him. "He's appointed by the Senator and PCO [the Privy Council Office]," Mulder told Cobb and Kennedy. "Those decisions are made by the minister and we are here to implement them."

It was a clubby arrangement. Both Byron and Murray sat on the party's national re-election committee and so did Raymond Boucher, the president of PNMD/Publitel. Boucher had done work for the Tories in the 1988 campaign, and his company received significant government work in the Tories' second term. When *The Citizen* reported that there was no competition for these contracts, Murray lost his temper and sent a barrage of angry letters to the paper. Of course there was a competition, Murray fumed. Six companies, he said, were invited to compete in June 1991, and a committee of five people had picked the winners. What he didn't say was that four of the companies were far too small in the opinion of government representatives on the committee to do the job, and one of these, Camp Advertising, was already up to its ears in government work. That left two — the two that won. There was a kind of competition, but the outcome was never in doubt. The competition consisted of an expensive dinner at Café Henry Burger in Hull at which the candidates chatted about how to design a two-page advertising spread for one of the July 1992 issues of *Maclean's* magazine.

One public servant, Chuck Guité, director of the advertising and polling section at Supply and Services, admitted he had not produced a written report for Murray rating the different pitches. All he did was brief him orally. And when he tried to explain to Cobb and Kennedy how the winner was picked, Guité became extremely defensive. Treasury Board policy was not followed in this instance, he said, because "the policy is a guideline. It's not a rule. We change the guidelines to fit the situation . . . It's not the first time it's been done and not the last time it will be done either." Guité tried to tell the reporters a rating system had been used, but he was contradicted by Ruth Cardinal, another bureaucrat who was at the dinner, who said no rating system of any kind was applied. The Tories were so angered by *The Citizen*'s stories that Harvie Andre stood up in the Commons and attacked Cobb and Kennedy personally. "They were really sensitive about this advertising contract," said Cobb later, "because it involved an awful lot of money." It usually did.

Ironically, even some executives from favoured Tory ad agencies were upset about the contracts that went to PNMD/Publitel. One of them was Yvon Martin, who had been so lucky with Canada Post and VIA Rail. The Canada 125 and constitutional referendum advertising had drained budgets for other projects, Ray Boucher had been the big winner, and Martin's firm was losing revenue. According to a senior advertising executive in Montreal, Martin complained to Fernand Roberge and asked for a piece of the constitutional action. This time, he struck out.

The experience of *The Citizen* in trying to find a copy of one written report concerning an advertising contract proved to be telling. During their investigations into allegations of kickbacks and bidding irregularities in federal advertising contracts, the Mounties made an astounding discovery: it was often impossible to obtain the written contracts the government had signed with ad agencies because in many cases no written contracts had been concluded. The contracts for which the police were searching didn't exist. The only way to confirm that an agency had received monies from a federal contract was to search the company's banking records for evidence of government cheques that had gone through the account. With photocopies of the cheques, the Mounties could then go to a government warehouse and have the government's original of the cheque pulled from storage. The cancelled cheques sometimes carried references to purchase orders but never to a contract as such. The Mounties were accustomed to following complex paper trails, but this was altogether beyond their experience.

RUNNING AFOUL OF THE BOSS

ULRONEY HAD MOVED INTO HIS SECOND TERM IN OFFICE FULL of confidence. Despite all the problems of the first four years, Canadian voters were not impressed with the performance of Liberal leader John Turner and his party, nor — despite the high personal popularity of leader Ed Broadbent — were they prepared to trust their federal government to the New Democrats. The Tories approached the 1988 election with poor support in the polls, but they ran an aggressive campaign. Mulroney fought it on the free trade issue, and the business community pulled out all the stops to support him. Ultimately, Canadians decided to give the Tories another chance.

And when they came back with their second majority, they made it perfectly clear to the public servants in Ottawa that they wanted no interference. If the Conservative government decided a thing was to be done, no guidelines, experts, regulations, traditions, or reluctant civil servants would stand in their way.

Lobbyists became even more powerful during Mulroney's second term; others matched Frank Moores in his ability to exert direct pressure on cabinet-level decisions. They made so much money that they swaggered around the town as if they owned it, and in a way they did. Threats, intimidation, bullying — all were familiar tools of the trade for a number of lobbyists. But, incredibly, they yearned for respectability. Ottawa has a way of exerting its own subtle pressure on vulgar carpetbaggers and after a while, some of these same individuals grew tired of being disliked, despised, or held in contempt. Changing their tack from bullying to charming, lobbyists began to court senior public servants and a few high-level Liberals, flattering them with salary offers and perquisites that were difficult to resist. In January 1993, old-line mandarins were shocked when they heard that Jack Manion, a former deputy minister and principal at the Canadian Centre for Management and Development, a federal agency, had joined Fred Doucet's lobbying firm, renamed The Government Business Consulting Group Inc.

Mulroney himself took an active role in ensuring that the people and companies he favoured were treated well, but he was able to do so more discreetly than his friends LaSalle, Roberge, Charbonneau, and Joe Stewart. He accomplished it in the privacy of his official residences. Lunch for him was a time to meet a few people and do a few deals, away from the glare of public life. Clinching the deal still meant shaking up a stubborn public service from time to time, and it infuriated him when they dug in their heels. He became involved in one nasty fracas that became all too public, although only part of the story has ever been revealed. It concerned a determined public servant, a flamboyant international banker, and Mulroney's close friend George Vari.

Vari and his wife Helen had become faithful and generous donors to the party; in 1988, for example, Vari donated $25,000 to the Tories, one of the highest personal (as opposed to corporate) donations received that year. In subsequent years his donations continued, although on a less munificent scale. In 1989 they dropped to a mere $789, but they rose the following year to $4,578. In 1991 Sefri Construction, Vari's company, donated $475, while the Varis personally gave $5,672.

As we know, the Varis were close to both Mulroneys, and they had befriended Toronto MP John Bosley and his wife, Nicole, as well. During an interview in the summer of 1994, Vari explained that he'd met the Bosley family many years ago and that John Bosley had been on Sefri's small board of directors for sixteen years. Corporate records show that Bosley was one of four officers of the company throughout his political career, which began when he was first elected in 1979 and includes the period between November 5, 1984, and October 1, 1986, when he was the Speaker of the House of Commons. Under the Mulroney conflict guidelines, Bosley did not have to declare his interest in Sefri nor resign from the company's board because he was not a cabinet minister, though he enjoyed cabinet rank. As Vari himself said, he was like a "godfather" to Bosley; when Bosley and Nicole were married in 1984, the Varis loaned them their Paris flat for their honeymoon. When George Vari needed a helping hand, Brian Mulroney and John Bosley were only too happy to assist.

It was not a small favour: in 1991 Vari wanted support for the financing of a new hotel in Budapest, in his native Hungary. Such a project did not qualify for CIDA aid or any other Canadian funds, but there was a route to public financing through two international agencies, the European Bank for Reconstruction and Development and the World Bank. Like the Federal Business Development Bank in Canada, these were international versions of last-resort lenders; both had Canadian representatives on their boards. Technically the World Bank loaned money to governments, but a subsidiary of the bank, called the International Finance Corporation, loaned money to private enterprise. "[The IFC] can't lend money to governments," said a former employee, "although it has sneaky ways to get around this rule. Its job is to operate at the cusp of bankable deals, to lubricate the deal to get market lenders, to do things just a little beyond the reach of risk perception. The acid test is whether their presence brings support from private lenders."

In July 1991, Vari announced he'd just bought his forty-fifth hotel, the Grand Hotel Royal in central Budapest, and that he planned to spend $100 million (U.S.) converting it into a luxury 380-room four-star hotel with new office, retail, and underground parking space. The work was to begin in October. Vari's partner in the project, with 50 per cent of the deal, was a French-owned construction company called CBC (Compagnie Générale de Bâtiment et de Construction); it was owned by the French conglomerate Compagnie Générale des Eaux. Sefri and CBC named their new Hungarian consortium Royal Beruhazo.

Vari went to both the EBRD and the IFC for financial backing for the consortium; he wanted about $28 million from the EBRD and $58 million from the IFC. With this kind of support from the two banks, he could approach commercial lenders for the rest of the money. The banks' endorsement was crucial.

Canada was only one of twenty-three countries that had banded together as partners to establish the EBRD, and it had contributed a disproportionately large $119 million in seed money. In May 1991, before the public announcement of the Vari plan, Don McCutchan, Canada's new representative on the board of the EBRD, was told by the PMO to arrange a lunch with Vari. McCutchan's job was an arm's-length position and he was supposed to be independent of the Canadian government, so the request from the PMO was irregular. But later, when the men relaxed over lunch at London's Connaught Hotel — a lunch attended by John Bosley, then chairman of the Commons foreign affairs committee, and Gaetan Laverture, a senior officer at the Canadian High Commission — the atmosphere was pleasant. Vari was charming and McCutchan liked him.

McCutchan had been a Toronto banker and an aide to Mike Wilson. He decided to check with his old boss about the relationship between Vari and Mulroney. Wilson told him he didn't know exactly; all he could say was that the construction millionaire was close to the prime minister. (Later, in Mulroney's last year in office, the Wilsons attended the prime minister's birthday party at 24 Sussex Drive. Vari was at the head table and, said one of Wilson's friends, "Mike was just another face in the crowd.")

The flamboyant new president of the EBRD, Jacques Attali, had also become a good friend of Mulroney. Mulroney thought he could enlist Attali's support for Vari's project, and he had talked to him about it in an unusual one-on-one meeting at Harrington Lake in June 1991, during a visit Attali made to Canada. The bureaucrats recognized immediately that Attali was held in high regard — he was accommodated at the government's guesthouse at 7 Rideau Gate, a residence normally reserved for heads of government. As they read the tea leaves of diplomacy, this put Attali in the most-favoured-guest category.

To ensure that Vari's hotel project stayed on the EBRD's agenda, Mulroney reminded McCutchan repeatedly to promote the loan. And McCutchan wasn't the only Canadian being harassed to push the project; those who know the players well say that Frank Potter, a former Bank of Montreal executive who was Canada's representative at the World Bank, was also feeling tremendous pressure to have his organization cough up the money through the IFC. Potter even received calls about the loans from the PMO, an unprecedented practice that had never occurred during his eight years at the World Bank. The calls were not from Mulroney himself but from one of his senior aides. Bosley also telephoned the World Bank staff frequently, using his position on the foreign affairs committee as an excuse for his lobbying, but on one occasion he let it slip to an interested listener — who wasted no time passing the news around — that he hoped to get a job with Sefri after he left politics. The bankers were unaware that Bosley was already an officer of the company.

On Christmas Eve, 1991, McCutchan was at home with his family, anticipating a performance by one of his children in a school concert that night. The phone rang; it was Bosley. What's happening to the Vari loan? he demanded. Is the EBRD going to support it or not? "John," replied a stunned McCutchan, "I understand it's important, but it *is* Christmas Eve."

"I don't give a shit," snapped Bosley.

McCutchan finally convinced Bosley that he could find out nothing for at least a week. All the banks in London, including the

EBRD, were closed for the holidays. Still, the coercion made the young banker anxious, and it also made him angry. After several years in Michael Wilson's office he was no political virgin, but this kind of lobbying, he thought, was unacceptable.

The truth was that neither McCutchan nor Potter could drum up much support for Vari's hotel project at their respective banks. There was a natural resistance to all the high-level heat that was being applied by the Canadians. For instance, Ron Freeman, an American who had been a successful merchant banker at Salomon Brothers in New York before joining the EBRD as second-in-command to Attali, was not keen on the hotel project. Nevertheless he was reluctantly supporting it because it was the only Canadian proposal among the 130 projects in the pipeline.

During a visit Freeman made to Ottawa in March 1992, Michael Wilson invited 150 of the country's top financial officers and bureaucrats to the ninth-floor dining room at the Lester Pearson Building for a dinner in Freeman's honour. In his remarks Freeman was extraordinarily blunt. There's a lot Canada could do in the rebuilding of Eastern Europe, he told them, but the EBRD had only one Canadian project before them. We're taking a serious look at it, said Freeman acidly, "despite the prime minister's unwarranted interference in it." His audience was shocked, but there were no reporters in the room and no Canadian bureaucrat would risk his professional skin by leaking Freeman's attack on Mulroney.

An example of the prime minister's direct interference occurred in April 1992. While EBRD officials were holding their annual meeting in Budapest, the London headquarters were badly damaged in a terrorist attack. During the meeting, word came that Mulroney was calling Attali. People were touched, assuming he was phoning at once to express his sympathy and concern. Attali excused himself to take the call. When he returned to the meeting, he was asked if Mulroney had commented on the attack. "No," replied Attali sourly, "he was calling about the Vari project again."

A few weeks later, in July 1992, Mulroney sent one of the government's Challenger jets to Washington to fetch Attali for another meeting in Ottawa; once again, 7 Rideau Gate was made available to him and his entourage. A meeting was scheduled at 24 Sussex Drive and officials hovered nearby on the front lawn, waiting for the signal that would summon them inside. One of them was Don McCutchan.

As the banker walked through the front door, Mulroney was waiting but did not greet him; all he said was "How are things going at the bank?"

"Good, sir," replied McCutchan.

"How about the Vari loans?" Mulroney demanded.

"Sorry, sir," replied McCutchan, while other officials, waiting to enter, shuffled nervously. "It hasn't come to the board yet. I expect it will be brought up at the next board meeting. I don't expect there will be a problem."

"There damn well better not be," Mulroney snapped. With a muttered comment about what McCutchan had to do if he valued his job, Mulroney turned away to greet the next visitor in line. The inference was unmistakable: Vari was to get what he wanted, or McCutchan was out of a job.

After the meeting, Attali took the government Challenger to Mirabel Airport to catch his flight to Europe, and McCutchan pondered his future. His career depended on his somehow persuading the bank to agree to loan the money for Vari's hotel. Potter was feeling similarly harassed; he had also been heavily lobbied by John Bosley, who had called him at least a dozen times. Neither Potter nor McCutchan could know that the whole problem would soon be taken out of their hands.

In August 1992 the EBRD and the IFC both approved the loans to Vari's consortium. The EBRD agreed to shell out $35 million; the IFC offered $25 million of its own money, another $25 million as a syndicated loan, and a final $10 million in what was called a "subordinated advance," all in U.S. dollars. But Vari wasn't popping champagne corks yet; troubling new problems cropped up. First, Vari was having real difficulty arranging the financing for his share of the project, and without an injection of equity from the consortium, the EBRD and the IFC would not be able to lend him the money.

Why he had so much trouble has never been explained, but international banking officials say it was because of a major scandal that hit Vari's partners at CBC. In February 1993, Gilbert Simonet, CBC's chief executive officer, was charged with misappropriation of CBC funds. Specifically, Gilbert was accused of giving a 20-million-franc payoff to French industrialist Roger-Patrice Pelat, a close friend of President François Mitterrand; the payoff took the form of work done on Pelat's château. The story got much worse. After Simonet was charged, it appeared that he had spilled some scandalous beans: he told the police that in 1986 Pelat had given former French prime minister Pierre Beregovoy an interest-free loan of 1 million francs (or $240,000) to buy a flat in Paris. Pelat died in 1989 and his heirs claimed in the press that the loan had been repaid with works of art and valuable books. As the investigation into Pelat's affairs enveloped Beregovoy, it became the worst insider-trading scandal in France's history. Beregovoy, sixty-seven, was shoved out of office, and five weeks later, on May 1, 1993, while walking along the banks of a canal in his home town of Nevers, he shot himself.

Because Vari's partners were so tangled up in this mess, the news was not helpful to his consortium as it struggled to find private lenders to make up its third of the project's budget. Over the next few months, EBRD and World Bank officials were flummoxed to find Vari trying to renegotiate his original loan requests. "Vari couldn't get private lenders," said a former member of the IFC. "So the pressure was intense to lend him *all* the money."

In the middle of these negotiations, Mulroney took an extraordinary step. In his 1992 Christmas list of patronage appointments he named Vari to SIRC, the Security Intelligence Review Committee, a much-coveted honour that brings with it an appointment to the

Queen's Privy Council and a title. From this moment on, Vari could call himself "the Honourable."

McCutchan was away when Vari attempted to reopen his negotiations with the lending institutions, and it was Frank Potter at the World Bank who took the heat. "But Frank didn't care," said one of his friends. "He didn't give a rat's ass about Vari." He may have been able to fend off Vari, but it didn't mean he was happy about it. According to a friend who knows Potter well, Potter told Michael Wilson that he had never felt so hounded in all his years at the World Bank. Vari was not happy with the cold shoulder he got from Potter and wrote a letter to Mulroney complaining about Potter's "unprofessional behaviour." By this time, however, nothing the two Canadians could have done would have budged officials at their institutions — there was no money for Vari, period. In the final analysis, he failed the demands of both the IFC and the EBRD that he raise a portion of the money himself.

In desperation Vari tried bargaining with Hungary's State Property Association (known as the AVU); as the Hungarian paper *Heti Vilaggazdasag* reported in September 1993, "Sefri-CBC was due to reopen the hotel this year. It tried to avoid paying the agreed $26-million price first by doing nothing, then by bargaining the price down with the AVU." By November 1993, the AVU had cancelled the deal altogether and was looking for a new buyer; by April 1994, it had decided to do the renovations itself. Vari explains the project's failure as the result of a dispute between city officials in Budapest and politicians at the national level over the land and the building. His own financing and the problems besetting his partners at CBC had nothing whatsoever to do with it, he insists.

The whole Vari mess was only one of the nails in Don McCutchan's professional coffin. At the same time that Mulroney and Vari were after him for the EBRD money, another uncomfortable situation was developing around the leadership of Jacques Attali. Over the years, Mulroney and Attali had become close friends. In many ways, the men were brothers under the skin; both had huge egos and quick tempers, and both were personally profligate in their spending. Like Mulroney, Attali was the son of a poor man; he was born in Algeria in 1943, the son of a Jewish perfume merchant. Eventually his father became extremely wealthy and was able to give his son an expensive education and see him become the intimate friend of powerful French politicians. Attali established a think tank for President Mitterrand that designed a plan for the massive nationalization of French banks and industry, a plan that was eventually discarded by Mitterrand himself.

"It is Attali's misfortune to have a face that is smug even at rest," wrote David Wall, an editor at *The Wall Street Journal*'s European edition, in an amusing and perceptive profile in *The American Spectator* in September 1993. "It lacks much in the way of a chin, and his mouth, indented, falls naturally into a shape that suggests superciliousness. Like French foreign policy Attali is ugly, yet vain. You miss the first five minutes of a conversation with him because you are dazzled by how well-dressed he is. He can be seen wherever the air is thick with consultation, with his matching Hermès tie and kerchief, his gold-plated Benjamin Franklin glasses, his subtle cuffs. One gets the impression he mousses each hair individually . . . He is famous for accepting invitations to three dinner parties an evening in Paris, and showing up at each."

The EBRD was another Attali brainwave, his own effort to launch a kind of 1990s Marshall Plan for the reconstruction of Eastern Europe, and he bragged about staffing it only with Nobel laureates. None came, but by dangling high tax-free salaries, he did attract about 700 very bright new people, including Canada's Don McCutchan, Mike Wilson's nominee. The fact that Attali became the first president, rather than a more popular Dutch candidate, was the result of the French government's agreement to having the bank headquarters in London as long as the first president was French. Mulroney supported Attali, which helped tilt the decision in Attali's favour.

Attali was put in charge of building and furnishing the EBRD's London headquarters. Needless to say, he spared no expense, something that irritated the British, who were paying the bills. It cost the British government £66 million, or about $132 million (U.S.). McCutchan had recommended a site in the Docklands area of Canary Wharf, where land was going for bargain rates; Attali vetoed his suggestion in favour of a more expensive location in the heart of the City, London's financial district. Attali's spending spun out of control. The new bank had an art collection worth $700,000, and its headquarters boasted nine restaurants. "The kitchen and wine cellar . . . acquired legendary status," wrote David Wall, "as did the mini-skirted receptionists." Other reports said he'd lavished £1.4 million ($2.8 million) chartering fifty-seven private jets for himself and his staff, while bank employees took another twenty-one trips on the Concorde that were deemed unnecessary. When an audit was done, the list of Attali's extravagances outraged European finance ministers: Attali had replaced the lobby's travertine marble with more expensive marble from Carrara at an extra cost of $1.5 million; he accepted hefty speaking fees, including one for about $40,000, which was against EBRD rules; he set up a Paris office without telling the bank's board; he routinely charged the bank twice for expenses; he spent $100,000 on a staff party; he loaded up his credit card with personal expenses and did not repay the bank until April 1993, after the stories of his follies appeared. The final blow came when it was revealed that Attali had spent a total of $400 million on operating the bank itself, twice as much as it had given out in loans for European reconstruction.

Who belled the cat? Don McCutchan. The Canadian director of the EBRD was the vice-chairman of the bank's audit committee, which uncovered the mess; and he was the only one of the bank's twenty-three directors who refused to sign the bank's 1993 budget of $210 million, although other directors were horrified. When he refused, all hell broke loose: McCutchan was forced to give reasons for his decision to senior Finance Department officials in Ottawa, to whom he was responsible, and he was warned that his action could well lead to his dismissal by a prime minister who was close to Attali. At the same time, Britain's *Financial Times* got wind of the story and published all the salacious details; financial circles in London and the rest of Europe were agog. Mulroney didn't hesitate. On March 5, Mulroney ordered a Challenger jet to New York to bring Attali to Ottawa for a private meeting. A few days after their meeting, Mulroney demanded McCutchan's resignation, a full year before the posting was due to end.

In the House of Commons, opposition MPs went after Mulroney, Mazankowski, now the minister of finance, and Michael Wilson, the minister of international trade. All of them refused to defend McCutchan, and all pretended that his recall was the end of a normal tour of duty. Taking McCutchan's part was *Globe and Mail* columnist Jeffrey Simpson; in one article he dismissed the government's excuses as "lies" and added, "The Prime Minister offered a series of complete evasions mixed with whoppers. It must have been excruciating for Messrs. Wilson and Mazankowski to listen to them." Wilson later told McCutchan that Mulroney was "pissed off" that Simpson had written that he'd lied. "The PM did lie," McCutchan retorted, pointing out that his term was for three years and Mulroney knew it. "Why has the prime minister fired the only person with the guts to stand up against this outrageous extravaganza?" demanded deputy Liberal leader Sheila Copps, in the House on April 22. There was no answer.

As Simpson went on to point out, "Mr. McCutchan went to London with specific instructions from Mr. Wilson to keep an eye on Mr. Attali's extravagance . . . In his meeting with Mr. Mulroney, Attali bad-mouthed Mr. McCutchan and made allegations against him, including the accusation that the Canadian representative had assaulted someone at the bank." External Affairs did a thorough investigation of Attali's smear and found the Canadian had conducted himself impeccably.

When reporters met with Mazankowski and Wilson in Paris in June 1993, they asked the ministers why Canada was treating McCutchan so badly at a time when officials at the EBRD were praising him as a hero. Mazankowski continued to bluster that the banker's return to Canada was part of the normal rotation; Wilson sat in glum silence, refusing to defend his friend and former aide. Wilson's lack of courage in this affair is criticized to this day. "We were all very disappointed in Mike," said a Toronto Tory who has known Wilson for years. "We all thought he had more iron in him." Other Tories reacted by having buttons printed and distributed at the Conservatives' 1993 leadership convention that read "F.O.D.M." — Friend of Don McCutchan.

When McCutchan was questioned by reporters, he was tactful. "It's unfortunate that it has come to this," he said. "The EBRD was Mr. Attali's idea, but by leaving he has probably ensured that the bank can in fact fulfill its mandate. Instead of worrying about various allegations, the bank can get on with doing what it was supposed to do — helping Eastern Europe."

While Mulroney was punishing McCutchan, other leaders were deploring Attali's behaviour, and within days the Frenchman was forced to apologize for his excesses and agreed to resign from his job. None of this helped McCutchan in any practical sense; he was out of government and definitely out of favour with Mulroney. He had failed on two counts: he had not been able to manoeuvre George Vari past the rules at the EBRD, and he had not looked the other way when Jacques Attali went out of control. These events hadn't helped the IFC's Frank Potter either. On June 16, Mulroney pulled the highly respected banker out of his job, returning him to a position in Finance based in Toronto, and replaced him with one of his own cabinet ministers, Robert de Cotret.

On the morning of June 25 at 11 a.m., Brian Mulroney signed his own letter of resignation as prime minister of Canada; at exactly the same moment in London, Jacques Attali signed a letter of resignation at EBRD headquarters. As witnessed by former Liberal finance minister Marc Lalonde, who just happened to be at EBRD headquarters that day, Don McCutchan's letter of resignation was faxed to Ottawa at 11:15 Ottawa time, fifteen minutes after Mulroney ceased to be prime minister and Jacques Attali agreed to leave the chairmanship of the EBRD. Not accidentally, and much to the annoyance of PCO Clerk Glen Shortliffe, who had demanded an earlier resignation, McCutchan had outlasted them both.

On July 16, 1993, Attali, now dubbed "Jacques Antoinette" by the European press, faced a new crisis. The bank's audit committee, with Don McCutchan present in his final official duty before he left London, held a press conference to discuss its report on Attali's spending. That same day Attali, who was still coming into the bank because his resignation had not yet taken effect, was forced to cut a deal with the EBRD's board of directors. He agreed to leave immediately if they would drop their investigations into his other questionable dealings at the bank. He declared grandly that he would waive his termination allowance of $290,000 to show his goodwill.

Later that summer McCutchan moved his family to Toronto; today he is happily employed as a financial adviser to the Reichmann family.

George Vari retired from the construction business in the summer of 1993. Sefri was acquired by a numbered company, which used the name Beddington Investments. Beddington, whose four directors included Vari and Bosley, then went into receivership. Asked recently whether Bosley was working for him, Vari said no, adding he had not seen Bosley for months and had no idea what he was doing.

CHAPTER TWENTY-ONE

MR. MULRONEY MEETS MR. BONGO

T WAS ONE OF THOSE BIZARRE EVENTS THAT DEFIED REASON. IN mid-October 1991, Brian Mulroney sat in Gabon's marble-lined Palace of the Renovation beside President Omar Bongo and announced that Canada would give the rich African nation, with its spectacular record of corruption and human rights abuses, $8.25 million for a hydro dam and a loan of another $15 million for incidentals. Although Mulroney would defend the decision later by saying that Bongo was trying hard to democratize his country and that in future Canada would tie its aid to countries exhibiting greater respect for human rights, it was difficult for the average person to understand why Canada was being so generous to Gabon. (The day after he made the pledge on human rights, Mulroney backtracked on linking aid to human rights. He claimed he hadn't really said it.) It was not the first time the Canadian government had lavished millions on Gabon, and one might ask if the country deserved Canada's largesse.

First, consider the demographics. Gabon, which received its independence from France in 1960, is a French-speaking country of 1.2 million people on the Atlantic coast of central Africa. Its citizens die early (men at fifty-one, women at fifty-five) and the infant mortality rate is among the highest in the world at 104 per 1,000 live births; 167 children per 1,000 die before age five. Forty per cent of the inhabitants are illiterate. Still, by Africa's standards, Gabon's citizens are rich. The country produces oil, and in 1991 the average per-capita income was about $4,830 a year, far higher than in any other African country. (South Africa, for example, had a per-capita income of about $2,400 a year in 1991.) This is the reason Gabon does not qualify for aid from CIDA. If Canada wants to give money to Gabon, it has to look elsewhere, as Mulroney's government did.

The second item to consider is the political character of the country, and here one cannot avoid the leader. Omar Bongo, who is protected by a private army of Moroccan and European mercenaries, became president of a one-party state in 1967; in 1990 international pressure forced him to work towards multi-party democracy. In the 1991 election, seven opposition parties elected members to the National Assembly, but Bongo's Gabonese Democratic Party held a majority. Bongo has hung on to power by establishing a thick network of obligations born of political patronage. "His followers receive administrative and economic privileges, commercial advantages and a share in the country's economic growth," reports a 1993 analysis from a U.S. political risk assessment service. "As much as 60 per cent of the government's budget has been spent on salaries and benefits for the president's supporters. He bestows appointments in the civil service and parastatal enterprises, drawing the money to reward his loyalists from state enterprises and presidential accounts." The risk of violent strife under Bongo's rule, the report concluded, was 85 per cent. It would drop to 10 to 15 per cent if the military or the opposition were to take over.

Several years ago, another publication reported that the World Bank had hired Coopers & Lybrand to do an audit on the national oil company in Gabon because it was receiving international assistance but appeared to be badly managed and funds were missing. The audit found the money in a Swiss bank account. Whose account, the audit did not state publicly. In 1990, there was widespread unrest in Gabon and rioting by unhappy public servants, including hundreds of Customs officials. "The president," reported *The Guardian*, "is being openly criticized for incompetence and corruption that has ruined the country but made him one of Africa's richest men."

Bongo's personal extravagance has been breathtaking. Aside from the Palace of the Renovation, with its 40-foot ceilings, he has ten other homes scattered around the country and keeps a fleet of bulletproof Mercedes-Benzes that are airlifted to Lausanne, Switzerland, for servicing every six months. (According to a 1991 report by *The Toronto Star*'s Bill Schiller, the Mulroney advance team "had to plead with Bongo's handlers not to meet Mulroney at the airport with a small fleet of Rolls Royces the Gabonese president owns.") No wonder there was resistance in Canada when some individuals in the Mulroney government started lobbying for money for a variety of projects in Gabon, projects that invariably involved one firm: a Victoriaville, Quebec, construction company called Entreprises Vibec. Lobbying for the first project began in 1986 when Gabon wanted Canadian money to build a new foreign affairs building. Because Gabon was too wealthy to qualify for CIDA assistance, the Tories promoting the project chose one of the country's biggest and most secretive government slush funds, "Section 31" at the Export Development Corporation.

The EDC is a financial institution established in 1944 to help Canadian exporters compete internationally by offering insurance and medium- or long-term financing both to the exporters and to their customers abroad. The insurance is one of the EDC's most important programs; it covers the risks Canadian exporters take when they are obtaining credits, ensuring performance, creating consortiums, and working in volatile political situations. When the EDC refuses to make a loan or offer insurance because the proposal makes no economic sense or cannot meet the usual requirements — in other words, when an international project cannot be justified in any customary terms — it can become a candidate for Section 31 money, funds that are simply allocated by the cabinet for political reasons. "Under Section 31 there is no limit to the loan," explained one bureaucrat who has worked in the area. The criteria are vague; basically all the rules require is that it be "in the national interest" that the thing be done.

Over the years, Mulroney's cabinet approved Section 31 money several times for Gabon — and wound up committing CIDA money for several projects as well, despite the country's supposed ineligibility. The money never went straight to Mr. Bongo, of course; most of it went to Quebec companies doing projects in Gabon.

Monique Landry, who began her Commons career as parliamentary secretary to the minister of international trade and went on to become minister of international development as well as minister of external relations, was a strong proponent of aid for Gabon. She too was interested in seeing that the contract went to Entreprises Vibec. Her assistant, Gilles Déry, called officials at International Trade on numerous occasions to track the contract for the foreign affairs building, the civil engineering for which was to be done by Vibec.

Another lobbyist for Vibec was Montreal communications consultant and lobbyist Richard Gervais. A close friend of Guy Charbonneau and part of the same social circle in Montreal, Gervais was registered not only as Vibec's lobbyist but as the lobbyist for Gabon itself. Gervais had worked as a spokesman for the Pharmaceutical Manufacturers of Canada and for Merck Frosst when the brand-name companies were battling for legislation to improve their patent protection against generic copies; he took up lobbying for these two organizations, and for the Port of Montreal, one of Charbonneau's business interests. All in all, Gervais was someone to be taken seriously; his clients were too important to Mulroney and other top Tories.

But Vibec had an even more powerful supporter in Guy Charbonneau, who was close to Vibec's president, Denis Roy. "Charbonneau was fronting the deal," said one of the officials at the EDC, adding that his office was not happy about Vibec's financial situation at the time, but Charbonneau insisted that the company be given the contract anyway. "His first stop was [John] Crosbie's office, where he was told it was not going to fly as a regular EDC loan." (Crosbie was then minister of international trade.) The fallback was Section 31. Today, Charbonneau willingly confirms that he became involved in the Vibec file. "They had some contracts and they wanted an extension of contracts," he says. "I thought it sounded pretty good."

After much internal wrangling, the cabinet finally approved Section 31 money to pay for 85 per cent or nearly $30 million of the $35-million cost of the foreign affairs building. The supervising contract went to a Quebec firm called Tecsult, one of the companies on Roch LaSalle's short list; the main engineering subcontract went to Lemay Vican, which soon afterwards changed its name to Entreprises Vibec.

Vibec seemed to be blessed. Charbonneau was determined to see it win other contracts, and more Section 31 money found its way to projects in Gabon that could use the assistance of the Victoriaville company. Once in a while extraordinary measures were necessary to secure the funds for these projects, as demonstrated by Mulroney's 1991 visit to Gabon, a twenty-four-hour stopover en route to a Commonwealth conference that baffled the journalists accompanying the prime minister on the trip. "What's a guy like our Prime Minister doing visiting a head of state like President Omar Bongo?" asked the *Star*'s Bill Schiller disdainfully. After briefing his readers on Bongo's self-aggrandizement at the expense of his people, Schiller asked again, "Is this really the kind of person — whose human rights abuses have been catalogued by Amnesty International — with whom we want our Prime Minister fraternizing?"

But Schiller figured out the answer all too easily, as anyone could. Mulroney was there to unveil the latest Canadian government loan, $23.25 million, which, once again, came from the convenient EDC Section 31 slush fund. Once that was taken care of, Mulroney was off by helicopter to Bongo's private hunting reserve at Wongua Wongue for a little heads-of-government R & R. Only flustered EDC officials knew that Mulroney's announcement was premature. It had not been officially approved, and there was still a lot of debate to be heard. By dropping into Gabon to play Santa Claus, Mulroney pulled the rug out from under those recalcitrant officials and politicians who had been raising objections. No one was going to embarrass the prime minister by forcing him to break his promise to a grateful Mr. Bongo.

Vibec was also most grateful and showed it in the time-honoured way; in 1991, the same year it won the contract announced by Mulroney in Gabon, it gave the PC Canada Fund a whopping $40,220.96. It followed this up in 1992 with another $11,696.50. In previous years its donations may not have been as spectacular, but they were always generous and steady. The bagmen could count on Vibec.

There was a third occasion when Charbonneau pushed for Vibec projects in Gabon. "Usually he had his secretary call to ask where the file was," said one official, "but twice he called himself." This time the money was for road paving. Although the country had over 4,600 miles of road, only 380 miles were paved; in 1992 a five-country international consortium won a contract to pave another 1,000 miles of a north-south Gabonese highway. The Gabonese didn't have the funds, of course, and no one asked Mr. Bongo if he couldn't help out by cutting back a little on his car tune-ups in Switzerland. "The construction project will be led by Quebec-based Vibec-Torno Enterprises," reported the *Export Sales Prospector*, a report on engineering construction and operations in the developing world. The two companies had set up a partnership for road construction in 1990 that was now getting the biggest share of the contract — 35 per cent of the total. Well, why not? Vibec was already so well established in Gabon, thanks to the prime minister and Senator Charbonneau.

By this time Michael Wilson was the minister for international trade. His officials didn't have to work too hard to persuade him of the folly of more assistance for Gabon. He resisted the commitment of more Section 31 money; according to some of his closest aides, he did not think the dam and the roads in Gabon were appropriate candidates for Section 31 loans. "Mike kept saying, 'No, no,'" recalled one of his officials. "And Mazankowski said, 'We'll put you down as a maybe.'" This was another project to which the government had committed CIDA money — about $30 million — while the EDC would contribute about $20 million. Once the Tories lost the 1993 election, astute observers in Ottawa said the project seemed to be dying.

Canada has given money to developing countries with appalling human rights records, many of them African nations with records worse than Gabon's. Canada has given more money to other developing countries than it lavished on Gabon. But no other African country had Gabon's wealth. And few companies had the good fortune to enjoy the kind of help that Guy Charbonneau could offer. Lavalin was certainly one of them. Vibec was another. It is clear that he never hesitated to wade in to help his friends; he helped the Favrettos and the Vocisanos win the RCMP lease for their Bona Building, and he helped Perez win the Chambers Building contract with the NCC. All these contracts were controversial, and on one occasion he himself was involved in a controversy over a contract.

One of the interesting things about this contract, which was with the Montreal Port Corporation, was that it was initially granted by the federal Liberal government. Charbonneau himself said the contract went to his consulting company, Charbonneau, Dulude and Associates, because one of his partners, Guy Dulude, was a friend of Port Corporation board member Romeo Boyer, who was a Liberal. His other associate in this company was (and still is) André Gingras, who became a board member himself in 1985.

When the Montreal Port Corporation was looking for new insurance policies in May 1984, it went to Charbonneau-Dulude for advice and then followed up with a consulting contract. Two months later the port gave its business to Pratte-Morrissette, Inc., a subsidiary of insurance giant Marsh & McLennan. Charbonneau not only was on the board of Marsh & McLennan, but he was chairman of the Pratte-Morrissette board. "They [Charbonneau-Dulude] planned the coverage, prepared the tenders, sent them out, submitted the list of competitors to the MPC, and made recommendations about which company should get the contract," said one source at the port corporation. "Other firms got some of the business, but Pratte-Morrissette got 90 per cent of it."

Perhaps this would not have been a problem had Charbonneau not been a senator. Although senators, even the Speaker of the Senate, as he was soon to become, do not have to follow the government's conflict-of-interest guidelines, they do have to abide by the Parliament of Canada Act. And Section 14 (1) of the act says: "No person who is a member of the Senate shall, directly or indirectly, knowingly and willfully be a party to or be concerned in any contract under which the public money of Canada is to be paid."

"I didn't know Pratte-Morrissette won on that proposal," Charbonneau said when he was asked in a 1990 interview about how his company came to have the lucrative port business. He said he had signed an agreement with Marsh & McLennan, Pratte-Morrissette's parent company, saying he would not help the firm get government business, nor would he share in any profits from government contracts. Dominic Taddeo, general manager of the corporation, said that three companies had bid on the insurance and that Pratte-Morrissette had emerged as the low bidder. Pratte-Morrissette was able to keep the bulk of the Montreal Port Corporation business for the next five years.

It was a nice contract to have. In the 1984–85 and 1985–86 fiscal years, the port paid annual premiums of $400,000 to Pratte-Morrissette. In 1986–87, the premiums soared to nearly $1 million. Pratte-Morrissette said the increase was due to a volatile market, which the company expected to cool down shortly. The next year, the premiums were down to about $800,000, and in 1989–90 they dropped to approximately $245,000. Pierre Neveu, a senior executive at Pratte-Morrissette, disputed these figures, saying the premiums were far less; when port authorities were asked to say whose figures were correct, they refused to do so. Pratte-Morrissette finally lost the port business in 1990 when the corporation decided to return to its original policy of placing most of its insurance under the corporate umbrella of the mother ship, the Canada Ports Corporation in Ottawa. Another insurance firm, Reed Stenhouse, a subsidiary of Alexander and Alexander Services Ltd. of New York, now has the bulk of the Canada Ports business. David Angus is on the board of Reed Stenhouse.

In an interview in 1994, Charbonneau displayed a thick sheaf of corporate documents to prove that he had sold all of Chardul to Marsh & McLennan several years ago. He'd kept the name and transferred some of his sale profits back into the company in case of claims against the company. This would explain, he said, why government records might still show that he owned the firm. He insisted Gingras had no role in it and that when he found from newspaper stories that Gingras was presumed to be his partner in the company, he had Gingras's name scrubbed from the records. If all this is true, neither the federal nor the provincial government has up-to-date information. According to the 1993 provincial registrations, Chardul is 100 per cent owned by Peerless, and Peerless is 100 per cent owned by Charbonneau. Although Gingras's name doesn't appear on provincial documents, it still shows up on 1993 federal registrations for Chardul.

The web of Charbonneau's business connections seems endless. In addition to his insurance interests with the Montreal Port Corporation, he is chairman of the board of Versabec Inc., a food service company that has the contract for cafeterias and catering at the port's offices. In 1991, another strand of the web connected Charbonneau to the infamous Bank of Credit and Commerce International, often called "the Bank of Crooks and Criminals." Government regulators around the world, led by officials at the Bank of England, seized BCCI's assets on July 5. BCCI's front man in North America was a Saudi national called Ghaith Pharaon; he illegally acquired two U.S. banks, the National Bank of Georgia and the Central Trust Savings Bank in Miami. In 1979 he had purchased Miron, Inc., a Canadian cement company based in Quebec, and had quickly loaded its board with powerful directors. Its members included Charbonneau; Jock Finlayson, the former president of the Royal Bank of Canada; Donald Macdonald, a former Liberal finance minister and high commissioner to Great Britain; Guy Saint-Pierre, the president of the huge engineering firm SNC Group, Inc.; André Bisson, a former senior officer with the Bank of Nova Scotia; and Joseph Husny, a Pharaon associate in Montreal who became Miron's president. Pharaon's stake in Miron Cement was held through a Panamanian company whose address was that of Husny's home in Montreal.

Miron was able to persuade the government of Canada to let it lease port land at Grand Cacouna, a small community on Quebec's South Shore, east of Quebec City. Miron had a cement operation there and wanted to ensure its access to the land around it. The lease terms were generous, to put it mildly; the government agreed to lease all the land around the port for just a few thousand dollars a year. And Charbonneau's business associate André Gingras was on the board of the Canada Ports Corporation.

In 1989 Pharaon sold his interest in Miron to Lake Ontario Cement Ltd. of Toronto, but the small team of directors who had worked with him moved almost intact to the board of another Husny company called Acme Signals. This company manufactures such useful products as road signs, the kind of item governments at every level will buy.

Pharaon's clout with senior Canadian politicians and businessmen was a thing of wonder to reporters in other countries. In August 1991, just a month after the bank was seized, *Wall Street Journal* reporter Pierre Goad described Pharaon's influence in Canada. "This March," he wrote, "the Université de Montréal's prestigious business school invited Mr. Pharaon to speak to a select group of movers and shakers at the city's Ritz-Carlton Hotel. A university spokeswoman said the business school organized Mr. Pharaon's visit at the request of certain Montreal businessmen she didn't identify. The university official who organized the visit declined to comment."

Halifax lawyer John Grant, one of the
top fundraisers in Atlantic Canada,
about to be disbarred after a financial
scandal in 1988, was found dead of
multiple stab wounds in a Dartmouth
motel. *(Canapress Photo Services)*

Montreal lawyer Bernard Roy,
Mulroney's first chief of staff in 1984,
left Ottawa in June 1988, unhappy
over allegations that he helped a client
obtain a federal government lease.
(Canapress Photo Services)

Happy Birthday, Prime Minister! Chef François Martin
presents Mulroney with a birthday cake in the dining room
of 24 Sussex Drive. *(Private collection)*

*Fred Doucet and his new bride, Alina Kawecki, cut the wedding cake,
cheered on by their hosts, Brian and Mila Mulroney; chef François Martin
made and decorated the cake. (Private collection)*

*Helped by Marina Culizo, François Martin (centre)
works with Kurt Waldele, chef at the National Arts Centre,
on a dinner party at 24 Sussex Drive. (Private collection)*

Montreal lawyer Michel Cogger was under RCMP investigation over allegations that he received improper payments while serving as a senator. (Chuck Mitchell/Canapress Photo Services)

Deputy Speaker Marcel Danis made an ill-fated trip to Guatemala during that country's election in 1985; his candidate lost. (Ron Poling/Canapress Photo Services)

*Former Tory MP Michel Gravel, convicted of influence-peddling in 1988,
and his wife, Louise, leave the federal tax court in Montreal in 1991 after
Gravel testified he passed on $35,000 in bribes to Public Works Minister
Roch LaSalle. (Canapress Photo Services)*

*Senneville (Que.) entrepreneur Guy Montpetit was flying high
on other people's money in Montreal and Saskatchewan until he was
brought down to earth by an investor's lawsuit. (Gazette)*

*After ducking Parliament Hill anti-corruption protester
Glen Kealey for months, Mulroney couldn't avoid him at the door of
the National Press Building in 1989. (John Hryniuk)*

*RCMP Assistant Commissioner Rod Stamler, an experienced
investigator in white-collar crime, left the force in 1989. He later complained
of interference in his investigations of some Mulroney friends,
especially Michel Cogger. (Private collection)*

Helen and George Vari, like parents to the Mulroneys, celebrate the May 1990 opening of Toronto's new Intercontinental Hotel, built by Vari's company, Sefri Construction. (Carrie Cockburn/Financial Post)

The guys of GCI, Ottawa's most powerful lobby firm during the Mulroney years, pictured here in one of the firm's publicity photos. From left: Gary Ouellet, Gerry Doucet, former Liberal communications minister Francis Fox, and Frank Moores.

From 1990 to 1991 former judge René Marin presided over an inquiry into the way the RCMP investigated complaints against Senator Michel Cogger; Marin absolved the police of any wrongdoing. (Fred Chartrand/Canapress Photo Services)

In 1993, a saddened Don McCutchan co-chaired a London press conference on the wild spending of Jacques Attali, president of the European Bank for Reconstruction and Development. Canadian High Commissioner Fredrik Eaton offered cheer with the inscription on this photograph: "Don — here you are pouring scorn and cold water on Attali — well done! Fred." (Private collection)

"Nobody will have to ask me to leave twice, I can tell you that,"
Mulroney told Tories in 1983, according to his biographer L. Ian MacDonald.
"You'll have the biggest parade of moving vans you've ever seen and, pow,
right back to Montreal." These three vans, at 24 Sussex Drive on May 27, 1993,
were among the parade of thirty-one that moved the Mulroneys out.
(Tom Hanson, Canapress Photo Services)

The Mulroneys' new $1.6-million Westmount home at 47 Forden Crescent
after renovation. All the windows were replaced, a portico was added,
and there is a new sun room at the side. (Peter McCabe Photo)

And *The Daily Telegraph* also took notice of Pharaon's political friends in Canada, adding a caustic note that Canadian banking regulators had refused to renew BCC Canada's licence in 1990. "Since then and until its closure, BCC Canada was allowed to operate only on short-term licences," the paper noted. "BCCI is now suspected of having used its Canadian subsidiary to run an extensive money-laundering operation."

CHAPTER TWENTY-TWO

PIE IN THE SKY

THE DETERMINATION OF BRIAN MULRONEY AND GUY Charbonneau to deliver tens of millions of dollars in contracts for projects in Gabon pitted them against a federal bureaucracy that was firmly opposed to the aid. Mulroney's unexpected announcement in Libreville angered official Ottawa. But there was another Mulroney initiative that had much more serious repercussions: his plan to privatize Toronto's Pearson Airport set politicians against bureaucrats in a war that damaged careers, drew fire from the provincial and municipal governments, and ultimately helped destroy federal Conservative support in Metro Toronto. It became one of the sleaziest affairs of his years in office.

By 1992 the government was looking for a private developer to take over two of Pearson's three terminals, Terminals 1 and 2. The new operator would have to spend some money on them but could then enjoy the benefits of milking one of the federal government's richest cash cows. Even in the middle of the recession, Pearson was a money machine. After Kennedy Airport in New York, it is the second-busiest international airport in North America, with an average of 21 million passengers a year. Pearson is responsible, directly or indirectly, for 56,000 jobs. Although its revenues declined from $170 million in 1990 to $134 million in 1991, primarily because of the impact of the privately built and operated Terminal 3 coming into operation in February 1991, the federal government was still able to cream off $42 million a year in profits, money that went to support smaller, money-losing airports in other parts of Canada.

It was too rich a prize to be relinquished to non-profit local airport authorities (known as LAAs), as the government had done with less profitable airports in Montreal and Vancouver. The Mulroney cabinet suggested early on that it would entertain a bid from a Toronto-based LAA, but there was little chance it would succeed. Most of the cabinet understood that the Pearson prize was intended for Don Matthews.

In June 1987 the federal government had awarded the right to build a third terminal at Pearson Airport to a private consortium put together by Toronto developers Huang and Danczkay. In the boom years of the mid-1980s, other companies had bid on Terminal 3, and among the disappointed losers was Don Matthews, one of the most powerful Tories in the party and co-chair of Mulroney's 1983 leadership bid. Even with the help of lobbyist Bill Neville, Matthews was unable to persuade the government that his proposal offered the best financial returns to the government. According to sources close to the process, Mulroney intended to make it up to Matthews.

In 1989, Matthews formed Paxport Management Inc., a consortium fronted by Ray Hession, a former senior Ottawa bureaucrat. Paxport put forward a secret, unsolicited bid for Terminal 2 in 1989. Even though it was turned down, informed people suspected it was just a matter of time before a way would be found to give Matthews's group a big piece of the airport.

Federal bureaucrats in the Department of Transport were completely opposed to the idea of privatizing Pearson. Federal policy decreed that there be airports in centres such as Corner Brook or Saskatoon that would never be financially viable; Pearson's profits helped to keep these airports open. Furthermore, air passenger traffic had dropped by 13 per cent during the recession, and the bureaucrats didn't support their political masters' claims that Pearson would grow by 3 per cent a year and would need extensive expansion to cope with the increased traffic. Why expand, they asked, when the three terminals are half empty? Why turn it over to the private sector when Air Canada and the taxpayers had spent $130 million in the early 1990s to renovate Terminals 1 and 2 and were on the hook for another $72 million in repairs yet to come?

No argument would dissuade the Tories; Mulroney was determined to privatize Pearson. In late 1991 and early 1992, a cabinet committee made up of Deputy Prime Minister Don Mazankowski as chairman as well as Transport Minister Jean Corbeil, Treasury Board President Gilles Loiselle, and two Toronto-area ministers, Michael Wilson and Otto Jelinek, met several times to decide whether to go ahead with a request for proposals from interested bidders. Hugh Segal, Mulroney's chief of staff, attended the meetings. During one wrangle, he piped up with a reality check that still rings in the heads of those who heard it: "Gentlemen, the prime minister wants this to happen."

In February 1992 angry federal bureaucrats tipped off their counterparts in the Ontario provincial government that the cabinet had decided to solicit bids for Pearson. On five hours' notice, provincial officials arranged for Ruth Grier, Ontario's minister responsible for the Greater Toronto Area, accompanied by four regional chairmen including Metro Toronto chairman Alan Tonks, to have an emergency meeting with Corbeil and Wilson at the Carlingview Inn near the airport. The meeting was acrimonious, to say the least. When Grier pointed out that provincial studies had shown a Local Airport Authority would earn $200 million more for taxpayers than a deal with private developers, Corbeil dismissed her comments with lofty disdain. "There are numbers and there are numbers," he said.

As if to underline their contempt for the province and the city, Corbeil and Wilson held a news conference the next day to invite companies to bid on the privatization. But when interested developers examined the fine print, they found that bidders would have only ninety days to submit proposals. Toronto writer Patricia Best pointed out two other bizarre elements in the bidding procedures in an article in *Toronto Life*: "The specifications were extraordinarily detailed, down to the colour of the paint on the walls. Was it written for bidders who had already done most of the work? Surprisingly, it did not require a company to demonstrate its financing — a 'description' of arrangements was all that was called for."

Other bidders, principally Montreal's Claridge Inc., the Montreal Bronfmans' holding company, raised concerns about the bidding process. Don Matthews and Paxport had been readying a bid for months, in contrast to the ninety days their competitors would have. The lack of interest in financing details was also understandable to Paxport's rivals: the Matthews Group was in shaky condition at the time with serious cash flow problems, and its books might not withstand close financial scrutiny. They weren't alone; by 1992 every real estate developer in the country was feeling the pinch, and many had gone into receivership or bankruptcy. Huang and Danczkay itself found its beautiful Terminal 3 half-empty, its high-end retail tenants screaming to be let out of their inflated 1980s leases. The company decided the enterprise was too rich for its blood and finally sold its interest in the terminal to Claridge Inc., which had pockets deep enough to outlast the recession. The only real winners were the lawyers, who pocketed more than $20 million in legal fees during the bargaining for Terminal 3.

To strengthen its financial position, Paxport brought in a number of partners including Agra Industries Limited, a Saskatoon-based holding company that controls Allders Duty-Free Shops. As part of the deal, Allders would have a twenty-five-year exclusive contract for the duty-free shops at Terminals 1 and 2. Matthews in turn would receive a $20-million loan — in effect an equity injection — from Agra, a company in favour with the Tories, perhaps thanks to the $275,854 it had donated to the party since 1985. The last donation on record, for $65,052, was made in 1992, the same year the airport contract was given; it was almost twice the size of any previous Agra donation.

Only Claridge and Paxport submitted proposals, and the government's evaluation took place between July and September 1992. Because there was acrimony over what appeared to be favouritism to Paxport, the government agreed to conduct a "fairness audit." A Montreal accounting firm was asked by Corbeil to evaluate the entire bidding process; after a few drinks one evening, the auditor on the case admitted to a senior Transport Department official that he had been ordered to "find it fair."

As expected, Paxport formally won the contest in early December 1992. The fine details of the privatization still had to be ironed out. Almost immediately it became clear to officials in the Department of Transport that Paxport remained too financially insecure to meet its obligations. "We had all sorts of documentation showing it was not a sensible deal," said one official who worked on it from the start. "The Matthews Group did not have the money to do this project. That's why, when the minister [Corbeil] made his announcement that we were to pick the best proposal, we asked about financial viability. When we said this is really questionable financially, we hired Deloitte & Touche to prove viability. Matthews was furious. The Prime Minister's Office said it was not necessary to negotiate the construction firm's financial viability — it would be proved over time."

The assistant deputy minister for airports at Transport wrote a letter to Paxport just before Christmas asking for proof that the firm had the $60 million in cash it would take to finance the deal. By New Year's Day, 1993, the impertinent bureaucrat was off the file and replaced by associate deputy minister Ran Quail. The tension between the bureaucrats and the politicians escalated until Glen Shortliffe, the clerk of the Privy Council, was put in charge.

"We were all operating under orders from Shortliffe," said one official. "Hession [Paxport's representative] was having lunch with Shortliffe every day," the official said. "Everyone stayed in Ottawa at taxpayers' expense while the deal was hammered out — at one time there were forty lawyers in the room." Those bureaucrats who could be counted on to take the PMO's side were routinely briefing the Paxport team on the government's strategy. One political aide who sat in on the negotiating sessions would periodically leave the room to report to Jelinek. Again and again, the message from top officials was, "The PM wants this to happen."

Some senior Transport bureaucrats were ordered to go along with decisions they couldn't accept, and a flurry of public service shuffles soon had the whole city buzzing. In March Shortliffe moved Ran Quail aside to make way for a retired deputy minister, David Broadbent, who was given the job of completing the privatization. Shortliffe also brought in a senior mandarin from the Privy Council Office, William Rowat, and told him to sign the contract. Rowat did. Then Shortliffe moved deputy minister Huguette Labelle out of Transport over to CIDA as the new deputy minister there, replacing her with Jocelyne Bourgon. "There's no question there was a fundamental difference of opinion between the government and some members of the ministry of transportation," Hession admitted to a *Toronto Sun* reporter in August 1994. "But who should be setting policy, the government or the bureaucrats?"

The government could push around the bureaucrats, but nothing could fix the essential problem with the deal: the Matthews Group didn't have sufficient financial strength to borrow the $700 million it needed to renovate the airport. Rumours circulated that Matthews's lender, the Royal Bank, had teamed up with Coopers & Lybrand to restructure the developer's finances. At this point Matthews hired Fred Doucet, bringing yet another lobbyist into the game. By this time the deal was wriggling with lobbyists. Paxport engaged Doucet, as well as Bill Neville, Hugh Riopelle, a former Air Canada public relations man who was close to Mazankowski, and John Legate, who had good connections to the Tory cabinet. Paxport's only competitor, Claridge, had hired Pat MacAdam, Gary Ouellet, David MacDonald, and Scott Proudfoot from GCI; Bill Fox and Harry Near from Earnscliffe Strategy Group; and former Chrétien aide Herb Metcalfe, a Liberal at the Capital Hill Group. At stake were potential fees of over $10 million for the lobbyists.

Glen Shortliffe stepped onto this crowded field once again when it appeared that Matthews's financial shortfall would jeopardize the privatization. Shortliffe brokered a partnership between Paxport and its former rival, Claridge, just weeks after Paxport won the bid. Claridge came in with enough money to take 60-per-cent ownership of the new Paxport-Claridge alliance called, with imaginative flair, Mergeco. The name was soon changed to Pearson Development Corporation, or PDC.

Claridge already had Terminal 3, and it wound up controlling the entire airport, making it more difficult for the Liberals to criticize the deal since two of Claridge's principals were both Liberals. Senator Leo Kolber had been the Montreal Bronfmans' most senior executive and was deeply involved in Claridge's fortunes, while the vice-president, Robert Rabinovitch, was one of the deputy ministers who had been fired by Mulroney for being too close, he thought, to the Liberals.

The fine print in the contract took months to negotiate, with further delays caused by Mulroney's announcement in February that he would resign. With so much attention and energy diverted to the battle to succeed him, it took until May 1993 to get the process rolling forward again. With the prime minister leaving on June 25, the Mulroney forces realized they were running out of time. Even with a reduced stake, Don Matthews needed the deal. No one could predict the support a new PM would bring to the agreement; he and his friends also had a good hunch the Conservatives would lose the election. The airport contract had to be settled quickly, but with one hurdle after another to jump, the negotiations dragged on through the summer.

At the same time, the Transport Department was having difficulties almost as trying with John Bitove and his catering contract at Pearson. Much of the Paxport affair eventually became public but the Bitove story has stayed under wraps, even though negotiations for both were going on at the same time and the PMO was deeply involved in both of them.

Bitove, who came from a Macedonian family, had built up a profitable catering empire in the Toronto area, and he was shrewd enough to cultivate powerful friends in politics. In January 1984, when the Liberals were still in power, he was successful in winning the airport food service contract from Cara Foods, owned by the Phelan family, by outbidding them by a few thousand dollars on a contract valued at some $70 million. He kept his advantage with the Tories by intense fundraising work.

In 1986 and 1987, for example, Bitove was the organizational mastermind behind Mulroney's annual fundraising dinners in Toronto, along with a series of pre-dinner events that were enormously popular and lucrative. One year it was an opportunity for donors to meet the Mulroneys along with Guy Charbonneau, Fred Doucet, Bill Fox, and several cabinet ministers. The next year he staged what he called a "VIP Ethnic Leaders' Cocktail Party." By 1988 his fundraising talent had become so legendary that he was appointed, along with Trevor Eyton, to run the Tories' election-year fundraising campaign. The pair brought in a record $25 million. Mulroney saw to it that Bitove was granted the Order of Canada, and all his closest friends donned dinner jackets to fly to Ottawa to celebrate the event. Eyton went to the Senate.

Bitove was not shy about seeking more than an O.C. One bizarre demand was that Canada recognize Macedonia as an independent nation. He paid Fred Doucet a fortune to lobby for this, but Doucet was unsuccessful in winning Mulroney's support in the face of strong opposition from officials at External Affairs. Bitove's business interests, however, were more successfully accommodated. In 1988 he began arguing with Transport Canada officials about his ten-year contract at Terminals 1 and 2, saying he wanted to renegotiate because his earnings would be affected when Terminal 3 opened. He was told to forget it. Then, explained one former airport official, Bitove argued that he deserved to have the contract for Terminal 3 because he already served 1 and 2. Again, officials told him no.

The next thing they knew, said two officials, orders came in from the PMO to keep Bitove happy and "make it happen." When one senior airport official continued to balk, he was fired; when another recommended against any changes, he was cut out of the negotiations and replaced by Glen Shortliffe, who was then the deputy minister of transport. The official who'd been banished from the talks was brought back in to sign the new contract, but he refused; he then received a Telex from Shortliffe ordering him to sign it, and this time he obeyed. The result was that Bitove had a new contract stating that his payments would be revised downwards, based on the number of passengers coming into Terminal 3. This new contract was extended for another ten years, in two five-year parcels.

Bitove was still after the food service contracts at Terminal 3, a contract worth at least $50 million a year. In 1991 Huang and Danczkay, which was still in charge at Terminal 3, told Toronto restaurant and catering businesses that they could compete for one or two of the three levels of food service at the new terminal — the fast-food areas, the full-service restaurants, and the bars — but they could not bid for all three. Combined bids would not be entertained, the developers said firmly. When an airport official told Bitove he did not have the right to all of the contracts, he went to see Mazankowski. Bitove then ignored the rule, bid on all three, and won all three. When the howls of protest went up from competing caterers, he faced them down without any apologies.

It didn't end there. Not long after securing the contract for Terminal 3, Bitove wanted to renegotiate its terms, just as he had for Terminals 1 and 2. Bitove was paying the government 27 per cent of his gross earnings at the time, a rate he thought was too high. After long and acrimonious discussions, during which Bitove kept dropping his payment offer lower and lower, he told the government that he should pay nothing on about $24 million in earnings from Terminals 1 and 2; rather, they should pay him to run the service, he told astonished public servants.

In June 1993 Bitove stopped paying altogether. Transport officials gave him until the end of July, but he produced only a partial payment at that time. Suddenly Corbeil, the minister, got into the act. On August 30, 1993, Corbeil met with Bitove in the boardroom at Pearson's administration building, but they could not work out an agreement. Finally, even Corbeil had had enough. Go ahead and take Bitove to court, he told his officials. Bill Rowat from the PCO was dispatched to give Bitove the news. Within fifteen minutes of telling Bitove, Rowat got a call from Mazankowski, who was in his dentist's chair. But this time the officials stared down the politicians. Transport Canada sued Bitove; the matter is scheduled to go to trial in the fall of 1994. Bitove hasn't remitted a dime for his food concessions for over a year, and the government claims he owes over $20 million. In his defence, his lawyers state that his contract was renegotiated with the government using a complex formula. According to their interpretation of that contract, he was entitled to withhold payments for the food concessions.

By the summer of 1993 many of the most senior people in Transport were so disturbed by all the favours being done for well-connected friends of Mulroney's, by all the pressure from lobbyists, by the loss to the taxpayers, and by their helplessness once the privatization deal was signed that they started to leak the details to the press. Reporters discovered that the government was subsidizing the developers handsomely; that the rate of return to the taxpayers was hundreds of millions of dollars less than would be the case if the public continued to own Pearson; and that the developers were going to make hundreds of millions of dollars for themselves.

Even as the stories poured out, the Tories tried frantically to have the deal finalized before the October 25 election. *Toronto Star* reporters David Lewis Stein and Bruce Campion-Smith obtained a copy of a letter from an official at Pearson Development Corporation to David Broadbent, the federal civil servant then in charge of the negotiations. "The company proposed that the agreement would set out the 'business principles' and that the actual details would be worked out in the following months," the reporters wrote. And they quoted another telling line from the letter's worried author: "While I understand that this may be considered to be a radical departure from the process in which we have been involved to date, I believe that it is absolutely necessary under the circumstances." The Tories agreed and the contract was signed, ready or not, on October 7, 1993, just eighteen days before the election. When the public found out the terms of the deal, it was game over for the Tories in Toronto. The details were damning.

• Paxport agreed to pay between $27 million and $30 million for a ten-year lease on Terminals 1 and 2. Yet Terminals 1 and 2 had generated $24 million in profit for the government in 1992 alone. (Add in Terminal 3 and the total profit was $60 million.)

• PDC was supposed to spend $700 million renovating the airport, but the final deal committed the company to spending only $100 million. It didn't have to undertake a second stage of development until the airport was serving over 22.5 million passengers a year. (In its best year Pearson had never handled more than 22 million passengers.) The only equity being put up was $65 million, which would be recovered within three years. The rest was debt financing.

• The government would pay one-third of any costs over $15 million needed to keep Terminal 1 operating until they were ready to tear it down, a project planned for the turn of the century.

• The developers could defer $33 million in rent in the first years of the lease.

• No other airport within 40 miles of Pearson could hope to receive any financial help from the government for expansion until Pearson was handling over 33 million passengers a year.

• PDC would be allowed to charge an extra fee or head tax on each passenger if it couldn't recover its renovation costs from the airlines. It was also allowed to raise its fees on everything from limousines to snack foods to retail rents to match the sky-high costs at Terminal 3, costs that had been fought vigorously but in vain by the retail tenants, limousine companies, and other businesses associated with the terminal.

The election campaign was in its last days as these revelations made the news. Encouraged by Toronto Liberals such as Senator Keith Davey and MP Dennis Mills, Jean Chrétien ignored the pleadings of Bronfman executives in Montreal and promised voters a review of the Pearson privatization if he won. He kept his promise and brought in former Ontario Liberal treasurer Robert Nixon to study the deal. Nixon began by asking some of the airport and Transport Department people what they thought; one can imagine what he heard. Among other things, Nixon and his colleagues found that the promises made to lobbyists were staggering; some, including Fred Doucet, had contracts to keep them on retainer until the year 2003 at $200,000 a year. "It was like a $2-million pension," said one observer. On Nixon's recommendation, Chrétien killed the deal, and since then Leo Kolber hasn't spoken to Keith Davey. The Liberal government decided it would not include lost lobbyists' fees when negotiating compensation for the disappointed members of the Paxport consortium. In February 1994 the Royal Bank of Canada, the Matthews Group's biggest lender, pushed the developer and its subsidiary, Matthews Construction, into receivership.

"The three biggest lobby campaigns during the Mulroney years," says John Chenier, the publisher of Ottawa's *Lobby Digest*, "were the Pearson Airport deal, the EH-101 helicopter contract, and the bridge to P.E.I. They were the most expensive and the most prolonged, and they succeeded despite enormous public opposition." (Others might argue that the lobbying for and against the legislation to provide extended patent protection to pharmaceutical companies was as fierce as any of these.) Although the Pearson privatization and the helicopter contract were cancelled after the 1993 election by the Chrétien government, lobbyists had far more successes than failures during the Mulroney years. And there is no argument as to which deal generated the most gossip and the wildest innuendoes in Mulroney's Ottawa: it was Air Canada's $1.8-billion contract to buy thirty-two Airbus 320 airplanes. One reason for the speculation was that the purchase took place before the Lobbyists' Registration Branch had been established, so even the minimal information the branch usually provides was not available. Another reason was the widespread belief that Frank Moores was the lead lobbyist on the deal.

Airbus Industrie was a consortium of four companies: Aérospatiale SA of France, with 37.9 per cent of the shares, Messerschmitt-Bolkow-Blohm GmbH of West Germany, with another 37.9 per cent, British Aerospace PLC with 20 per cent, and CASA of Spain with 4.2 per cent. The consortium had poured nearly $2 billion into the development of a mid-range passenger jet, the A320, and was anxiously looking for customers, a hard sell given that Boeing of Seattle still held the lion's share of the global market for commercial jets. Under French law, Airbus was permitted to keep its financial figures to itself, but it was well known that the company was not making money; indeed, it was heavily subsidized by its member governments. "Airbus looked at Canada as a back door into the United States," explained a senior U.S. businessman who has studied the company carefully. Canada seemed a good bet for the consortium, and a nice coincidence looked like a good omen for its partners: Franz Josef Strauss, the popular leader of the Christian Social Party, was chairman of the seventeen-member supervisory board of Airbus, and he already had a strong salesman in Canada in the person of Karl-Heinz Schreiber. It was Schreiber who was responsible for Strauss's personal holding companies in Alberta under the umbrella of Bitucan Holdings Ltd. and who had become so close to Elmer MacKay in the course of promoting the Bear Head project.

When GCI hung out its shingle in 1984, one of its first clients was Mercedes-Benz. Very quickly, Moores was invited to join the board of Mercedes-Benz, which became, within a few years, the major shareholder in Messerschmitt-Bolkow-Blohm, one of the Airbus partners.

Another early client was Schreiber's Bitucan Holdings; a third was Bear Head Industries, the Thyssen subsidiary Schreiber also represented. Schreiber became a valued GCI client, and he would eventually hire Greg Alford away from GCI to run Bear Head's Ottawa office.

There was yet another factor that made Moores the natural choice as Airbus's lobbyist. While Moores and Ouellet were building GCI into the city's most powerful lobbying firm, Moores and several other Mulroney supporters — David Angus, Ken Waschuk, and Fern Roberge — accepted appointments to the board of Air Canada. At the time of the appointments in March 1985, the Air Canada board was under the supervision of Moores's old roommate, Transport Minister Don Mazankowski. In July 1985, there was a flurry of critical press coverage when it was revealed that GCI was the registered lobbyist for two of Air Canada's competitors, Nordair and Wardair. Moores claimed these accounts were handled by other GCI personnel and that there was no conflict with his Air Canada responsibilities. But Claude Taylor, Air Canada's chairman, demurred; in his view, there was an appearance of conflict. Moores dropped the clients rather than lose his Air Canada directorship.

GCI's connection to Airbus Industrie began to surface that same summer when an official in the Department of Industry told reporters that Moores was trying to drum up business for Airbus, which was eager to sell its aircraft to Air Canada. Ottawa reporter Bob Fife was told that Moores had arranged a meeting with government officials to discuss a number of issues, including a possible Airbus sale to Air Canada. If an Air Canada director was lobbying on behalf of a company trying to sell planes to the airline, there was more than the appearance of conflict of interest. Moores discovered that Fife was pursuing the story and invited him over to 50 O'Connor to talk; when Fife arrived, Moores was waiting with his resignation from the Air Canada board. In return for the scoop, Fife said afterwards, Moores asked him not to mention his relationship with Airbus. Sorry, Fife told him; it's part of the story. Moores took Fife's response philosophically; because he'd had to drop Wardair and Nordair as clients to stay on the Air Canada board, he joked to Fife that maybe now he'd get them back.

To this day, Moores publicly denies that he ever lobbied for Airbus. His client, he insists, was the helicopter division of Messerschmitt-Bolkow-Blohm, not the division that made up part of the Airbus consortium. "I don't know where the hell the rumour came from," he says. Moores blames Boeing executives for initiating gossip, but others, including senior bureaucrats and political staff, have confirmed the story.

Boeing did have reason to be unhappy; Airbus was trying to sell to Wardair as well as Air Canada. Max Ward was in the market for a dozen new planes, and the consortium thought it could convince him to switch to the A310-312 instead of taking the Boeing jets he'd already ordered. Air Canada had been looking at Boeing planes too; in fact, Boeing representatives said that by 1986 Air Canada's new fleet plans were designed around Boeing aircraft. A massive effort began to shift Air Canada away from Boeing and over to Airbus. The players, explained an industry source, included Schreiber, Moores, Ouellet, and lawyers from Stikeman Elliott, David Angus's firm. One Boeing executive says he spent hours with Angus discussing the deal; "[Angus] said to me, 'Don't you know this country is a banana republic?'" The executive laughs heartily at the memory of this conversation. One of the key meetings was held in offices in the PMO in late 1986; among those present "to set the internal game plan," as the industry source described it, were Lucien Bouchard, then Canada's ambassador to France, Moores, and Ouellet. Mulroney wisely kept his distance.

"The first thing they went after was Max Ward's plan to buy three Boeing 767 aircraft," the source said. They convinced Ward to switch to the Airbus instead. He ordered twelve Airbus 310-312s, telling the press in January 1987 that size and cost were factors in his decision not to buy the Boeings. But Boeing officials became extremely alarmed at Ward's change of heart and at the intelligence they were receiving out of Ottawa. They went to the U.S. ambassador in Ottawa, Tom Niles, for advice and found that Niles, a soft-spoken but very tough diplomat, was even more concerned. He believed that Moores and Ouellet were successfully persuading the cabinet, the Transport Department, and Air Canada — still a Crown corporation — to consider the Airbus instead of the Boeings. Niles wasn't politically naive, but he was appalled that cronies of the prime minister could have such influence.

The lobbying went on from both sides through 1987. In early December of that year Boeing, not to mention much of official Ottawa, was stunned by the news that Transport's deputy minister, Ramsey Withers, a man closely involved with the Air Canada file, was leaving government to join GCI. Withers, a former chief of defence staff, was the first top mandarin to bolt for a lobbying firm. Boeing was again upset; it suspected that Airbus, for which Moores was lobbying so strongly, had the inside track on the Air Canada purchase. When the issue was raised in the House of Commons in February 1988, Transport Minister John Crosbie defended Withers as "a man of complete integrity, honour, faithful service and rectitude," who had no connection with Air Canada's fleet replacement plans.

Crosbie's assessment of Withers's character may well have been correct, but he was wrong about the deputy's knowledge of the fleet plans. In April, *The Toronto Star*'s Linda Diebel cited a letter dated December 22, 1987, to Ottawa aerospace industry consultant Ian Macdonald in which Withers described Macdonald's understanding of Air Canada's fleet plans as "inaccurate in some significant areas." Boeing fought on, but it knew the struggle was futile. As one of its spokesmen, Craig Martin, told Diebel, he believed the deal was part of a package that included a contract for Canadair in Montreal to build fuselage parts for the A320. When Liberal transport critic Brian Tobin claimed the fleet-replacement decision was "lobby-driven," Gary Ouellet (who, like Moores, insisted that MBB was their client, not Airbus) responded with a cheerful denial: "There's no dire plot to lobby anyone." On April 1, 1988, Ramsey Withers became president of GCI.

On July 20 Air Canada held a press conference to announce its decision to buy thirty-four Airbus 320s to replace a fleet of thirty-three Boeing 727s, with delivery to begin in 1990. The cost of the planes was set at $1.8 billion, the largest civilian aircraft purchase in Canada's history. And just as Boeing had predicted, the deal included a $1-billion contract for Montreal's Canadair plant to manufacture Airbus parts. Predictably, Boeing officials were annoyed. Spokesman David Jimenez said the deal made no sense when Air Canada could have bought fourteen Boeing 737s and kept most of its 727s, which were still relatively new planes. But Benoit Bouchard, the new transport minister, stoutly defended the purchase. It was a time of celebration at GCI headquarters, in the PMO, and in Munich, where Airbus chairman Franz Josef Strauss heaved a great sigh of relief.

A few questions remained, not the least of which was how Air Canada intended to pay for the planes. The answer was that approximately $320 million was expected to materialize when the government implemented a cherished plan to privatize the airline, a process that began with the announcement that RBC Dominion Securities would be the lead underwriter in selling 45 per cent of the company's shares. The issue came to the market at the end of September 1988, just a few weeks before the federal election.

Karl-Heinz Schreiber did not relax after the Air Canada purchase went through; he still hoped to complete a deal with the federal government for the Bear Head plant in Cape Breton. But there was bad news on October 3: Strauss had collapsed while hunting deer on the estate of Prince Johannes von Thurn und Taxis; he died of heart failure shortly afterwards in hospital. Germany mourned the loss of its most charismatic politician.[1]

Strauss's death caused barely a ripple in Ottawa; people there were gossiping about the value of the commission paid to GCI for helping to land the Air Canada contract. Estimates fluctuated wildly between $20 million and $70 million. Boeing conducted an investigation into the whole affair, one that involved police forces in both Canada and the United States; it concluded that a commission in the order of $20 to $30 million was paid to Moores and Ouellet. The partners always dismissed such stories, and today Moores makes light of the rumours that he had tucked away millions from the deal. "I read that stuff and I wish it were true," he chuckles.

However, there is little question that Moores was prospering. The best evidence of his new-found wealth was the purchase of a luxury fishing camp with about twelve miles of one of the Gaspé's richest salmon rivers, the Grand Cascapédia. Well-informed Quebeckers say he paid an American family close to $2 million for the camp; Moores claims he and Montreal businessman Brian Jones paid less than $200,000. Whatever the purchase price may have been, the camp is now worth a fortune; he has done extensive renovations at a cost of about $1 million, according to sources.

Boeing finally decided to stop squawking about its loss in Canada, but the Airbus story doesn't end with Boeing's acceptance of defeat. Early in 1989, when his airline was facing bankruptcy, Max Ward sold Wardair and his new Airbus planes to Canadian International Airlines for $70 million. Later the same year, Lavalin's Bernard Lamarre decided to get into the aircraft leasing business, and he bought Ward's Airbuses from Canadian with a loan from a French bank, the Caisse National de Crédit Agricole. But Lavalin was also in deep financial trouble, and after taking delivery of two of the planes, Lamarre cancelled the remaining order. Crédit Agricole petitioned Lavalin into bankruptcy in October 1991 and repossessed the planes.

In the summer of 1992 National Defence bought three of the old Wardair A310-312s to give struggling Canadian Airlines a much-needed cash infusion; and in February 1993, the federal government bought the two Lavalin Airbuses for $43 million each from Crédit Agricole. To no one's surprise Canadair was awarded the contract to refit four of the aircraft for military use, and the fifth was

sent to Innotech Aviation of Montreal for a $3.5-million luxury refit
ordered by Mulroney. The plane, dubbed "Air Force One" by the
amused Americans in Ottawa who knew its history, was to be used
for Mulroney's travels. The refit, which took until July 1993 to complete, included a new executive cabin with a dining-conference room,
a lounge with two fold-out beds, and an office. Chrétien ordered the
plane sold, but so far the government has not found a customer willing to pay the $56-million asking price. The only VIP it has served
so far is Queen Elizabeth who used it during her Canadian tour in
the summer of 1994.

As the Tory regime drew to a close in Ottawa, Frank Moores,
who had been semi-retired since the 1988 federal election, saw that
it was time to go. "Four of our key people wanted more of the
action," says Moores, "and some of the partners weren't prepared to
give up their shares so they decided to go off on their own." Led by
Ramsey Withers, the discontented executives left in 1993 to form
IFRG Industry Government Relations. Gary Ouellet, fulfilling a lifetime dream of a career as a magician, went into partnership with
U.S. entertainer David Copperfield. With the firm a mere remnant of
its former self, Pat MacAdam departed in the spring of 1993.

In the fall of 1993, just before the federal election, Pierre
Bourque, Sr., and Moores sold what was left of GCI to Arthur
Nightingale, a former president of Saint John Shipbuilding, who'd
been in Ottawa for two years representing the interests of the Irving
family, owners of Saint John Shipbuilding. Nightingale and his wife,
Marie Blouin, changed the name of the firm to Blouin-Nightingale,
scaled the office down to a quarter of its original size, scrapped the
traditional Christmas "screech-in" (a high-spirited cocktail party
fuelled by Newfoundland rum) in favour of a sedate family get-
together with Santa Claus, and tried to carry on, with Moores acting
as an adviser. It didn't work out, as Moores candidly admits. "He
wanted the accounts but he didn't want the potential obligations. He
and I had a bit of a difference of opinion as to what I was supposed

to do with those bills . . . That was the last I saw of him."

Even Pierre Bourque admits his investment in GCI "was not one of my best ventures. I was led down the garden path when I negotiated with Moores and Ouellet. I lost a considerable amount of bucks there . . . Ouellet was managing the company and Moores was flying around the world as a travelling salesman enjoying life, and the money was always spent before it got to me."

Times were tough, the Grits were in power, and all that was left on the thirteenth floor of 50 O'Connor was the ghosts of the fun-loving buccaneers who'd taken their winnings and run. By the spring of 1994 Blouin and Nightingale had called it quits and moved to Cuba. The few remaining files of Ottawa's mightiest lobbying firm were transferred to Moores's secretary's house in Orleans, an Ottawa sub-urb, where an answering machine picked up messages. In the summer of 1994 Moores officially informed the Lobbyists' Registration Branch that he was no longer in business.

LIFESTYLES OF THE RICH AND FAMOUS

VEN HER HUSBAND WOULD HAVE TO ADMIT THAT MILA Mulroney is not low-maintenance. Beautiful, chic, charming, smart, and ambitious — Mila was and is all these things. She is a loyal and loving wife to a demanding partner, a caring mother to four well-liked children, a devoted daughter to her parents who have been through difficult times with her father's poor health, and a delightful companion of the "ballet group," the circle of close women friends who surround her in Montreal. Given the demands of her husband's years in power, few women could have managed all these relationships and responsibilities as gracefully as Mila did. What failings she had during those years were human — she wanted so badly to do things beautifully, to entertain stylishly, to make sure the official residences were elegant, that she lost sight of how she achieved it. For Mila Mulroney, a perfectionist in all things, the ends wound up justifying the means. And therein lies her fatal flaw. She had it all, but the means by which she grasped for even more gave her the indelible image of a person obsessed with the perquisites and luxuries of power.

When Mulroney joked about his wife's spending habits, he wasn't being entirely funny; they were legendary. Once or twice every week, followed by an RCMP security car, driver Derek McSweeney (Michael McSweeney's brother) would chauffeur Mila to Montreal to shop, see her parents, keep a medical appointment, or have lunch with friends.

Usually she stayed in the eighth-floor royal suite at the Ritz-Carlton, which normally costs $1,650 a night. The suite boasts a large living room with a massive armoire whose doors swing open to reveal four television monitors. The master bedroom holds an immense Chinese chest whose lid swings up at the push of a button to produce yet another television set. The Mulroneys used the suite on a regular basis for nine years; who paid for it is not known. It's possible there was no charge, given that Mulroney had served on the Ritz board and that hotel manager Fern Roberge was a long-time supporter.

Every few months, Mila took shopping trips to New York. Thanks to the airline passes she was entitled to as the wife of the prime minister, she flew first-class at public expense. She routinely stayed at the Pierre, where a luxury room is priced at about $800 a night. Neither chef François Martin nor others who were familiar with her routine could say who paid for the hotel. "I remember one time," said Martin, "that she was going to New York for two and a half days and needed $13,000 to $15,000, but Bonnie [Brownlee] had trouble getting her the money. 'I don't know what to do, François,' Bonnie told me. 'Where can I get the money?'" The chef was sympathetic but baffled, and said he had no idea. "But eventually she got the money."

As the years passed, Mila's taste for couture clothes developed rapidly. With her height and perfect figure, she could vie for anyone's best-dressed list. By the early 1990s Mila's friends noticed that she wore Chanel more than any other couture label. On Montreal's Sherbrooke Street she was a regular at Holt Renfrew, Emanuel Ungaro, and the Ralph Lauren Polo shop; she was also a valued client of Eleni Haute Couture on Monkland Avenue, where she had been introduced by Yolande Charbonneau. As the *Gazette*'s Tommy Schnurmacher reported in 1991, many of her outfits came from Serge and Réal, where a simple silk day dress starts at $4,000. The two designers, Serge Senecal and Réal Bastien, create outfits for Montreal's wealthiest women; Mila had been a customer for years.

Many of her hand-knit sweaters are purchased from Montrealer Linda Laing for $425 each and, wrote Schnurmacher, "Mila had been known to pop by Les Fourrures Sylvère on de Bleury St. for a drop sable coat or a mink jacket." Then there are the days when Mila just can't get out to do the rounds. "On those rare occasions when Mohammed doesn't want to go to the mountain," Schnurmacher added, "the mountain comes to Mohammed. In other words, boutique owners cheerfully shlep their wares over for Mila's perusal in the royal suite of the Ritz-Carlton."

Although Sally Armstrong wrote in 1992 that Mila owned only sixty pairs of shoes and dyed many of them to go with different outfits, she did not buy cheap shoes. A February 1993 article in *The San Francisco Chronicle* noted an upcoming fashion show from "hot Milanese designer Claudio Merazzi who counts Princess Caroline, Danielle Steel Traina, Mila Mulroney, Ann Getty, Georgette Mosbacher and Denise Hale among those he has shod." Mila, said household staff members, rarely paid less than $450 for a pair of shoes and she had far more than sixty pairs; her shoes were kept in two attic storage rooms at 24 Sussex and a large dressing room.

Trips abroad offered more shopping opportunities; the goods were shipped separately back to Canada. Mila's errand runner and odd-job man, Robby McRobb, had a friend at Customs who could clear the parcels quickly. When the Mulroneys travelled, they were given the most perfunctory Customs clearance allowed any Canadians; as a courtesy to the prime minister and the governor general and their companions or entourages, Canada Customs officers board their VIP aircraft with Customs forms that they are required to complete, like other Canadians. Unlike other Canadians, however, they never have their bags searched and they are never questioned about purchases.

On one occasion, Mila's habits aroused a protest. On a trip to New York in 1985 she was accompanied for security reasons by RCMP Chief Superintendent Jean Poirier, the head of VIP security for the force, and Inspector Roy Berlinguette. They were with her when she purchased some expensive jewellery in a Manhattan store. On their return to Canada, the officers realized they were expected to carry Mila's hand luggage through Customs and they believed the luggage contained the jewellery. As peace officers sworn to uphold the law, the two Mounties were disturbed by the notion that they should assist the prime minister's wife in sneaking jewellery into the country that they believed she had not declared. They refused to do it. They also felt they had a duty to report the incident to their superiors — a career-threatening move if there ever was one. The matter went all the way to Commissioner Robert Simmonds, but a decision was made to overlook the affair. After all, someone said, the officers could have made a mistake.

The bottom line was that Mila needed substantial infusions of cash every week or two as walking-around money. After François Martin came to work at 24 Sussex Drive, one of his regular chores was a visit to Fred Doucet's office in the PMO. Their meetings were always brief and businesslike; after they exchanged a pleasant word or two about the weather or some social event at the residence, Doucet would hand over a thick, unsealed letter-sized envelope to Martin. On several occasions the envelope contained thousands of dollars in $1,000 and $100 bills. Martin was not the only staff member asked to pick up the money for Mila; others also took turns doing the job.

Martin was sometimes asked to do banking for Mila. Late at night, just before he went home from work, she would give him an envelope with thousands of dollars in cash and ask him to deposit it in her account at the Wellington Street branch of the Bank of Montreal. "I was nervous because I had to take it home overnight," he said; fortunately, he never had a problem. On his way to work the next morning he would pass by the bank and make the deposit. "Cash came in like it was falling from the sky," says Martin.

Near the end of the first term, when Fred Doucet left the PMO to take on a new job organizing Canada's participation at international summits, Martin's cash pickups for Mila ceased and the system changed. Thereafter cash was kept at the house. A wall safe, hidden behind a picture in the hallway leading to the prime minister's study, was not considered secure enough. Instead, a safe the size of a refrigerator was installed in Martin's basement office. Rick Morgan, the prime minister's executive assistant, would deliver and retrieve the cash from the safe. On two occasions, Martin was working in the room when he saw Mulroney remove some money.

It was all very well for Mulroney to kid about Mila's extravagance, but he was no slouch himself. "He always lived up to the hilt," said one of his oldest friends. Like Mila, Mulroney enjoyed living and working in luxurious surroundings decorated with fine furniture and good paintings; when he went to Iron Ore, he tossed out Bill Bennett's simple Eaton's-style office appointments and had the whole place lavishly redecorated with antiques. He did the same with his offices in Ottawa, having more decorating done just a few months before he stepped down. And he too liked expensive clothes. In the mid-1980s he would buy several $2,000 suits at one time from Bijan in Manhattan, one of the most expensive stores in New York, and of course he has long indulged a weakness for Gucci loafers at about $500 a pair.

One individual who has known Mulroney well since his days at Iron Ore is Conrad Black. In his 1993 autobiography, *A Life in Progress*, Black patronizingly described the Mulroney he knew in the 1970s. Even though Mulroney had become successful, wrote Black with the confidence of someone to the manner born, "he still felt himself quite keenly to be the underprivileged lad from Baie-Comeau, son of the foreman in the Chicago *Tribune*'s newsprint mill, who identified more with the French than the English in Quebec, and more with the lower economic echelons than with the scions of wealthy Westmount . . . He had the attitude to money of someone who didn't have any himself but had seen others scatter lavishly: he appreciated it more in the spending than in the accumulation, the latter a process he tended to oversimplify. And politically he had the attitude to money of someone who came to maturity in the last years of Duplessis when the tangible fruits of a long incumbency were being extravagantly dispersed. He had the heart of a working man but the tastes of the rich."

Maintaining the Mulroneys' lifestyle literally cost a fortune, but while they had far more money than most Canadians, they were not multimillionaires. When Helen Vari told Joe Plaskett they were "very poor," they were — as seen from the world of the Varis. In his last year in office, 1992–93, Mulroney earned $159,300 a year, a figure that included his basic MP's salary, a tax-free expense allowance, and an extra salary for being prime minister. Nine years earlier it was less; in 1984–85, his first year as prime minister, he earned a total of $130,700. Even with free housing, free cars, free servants, and generous support kicked in by the PC Party, it was not enough for a couple who lived the good life in New York, Palm Beach, and Paris, or for a woman who wanted to travel in the international fast lane with wealthy girlfriends like Helen Vari, Jacqueline Desmarais, and Laurie Johnson, the wife of former Nabisco chief Ross Johnson.

Whenever she was asked about their extravagances, Mila explained them away by saying she and Brian were able to enjoy a comfortable life thanks to the excellent investments he'd made before he entered politics. "Brian's investment income [from the Iron Ore days] supplements his present salary and enables us to do some of the things we enjoy," she told her biographer, Sally Armstrong. Certainly, Iron Ore had paid him very well, but never generously enough to support their later lifestyle. Records filed by Iron Ore's parent company, Hanna Mining, with the U.S. Securities and Exchange Commission show that no Hanna executive earned over $400,000 a year, even with bonuses, during Mulroney's time at the Canadian branch plant. The documents list no bonuses for Mulroney. Once he'd been made a director of Hanna and elected to the board, the 1983 SEC circulars reveal that he was given 600 Hanna shares, a pittance compared with the thousands of shares held by other Hanna executives.

During his years at Iron Ore, Mulroney was paid well enough to make investments, but they were not all successful. When he invested $15,000 in East Coast Energy, the Doucet brothers' company that foundered in 1983, he lost every penny of it. Even earlier, in 1979, Mulroney had been interested in building a hotel in Labrador City with Sam Wakim and Jean Bruyère, using Iron Ore pension fund money and a mortgage from Montreal Trust to finance the project; that fell through. Through his broker, Jonathan Deitcher, he invested $50,000 in an Alberta tax shelter that also ran into financial difficulties. When Mila sold their Belvedere Road house back to Iron Ore in 1981, reported John Sawatsky, the couple cleared $350,000. Charbonneau has suggested this money was the foundation for their wealth. David Angus claims Mulroney was a "substantial millionaire" before he entered politics; George and Helen Vari do not agree. Even in the summer of 1994, the couple said in an interview that they believed the Mulroneys did not have much real wealth, although, said George Vari, they knew that as president of Iron Ore Mulroney "had been in good financial shape."

Other Montrealers who knew the Mulroneys well during the Iron Ore days say quite categorically that the couple did not become millionaires during this period. "Mila had good taste and knew where to get bargains," said one friend who frequently went shopping with her. "But they didn't have any real money."

When the Mulroneys moved to Ottawa in 1983, they completely redecorated Stornoway, the residence of the leader of the opposition, with the help of designer Giovanni Mowinckel. But the reputation for New York shopping binges, Palm Beach holidays, and living well beyond their means did not come until after they moved into 24 Sussex Drive the following year. The prime minister's salary would not have covered all their expenses. One source of support was clearly the PC Canada Fund. David Angus controlled the fund and only he and Nick Locke, the fund's executive director, who had to co-sign the cheques with Angus, knew exactly how far the party would go to assist the Mulroneys. Friends of Locke's say he was a straight arrow who was uncomfortable about some of the decisions that were made.

The fund was tapped for some of the Mulroneys' personal travel expenses, as the trips to New York and Paris in 1985 and 1986 illustrated. Angus admits that between 1984 and 1986 he signed several postdated cheques totalling $324,000 to cover furnishings for the residences; the fund also provided cheques to cover the cost of a bank draft to pay for a $3,200 necklace Mila ordered from Bulgari in Rome in 1985. After Mowinckel threatened to sue the Mulroneys in 1986 for $51,000 they had owed him for eight months — Mila had racked up the bills by charging furniture and other goods to his account at several stores — the fund helped them out again. Robby McRobb sorted out the bills, and most of the charges were picked up retroactively by the National Capital Commission, but Angus agreed to pay $5,494.26 for several items, including eight antique armchairs and several lamps.

All PC Canada Fund cheques were supposed to carry the signatures of both Locke and Angus, but on this occasion Angus wrote the cheque on CIBC account number 72-1112, the account he controlled in the CIBC's main branch on Boulevard René-Lévesque in Montreal. The cheque did not carry Locke's signature nor any PC Canada Fund logo, but the bank confirmed it was a fund account and that Angus had signing authority. The account was unknown to Robert Foster, the man who succeeded Angus as chairman of the fund in 1993. As far as Foster knew, every single cheque issued by the party had to come from the fund's only bank account, number 0105015 in Ottawa; he had no idea the fund had a second account. Only the Ottawa office was supposed to issue cheques, Foster said, and no office had more than $250 in petty cash on hand. Angus admitted the Montreal account existed and that he had sole signing authority for it; he said he sent the cheque only because Mowinckel needed the money in a hurry and the fund's Ottawa office was closed. (Perhaps, but it still took him several days to send it.)

Such glimpses into the inner workings of the PC Canada Fund are rare, and the board has always remained secretive about its arrangements with Mulroney. "We had a private, gentlemen's agreement," Angus said in 1987; when the Mulroneys incurred expenses in the course of party duties or in promoting the party's image, the fund would cover them. A little more light was shed by former British Columbia MP and party president Gerry St. Germain on July 18, 1991, the eve of the party's national convention. That's when reporters questioned him about a mysterious story that had surfaced in Ottawa about Mulroney's earnings. An anonymous Revenue Canada official leaked a report to Bob Fife that Mulroney had filed a tax return for 1990 claiming income of about $300,000, almost twice as much as the annual $164,200 he was earning as prime minister. The story said Mulroney filed three T-4 slips, including one for pay from the party, which added up to more than $300,000.

"The party does give assistance to the leader of the party," said St. Germain, "and what the prime minister actually declares as income is his business. I haven't got any information as to amounts." But he added that the extra money wasn't a supplementary income for Mulroney, and that the accounting procedures were all open and above board. What he refused to provide was details: Did Mulroney have to submit receipts? Was the money paid in lump-sum amounts? He wouldn't say. But later the same day, the embarrassed party president had to qualify his remarks. Claiming his earlier comments had been distorted, St. Germain huffed that "the PC Party of Canada does not supplement the income of the leader." Then PMO spokeswoman Sunni Locatelli moved in to smooth things over: "The prime minister does not receive any salary or income from the Progressive Conservative Party," she said. The party covers only the cost of political events such as trips to Toronto for party fundraisers.

Again in July 1994, Angus repeated his earlier statements that the Mulroneys had received no extra income from the party, but his explanation of what did happen was convoluted. When he took over in 1983, Angus said, Mulroney consulted other party leaders; based on their advice, he told Angus that the party could wind up paying for things that might be considered personal. "And I would like you to keep strict track of the expenses of a personal nature and bill me on a regular basis," Angus quoted Mulroney as saying. He even sent a letter to this effect, said Angus. "Periodically I would invoice Mr. Mulroney for any expenses paid by the party that we considered to be of a personal nature and he would pay me immediately. And I know of no other payments that were ever made to him by the party while I was chairman."

All this sounds clear. Some of the money the couple spent could well have come from the Mulroneys' personal funds, but when David Angus was asked about the source of the cash that was picked up regularly by staff members such as François Martin, he replied that he had no idea where Mila got it — unless it came from the regular monthly cheque he gave the Mulroneys for expenses. Angus would not say how much money he provided to the Mulroneys; all he would admit to was that it was a "modest" figure. He sat down with the Mulroneys every year, decided what their expenses would be for the coming year, and then set aside a portion of the fund's annual budget for these. "We tried to even out the cash flow so they would have monies available to them to pay these expenses on a regular, even, sort of ongoing basis," said Angus. So he would divide the total amount into twelve monthly cheques made out to Mulroney's chief of staff in trust. Until he left the PMO in 1987, the person who handled the money was Fred Doucet. Concerned that there might be a tax consequence for these expense cheques, Angus said he obtained a ruling from Revenue Canada to ensure that the procedures were correct. "It was all cleared with the PC Canada Fund board," he added. "Everything that was done with any cent of party funds was known by the board of the PC Canada Fund." Except for rare occasions the money was not used for entertaining; one exception was a summer press gallery barbecue, and another was when Mulroney paid for some musicians to play at a gathering at 24 Sussex.

Bonnie Brownlee agrees that the money Martin says he picked up could have been the money Angus provided. After Doucet left, she said, it would have been another trusted staff member who handled the cheques from Angus; "it was always Doucet or Burney or Marjory LeBreton that handled those types of financial things." All of this appears to support the comments made by poor Gerry St. Germain before he was forced to backtrack: the party did indeed pick up many expenses for the Mulroneys.

During the Mulroney years, the PC Canada Fund raised millions, but it also spent about $10 million a year maintaining offices and staff across the country, running a sophisticated direct-mail system — and contributing to the comfort and happiness of the leader. When he left in June 1993 the party had $2 million in the bank; by June 1994 it was carrying a debt of $5.7 million. After the disastrous 1993 election, Foster and party president Gerry St. Germain shut down PC Canada Fund offices across the country and drastically downsized the Ottawa headquarters. "Given the new reality," said Foster grimly, "we had to bring our overheads down."

But the old reality, in the heady 1980s, was that there was money for jam — although Mila did not count on the PC Canada Fund for everything she wanted. As she acquired the clothes, jewellery, art, and furniture she had always longed for, Mila found ways to economize. In the early days, for example, when she poured so much energy into decorating the residences, some of her close friends in Montreal asked local antique dealers to donate pieces. The answer, in a city where Mila's spending habits were legendary, was usually no. On other occasions she used her privilege as the wife of the prime minister to buy gifts for foreign dignitaries at a Toronto store. Allowed under the regulations to spend up to $1,000 on such gifts, she on one occasion bought a gift for a foreign dignitary for about $250 and then spent the rest of the money on yellow-patterned

Ginori breakfast china for herself. The merchant was instructed to send the entire bill to External Affairs. When this practice was queried under two access-to-information requests, based on invoices provided by the merchant in the case, the response was long delayed. In one case, the access officials said, she had repaid the money owing to External Affairs. In another, officials refused to answer the request, claiming that to do so would jeopardize relationships with a foreign country. Finally, there was the privilege of a tax number from Revenue Canada, which allowed them to buy goods for the house tax-free. Mila did not use the tax number when she was shopping herself, but members of the household staff used it to buy goods of all kinds on her behalf.

Unhappily, one effort to enlist the aid of a government agency to buy goods for her almost ended in a fiasco. Because 24 Sussex did not have enough matching china for the fifty or so guests the Mulroneys liked to assemble at dinner parties, Mila began hunting for a new dinner service. Staff at the National Arts Centre, which did most of the Mulroneys' catering for large parties, gave her catalogues for china and other luxury items that she could order wholesale. In one catalogue from Fitz and Floyd, a Japanese company that manufactures beautiful china, she found a blue pattern called Starburst. A service for fifty — 560 pieces in all, with fifty extra luncheon plates, two coffee pots, two cream jugs, and two sugar bowls — would cost about $23,000 wholesale. To the joy of the Fitz and Floyd salesman who priced the order, she decided she'd take it. A problem arose some time later when she found, to her surprise, that the NAC did not have the money in its budget to pay for the china; they would have to cancel the order. But the company would not take the china back. Mila came up with a solution. "You buy it," she suggested to an Ottawa businessman of her acquaintance. "I'll pay you back $1,500 a month." Very reluctantly he agreed. He paid the shot on the china and Mila made irregular installments on the debt. Most months he had to ask for it, and frequently more than once. Mila wound up owning a spectacular set of china for fifty people. When the Mulroneys left Sussex Drive, this china was among the items she tried to sell to the National Capital Commission. She wanted her full purchase price — $23,000. It was worth it, she reasoned; after all, she got it wholesale.

Over the years Mila used the same NAC catalogues to make other wholesale purchases. She bought a set of china to give Bernard Roy and his wife, pieces of which were given to the Roys over a period of time. The set was kept in a cupboard in Martin's basement office; whenever she wanted to give them a gift, she would retrieve a few items. Rumours circulated around Ottawa about this china; a source familiar with its purchase said it was paid for through the PMO.

Another luxury Mila indulged in was hairdressing for herself and her family from Ottawa stylist Rinaldo Canonica. When Mila appeared at his salon in downtown Ottawa she was treated like royalty; Canonica would immediately drop his scissors and comb, turn his waiting client over to another hairdresser, and attend to Mila. Other customers noted with wry amusement that she would be served her coffee in a china cup and saucer while theirs arrived in paper cups. The royal treatment was not reciprocated — Mila became famous for her parsimony in the salon because she rarely tipped any of the staff more than $5. But that didn't bother Canonica. He appeared so often at the residence to fix her hair for special occasions that he seemed like one of the household. Even today, one well-placed source has said, Canonica will drive to Montreal to cut her hair.

Canonica's staff were less cheerful about the arrangement. Mulroney never came into the salon; a hairdresser was dispatched to his office or to his home. The woman who cut his hair during his first two years in Ottawa went to the residence frequently or to his Commons office, where Mulroney would perch on a chair in the corner, the rug rolled back. When the hairdresser was finished she'd receive a warm smile and thanks, but no money, not even a tip, and never the customary present at Christmas. Perhaps Rinaldo sent the Mulroneys a bill, but if so he didn't pass the payments along: he didn't pay the hairdressers who went to the residences or the offices. "We worked on commission," explained one, "and if we didn't cut the hair in the salon, we didn't get paid." When one of Canonica's disgruntled employees went so far as to obtain legal advice on how to collect the money owed, the advice was to stop cutting the prime-ministerial hair and write it off to experience.

When the first hairdresser found excuses to avoid the chore, another was sent out, and often the trip was to Harrington Lake. This hairdresser did the couple's hair for several years, usually taking care of Mila in the salon three or four times a week. When called to the residences, sometimes as early as 5 a.m., the hairdresser was not reimbursed for the service nor for mileage. But the Mulroneys tried to show their appreciation by arranging for the hairdresser to be able to use Room 200, one of the most impressive House of Commons committee rooms, for a summer wedding reception. Such rooms are highly prized and rarely available to people who are not parliamentarians; the official who scheduled such bookings at first said it was already booked. Only when Mulroney personally intervened did the couple receive their choice of Saturdays in August.

A few months after the wedding, when the hairdresser was returning to Ottawa from Harrington Lake one chilly fall morning at about 7, the car skidded on the slippery, dew-slicked road and crashed into a tree. After a patrolling RCMP officer discovered the wreck and ordered an ambulance, the hairdresser was hospitalized with severe injuries for weeks. The Mulroneys never called or even sent a card.

For years Canonica's wife, Pat McCaffery, was involved in Mila's charitable activities, especially her pet charity, cystic fibrosis. In April 1986, McCaffery was on Mila's committee to stage a $5,000-per-ticket hockey game to raise money for cystic fibrosis research and was given the special responsibility of persuading Ottawa's city councillors to rent the Civic Centre rink at cost.

Using public money, the Mulroneys found an old but reliable method to repay the couple's generosity. Both Canonica and McCaffery were on the Sussex Drive invitation list and included in many glittering government galas. In February 1991, Canonica was named to the sixteen-member board of the Federal Business Development Bank for a three-year term. When *Citizen* reporter Kathryn May asked Nancy Cormier, an assistant to Small Business Minister Tom Hockin, why he'd recommended Canonica, the answer was that Hockin "trusts his judgment on small- and medium-sized business needs, and he has always been interested in being nominated to the board." Cormier wouldn't tell May who told Hockin to appoint Canonica, nor whom Canonica had told he wanted to be on the board. In 1993 McCaffery was appointed to the board of the Official Residences Council.

On October 1, 1991, Mila turned up at Canonica's new purple and coral salon in Ottawa's World Exchange Plaza to cut the ribbon for its opening and to say a few words. She was "one of the many pampered Ottawans who spend time at Rinaldo's," she said, calling it "a place where kindnesses are offered." The Montreal *Gazette*'s report of the opening quoted an "Ottawa observer" as saying Mila's appearance at the event was tacky. "Imagine the prime minister's wife endorsing a commercial enterprise."

For years Brian Mulroney trumpeted the fact that he paid for his own groceries. Records released by the government in 1992 show that from 1984 to 1991, he wrote cheques every six months or so for roughly $4,000 (or about $8,000 a year) for his family's food. In September 1993, a Privy Council Office official told *The Toronto Star*'s David Vienneau that Mulroney had paid a total of $74,598.75 for food consumed by his family since September 1984. That works out to $171.03 a week, or $684.12 a month, for his family of four children and two adults.

But that figure bears no resemblance to what the household

actually spent on food. In the first four months of 1985, the grocery bills ran between $3,742 and $4,795 a month, and by the summer they were averaging $5,700 a month. During Mulroney's first year in office, the total grocery bills added up to $42,125. The Loblaws bill alone was never less than $1,200 a month, and often it was over $2,000. The bills from Albert's Meat Market were about $1,000 a month. Lapointe Fish Market charges ran at about $260 a month, while the ones from Ontario Fruit Market were between $400 and $800 a month. Items from Boushey's, a luxury convenience store on Elgin, cost the household between $151 and $338 a month. Wine and liquor bills from Quebec's Maison des Alcools ran to $2,000 a month. Although Mulroney himself was a teetotaller and Mila drank very little alcohol, fine wines were always served at their parties. (For Mulroney, Martin was required to keep a large stock of NyQuil on hand. This over-the-counter cold remedy is, after booze, America's number two "drug of choice," reported *Time* magazine in 1994.)

Every year the food and wine costs multiplied. "By the time I left in 1989," said Martin, "I was spending up to $7,000 a month." These figures are confirmed by 1988-89 Privy Council records, which show that the food and liquor bills were up to $83,715; by 1989–90 they'd grown to $90,000. The next year, 1990–91, they'd soared to $105,476, and in 1991–92 they were up again to $141,688. In 1992–93 the Mulroney food and liquor bills were $153,128.

And except for Mulroney's contribution, the taxpayers paid them all. The Mulroneys were obviously not consuming all this themselves; the household kitchens fed a staff that had grown to twelve by 1993. (Their salaries cost the taxpayers $338,512 a year by the time the Mulroneys left Ottawa.) The government could and did argue that this budget was covering official entertaining by the prime minister, and there is some truth to this assertion. But the chef was also sending regular care packages to Mila's parents in Montreal and to her sister, Ivana, in Toronto, packages stuffed with food, cases of wine, flowers from the greenhouses at Rideau Hall, even cleaning supplies such as cans of Comet and boxes of Tide. ("When you pay your own bills," sniffed their press secretary Luc Lavoie when Martin made these revelations in 1990, "you can do what you want with the food, the wine, the flowers.") And for most large formal political events, such as the regular summer garden parties for the party faithful, the press, or the PC caucus, the Mulroneys used the catering arm of the National Arts Centre, and the party covered the costs. Parties and dinners for foreign dignitaries were paid for by External Affairs.

Canadian taxpayers also subsidized three weddings, all catered by François Martin. The first was Fred Doucet's wedding to Alina Kawecki on Saturday, March 22, 1986. Mila, said Martin, did not want to host this wedding; for all the ties between Doucet and her husband, she herself was uneasy around him. Only when Brian insisted did she finally agree that the reception could be held at 24 Sussex Drive. Over 140 people were invited, most of them just as close to the Mulroneys as they were to Doucet. The usual cast of characters was in attendance: Frank and Beth Moores, Guy and Yolande Charbonneau, Robert and Trudy Shea, Bonnie Brownlee and Bill Fox, Pat and Janet MacAdam, Sam and Marty Wakim, David Angus and "guest," Michael and Kelly Meighen, and Don and Phyllis Matthews. Martin made the three-tiered wedding cake but because Mila was irritated with the whole event, she would not let him decorate it at the top of the staircase, which was the only out-of-the-way place large enough to hold the square mirror he used as a tray. As a result, he put it all together in the kitchen; then he and Mulroney had to tilt the mirror at a dangerous angle to lift the whole edifice through the dining-room door. Martin took wine and champagne from the basement wine cellar; some of it was a fine Bordeaux packed in wooden boxes and imported from France, a gift from an admirer of Mulroney's.

Then there was the wedding of Bill Fox and Bonnie Brownlee. This time it was Mila who insisted on hosting the wedding and reception for the pair, each of whom had been married before. As Brownlee herself admits, she was not keen to get married at 24 Sussex Drive; she wanted a small wedding and she wanted to be in control. But Mila pressed the issue. Mila even called Bill Fox to say she'd found the perfect engagement ring; Fox thought choosing the ring should have been his job. At least Brownlee was prudent enough to pay the bills for the food and wine herself. On this occasion, Martin was allowed to decorate the cake on the mirrored square at the top of the staircase. He listened to her recite her vows at the foot of the stairs while he feverishly piped the last swirls of icing on the cake. Then he swathed it in bridal tulle and carried it down triumphantly.

The third wedding was more of a chore. This was the September 1988 wedding of Mila's brother, John Pivnicki, the same young man who had travelled to Paris in 1986 with his sister for a holiday at the Plaza Athénée. After deciding a $10,000 estimate from a Montreal caterer was a little steep, the family asked Martin to prepare a cocktail reception for 180 guests at a reception hall in Montreal. For two weeks he laboured over Chinese dumplings and baby spring rolls and baked yet another three-tiered wedding cake. After two trips to and from Montreal in a van laden with food and supplies, Martin was up all night before the wedding doing the flowers, scrubbing the floor, decorating the tables, and getting the food ready.

Characteristically, the PMO press officer dismissed Martin's revelations with his usual insouciance: "The chef works out of the house for the family," said Luc Lavoie, who was soon to go off to Spain as the Canadian ambassador for the 1992 summer Olympic Games, and apparently had stopped worrying about trying to make sense of the Mulroneys' spending habits. "It doesn't matter if he works one day on a wedding."

Over the years, the Mulroneys grew fond of certain journalists and their names appear frequently in the guest lists: Baton Broadcasting's Mike Duffy, Jeffrey Simpson of *The Globe and Mail*, Bernard Dérôme of *Le Point*, Lloyd Robertson, host of the CTV National News, and Peter Mansbridge, the host of CBC's national television news shows.

Media tycoons — men like Kenneth Thomson, Conrad Black, and Douglas Bassett — were familiar guests. But the one journalist who became closer than all the others to Mulroney, especially in the second term in office, was William Thorsell, editor of *The Globe and Mail*. Mulroney was shrewd to cultivate influential journalists, and he was only doing what any smart politician would have done. But he and his staff never forgot a slight, and any hostile journalist soon became persona non grata at 24 Sussex Drive. When one Toronto journalist on Mulroney's blacklist had to be included in a 1986 state dinner for the prime minister of Japan because her husband was a senior Ontario government official, the two were seated in the farthest corner of the hotel ballroom with one other couple, at a table for ten.

Despite meticulous planning by Mila and her staff, not every party at 24 Sussex Drive went off without a hitch. On one occasion Montreal media baron Pierre Péladeau arrived for dinner with a woman who was not his wife. Mulroney stormed into the kitchen and told the staff they would have to change the seating plan because he didn't want to sit beside the woman. And not everyone was thrilled to be invited. The Mulroneys invited hockey star Wayne Gretzky for dinner three times before he finally accepted; movie star Michael Fox declined several invitations and never did come.

On other occasions, guests who accepted lived to regret it. Bobby Orr, another hockey great, was invited to Harrington Lake for a few days with his wife and two children. Harrington has its own guest cottage, a rustic two-bedroom cabin in the woods well over a mile from the main house. It's very pretty and when visitors stay, the staff make sure there are plenty of cold cuts, candy, beer, and soft drinks to snack on. It should be idyllic. The problem with the place is that it is completely infested with mice, and no one has figured out how to get rid of them. Bobby Orr and his family lasted one night, then packed their camper-van and fled the next day, muttering apologies. Fred Doucet, said one former staff member, put up with it for a few hours; he drove back to Ottawa the same day. Finally, when the Mulroneys proposed to put visiting French president Jacques Chirac in the guest cottage, the National Capital Commission hired a team of exterminators to drive the mice out just long enough for the visit. (In the 1992–93 fiscal year the NCC spent $12,348 trying to rid official residences of mice, squirrels, and earwigs; $3,209 of that amount went to pest control at Harrington Lake.)

As the years went on, the Mulroneys collected more and more beautiful furnishings for the houses. A visiting head of state gave Mila a grand piano, for example, which went with them to Montreal. Under the government's 1985 conflict-of-interest code, which was introduced by Mulroney, a holder of public office is supposed to declare any gifts worth more than $200 to the assistant deputy registrar general. Although not technically the law, it is a condition of employment for the officeholder. Having made the declaration, he or she can keep the goods. The spouse of an officeholder, however, is exempt. In practice, many politicians leave behind gifts valued at more than $1,000, and they are usually held by the department in which the minister served. Mulroney is considering giving his booty to the National Archives (for which he will get a tax writeoff) and there's plenty of it — the list, for his nine years in office, fills nineteen pages.

The Tories themselves knew Mulroney's taste: he wanted artworks and they gave him plenty, starting with a print by Ottawa artist Henri Masson at Christmas in 1984. In 1986 the Halifax Tories' 500 Club gave him a painting by Kenneth Tolmie; his own staff in Ottawa chipped in for a painting by Robert McInnes. In 1992 the PC Canada Fund gave him a painting called *Emergence* by John Young, the Quebec Tory caucus gave him an Inuit sculpture, and the whole caucus presented him with another painting titled *Leighlinbridge*. The following year the caucus gave him three paintings — one for his birthday, one for his wedding anniversary, and one as a farewell present. His riding association in Charlevoix bought him a goodbye painting, as did the officials in the Privy Council Office. And over the years, Mulroney received three unsolicited portraits of himself.

To their chagrin, one piece that did not go with the Mulroneys to Montreal was a valuable painting by the legendary Quebec artist Jean-Paul Lemieux. Called *Le Réfectoire*, it was a long horizontal piece that hung over the sideboard in the dining room; it was loaned to the house by the artist when his friend Pierre Trudeau was in residence. After Trudeau's retirement in 1984, when John Turner became prime minister, the Lemieux family agreed that the painting could remain on loan. The same decision was made a few months later when Brian and Mila Mulroney moved into the house.

One day François Martin, an aspiring artist himself, told Mila how much he admired the painting and how he would like to buy it. Mila told him the Lemieux was out of his reach, and besides, remembers Martin, "she said she owned it herself. Brian had bought it for her a long time ago for $17,000." Bonnie Brownlee later told Martin she didn't know why Mila would have said that. "Mrs. Mulroney doesn't own the painting," Brownlee declared. "It belongs to Mr. Lemieux." The Mulroneys did, in fact, own a different Lemieux — a numbered lithograph presented by the painter and his family in 1985.

In the late 1980s the painter decided he wanted *Le Réfectoire* returned; he had a buyer for it. When Brownlee relayed this message to Mila, Mila told her to call him back and arrange a meeting to see if the picture could remain in the house. Lemieux ultimately agreed it could stay. Lemieux died in 1990 and the painting remained at 24 Sussex until the spring of 1993, when Mila tried to buy it. She called Lemieux's daughter, Anne-Sophie Lemieux of Sainte-Foy, Quebec, who had inherited her father's estate, and offered her just over $50,000. Lemieux's daughter did not respond well to the proposal. Between 1992 and 1993 three art galleries, including Klinkhoff in Montreal, had evaluated the painting and declared it worth $150,000. Lemieux's canvases, especially the bleak and lonely winter landscapes for which he was so famous, were widely reproduced. In the summer of 1993 the Montreal Museum of Fine Arts showed a major retrospective of 115 works, many of which have never been seen before. Such a retrospective, which creates great public interest, helps drive up the value of an artist's work. Mila's offer was promptly rejected and the painting was removed less than two weeks later.

Gifts to the Mulroneys from foreign leaders were certainly interesting if not always splendid; one has to wonder about a set of "three-dimensional Canadian flags" from the Reagans presented during a 1993 visit to the Reagan library in California. In 1986 alone there was a silver cigarette box from the president of Peru, a porcelain vase and a gold cup from French president François Mitterrand, two antique maps from Laurent Fabius, the former French premier, a decorative tray, two cultured pearls, and a cabinet from Premier Nakasone and silver vases from Emperor Hirohito of Japan, a piece of Roman glass from Shimon Peres of Israel and a samovar from Edward Sheverdnadze, the foreign minister of the Soviet Union. King Hussein of Jordan gave him a backgammon set in 1990 and the prime minister of Malaysia gave him a gong. In 1992 the gifts came from the presidents of Korea and Hungary, the foreign minister of India, and the queen of Denmark. The Dene and Métis nations gave him a parka in 1988 and a rifle in 1989.

Unlike her husband, Mila did not have to declare any of the gifts she received over this period. So any jewellery, paintings, clothing, wine, crystal, china, pianos, or other goods that came her way are hers to keep without a peep to the bureaucrats. One foreign dignitary gave Mila a stunning golden brooch set with diamonds and rubies mounted around his initial, which was "H"; she had the piece melted down by Montreal jeweller Lou Goldberg and made into a more discreet piece with matching earrings. These pieces formed part of a growing jewellery collection, one that became dazzling by the time the Mulroneys left 24 Sussex Drive. It included a Piaget watch and a 3.5-carat diamond ring from Goldberg's, according to the *Gazette*'s gossip columnist Tommy Schnurmacher. Mila told Sally Armstrong that she does not have a lot of expensive jewellery; much of what she wears, she said, is fake. Nonetheless, Mila had Joe Kovacevic, who was a gifted carpenter as well as the general caretaker at 24 Sussex, make a large polished wooden cabinet to hold her collection.

While he was still the chief executive officer of RJR Nabisco, their friend Ross Johnson made sure that boxes of food — including the company's much-loved Oreo cookies — showered the residence almost every month, boxes they would often pass on to their friends. Montreal cosmetics queen Lise Watier sent selections of her expensive perfume, makeup, cleansers, and other luxury cosmetic items. Their friend Marty Wakim regularly visited with pieces of the Hungarian china that Mila collected. Another friend sent two cases of Louis Roederer "Cristal," a wine that retails for $125 a bottle.

So many gifts rolled into the house that the Mulroneys couldn't begin to use them all, and Mila set many aside in storage. When they needed a present for someone, the hoard provided a ready selection. Every Christmas they had a major wrapping session at the dining-room table, finding homes for many of the unwanted items.

It was difficult for the household staff to think of things to give Mila at Christmas; what could they give a woman who had everything? A woman who once gave the male servants watches and the maids diamond studs from Lou Goldberg? One year, the staff decided to pool their resources and let François pick out something from all of them. After he passed the hat, he had only $80 to spend. What on earth can I buy with this? he wondered. But a day or two later, when he was tramping around a discount store in Hull, he spied a pretty nightgown with a Sweet Baby Jane label stitched into the neck. Back at 24 Sussex he asked one of the maids to razor the label out and replace it with a label from Holt Renfrew. When Mila opened it on Christmas Eve, she shrieked with delight. "She loved it," Martin said with a hearty laugh.

One morning in 1989 François Martin walked upstairs to the master bedroom to hand Mila his letter of resignation. For four years he'd worked for the Mulroneys from 6 a.m. until midnight, rarely taking a day off. But it wasn't long days and hard work that did him in, Martin says, nor the fact that a new household coordinator had been hired at a higher salary than his. "I quit because I was afraid if I stayed any longer I would become like them." His parents, he says, raised him on strict principles, and he simply didn't like working for the Mulroneys. Another staff member who lasted the full nine years agreed it was always stressful, but the chance to work for a prime minister, no matter how demanding, was a once-in-a-lifetime privilege. That's how Bonnie Brownlee sees it too, and her job was probably the most difficult of anyone's. "I was working for my country," she says today.

On the morning that Martin finally handed Mila his letter of resignation, she was sitting up in bed, eating breakfast, and flipping through magazines. After reading his letter, she looked up at him in shock, then tried to persuade him to change his mind. The answer was no.

So the Mulroneys hired a new chef, John LeBlanc, who was, like Martin, a protégé of Kurt Waldele, the chef at the National Arts Centre. LeBlanc lasted the remaining four years of the Mulroney period in Ottawa because he followed some wise counsel from a senior staff member. It's a busy household, he was warned, a crazy household, a demanding household. There are kings coming to visit and you need caviar, but there are kids running around too and you need pizza. Work late when you have to, but make sure you take time off when they go away. Don't try to do everything yourself — you'll burn yourself out. LeBlanc followed this advice and survived.

JUSTICE FOR SOME

IN BRIAN MULRONEY'S SECOND MANDATE, THE MAN HE AND HIS colleagues had dismissed as a crank and a sore loser returned as a genuine nightmare. Glen Kealey's anger at being asked for money by Roch LaSalle and later losing the MICOT project when he refused to pay did not go away. Other business people have had to wrestle with the question of whether to pay up; some write it off as the cost of doing business, others quietly refuse and quietly suffer. And the odd person will protest, loudly and vehemently, and will be labelled a crackpot for his pains.

That's what happened to Kealey. Having drawn his personal line in the sand on the matter of paying what he saw as a kickback, he remained silent even after he was ruined financially. In May 1988, however, he began to see things differently when Quebec organizer Pierre Claude Nolin and three other party organizers arrived at a meeting of the Hull-Aylmer PC riding association, of which Kealey was a board member, to ensure the election of their choice for president, Hull businessman Pierre Moreault. After seventy-nine ballots were collected from the seventy-two people present, furious riding association members demanded that party headquarters overturn the election. When their demands were ignored, Kealey went to the RCMP to tell them, for the first time, the whole story of his meeting with LaSalle. He also held a press conference to detail his grievances. No one paid much attention then, nor did many people vote for him when he ran as an independent in the Hull-area riding of Pontiac-Gatineau-Labelle in the fall 1988 election, campaigning for integrity in government. With nothing more to lose, he decided to start picketing Parliament Hill, embarking on a crusade that captured the imagination of many Canadians.

Although he never filed for bankruptcy, all of his assets, including his home and car, were seized by creditors, and he was left with just his clothes and a few bits of furniture. He was living rent-free in a small, leaky house in Hull that belonged to a friend; former business colleagues gave him enough money to cover the heat, electricity, and telephone. They also loaned him equipment to print the unending river of words he generated: faxes, letters, press releases, and something he called his "data base" — a list of all the players in the Mulroney government who were part of what he believed was a conspiracy to extort bribes and kickbacks on government contracts.

In late November 1988, he began a campaign of personal harassment against them. Every morning for three years, no matter how foul the weather, Kealey stationed himself near the west door of the Centre Block with his placards. "RCMP always get their man — but not their politicians," blared one of his signs. "Where were you when Brian Mulroney was destroying Canada?" demanded another. Even worse, for the targets of his fury, were the shouted taunts: "Noriega, Ceausescu, Mulroney!" he would yell. "Two down and one to go!"

Despite these bizarre tactics, Kealey won attention and some grudging respect. Unlike some other Hill protesters, Kealey kept his hair trimmed and his beard shaved; he wore clean shirts, silk ties, and good suits. His greatest assets, however, were a keen intelligence and a quick sense of humour. Reporters, Mounties, and tourists began to enjoy their conversations with him; before long even opposition politicians would stop on their way into the House for a few minutes' chat. Once in a while someone would offer to buy him lunch, and he would cheerfully down tools and go off for a hamburger on the Sparks Street Mall, where he would explain why he believed Mulroney and his gang were all crooks. And he had a formidable memory. He remembered everything everyone told him, all the tips, all the connections. As soon as he got back to the little house in Hull, he'd settle at the kitchen table to write it all down.

As the months passed, Mulroney and his ministers grew increasingly frustrated with Kealey's irritating presence. In March 1990, the Commons passed a law forbidding demonstrators within 150 feet of the doors of the Parliament Buildings. Intended to silence Kealey, it backfired badly when Canadians realized that the new law prevented citizens from expressing their opinions on the Hill. The "Kealey law" became a hotly debated freedom-of-speech issue around the country, and Kealey simply ignored it. He and another picketer, Roman Catholic priest Tony Van Hee, an anti-abortion protester, were hauled off by police to a detention centre where they were thrown into a large cell with a group of hostile bikers. Only the threat of press coverage got the pair moved to a cell by themselves, one so small that for the next four days Kealey slept on the floor with his head wedged under the toilet bowl.

This was the first time he went to jail, but it wasn't the last. Kealey wound up in jail on several occasions for hanging "Impeach Lyin' Brian" posters on the Ottawa bridges, disobeying the picketing law on the Hill, and braying at politicians. In March 1991, he was arrested four times for worming his way past barricades put up to prevent Gulf War protesters from storming the Hill, barricades that remained in place after the war's end to keep him at bay. All the while, he was assembling a legal case against Mulroney and his friends, gathering evidence, documents, and witnesses.

In February 1991 Kealey was finally able to persuade a local justice of the peace, Lynn Coulter, to listen to his reasons for wanting to lay charges against these politicians, aides, and police officers. Coulter was a tough-minded woman with thirty-two years of experience; one courtroom employee described her as having a "built-in bullshit detector." If fate hadn't sent the JP on duty for a cup of coffee, letting

Coulter sit in for him for a few minutes, she never would have dealt with Kealey in the first place. She wasn't happy about it; her face, on the first day of the first hearing, was glum, and she would snap at Kealey whenever he rambled in his delivery.

Although this hearing began in public, the Justice Department quickly rolled in its big guns, senior lawyers who argued successfully that the hearings should be held in camera. Media lawyers representing *The Globe and Mail*, Southam News, and the CBC protested, and the legal wrangles delayed the hearing for several months. Finally, the Ontario Court of Appeal sided with the federal Justice Department's argument for an in-camera hearing, and it began in July 1991. Friends had raised $10,000 to pay a top Ottawa criminal lawyer, Arthur Cogan, to assist Kealey, but in the last weeks before the hearing began, Cogan stopped taking Kealey's calls. A day before the hearing, in desperation, Kealey hired another lawyer, Richard Bosada, to step in. (Cogan eventually returned $5,000 of the money.)

In this procedure Kealey was allowed to subpoena witnesses, and he did it with a vengeance. For the next seventeen days, they filed in: six RCMP officers or former officers, kickback artists like Frank Majeau and Michel Gravel, former cabinet minister Suzanne Blais-Grenier, and police informant Émilien Maillé, who had been the key witness against Gravel in his trial. Their testimony was astounding. Although neither Kealey nor his lawyer was able to obtain transcripts of the hearing, several people in the courtroom took extensive notes that have been compiled into a general account of the testimony that was given that summer.

RCMP Staff Sergeant Richard Jordan led the team of twenty-five police investigators in the 1989 Doug Small budget leak case and had refused to lay theft charges against Small for lack of evidence. Jordan, who has since left the RCMP to practise law in Ottawa, testified that there was little direct interference by senior officers in sensitive political investigations; instead, he said, those in charge kept saying the investigators did not have enough information. "They don't call it interference," he said. "They don't do it in that way. It is couched in terms of 'lack of reasonable and probable grounds' and . . . flexible standards."

Former assistant commissioner Rod Stamler also testified, making statements he was later to repeat in Paul Palango's *Above the Law*. In his testimony before Coulter, Stamler said the RCMP had gathered convincing evidence of a secret commission of hundreds of thousands of dollars paid to a senior Mulroney aide by the Metropolitan Life Insurance Company to secure federal leases at its new Ottawa headquarters. The crucial evidence needed, he testified, was in the hands of the FBI in the United States, and the FBI refused to give it to the RCMP. Stamler suggested there had been a tradeoff between the U.S. and Canadian governments during last-minute free trade negotiations; he said the same thing to Paul Palango nearly three years later.

Inspector André Beauchemin testified that he had investigated the activities of lobbyist Gervais Desrochers and his company, Inter Gestion GD Ltée, because of allegations that Desrochers had received kickbacks on the lease with Metropolitan Life for the free trade negotiators' office. Beauchemin said an investigation of Desrochers's bank accounts showed Metropolitan Life had made three payments to Desrochers: two cheques for $6,000 each and a third for $33,000. Although the Desrochers material grew to several files, Beauchemin said he did not lay charges because he needed more evidence.

Beauchemin also testified that he had worked on the RCMP's investigation of the COSICS deal, which found that sensitive information appeared to have been leaked to Senators Charbonneau and Cogger. Cogger's file, said Beauchemin, filled an entire cabinet at RCMP headquarters. No charges were laid in the COSICS investigation, the inspector added, explaining that "there is a difference between reasonable and probable grounds and evidence." The decision is the Crown prosecutors', he said, and they chose not to lay charges. Coulter was starting to get interested; each day her scepticism about Kealey's notorious paranoia lessened.

Inspector Raymond Bérubé, who had been in charge of the Economic Crime Unit at the RCMP's Montreal headquarters, testified that he had been one of the investigators in the Gravel case and had also investigated LaSalle and Richard Grisé. Bérubé told Coulter that he had wanted to raid Grisé's home and office before the 1988 election, but had been told by his superior, Brian McConnell, to delay the raids until after the election. Following the Grisé affair, Bérubé was brought back to Ottawa and placed in charge of the force's equestrian unit, which includes the Musical Ride. Putting the best face on it, this was a lateral move for an ambitious cop and a clear signal to other officers.

Bérubé made the same point that Beauchemin had made concerning the final decision to lay charges: when senior politicians were involved, the police were told to be especially careful. "They make doubly sure of the wording of the charges," he explained, "and only after their supervisor has agreed are they allowed to discuss the case with the Crown attorneys." The Crown, he said, can choose to "refine" the information, and the Crown would advise the commissioner about the precise charge and the date it would be brought. In the Gravel case, the Crown prosecutor, Valmont Beaulieu, had been specially appointed to handle the case; he struck a deal with Gravel's lawyer, Gabriel Lapointe, for a guilty plea after the 1988 election. The Crown decided not to prosecute the men who had paid bribes to Gravel.

Suzanne Blais-Grenier took the stand very reluctantly. Still smarting from attacks by her former Tory colleagues, she came to Ottawa under force of a subpoena. Once there and under oath, however, she spoke frankly, as if it was a relief to talk. She had been made aware of kickbacks from many sources almost as soon as her party took office, she said, but she had hoped Mulroney would stop it. He didn't. The party merely differentiated between good and bad patronage, she explained to Coulter; good patronage was patronage that benefitted Tories. She testified that LaSalle had dubbed himself "the minister of patronage," but that the distribution of the big contracts was controlled by Bernard Roy in the PMO.

Blais-Grenier told Coulter that she believed Frank Moores had far more influence on contracts than any lobbyist ought to have, and that associates from his firm often attended federal department meetings about contracts. They became aware of sensitive information, she said, that would benefit their clients. She said that public servants often told companies to hire GCI "because they have an ear in the PMO."

Blais-Grenier also testified to the existence of a secret PC fund that came from the 5-per-cent kickbacks extorted from businesses that won federal contracts. She said it was her belief that the money was routed to an offshore account (she mentioned Luxembourg). The money, she testified, was a retirement fund for Mulroney. Another matter Blais-Grenier discussed was the way contracts were determined ahead of time and unsuccessful bidders told to wait their turn — the system Frank Majeau had perfected when he worked for LaSalle. She talked about Nolin's informal lobbying efforts, when he was a chief of staff to LaSalle, on behalf of his father-in-law's construction firm, Desjardins et Sauriol (later called Dessau). LaSalle and his chums were competing with the Roy-Mulroney-Charbonneau alliance, she said, and they did not like LaSalle's efforts to direct contracts to his own cronies.

Blais-Grenier saved her last salvo for the RCMP. "At some level, the RCMP is as corrupt as the politicians," she told Coulter. They had harassed her, she claimed, and tried to install a bug in her riding office. If they would be equally zealous in investigating more senior politicians, she declared, they might be more successful. "The RCMP do not identify crime at that level," she said. "They protect power." Only a royal commission, she told Coulter, could examine the whole contracting system and clean it up.

Majeau, Gravel, and Maillé gave the justice of the peace first-hand accounts of all the crooked practices they had witnessed and taken part in themselves. Maillé admitted he had become an unpaid

RCMP informant early in 1986 after failing to win government contracts he'd been promised by Gravel and other politicians, and his testimony was full of tales of Swiss bank accounts and blackmail, intimidation, and other nefarious activities going back to the 1970s.

After listening to thirteen witnesses and studying the files provided by the RCMP officers, Coulter had heard and seen enough. On Wednesday, July 17, 1991, she ruled that Kealey had "reasonable grounds to believe a crime had been committed," and she said she would sign Kealey's charges against thirteen of Mulroney's closest associates and against Canada's three most senior police officers.

Those charged with conspiracy to commit fraud were Sports Minister Pierre Cadieux (Gravel's former roommate); former cabinet ministers Roch LaSalle (who was also charged with asking Kealey for a bribe), André Bissonnette, and Michel Côté; Bernard Roy; Michel Cogger, Jean Bazin, and Guy Charbonneau; Frank Moores; three former Hill aides, Pierre Claude Nolin, Pierre-Paul Bourdon, and Michel Deschênes; and Gervais Desrochers. The three policemen charged with conspiracy to obstruct justice included RCMP Commissioner Norman Inkster, Deputy Commissioner Michael Shoemaker, and former deputy commissioner Henry Jensen.

The testimony given during the hearing was not allowed to be reported, although bits and pieces of information leaked out. Kealey himself was remarkably tight-lipped for a man who believed in sharing his information with the world, but he also believed in Lynn Coulter and the process she had initiated in her courtroom, and he did not want to let her down. When Canadians, who had heard none of the testimony, learned of her decision, they were stunned. The news made banner headlines across the country and in the United States, Europe, and Great Britain. Within hours of the announcement of the charges, the dollar had dropped three-quarters of a cent on world money markets, from 87.11 cents U.S. to 86.36 cents, forcing the Bank of Canada to raise interest rates. The accused men were ordered to appear in an Ottawa courtroom on September 16.

It was a victory and a vindication for Kealey, now mobbed by reporters who had previously mocked him. As for Lynn Coulter, the local legal community backed her decision with praise for her reputation as a fair but tough court officer. "She does not suffer fools gladly," well-known Ottawa lawyer Robert Meagher told the Ottawa *Citizen*. "It doesn't matter if it's the Crown, the defence, or a witness." Even Arthur Cogan, the lawyer who had abandoned Kealey, was quick to endorse an official he had known for twenty-five years: "Lynn has a good judicious mind and she is a super person," he told the paper. "A hearing before her is as good as any judge. She is very even-handed. She is as quick to jump on a Crown as she is on a defence attorney."

Kealey's euphoria did not last long. As the September court appearance drew closer, rumours began to drift around Ottawa that the charges would be dropped. Comments about Coulter's competence floated here and there, whispers that she wasn't skilled enough to handle such a complicated case. The initial shock of the charges was displaced by the old scepticism about Kealey's sanity or speculation about his ability to hoodwink a naive justice of the peace. Norman Inkster rushed to Solicitor General Doug Lewis's home in Orillia to brief him on events; within days of the hearing, Lewis was telling reporters that he was sure all charges would be dropped and "any investigations will prove that there is no foundation to the charges." Liberal justice critic Russell MacLellan jumped on Lewis for inappropriate behaviour; as the minister responsible for federal policing, Lewis had no business commenting on the case, MacLellan told reporters.

But Lewis was right in his prediction. On September 16, while Coulter was on a long-delayed holiday abroad, the Ontario Crown attorney's office announced it was withdrawing the charges against everyone except Roch LaSalle. Brian Trafford, the director of criminal prosecutions in Ontario, called Coulter's decision to allow the process to go ahead "a miscarriage of justice." Tory Ottawa heaved a collective sigh of relief; Kealey was nuts after all. There was much chest-thumping from members of the group who had been charged, and from their lawyers came threats of lawsuits and reprisals, but nothing resulted. Instead, a ten-person team of officers from the Ontario Provincial Police started a massive new investigation into the activities of Roch LaSalle. This investigation, led by OPP Superintendent Earle Gibson, cost over $1 million and ended in 1993. To this date, the team has issued no report. The charge against LaSalle was dropped in 1992; after a year without action being taken, the charge is dropped automatically.

The failure of his court challenge against the Tories did not discourage Kealey. Although he ceased picketing when he got his day in court, he set up a non-profit organization he called the Canadian Institute for Political Integrity, which he still runs on donations from fans across Canada. Every day he receives calls or letters from people with their own tales of government or police corruption; CIPI's job is to try to help. Unfortunately, like many whistle-blowers who are alienated from the mainstream, Kealey has become a captive of groups using him to promote their own agendas, and he damaged his own reputation when he agreed to speak to some right-wing hate groups in western Canada and in Ottawa. "I'll speak to any group, left-wing, right-wing, anyone," Kealey said defensively when asked about this not long ago. Today his conversation has become infused with descriptions of the evils of the Rothschild banking empire, and his once-tolerant listeners have begun to drift away, more than a little saddened.

Given the catalogue of scandals Canadians endured through the Mulroney years, any reasonable person would have to ask how it happened. Where were the police? The prosecutors? The courts? The answers are not pretty.

For starters, politicians overhauled the law of the land to protect themselves from police investigators; they even arranged to have the taxpayers foot their legal bills. Police investigations went awry over administrative bungles that seemed almost deliberate. When some investigations concluded that charges should be laid against politicians or their friends, officers often found themselves arguing with nervous Crown prosecutors who did not want to lay any charges, or only the fewest possible. Some Quebec prosecutors used an unusual legal process called a pré-enquête to shield certain suspects from public exposure.

The move to change the law began in the winter of 1989. On December 12 of that year, RCMP Commissioner Norman Inkster rocked the House of Commons justice committee with the information that fifteen MPs and senators were under investigation by his Mounties. Furthermore, he added, the RCMP had studied a total of thirty cases involving abuses by MPs since 1985, a figure that did not include political staff or organizers, and more investigations were yet to come. Inkster's figures made headlines and frightened certain parliamentarians who made up their minds to get the Mounties out of the business of parliamentary administration.

Interestingly, Inkster's totals were *down* from numbers he'd revealed six months earlier to the same committee; the difference was that no journalists had noticed. Even MPs must have been asleep at the switch on June 13, when the commissioner said that the force's Special Federal Inquiries Unit had conducted sixty-five investigations since 1985. Inkster said that twenty-two were still under investigation, thirty-eight had been concluded without charges, and five had resulted in charges being laid. The figure of thirty-eight cases concluded without charges was intriguing; what happened to them all?

Once the politicians took in what Inkster had said, they were determined to change the system. As described earlier, many of the investigations and the fraud and corruption charges had resulted from the mishandling of MPs' office budgets. At $165,000 annually, these budgets were irresistible to some. "Many of these guys hadn't seen so much money in their lives," chuckled David Angus in the spring of 1994, as he tried to explain why so many of them fell victim to temptation.

Many MPs believed that how they spent their Commons office budgets was their business, and no Mountie should be telling them what they could or couldn't do. When they got wind of yet another RCMP investigation into the misuse of government telephone calling cards — one politician's card number was used by an illegal laboratory processing narcotics north of Montreal, for example — they were terrified. Most knew that their children and their friends were using the cards (as had happened in the Liberal era as well) and that the system was completely out of control. MPs suddenly saw themselves facing scrutiny over thousands of dollars' worth of phone bills. The Mounties had to be stopped.

An all-party committee of the House designed a clever new law for the purpose. The thrust of Bill C-79 was that the powerful and secretive all-party Commons executive committee, called the Board of Internal Economy, would have exclusive authority to decide whether an MP's use of his or her Commons budget was appropriate. Before police could raid an MP's office, the RCMP would have to seek an opinion from the board and take that opinion to a judge in any request for a search warrant, wiretap, summons, or arrest warrant. The judge did not have to agree with the board's opinion — the police could get their warrant or wiretap in the face of board opposition — but the new law meant at least a delay and the possibility that the politician under investigation would be warned well ahead of time.

The very notion of such a law unleashed numerous editorials calling on the MPs to come to their senses. To their credit, the NDP opposed the bill, and Nelson Riis, the party's representative on the Board of Internal Economy, fought it openly. He was outvoted by the board's Tory majority. But it was the way the law was enacted on May 7, 1991, that was most disturbing. By that date, Bill C-79 had received the requisite three readings in Parliament but was not yet law. Later that day, it was suddenly proclaimed law (as an amendment to the Parliament of Canada Act) by a hastily arranged Order-in-Council, one that required approval from four cabinet ministers and a signature from the clerk of the Privy Council. A copy of the Order-in-Council was then faxed to Tory MP Gabriel Fontaine at 4:51 p.m., nine minutes before the end of the civil service workday. The next morning, on May 8, Fontaine invoked the new law in his defence when he appeared for his preliminary hearing in Quebec City on fourteen charges of fraud, breach of trust, and conspiracy.

When reporters got wind of this fortuitous bit of timing, most government spokesmen stonewalled, but one person blabbed. Guy Côté, the assistant clerk of the Privy Council, told Southam News that he was telephoned by someone in the office of Tory House leader Harvie Andre on May 7 and ordered to pass the Order-in-Council that day. "We were told it was urgent," Côté told Southam. Andre's office denied any link between Fontaine's hearing and the rush to pass Bill C-79.

On May 10, 1991, *The Globe and Mail*'s Geoffrey York shed some light on the timing of the bill with a report that it had been enacted just four days after the RCMP raided the office of Lotbinière Tory MP Maurice Tremblay. York reported that the law was proclaimed after Tremblay telephoned Harvie Andre's office and the Speaker of the Commons. Responding to opposition questions about whether Tremblay's call could be an attempt to obstruct justice, Andre admitted only that he had pushed the bill through. "When I became aware, as a result of a conversation with a member of Parliament whose offices were being searched by the RCMP at that time, that C-79 had not been proclaimed, I was on my way out of town. Three days later when I got back, I asked my staff to have it proclaimed." Andre insisted that Tremblay had not acted improperly and that the call was meant only "to inform me that the search was under way and not to ask for any action." It certainly came in the nick of time for Fontaine, who has been able to use it to delay his trial until late in 1994. And within two weeks of the law being passed, two more Quebec MPs invoked it. Gilles Bernier and former MP Richard Grisé (charged with breach of trust in a case unrelated to his first conviction) raised the C-79 amendment at their preliminary hearings on May 28, 1991.

When Bill C-79 was passed, the RCMP was in the thick of several political investigations, and some opposition members charged that the legislation amounted to outright tampering. Few MPs had much luck using the new law to clear the charges against them; both Bernier and Grisé were told by a judge that it did not apply retroactively, and when they appealed the rulings their appeals were dismissed. Three years later, Grisé was convicted of charges of misusing his House of Commons funds; Bernier was acquitted in June 1994. Tremblay was convicted in December 1992 of spending $5,000 from his office budget to send six members of his riding association to Acapulco. After his conviction by an Ottawa jury, Tremblay angrily offered the explanation that the jurors had found him guilty primarily because of the Tory government's unpopularity in the nation's capital. Then his lawyer, Serge Ménard, offered another view that was equally insulting to the Franco-Ontarian jurors, saying he doubted that they really understood French.

One of the junketeers on the Mexican trip was Jean Lassonde, Tremblay's riding association vice-president, who was convicted in Ottawa in March 1993 of fraud for his role in planning the holiday caper. The Mounties had wanted to charge Lassonde with obstructing justice; as they listened to wiretaps of Lassonde and others, the police officers had heard Lassonde coaching his fellow travellers on the version of events they should offer investigators. "They had agreed upon a story to give the RCMP that they had worked [to earn the Mexico trip] and that if the six or seven of them said the same thing [to the RCMP], that [the RCMP] would not be able to prove the contrary," noted Judge Hector Soublière.

Since the offence occurred in Quebec, the Mounties took the wiretap evidence to a Quebec Crown prosecutor to ask that an obstruction charge be laid. The Quebec Crown prosecutor refused to lay the charge. Unfazed, the Mounties took the fraud case to an

Ontario Crown prosecutor in Ottawa, where Lassonde was charged, tried, and convicted of fraud, although they were not able to charge him with obstruction of justice because that offence had been committed in Quebec. What gave the Mounties the loophole to move the case was that the money for Tremblay's office budget originated in Ottawa. A fraud could be prosecuted at the origin of the funds.

The Board of Internal Economy's assistance to beleaguered politicians did not end with the passing of Bill C-79; it also decided that MPs who'd been charged with fraud or other crimes concerning their offices, staff, or budgets should have their legal bills paid from public funds. Robert Marleau, the clerk of the House of Commons, explained in 1993 that the Commons would pay for all bills from the beginning of a police investigation through the preliminary hearing, including motions by the MP to quash search warrants and charges. While Fontaine pursued his case through the courts, claiming that the C-79 amendment shielded him, the Commons was paying. MPs have to dig into their own pockets to pay their lawyers only if a case goes to trial.

"In all cases, the assistance stopped once the trial began," Marleau said, "which does not mean that the board would be prevented from reviewing a case once the trial was over. The distinction is important because otherwise there is a danger of the impression being created that blank cheques are being handed out, which is not happening." Perhaps not, but paying legal bills was certainly a high priority for the board. From 1991 to 1993, the board approved paying legal fees for Fontaine, Bernier, Tremblay, Jean-Luc Joncas, Carole Jacques, and Pierre Cadieux. According to the minutes of the board tabled late in 1993, several other MPs also had their legal bills paid, but they were not named. The issue of the legal aid plan for the MPs was a hot topic at board meetings; in fact, it was the one item of business that came up more frequently than almost any other. The board held thirty-seven meetings between 1991 and 1993; at sixteen of them, there was discussion or decisions were made about legal bills for one MP or another.

Taxpayers will have to take Marleau's word that the Board of Internal Economy is not signing blank cheques in paying the legal fees. The board does not make public how much of the annual $240-million budget of the House of Commons goes to MPs' lawyers; when Marleau was asked to provide the figures, he declined. At the board meeting in June 1993, the last before the end of the session, members approved reimbursement of legal fees for Gilbert Parent, the Liberal MP from Welland–St. Catharines–Thorold, who was then under RCMP investigation for misuse of his office budget. The Mounties announced on December 10, 1993, that they had ended their investigation and that evidence available would not result in a conviction. Parent was elected Speaker of the House of Commons on January 17, 1994, a position that automatically makes him the chairman of the Board of Internal Economy. As a grateful recipient of the board's largesse he is most unlikely to change the system.

Bill C-79 and the payment of legal bills are only two of the ways MPs found to protect themselves from what they saw as RCMP harassment. From the point of view of the Mounties, their job was made difficult by far more serious obstacles. Back in April 1989, two months before Inkster jolted the justice committee with the numbers of MPs under investigation, Rod Stamler, the assistant commissioner responsible for commercial crime, resigned from the force. It was time for a career change, he said. In fact, he had left because he disagreed with Inkster's handling of the ongoing investigation into Michel Cogger. Stamler remained quiet for five years, working as a senior partner at Lindquist Avey Macdonald Baskerville, a Toronto-based forensic accounting practice. Stamler became one of the firm's rainmakers, hauling in plenty of business thanks both to his international reputation as an honest cop and to his friendly and gregarious style. On the subject of RCMP life under the Tories, however, his cheerfulness disappears.

Stamler describes a "leaky sieve" investigation system so porous that the solicitor general and his staff knew "virtually anything they wanted to know" about Mountie investigations. It is an open question whether investigations into politicians were compromised. According to Stamler and other police officers, the Solicitor General (who is responsible for the RCMP) and his political staff received frequent briefings about sensitive RCMP investigations, particularly the political ones, and the Mounties learned to expect requests for information from the solicitor general on a regular basis.

"The problem is not the solicitor general," Stamler says. "They are, for the most part, straight, honourable people who would maintain secrecy. But they have a political staff that has access to this information, and they deal with political staff at the PMO and everywhere else. So you've got a circle of these people [around] the ministers who become privy to all the information. Now does that get back [to those under investigation]?" Stamler believes that it did. The Mounties' investigation files were not given over to political aides, Stamler explains, but the information that was provided by other means was extremely detailed. "Letter books and briefing notes went forward on a regular basis to the solicitor general from the commissioner. That's formal. It's policy." Questions would come back from political staff in the minister's office, very specific questions on political investigations: Were the Mounties planning to take out a search warrant? And later, what had been seized? They would ask similar questions about wiretaps. We lost the element of surprise, says Stamler, stating the obvious. When the Mounties showed up with search warrants, they knew that in many cases no incriminating evidence would be found.

At least three members of the solicitor general's staff were in a position to have access to the sensitive information, the chief of staff, the executive assistant, and the press aide. Others were being briefed in the Prime Minister's Office. "By briefing [politicians and aides] daily or twice a week about what the investigator is doing, by briefing the commissioner and then the solicitor general — these are the subtleties that undermine investigations," Stamler said bluntly. "It's a big circle. Can you imagine doing the Cogger investigation and briefing every day, or at least once a week, on the nature and the extent of the investigation to the solicitor general's staff and then on to the Prime Minister's Office? But that's the policy."

It was never intended to be policy. The 1980 McDonald commission, which looked into evidence of wrongdoing by RCMP officers — especially those officers who burned separatists' barns in Quebec during the FLQ era — recommended splitting off political intelligence and security work from the RCMP and setting up a separate service, the Canadian Security Intelligence Service. Thereafter it was CSIS, rather than the RCMP, that ran security checks on political staff and patronage appointees. McDonald said that the solicitor general ought to be kept aware of operational matters so that he had enough information to be fully accountable to Parliament for the activities of CSIS. But McDonald agonized over the fine line that divides the possession of sufficient information to be responsible and the actual hands-on management of the organization. Elmer MacKay, the first solicitor general in the Mulroney government, was very keen to direct operations. This made many police officers nervous; the minister was not supposed to micromanage what they did or even know everything that they did.

Although the McDonald commission's recommendations were intended to apply to the new security service, in the end the solicitor general's office wanted briefings on all high-profile cases, whether they were CSIS or RCMP files. The two services began briefing the solicitor general as a matter of policy, though in the early 1980s, the information was kept to a minimum. During the Inkster years, senior Mounties confirm, the information flow increased dramatically. This was not a policy that began with the Mulroney government, but it was one that it exploited more insistently and pervasively than its predecessor. Stamler tries to be cautious about the implications here. There is no way to know for certain, he warns, that details of the RCMP's political investigations were being leaked to suspects. The records of each case would have to be reviewed carefully. "It would be interesting to look at the letter books — which show who knew what, and when — and the briefing notes," he says.

The Mounties weren't the only ones upset about the policy of briefing political aides about investigations. CSIS staff didn't like it any better than RCMP officers did. In 1992 CBC Radio's Jason Moscovitz reported that CSIS routinely gave the names of its most sensitive sources to politicians. Moscovitz said that every year the federal solicitor general is shown the names of up to 100 highly placed informants; a 1986 directive obliged CSIS to cough up the information. The directive instructed CSIS to advise the solicitor general of any sensitive sources they intended to recruit. Who exactly is a sensitive source? Well, certainly one of the most sensitive was Claude Morin, a leading Quebec separatist and lieutenant to Parti Québecois leader René Lévesque, who was recruited in the 1970s by the RCMP and whose role was not revealed until 1992. CSIS had at least 1,000 informants, and the solicitor general would know their identities, information that goes well beyond the basic rule of any intelligence organization: only those who need to know should have the information. The list of its confidential sources is simply the most closely held secret of any police force or intelligence-gathering organization.

The Globe and Mail pursued the Moscovitz story and reported that when the practice began, CSIS officials were horrified that the solicitor general and his staff demanded and were given top-secret CSIS files. "People who didn't even know where they had parked their cars would go off with files and squirrel them away," said one security expert. "And when we objected they would just sit there and grin at you." Although the deputy director of CSIS wrote the *Globe* to deny it, other security officials insisted that political aides attended meetings between the solicitor general's office and the targeting and recruitment committee of CSIS, a committee that decides where sources are required and who might be likely candidates for recruitment. One former solicitor general, James Kelleher, justified the practice by saying he was too busy to attend all the meetings and would send trusted aides in his place; he also said he wanted these aides at his side when he did attend. One of his aides was Bill Pristanski, his chief of staff for many years — recruited, explained Kelleher, because he was a "Sault boy" like himself. Now an Ottawa lobbyist, Pristanski had been Mulroney's executive assistant before his promotion to the solicitor general's office; he was soon known in Ottawa to be fully aware of RCMP investigations. "Pristanski had a personality of his own," said Stamler. "He was an aggressive aide to the solicitor general. He had a style like that: to assess the situation and to get as much information as possible." Pristanski and other political staff members justified their questions about sensitive investigations by saying that opposition MPs might ask the solicitor general related questions in Question Period. That excuse doesn't make any sense, responds Stamler; it was government policy not to answer opposition questions in the Commons about ongoing police investigations.

This practice came back to haunt the Tories in the summer of 1994 when Brian McInnis, a press aide to former solicitor general Doug Lewis, revealed that he possessed confidential CSIS documents showing that the organization had recruited Grant Bristow, a member of the right-wing hate group the Heritage Front, and that Bristow had not only infiltrated the Reform Party, he'd also signed up dozens of Heritage Front members as new Reform Party members. As the story unfolded, it became clear that Bristow had briefed his CSIS handlers on what he knew about a CBC documentary being made on the Heritage Front, a revelation that suggested CSIS was kept informed of sensitive projects being pursued by journalists. Not only were Reform MPs suspicious that the Heritage Front infiltration was a dirty-tricks operation by the Mulroney government to destroy their party, which was threatening traditional Conservative support, but it looked as if taxpayers' money had been used to finance Heritage Front operations. The story illustrated that a relatively junior political aide not only had access to top-secret CSIS material, but was able to take it home. The need-to-know rule became quite elastic, and information was given to a fiercely partisan group of aides who were, for the most part, young and inexperienced and whose primary tasks were protecting their ministers and riding herd on recalcitrant public servants.

The Mulroney years also saw a justice system that seemed out of kilter when politicians ran afoul of the law. There is no better example than the RCMP investigation of Michel Cogger.

Takayuki Tsuru's lawsuit against Guy Montpetit was launched in October 1988, in the middle of the federal election campaign. As more evidence of Cogger's involvement emerged, Rod Stamler became exasperated at the roadblocks thrown up by his superiors. A significant handicap was the force's failure to address the interprovincial nature of the offences. "Overall," Stamler says, choosing his words carefully, "there was a reluctance to mobilize the units that had to be mobilized. We were not able to put together a solid team of investigators that would have involved Montreal, Ottawa, Saskatchewan, and wherever else. It was all fractured." As an assistant commissioner, Stamler did not have the power to order the deployment of manpower; that decision was Inkster's.

In Saskatchewan, where the RCMP is under contract to provide policing throughout the province, officers looked into the GigaText deal, but only to determine whether provincial officials had committed any wrongs. "The Cogger part of the investigation," says Stamler, "was the part that needed the coordination, and that's what was more difficult to get." Other officers familiar with the eastern Canada investigation of Cogger have concurred with Stamler, saying that the whole operation suffered from a lack of central coordination. Officers needed to be assigned who would investigate all facets of the case and gain an overview of the deals.

While adequate RCMP manpower was not being provided for the investigation of one of Mulroney's closest buddies, the necessary resources were available to another inquiry. Former Liberal cabinet minister John Munro was suspected of wrongdoing in connection with funding that went to native groups while he was minister of Indian affairs in the Trudeau cabinet. "The investigation involving John Munro went on and on and on," says Stamler. "There were no problems in terms of maintaining that investigation." (After an exhaustive investigation that lasted three years, Munro was tried and acquitted.) Such decisions are subtle at the RCMP, Stamler explains.

Inspector Tim Quigley, who was based in Ottawa and worked under Stamler, spent about a year on the Cogger investigation before he was suddenly reassigned, doing great harm to the investigation. When Quigley left, Inspector Antoine Couture was brought in. Couture was a good man, says Stamler, "but that is not the point. The point is you cannot pick up the thread of an investigation like that when you come in a year later."

In the Munro investigation, sudden personnel changes never happened. Henry Kennedy, the officer handling the Munro case, won promotions but remained on the case. "Here's two investigations ongoing at the same time," says Stamler. "In the Munro case, the guy is promoted to inspector and he's transferred, but he remains on the investigation. In the other case, the guy is moved." For Stamler, it was a clear signal that Cogger was receiving special treatment. By April 1989, Stamler had had enough and he resigned from the force. "The entire investigation left me in a position where I could not continue with this type of work."

The RCMP investigation cranked up again when *The Gazette* ran stories about Cogger's bills to the FBDB and his other questionable business activities. On January 18, 1990, the Ottawa *Citizen* reported that Cogger had been the target of an RCMP sting operation. When Mulroney found out, according to Paul Palango, he kicked an RCMP car on the Hill in a fit of anger, hissing at the shocked officers, "You stupid bastards!" The message was received loud and clear at RCMP headquarters. Inkster ordered the Marin inquiry to look into Cogger's complaints about RCMP harassment, and he distanced himself from the officers who were investigating the senator. "The investigators all became persona non grata," Stamler says. "Some officers were really concerned for their future. The fact that the prime minister is angry should concern the commissioner, but it shouldn't concern him to the extent that it did. The Marin inquiry was a reaction of a commissioner that far exceeds the requirement. That was never done before in RCMP history — that you'd stop an investigation over the complaint of a senator who is under investigation."

The inquiry was meant to soothe Mulroney, but to the prime minister's chagrin, Marin cleared the Mounties of any misconduct. "I find there were reasonable grounds that [Cogger] was using his position as a senator to exert influence," Marin stated. "Such grounds . . . provide legal justification for police attempts to set up opportunities for law breaking."

While Marin had been reviewing the ethics of the RCMP's treatment of Cogger, Couture continued his work in Montreal. Numerous search warrants were executed: at Cogger's home near Knowlton, Quebec, at his Montreal apartment, at his Montreal office, and at his Senate office. The Mounties searched his bank accounts and his Mercedes-Benz. The warrants showed that the RCMP believed Cogger had committed three acts of influence-peddling, one act of defrauding the Federal Business Development Bank of $74,250, and one act of accepting a $5,000 benefit from a business partner, Meyer Lawee. Finally, three years after their first investigation began, the Mounties had put together what they believed was a solid case against Cogger. They were ready to go.

In most provinces the RCMP can lay charges themselves, but with serious offences such as influence-peddling they would do so only after consulting the Crown. Couture had laid about a dozen fraud charges during four years in commercial fraud in Ontario, and he almost always won convictions. In Quebec, however, there was an added wrinkle: the law permits the police to be complainants only; it is the Crown prosecutors who always have the power to lay charges. Couture and his partner, Inspector André Beauchemin, had to convince three Crown prosecutors, among them Pierre Lévesque (son of the late premier, René Lévesque) and Serge Authier, that they had the goods to convict Cogger. To their frustration, Lévesque agreed after three days of arguing to go ahead with just one charge, not the five the Mounties were asking for. We'll charge Cogger with peddling his influence to Montpetit, he said.

As criminal prosecutions go, the Montpetit case was the obvious and easiest case for Lévesque to prosecute. The Supreme Court of Canada has defined the standard for influence-peddling. The mere act of opening the doors of government to people seeking government favours, and charging for it, constitutes influence-peddling, even if the person has no influence. Cogger had sent a bill in the amount of $110,000 to Montpetit, itemizing his efforts with several senior government officials on Montpetit's behalf. Cogger's bill to Montpetit said it all.

The police were devastated by the fight with the prosecutors: three years to assemble the case, and it was reduced to a single charge. Cogger's preliminary hearing was held under a publication ban, and in the end, no jury ever heard the case. Crown prosecutor Lévesque agreed to a suggestion from Cogger's lawyer, Bruno Pateras, that no public trial be held; they simply filed the evidence from the preliminary hearing with the trial judge, Jean Falardeau. No witnesses, no press reports, no public scrutiny of the testimony.

Lévesque's move caused a stir within the legal community. McGill University law professor Ron Sklar questioned its legality and expressed astonishment with the tactic. "It's a short-circuiting of the normal procedure," he told the *Gazette*, "and it's a muzzling of the press [to keep them] from scrutinizing the court process." Other lawyers consulted by the *Gazette* agreed; only one, Toronto lawyer Edward Greenspan, sided with Lévesque. He said that although it was an exceptional case, he had seen a trial without witnesses. Greenspan added that he applauded the move because it saves time and money.

The Ottawa *Citizen* raised its concerns about the unusual accommodation of Cogger in a February 10, 1993, editorial. "Taking unusual steps, especially where the verdict has implications for public trust in political institutions, raises suspicions about special treatment for the well-connected. To be sure, Cogger's case only strengthens those suspicions. While some of the political scandals that have rocked Brian Mulroney's government ended in resignations, firings, dismissed charges, or acquittals, too many have supported the perception of justice being manipulated by law-breaking lawmakers."

As we know, Judge Falardeau acquitted Cogger on June 17, 1993, noting that he "was not convinced beyond a reasonable doubt that the accused committed the actions with a guilty mind or blameworthiness necessary to lead to a conviction." It's instructive to compare Cogger's case with that of a public servant tried by Falardeau just two weeks before Cogger's trial began. Falardeau had convicted federal civil servant Jean Rivard of defrauding the government by claiming an extra $5,000 in real estate fees for the sale of his house. (Rivard's job required him to relocate from Mirabel to Montreal.) In his ruling, Falardeau did not give Rivard the benefit of the doubt. He did not wonder whether the middle-level civil servant had a guilty mind or showed blameworthiness. Instead, Falardeau said that the "intention of an individual can be deduced from the actions he carries out," and as far as Falardeau was concerned, the act of overbilling revealed the man's criminal intentions.

Mounties investigating political corruption in Quebec began running into another brick wall, the use of the pré-enquête, a closed hearing that prosecutors often insisted on before charges were laid against a politician. Evidence is presented behind closed doors to a judge or a justice of the peace in the absence of the suspect. If the judge is satisfied, he or she initials the charges and the case then proceeds like any other criminal prosecution. In the rest of Canada, the pré-enquête is such a rare legal procedure that it is almost unheard of. (One small irony here is that Glen Kealey used a pré-enquête to lay his charges.)

In Quebec, this procedure became the norm for political corruption cases. After the RCMP had gathered evidence to charge Lévis MP Gabriel Fontaine with fraud, breach of trust, and conspiracy, they discovered that prosecutor Pierre Lapointe had decided to hold a pré-enquête. "It is a general policy of the attorney general of the province that in those cases [involving politicians] we always have pré-enquêtes," Lapointe explained, "if it is a politician and if it has to do with his duties and his riding budget. Why? For reasons of prudence, I guess. Essentially for reasons of prudence. We are more prudent [with politicians] than with others because of the consequences of the charges."

Admitting that there was no written policy to that effect, Lapointe also conceded that Crown prosecutors would inform the deputy attorney general, who was in effect their boss, about the progress of the case. "Obviously when charges of that nature are involved . . . everyone is notified. It goes up the hierarchy. I would not have acted in any other way than to have had a pré-enquête." How could he justify treating politicians differently than normal citizens accused of breaking the law? His answer was frank: public servants were simply covering their rear ends. "You must understand that there is a question of civil liability that is relatively important," Lapointe argued. "It's the type of charge that is most likely to expose the attorney general to a damage suit, and the fact that there is a pré-enquête means that we ask a justice of the peace, an independent person, to decide on a question that in principle the attorney general decides upon. There is a double-check by the justice of the peace."

That's a convoluted way of saying that Crown prosecutors in Quebec are more careful about laying charges against prominent people than they are when pressing charges against an ordinary citizen. They take the precaution of holding a pré-enquête, which gives them greater comfort against possible suits for wrongful prosecution, and the minister of justice is always alerted when such a special hearing is to be held. One Hull prosecutor, Valmont Beaulieu, had opposed the practice back in 1986 when he refused to hold a pré-enquête in the Gravel case despite pressure from his Quebec City superiors. In 1989, however, a pré-enquête was held at the end of the RCMP investigation into Jean-Luc Joncas, the Tory MP for Matapédia-Matane, and Quebec Court Judge Jean Bécu signed off on twenty-four counts of fraud, breach of trust, and forgery. (Joncas was later acquitted of all the charges when the presiding judge, Charles Quimper, lit into the national press and the RCMP, charging them with conducting a "witch hunt" of Joncas. Quimper had once been a lawyer with the RCMP; his outburst was never explained, although it appeared he believed that the media had convicted Joncas before his trial and that somehow the RCMP was behind the media's actions.)

Another pré-enquête was held in 1993 when the Mounties wanted to bring influence-peddling charges against Carole Jacques and her political organizer, Jean-Yves Pantaloni. The Mounties trudged to the Montreal Crown's office with a thick book outlining the case against Jacques, and once again the three Crown prosecutors, led by Serge Authier, declined to lay charges. Instead, the Mounties were invited to let a judge decide in a pré-enquête. Alexander Rack and Marc Paquin (the son of murdered Saint-Laurent developer Henri Paquin) came to testify at the closed-door hearing on July 12, 1993, before Judge Claude Joncas. Moments after their testimony, Joncas signed the charge sheet, which held a total of twelve counts of influence-peddling, breach of trust, and conspiracy.

Although Canada's Criminal Code is a federal law, under the Constitution Act of 1867 the provinces have authority over the actual administration of justice, including the hiring of Crown prosecutors. Although there is no obvious explanation for Quebec Crown prosecutors' frequent reluctance to prosecute RCMP cases against federal Tory MPs, there is an opinion in nationalist Quebec that the

RCMP is a federal police force, which, when investigating crimes in Quebec, is pursuing an agenda that has little relevance to Quebeckers. That attitude — along with the long-standing close relationship between Robert Bourassa and Brian Mulroney and the fact that Bourassa's justice minister was always briefed on impending political prosecutions — cannot be overlooked when pondering the overall attitude of the Quebec Crown.

How a prosecutor is selected for a particular case is another delicate issue. The prosecutor originally assigned to the Cogger case was Michel St. Cyr, who had been prosecuting political corruption cases in the province for sixteen years. Despite his scruffy shoes, wrinkled suits, and hangdog smile, St. Cyr's plodding and unflappable style had proven effective. In the early 1980s, St. Cyr had prosecuted former Liberal cabinet minister Bryce Mackasey on influence-peddling charges; although Mackasey was ultimately cleared, St. Cyr won convictions against Mackasey's accountant, Robert Harrison, on numerous corruption charges. The other co-accused, Jean Bruyère, pleaded guilty to the same charges.

St. Cyr met with the Mounties several times on the Cogger case, reviewed their search warrants, and got up to speed. Six months into the Cogger file, St. Cyr was transferred from Montreal to the two-man Cowansville office at his own request, but he told his bosses he was willing to continue with the Cogger case. All he'd need was a replacement to fill the gap in Cowansville, an hour's drive away, whenever he was out of the office. The answer was no, and Pierre Lévesque took his place on the Cogger prosecution. Lévesque's early career had been with Michel Proulx, one of the top criminal lawyers in Canada, but Lévesque did not last in the practice and after a stint in another struggling firm he joined the Crown's office with its guarantee of a regular paycheque. He had never prosecuted a political corruption case.

The same thing happened in the prosecution of André Bissonnette, the Mulroney cabinet minister charged in the infamous

Oerlikon affair. The Montreal Crown prosecutor's office had half a dozen prosecutors who specialized in white-collar corruption. Rather than draw from that group, the Crown assigned Ellen Paré, a young and inexperienced prosecutor from the Montreal suburb of Longueuil, to prosecute Bissonnette and his friend Normand Ouellette. Paré, like Lévesque, had never prosecuted a politician in her career, and she was easy pickings for the two skilled and senior Montreal defence lawyers, Bruno Pateras and Jean-Claude Hébert. The result was expected: Bissonnette was acquitted while Ouellette, his riding association president, was convicted.

What about our judiciary? Do they have something to answer for? We have seen many examples of extraordinary decisions by judges when politicians appeared before them, though few can top Judge Falardeau's decision that Michel Cogger was innocent because he didn't have a criminal mind. Another judge displayed unusual behaviour in 1991 when Michel Gravel was before her on an income tax appeal. Judge Louise Lamarre Proulx, a sister of Lavalin boss Bernard Lamarre, had been appointed to the Tax Court of Canada by Mulroney in 1988. Two days into the hearing it was clear that Gravel's feisty and clever lawyer, Claudine Murphy, intended to call a stream of witnesses, including RCMP officers, to testify in open court on the same issues they'd talked about in the closed-court Kealey hearings. "I'll go all the way to the top if I have to," she told Montreal lawyer Roger Baker, a friend of Mulroney's who had been defending LaSalle in Frank Majeau's wrongful dismissal suit.

Alarmed that her court might become a media zoo, Lamarre Proulx used a temporary break in the proceedings to seek advice from officials in Ottawa. Her next step, although neither side had asked for it, was to issue a reporting ban on any further testimony in the Gravel appeal. Media lawyers objected successfully, and after a few weeks' delay, she reopened her court to reporters. By that time Murphy was off the case, and Gravel was dependent on a junior lawyer whose experience had been in real estate and family law, not criminal work. His defence fizzled out. In 1992 Lamarre Proulx ordered him to pay the income tax on the money he said he had raised for LaSalle, and the case was closed.

The buzz around Montreal was that Murphy had been pulled off Gravel's case after a visit to partners in her firm by both Marcel Danis and Carole Jacques. "Yes, it's true that my bosses were quite concerned for a while," said Murphy. "Yes, Marcel Danis was close to my bosses and Carole Jacques used to work at my firm. Yes, they talked to my bosses."

But, Murphy claimed, the partners in her firm were not the kind of people who could be pushed around. "They are non-political, they represent people from all parties." The reason she dumped Gravel as a client, she explained, was that they disagreed about her fees. Still, it is unusual to leave a client in the middle of a court appeal. Murphy also acted for Frank Majeau in his wrongful dismissal suit. At one stage in the Majeau matter, she went to Roger Baker informally to try to reach a settlement. Baker's interpretation was that she'd tried to threaten him, and he filed a complaint with the RCMP. The RCMP told her they might have to lay charges against her, and Murphy was forced to retain a criminal lawyer to act on her own behalf. The investigation went nowhere, but the experience unnerved her. On his last day in office Mulroney appointed Baker to a judgeship, as he did Brian Trafford, the director of criminal prosecutions in Ontario who had been in charge of the Kealey prosecutions following the Coulter hearings, the same prosecutor who had called the process in Coulter's courtroom "a miscarriage of justice."

The legacy of the Mulroney years is a sad one for several of Canada's major institutions. The RCMP has been demoralized by its inability to effectively address the wrongdoings of MPs, MPs' aides, and senators. Norman Inkster retired from the force in June 1994, his career clouded by allegations of favouritism to his political masters.

But the Mounties were not the only ones to be tarnished and

humiliated. Parliament has been stained by the sheer numbers of politicians investigated and charged with fraud or breach of trust. There was even the apparent attempt to influence a judge, René Marin, by persons at the highest levels of government. After nine years of watching politicians, lobbyists, backroom boys, bagmen, and other associated hangers-on dining so splendidly at the public trough, many Canadians have lost their faith in the political system and their trust in elected officials. Every political party in or out of power has its crooks and scoundrels, its scandals and patronage binges; it was our bad luck to endure nine years of a regime that overlooked, condoned, and sometimes even encouraged such behaviour. But the damage is not irreparable. Some have suggested that a royal commission with full subpoena powers should call to account those who arrived in Ottawa after 1984 with the singleminded goal of lining their pockets. Whether or not such a commission is held, the issue of integrity in government has not been resolved by the defeat of the Conservatives. Many of the Tories' best tricks were copied from previous Liberal governments.

Reforms are needed to ensure that the justice system is not taken hostage again. The Mounties must regain their independence; they should not be briefing the solicitor general about ongoing political investigations. It would help if the commissioner were outside the deputy minister structure, removed from any immediate pressure from the solicitor general's office or the prime minister. He must be free to have his officers investigate the crimes of parliamentarians. Parliament could also pass legislation to deal specifically with government corruption, legislation that would establish a group of federally appointed lawyers whose only job would be to prosecute those cases. The law would also stipulate the penalties for those found guilty.

Money-laundering expert Mario Possamai notes that other jurisdictions have had problems like Canada's with corrupt politicians, and three are currently developing effective solutions. In the 1980s, the Australians of New South Wales found that the police could no

444

longer investigate political wrongdoing, partly because of their lack of independence, partly because senior police officers themselves were implicated in other crimes. New South Wales faced an acute crisis, and the government responded by setting up an independent commission whose sole task was to investigate corruption. Public awareness campaigns were also launched to make the point that everyone pays a price when there is such corruption.

The serious situation in Italy is known all over the world. For the past few years Italy has pursued the "Clean Hands" project, a drive to clean up a Mafia-ridden political system structured on bribes and kickbacks at every level. Italy was able to undertake this campaign, says Possamai, because its magistrates are independent under the country's constitution. They are duty-bound to investigate criminal acts, including those committed by corrupt politicians, and they are duty-bound to prosecute. Leading the way has been Antonio Di Pietro, the chief magistrate of Milan, who initiated the "Clean Hands" project in 1992 in answer to numerous complaints from business people who were fed up with paying bribes and kickbacks. When Di Pietro began pulling the threads, he unravelled the biggest political and business scandal in Italy's history, one that has seen four former prime ministers indicted.

Hong Kong is another example of a jurisdiction that had to overhaul its method of dealing with crooked politicians. Here the citizens realized in the 1970s that corruption does not just line the pockets of politicians; it exacts a very real financial and social cost. When decisions are made on the basis of benefitting friends of the government instead of making the best deal possible for taxpayers, markets cannot operate freely and a country's ability to compete internationally is ultimately affected. The very practical Chinese have decided that it simply makes good business sense to operate honestly.

The model most suitable for Canadian needs, Possamai suggests, may be Australia's: an independent commission, free from political interference. In a sense we have such an institution in place now with Elections Canada, an independent agency that operates at arm's length from the government. It can initiate its own investigations, arrange its own prosecutions, and accept public complaints, and it is duty-bound to investigate complaints. The essential ingredient, adds Possamai, whatever the agency or vehicle, is the independence of the investigators and the prosecutors.

During the Kealey hearings, Justice of the Peace Lynn Coulter made an appropriate observation. Quoting the famous line attributed to Edmund Burke, she commented, "The only thing necessary for the triumph of evil is for good men to do nothing."

YES, PRIME MINISTER

B
RIAN MULRONEY WAS THE PRIME MINISTER OF CANADA FOR
nine years. How did he conduct himself while in office?
What motivated him? What did he do all day? At the end
of the Mulroney era, those close to him have been more
forthcoming than they were during his time in power, when anyone
he suspected of betraying him was given swift and brutal punishment. Mulroney himself awaits what he believes will be the positive
judgment of history; in the meantime, a picture of Mulroney in office
is coming into sharper focus.

Mulroney was undeniably a charmer when he wanted to be. The
best evidence comes from his own critics in caucus, who would attend
every Wednesday morning in the Railway Committee Room (and
later in the converted Reading Room) while he accepted their questions, complaints, gripes, and bickering. No Conservative leader in
living memory handled caucus better than Brian Mulroney. He was
humble about his failings, he grieved over his mistakes, he waxed
righteous over the fallen sinners, he acknowledged the problems.
Then he would set all that aside, tell the troops how well they were
doing, what great developments were in the works, how feeble was
the opposition, how much he loved them all. It was a masterful performance, one that renewed their spirits and refreshed their souls. By
noon, when the meetings ended, Mulroney would emerge surrounded
by a cheerful and feisty band of believers. "The Boss listened to me

and I really gave it to him," they'd tell the folks back home. "There'll be some changes made, I can promise you that." Nothing changed, but the backbenchers believed that their opinions had registered and that they were taken seriously.

No one knew better than Brian Mulroney what it felt like to be down and out, and no one knew better how to comfort those who found themselves in that slough of despond. Even old enemies became stout friends when he helped them in their troubles. Bill Neville had been one of Joe Clark's fiercest supporters, but when his son died tragically and he lost his job as Clark's chief of staff after the 1980 election defeat, it was Mulroney who was there to comfort him and his wife, Mulroney who arranged a vice-president's job for him at the Bank of Commerce. Neville remained close to Clark, but he developed a steadfast loyalty to Mulroney that continues to this day. When *The Financial Post*'s bureau chief, Hy Solomon, and later *Citizen* columnist Marjorie Nichols became mortally ill with cancer, Mulroney called and visited them in hospital. Their families and friends appreciated these gestures and so did the journalists, neither of whom had been especially kind to Mulroney in print. When kids of caucus members got into trouble or there was difficulty in a marriage, Mulroney offered sympathetic help. Mila was likewise carefully thoughtful. During her years as chairman of the cystic fibrosis charity, she made herself available to many families of sick children and to the children themselves; some would phone just to chat, and she always cheered them up. At 24 Sussex Drive, she made sure her staff kept a list of the birthdays of friends and godchildren. In the midst of his own difficulties Michel Cogger was proud to tell a Senate staff member that he'd received a remembrance from the Boss on his birthday.

When political adversaries fell on hard times, Mulroney was also quick to make contact. After David Peterson's defeat at the hands of Ontario voters in 1990, Mulroney was on the phone; months later he still called to ask how things were going. Likewise the master of networking never failed to notice an important new appointment; within twenty-four hours of William Ardell taking over as head of Southam Inc., one of Canada's largest publishing empires, Mulroney was on the line to offer congratulations.

"He's an old-style Irish pol," said one former deputy minister who watched Mulroney up close for some years with a mixture of awe and contempt. "He had some very attractive traits but they were traits he demonstrated in private. You have to respect him for these. He was always phoning sick people because he believed it was the right thing to do. He had the ability to make people in a room feel comfortable. What I didn't like was the bullshit, the exaggeration, and the stroking."

Despite his mastery of caucus and his ability to reach out to people, Mulroney found it impossible, even after nine years, to win the hearts or minds of most of the senior public servants who worked for him. One of the few exceptions was Paul Tellier, the clerk of the Privy Council for most of the Mulroney years, who had risen high in the public service with the Trudeau Liberals but adapted even better to the Tories and to Mulroney. He too came to display the prime minister's bullying arrogance. Another was Tellier's successor, Glen Shortliffe, who developed a reputation as another my-way-or-the-highway Mulroney clone, but without the charm. A third was Marc Lortie, a courtly diplomat from External Affairs, who came into the PMO as press secretary and soon adopted the brusque swagger of the people who worked for the Boss.

Others in this circle did not succumb as easily. Waiting for Mulroney to get down to serious policy discussions was a frustrating business for mandarins, and some realized that reading briefs was not one of Mulroney's priorities. "He depended on news reports to brief him on the issues we were dealing with," said one public servant who served on more than one cabinet committee.

Senior bureaucrats in the Privy Council Office tried many techniques to draw the prime minister's attention to important issues, but no one could devise a way to interest him in reading his briefs. Finally two bureaucrats resorted to illustration. They used cartoon figures to represent a series of choices and — fearing they were right off the dial and might insult the prime minister — completed the presentation with two possible options for his consideration. One option had a big "X" marked across it to show this was not the recommended choice. Mulroney's reaction? "He loved it," said one official.

The days of most Canadian politicians are sliced into ten- or fifteen-minute segments, filled with meetings and calls that begin before breakfast and end late at night over briefing books. Pages from Mulroney's daily, weekly, and monthly diaries show that his days were not carved up in this fashion; instead large blocks of "private time" were set aside. This was not unusual, say those who knew his schedule well. What the diaries seem to suggest is that he was just not that busy, at least not busy on government business. He spent at least six hours a day on the telephone, plumbing his networks for gossip, feedback, and business news. And he passed hours with his cronies over lunch at 24 Sussex, at Harrington Lake, or in Montreal discussing deals, patronage appointments, and party business.

When he did meet with them, deputy ministers and other senior officials were frequently annoyed by Mulroney's habit of opening cabinet committee meetings with a twenty- or thirty-minute discussion of the day's press coverage. He drew attention to flattering stories and editorials that endorsed his point of view on events or presented a favourable interpretation of some new government initiative. The lesson would go on at great length while frazzled deputies peeked at their watches and slid resigned glances at one another. In their minds these self-congratulatory rambles served only to highlight the prime minister's vanity and his obsession with media coverage.

"You have to understand the tremendous amount of media monitoring we did," said one former communications official. "We got three or four packages of stories a day, and that was just the print journalism. The PM was preoccupied with the press, and nobody wanted to be caught out missing something. For the people in the communications office it was a nightmare; they couldn't skim the papers fast enough to keep up with him." It cost taxpayers about $840,000 a year to keep Mulroney informed, reported Southam News in 1993. Using material gathered by researcher Ken Rubin, the news service discovered that the PCO produced at least nine daily reports about what was in the papers and being broadcast. The reports began to flow in at 7:15 a.m. with The Early Bird, a collection of clippings from the Toronto, Ottawa, and Montreal papers, a service that cost $94,000 a year. The most expensive service was provided by ACF Communications, which charged $313,331 annually to produce Media Day at 8:30 a.m., a summary of electronic and print coverage.

Mulroney's press secretaries and communications strategists, people like Bill Fox and Ian Anderson, combed negative stories for facts they could challenge. "When Mulroney didn't like a story, you had to get somebody to dig out facts they could refute, rebut, or show to be inaccurate," said one media adviser. "Failing that, you had to write the editor. You couldn't refute opinions so you'd go after the reporter personally." This favourite Republican tactic was picked up by Mulroney's staff: start a high-level letter-writing campaign against the reporter or columnist, complaining about bias, tone, accuracy — anything but the actual content of the story. By the time an editor, publisher, or producer had been bombarded with indignant letters from senior officials and politicians, he or she would be a little gun-shy on the reporter's next story. It made everyone nervous or cautious, which was exactly what was intended. A typical example was the barrage of letters the Ottawa *Citizen* received following publication of the stories by Mark Kennedy and Chris Cobb on the advertising and polling contracts given to Tory agencies during the Yes campaign.

Many critics have complained that *The Globe and Mail* gave up serious investigative reporting on political corruption because of Mulroney's influence with the paper's editor, William Thorsell, and with its publisher for many years, Roy Megarry. Thorsell had no taste for these stories, but it must be said that under his predecessor

Norman Webster and under Thorsell himself, the *Globe* pursued these stories with more vigour than any other newspaper. The Montreal *Gazette* frequently matched the *Globe*'s efforts in this area. Canadian Press reporters in Ottawa such as Bob Fife, Tim Naumetz, Edison Stewart, Derik Hodgson, David Blaikie, and Warren Caragata were diligent even after most moved on to work for newspapers, but most also became discouraged as the flak from the PMO increasingly unsettled their managers. Blaikie had one of the more sobering experiences; his beat was Canada Post, and his persistent probing of the corporation's secretive practices so enraged Harvie Andre, the minister for Canada Post, that Andre's press secretary wrote Blaikie's boss at Canadian Press to recommend they fire him. By the end of the Mulroney era, rather than pursue stories about political corruption at the highest levels in Ottawa, Canadian newspapers largely chose to look the other way. With falling advertising revenues, newspapers were less eager to pay hefty fees to libel lawyers to vet stories before they were published and to defend reporters afterwards if they were sued. It was safer and cheaper to ensure that the stories didn't offend before they went out.

Mulroney's relationship with the press became increasingly complicated over the years. Although he craved attention, he was wary of most Canadian reporters, and in his last two years in office he preferred to grant interviews to foreign journalists at *The Washington Post*, *The New York Times*, PBS, and C-Span, the broadcasting service of the U.S. Congress; they were invariably friendlier. Inaccessible to reporters at home, Mulroney appeared on *Larry King Live* and on C-Span to do colour commentary during the 1992 Vancouver Summit between Boris Yeltsin and Bill Clinton. At the same time he did grow fond of William Thorsell. They talked on the phone every few days and still do today. Friends visiting Thorsell at home always knew when it was Mulroney on the line; Thorsell's voice would drop, and he would mutter quietly into the phone. One bureaucrat remembers Mulroney bragging at cabinet committee meetings about the influence he'd had on a Thorsell Saturday column in the *Globe* or on an editorial he'd had a chance to discuss with Thorsell before it was written. "Thorsell's got it right again," he would crow at the meeting, before going on to quote from the approving piece for his glassy-eyed audience.

Television was much easier to control. During Mulroney's tenure in Ottawa, the CBC's national television bureau in Ottawa had shied away from stories about Tory corruption. Unless it was a major scandal that couldn't be ignored — an Oerlikon, a Stevens inquiry — the bureau either overlooked them altogether or underplayed them. The very occasional skirmish between a cabinet minister and a CBC reporter would be pointed to proudly as evidence that the CBC was tough and held the government to account. The truth was that CBC managers were so terrified of the cuts being made to the CBC budget by a Tory-appointed board of directors that they grew ever more reluctant to take on the government. When CBC chairman Patrick Watson resigned in June 1994, a year before his contract ran out, he was explicit in his criticism of the government's attempts to meddle with the corporation's news programming. "There were a number of calls, trying to stick their fingers into the program process," Watson said after resigning. "They were people very close to the Prime Minister's Office. And that's not unheard of in the history of the CBC." But, Watson added, these calls — and there were about six of them — "were a little more diligent than what the corporation is used to." Most of the calls were made during the fall of 1992 when Canadians were preparing to vote on the Charlottetown constitutional accord. Watson won't say more because he's writing a book about his experiences.

Veteran broadcaster Knowlton Nash is also scathing in his criticism of the Mulroney government's interference in the CBC's management. His book *The Microphone Wars: A History of Triumph and Betrayal at the CBC* documents the Tories' determined but unsuccessful efforts to dump CBC president Pierre Juneau, an old friend and colleague of Pierre Trudeau who was appointed in 1982. And Nash vividly remembers the night in 1984 when he was anchoring the national news and received one angry call from Gary Mulroney and three from Mulroney himself, who was sputtering with rage. What had made him so angry was the CBC's reporting of a Mulroney pep rally in Montreal in the spring of 1983, Nash says. "He complained that we had underestimated the size of the crowd and the importance of the people who were there." Throughout the years in power, he adds, Mulroney repeatedly complained about the CBC's coverage.

Nor did CBC Radio escape the notice of the politicians. Just a few years after Mulroney came to power, senior managers were forced to keep computerized records of airtime given to each party during election periods, even tracking whether the tone of the broadcast had been negative or positive. The message from CBC managers to producers was clear: the government views the broadcasts, and especially the commentators, as too liberal, too left-wing. "That message was conveyed to us regularly," said one producer. And it came home very clearly in one case in June 1992, when a senior CBC radio producer worked with reporter Jason Moscovitz on a series of stories about the politicization of CSIS under the Tories. The stories described how the identities of CSIS informants were jeopardized by the insistence of the solicitor general that his political aides be present at sensitive briefings. As the series ran, the producer discovered that Bill Neville, a CBC board member, had written to the corporation's president, Gérard Veilleux, to complain about the liberal slant of another series for which the same producer was responsible. CBC management immediately reassigned him to a job that did not involve any broadcasting duties.

Over at CTV, the situation was different and in some ways worse. Reporters at its Ottawa affiliate, CJOH, became accustomed to orders to pull items unflattering to the Mulroney government. When the entire Ottawa press corps was pursuing the question of whether Mulroney was drinking heavily after the 1990 failure of the

Meech Lake Accord, CJOH reporter Richard Ghizbert was yanked away from the gates of Harrington Lake after Doug Bassett, the owner of Baton Broadcasting, called the head of the CJOH newsroom. On another occasion, footage of Mila injuring herself in a charity volleyball game was also pulled on orders from management. Then there was the time François Martin was booked to go on CTV's *Canada AM* to discuss his experiences at 24 Sussex and found his appearance abruptly cancelled at the last moment.

At a journalism convention in the spring of 1994, not long after he'd joined the lobbying firm of Earnscliffe Strategy Research, the CBC's former senior producer in Ottawa, Elly Alboim, lamented the state of political journalism, declaring that reporters should be covering the government's agenda. Rooting around in scandals, he suggested, was irresponsible and unprofessional. That opinion was certainly shared by Mulroney.

In the words of Erik Nielsen, "Brian was overwhelmingly preoccupied with his own likeability and acceptance. That's why he surrounded himself with sycophants who would praise him to the high heavens. People like Roy and McMillan and that man who wanted to be called 'Doctor' . . . If he ever asked my opinion I told him." Mulroney soon stopped asking. His need for praise did not diminish in his ten years in Ottawa; he demanded it from his cabinet colleagues and senior mandarins as much as he wanted it from the press. Toadyism became the fashion for those dealing with him on a regular basis. In earlier times, said one deputy minister, "whether it was a Trudeau or a Clark, there was a discipline in the system and you could vigorously argue an opposite point of view, and if, at the end of the day, you didn't win, the fact that you didn't win wasn't held against you." In the Mulroney years, it wasn't smart to argue vigorously against the prevailing opinion. It *was* held against you. "We can't afford boosterism," the deputy said. "You have to allow professionals to speak their minds." When they don't or when they can't, he explained, they become risk-averse, cautious, and ultimately useless.

Nobody denied that the public service was demoralized during the Mulroney years. The signal had been sent early in his mandate when the new Tory leader boasted that his government planned to give bureaucrats "pink slips and running shoes" as soon as they took power; the intent was underlined by the imposition of chiefs of staff in each department. By 1988 a Woods Gordon study had found that Ottawa's senior managers involved in the administration of income security programs were suffering from extremely low morale, and even the government's 1988 Public Service Commission annual report made the same point. PCO Clerk Paul Tellier's reaction to the bad news was to bring the government's deputy ministers together for a breakfast and order them to pass the word to the troops: Morale is just fine.

More studies showed that Tellier's enforced cheeriness was wrong; University of Ottawa professors David Zussman and Jak Zabes did major studies in 1986 and 1989 that demonstrated the plummeting morale of the civil service, especially at senior and middle management levels. If there was one event that highlighted the simmering anger felt by so many, it was the 1989 Al-Mashat affair, in which senior politicians publicly blamed a senior foreign service officer, Raymond Chrétien, for botching the normal immigration process and allowing into Canada Mohammed Al-Mashat, the former Iraqi ambassador to Washington.

"There was no question," admitted a chief of staff for one of the most powerful cabinet ministers. "From the beginning we were told that the public service was the enemy and that it wouldn't do to get close to them." The final straw was a hasty and poorly thought out government reorganization implemented in June 1993 to show Canadians the government was serious about downsizing. It collapsed thirty-two departments into twenty-five and displaced several of the city's deputy ministers and assistant deputies; as Arthur Kroeger, one of Ottawa's best-respected and most experienced former deputies told *The Globe and Mail's* Giles Gherson, "That reorganization was a travesty. It was ill-conceived, ill-timed and deeply destructive of public service morale."

But the best line goes to another one of Gherson's contacts, a senior bureaucrat who told him the day after the Chrétien government won, "I felt like a kid abandoned by his parents for nine years and left in the hands of an abusive babysitter."

We can't say that Brian Mulroney didn't warn us. "Ya dance with the lady what brung ya," he told Canadians, long before his first government was elected. It was a succinct summation of the one principle by which he governed. Interpret it as simple loyalty to one's friends or confirmation that to the victor go the spoils; the result is the same. Canadians didn't take it in at first; a year or two passed before we understood the Mulroney agenda. His record shows that he was driven by ego to become the most powerful political figure in Canada, and that once prime minister, he oversaw a government that put the country's treasury at the disposal of himself and his supporters. Those who had been there the longest, fought the hardest, and stood by the most faithfully won the richest rewards, the best jobs, the lucrative contracts and leases, and the crucial legislative changes. The others, the minor figures attached to his victories, had to be satisfied with the inferior contracts, the lesser appointments, the cocktails with cabinet ministers instead of dinners at Sussex Drive. But mogul or small fry, if they had been there for the Boss, they were taken care of.

"There's no whore like an old whore," he chuckled in 1984 when he heard that former Liberal cabinet minister Bryce Mackasey had been given a patronage plum by outgoing prime minister Pierre Trudeau. It was an unfortunate remark that came back to haunt him; many Canadians thought his cynicism reflected his true political philosophy. His behaviour at the end of his years in power simply reinforced the comment he'd made at the beginning; it was time to take care of the folks who'd brought him to the highest political office in the land.

In fact, astute observers realized Mulroney was on his way out when they saw the pattern of patronage appointments shift subtly in the late fall of 1992. Any close friend or crony of either Brian or Mila who still needed a job got one, and in most instances these jobs were "good behaviour" positions — the occupants couldn't be removed during their fixed terms unless they committed a serious misdemeanour, at least not without a handsome severance. And for those already ensconced in secure positions, Mulroney broke appointments before their renewal dates, then reappointed them for another full term. If it can be done with a lease for Pierre Bourque, it can be done for a friend on the Immigration and Refugee Board.

Some people, of course, suffered disappointments as Mulroney prepared to leave office; either they did not get what they wanted or their luck had run out. Joe Stewart hoped to the last minute for a call to the Senate, but the Nova Scotia slots went to others. Joe remained on the sidelines in New Glasgow, fending off hostile Revenue Canada investigators. Another Senate hopeful had been Patrick MacAdam, but after the dust-up over the Bourque lease, the steam went out of a campaign to get him into the upper house. Then there was Marcel Danis, who did not receive an invitation to join the Federal Court as had been expected. The former labour minister and deputy Speaker of the House is back teaching political science in Montreal.

The list of satisfied customers is much longer, too long, in fact, for these pages. What follows is the highlights, beginning with Mila's friends. In March 1993, Mila arranged for Judy Parrish to get a five-year appointment to the Citizenship Court of Canada, a job worth $66,000 a year. Until she was given the judgeship, Parrish was working as a receptionist; her estranged husband, Paul Dick, who was defeated in the 1993 election after twenty-one years as the MP for Lanark-Carleton, had been ordered to pay her $3,200 a month. Nine months later an Ontario judge cancelled the support payments, ruling that Parrish was now well able to support herself. "Paul took a lot of heat on that appointment," said one of Dick's close friends, "but he had nothing to do with it." The appointment was the Mulroneys' idea, he explained, and no one in cabinet was consulted.

After the Dicks had separated, the friend related, Mulroney himself had called Dick. "Get over here," he ordered. Mystified, Dick obliged and found to his chagrin that Mulroney, prodded by Mila, wanted to know if there was someone else in Dick's life. "Paul denied it," said the friend, "and so Mulroney tells the missus there's no one else." A few weeks later Michael McSweeney, the man who had been general factotum, babysitter, and sometime driver for the Mulroneys, spotted Dick skiing at a Quebec resort with a woman who was not his wife. McSweeney reported back to Mulroney. "This destroyed what little relationship there was between Paul and Mulroney," the friend said. Mulroney would not have done Dick the favour of looking after his ex-wife; he did it for the ex-wife.

Then there was the appointment of Pat McCaffery, Rinaldo Canonica's wife, to the board of the Official Residences Council. Annelie Bubalo was part of Mila's small circle in Montreal; her husband, Drasko Bubalo, a Serbian like the Pivnickis, was given a senior job on the Immigration and Refugee Board. Harvey Corn, the Mulroneys' notary and chairman of Telefilm Canada, won a five-year full-time position on the Canadian Pension Commission. Two foot-soldiers who'd served for many years were also well taken care of: for Rick Morgan, Mulroney's trusted executive assistant, there was a senior job at Bombardier. For the multi-talented Michael McSweeney, there was the presidency of the Standards Council of Canada, a position worth $106,000 a year.

At Christmas, 1992, the patronage payoffs began in earnest when Mulroney found nice berths for other former aides. Camille Guilbault, his deputy chief of staff, became the commissioner of Canada's pavilion for Expo '93 in Korea, while Denise Cole, another former PMO staff member, was named to the board of the Advisory Council on the Status of Women. York University professor and former lobbyist Charles McMillan was reappointed to his job on the board of the Asia-Pacific Foundation. There was a five-year term on the Canadian Pension Commission for Ottawa lobbyist Keith

Hamilton, the man who had tried to help Glen Kealey get the MICOT deal while he was still working on contract in the PMO. Former press secretary Marc Lortie was named ambassador to Chile.

Marketing expert Jean Dugré of Montreal, who set up a fundraising committee in 1983 called The Friends of Brian, was given a full-time job at the Parole Board. Another name on the 1992 Christmas list was that of Montreal lawyer Jacques Courtois, a partner at Stikeman Elliott in Montreal. Courtois was a former president of the Montreal Canadiens hockey team, an adviser to the founders of the Bronfmans' Edper group, a director of the Ritz-Carlton Hotel in Montreal, chairman of McGraw-Hill Ryerson Ltd., and the father of Nicole Eaton, wife to Thor Eaton of the department-store family. As important as all this was Courtois's role as a Mulroney fundraiser, going back to the 1976 leadership campaign. His reward was the chairmanship of the Security Intelligence Review Committee. George Vari was appointed to SIRC at the same time.

Between December 17, 1992, and early January 1993, the Privy Council Office processed a total of 178 appointments, most of which went to former political aides and senior Conservative Party organizers. Vancouver lawyer and Tory organizer Lyall Knott, a partner at Clark Wilson, which had received plenty of federal legal work, went to the board of the Vancouver Port Corporation. Old Mulroney friend Jean Riou, a former party vice-president and another lawyer who had received government legal work, had his directorship on the board of the Montreal Port Corporation renewed. New Brunswick's Harry Gaunce, a former chairman of the party's finance committee, was reappointed to the port corporation in Saint John. Toronto lawyer and PC Canada Fund board member Donald Guthrie won a three-year renewal to the board of the CNR.

The folks back in Manicouagan and Charlevoix also knew it was Mulroney's last Christmas in office. In December the cabinet passed an Order-in-Council to give Sept-Îles, located in Mulroney's former riding of Manicouagan, a $1.5-million grant for a new performing arts centre. This was in addition to $120 million granted for a new aluminum smelter. Newsletters to constituents in Mulroney's current riding of Charlevoix bragged that he'd pumped at least $20 million in grants into the riding during the previous four years, an amount that included a 1992 grant of $250,000 from Agriculture Canada to Biôme Dépollution, a French company that promised to rid the air of the stink of pig manure.

On February 24, 1993, to no one's surprise, Mulroney announced he was leaving politics. Thereafter the appointments rained down thick and fast until June 24, his last day in office. Following his appointment of two new senators — Saskatchewan lawyer Raynell Andreychuk and Jean-Claude Rivest, one of Robert Bourassa's most senior advisers — within days of revealing his retirement, Kim Campbell, the leading contender in the race to succeed Mulroney, commented publicly that the appointments should have been held until after the election. Just hours after she made her remarks, Mulroney appointed two more senators, Alberta's Ron Ghitter and Manitoba's Terrance Stratton, long-time Tory activists who were in charge of the party's 1993 election campaigns in their home provinces.

Mulroney blustered that most of the appointments in the last six months were routine, non-patronage positions, but that was not true; he also stated that his patronage record was not as bad as that of former prime minister Pierre Trudeau, who, he said, made 225 appointments in one week before he left. That was also not true. Trudeau made 225 appointments during his last two months in office — and as of June 5, 1993, Mulroney had surpassed Trudeau with a total of 241 appointments. He left office on June 25, making another large batch of appointments in his last days, indeed in his last hours, in office. On June 24, he named Helen Vari to the board of the Canada Council.

Putting aside a series of senior RCMP appointments, the prime minister made 655 appointments from December 17, 1992, to June 10, 1993, and only 73 of them were public-service positions. Four appointments went to high-profile Liberals and New Democrats:

Lucie Pépin, a former Liberal MP from Montreal, was given a ten-year appointment on the National Parole Board; Rosemary Brown, a New Democrat from Vancouver and head of the Ontario Human Rights Commission, was appointed to the Security Intelligence Review Committee; Liberal MP Marcel Prud'homme was named to the Senate as an independent; and New Democrat MP Derek Blackburn became a member of the Immigration and Refugee Board in Toronto. Almost all of the remaining 500 appointments were highly partisan. There were jobs for at least ten of his former aides, nine former politicians, twelve failed Tory candidates from federal elections, six relatives of senior Tories, and thirty-three high-profile backroom organizers or party donors. The balance went primarily to party workers and riding fundraisers.

Senate appointments went to Len Gustafson, a Saskatchewan MP who was Mulroney's parliamentary secretary; Duncan Jessiman, a Winnipeg lawyer and Tory fundraiser; Mulroney's long-time crony Fernand Roberge, who had left the Ritz-Carlton to run Stratcorp Inc., an import-export firm; appointments chief Marjory LeBreton; former LaSalle chief of staff, PMO aide, Quebec organizer, and lobbyist Pierre Claude Nolin; PC Canada Fund boss David Angus; and party president Gerry St. Germain.

A number of Tories received judgeships, among them David Jenkins, a Tory campaign manager in P.E.I., who went to the province's Supreme Court; and John Edward Scanlan, whom we met earlier, Elmer MacKay's campaign manager in 1988 and former president of the Central Nova Conservative Association.

The Parole Board became a much-desired resting place for well-connected Tories because it pays so well; the forty-five full-time members earn between $80,100 and $94,500, while part-timers take home $400 to $475 a day. Among the final appointments were Pierre Cadieux, the campaign manager and law partner of Sports Minister (and namesake) Pierre Cadieux, who was responsible for the Parole Board when he was solicitor general in 1990; Claire Carefoot, Joe

Clark's former riding campaign manager; Michel Dagenais, a Montreal lawyer and long-time Conservative Party worker in Quebec who was promoted from vice-chairman to chairman for a ten-year term (and was subsequently dumped by the Liberals as chairman — but not as a member — in the spring of 1994); Stan Graham, a former Tory MP from the Kootenays, B.C.; and Keith Morgan, a former Mulroney aide, husband to Gisèle and father to Rick, who was appointed vice-chairman of the Quebec region of the Parole Board. Mulroney's secretary, Nicole Guénette, was sent to Paris as chief of staff to Benoit Bouchard, the new Canadian ambassador to France. Among several appointments to the Canadian Pension Commission, jobs that bring in $73,400 to $86,400 a year, were Joan Fennimore, an assistant to Elmer MacKay, and James Ramsay, former chief of staff to International Trade Minister Michael Wilson.

The National Transportation Agency provided a comfortable bolt-hole for several Tories in need of high-paying, full-time employment. Among those lining up for salaries in the $88,000-to-$103,000 range were George Minaker, a former Tory MP from Winnipeg; James McGrath, former Tory MP and former lieutenant-governor of Newfoundland; and Gilles Rivard, a Quebec City lawyer and Tory organizer who was involved in the 1988 scandal surrounding the resignation of Michel Côté. Ports Canada was always a favourite for Tories interested in real estate, and here two Montreal insiders, Jean Riou and André Gingras, were given three-year renewals of their previous appointments. Gingras's appointment as chairman of the Montreal Port Corporation was also renewed for another three years.

Over at the CNR board, another haven for those with real estate interests, Maurice Mayer won a three-year renewal. At VIA Rail, Marc LeFrançois, the Quebec City developer and Tory organizer who was also linked to Michel Côté, was first appointed to the board in 1985 and then served a five-year term as chairman; Jean Sirois, the Montreal lawyer, Tory bagman, and former Telefilm chairman, was appointed to the board; Hugh Smith, a Halifax investment company executive and Tory organizer who hosted the party for Don Mazankowski when he received his honorary degree at the Technical University of Nova Scotia in 1987, had his appointment renewed for three years. A newcomer to the VIA board was Stuart Hendin, the Ottawa lawyer and lobbyist who worked closely with Guy Charbonneau on many projects.

Mulroney didn't forget the CBC board; here he renewed Bill Neville's term for another three years and added Brian Peckford, the former Conservative premier of Newfoundland, for a five-year term. At the Export Development Corporation, the source of the Section 31 money for Vibec, Mulroney found a spot for his old friend and fellow Irishman Brian Gallery, who had had to resign from the vice-chairmanship of the CNR when he tried to bully the advertising department into keeping up its level of advertising in his shipping magazine. (Ports Canada and several of its port corporation affiliates in Montreal, Halifax, Quebec City, and Vancouver, as well as a Ports Canada company called Advantage Canada, run by former Mazankowski aide Pat Walsh, continued to advertise heavily in Gallery's magazine.)

Mulroney put Don Matthews on the board of the Bank of Canada for a three-year term in the middle of the final negotiations for the Pearson Airport deal; he also appointed Arni Thorsteinson, chairman of the PC Manitoba Fund, to the Bank's board, but Thorsteinson had to withdraw almost immediately when it was discovered that he had defaulted on $6 million worth of mortgages due to the Manitoba government.

There was another board much favoured by Mulroney and his friends, where the jobs paid well and seemed to suit so many of the wives, widows, and girlfriends. It would be unfair and sexist to suggest that all of the women on the Immigration and Refugee Board fell into these categories, but an interesting percentage certainly did. For a lot of Tories, it was cheaper to secure the girlfriend a job on the IRB than to support her. The pay runs at about $80,000 a year, and the jobs are held on good behaviour.

In Toronto, Mulroney found a space for Marty Wakim, the wife of one of his oldest friends, Sam Wakim. The prime minister pushed through the seven-year appointment on June 24, his last day in office; it runs to the year 2000. In Montreal, Denyse Angé, Mila's friend at the Fur Fashion Council, was first appointed in 1985; her appointment was renewed for five years. The appointment of Roger Nantel's widow, Lucienne Appel, was extended for two years. Marthe Carrière, Guy Charbonneau's friend, did even better: she was initially appointed to the Montreal IRB in 1989, and her term was broken and renewed to 1997. Paule Champoux, the widow of Peter Ohrt, a former Mulroney campaign organizer and aide, had her initial three-year term on the board extended for another five years. Régis Dionne, a Baie-Comeau lawyer and former Mulroney campaign worker who is also a close friend of Keith Morgan, had his appointment extended to 1997. Francine Latraverse, who is married to Jules Pleaux, a Tory organizer in Quebec and later chief of staff to former Treasury Board president Robert de Cotret, had her initial two-year term renewed for five years. Then came Madeleine Marien-Roy, wife of Montreal lawyer and former chief of staff Bernard Roy, who was appointed in 1990 for two years, renewed for a further two years in 1992, and then saw her appointment cancelled on April 15 so that the term could be renewed for a further seven years until the year 2000.

Gisèle Morgan, the former national director of the PC Party, was named deputy chairman of the Montreal board. Liliane Poiré, Roch LaSalle's invaluable former aide and the woman who worked as a liaison between his office and Guy Charbonneau's, was appointed to the IRB in 1988 with a renewal to 1994 (but she is now back in Ottawa, working for a Tory senator). And finally, there were the Raymond sisters, whom we met in the days of the break-ins at Tory offices in Montreal. Denyse and Louise Raymond joined the Montreal board within a few months of each other nearly five years ago. Denyse had been working for Charbonneau on Tory activities in Montreal; her appointment lasts until 1997. The appointment of

Louise, who worked for the PC Canada Fund, ran out in 1993. Of all the appointments except those to the Senate, the IRB's positions involve the most manoeuvring and excite the most envy. It is not an old boys' club, like the CN and VIA boards or the ports boards or the board of the Bank of Canada. The boys kept the boys' clubs for themselves; they used the IRB to take care of the women.

A few days before Kim Campbell won the leadership of the party, the Mulroneys made a farewell visit to Charlevoix, dispensing a last little something for the good voters of the riding, a $3-million federal grant towards a new environmental centre. When reporters asked about the rewards he'd been scattering through the ranks of the faithful, Mulroney's response was entirely typical: "It is an undeniable fact that Brian Mulroney, as prime minister of Canada, nominated more New Democrats, more Liberals and non-Conservatives to posts of power in Canada. It's a historic fact."

Even the Conservatives blushed when they heard this whopper, but for a small group of mutineers in Supply and Services Minister Paul Dick's office, it was just the kind of line they loved. Perhaps because they knew their boss was on the outs with the prime minister, or maybe just as a bit of gallows humour in the last days of the Tory regime, Dick's staff kept a Wall of Shame in the kitchen of the ministerial suite. Prominently displayed was every embarrassing news story, shameless patronage appointment, and appalling comment from the prime minister. Most of the items were simply clipped and tacked up, "but Michael McSweeney's appointment was a framed addition to the Wall of Shame," said an aide. "Who did this? We all did. The whole staff did it. We pinned up every self-promoting press release that came from Perrin Beatty's office." The $150,000 furniture deal struck between Mila and John Hoyles, the general manager of the NCC, created a frenzy of activity. "After this announcement, the Wall of Shame received daily additions," the aide said. "You'd stand by the fax machine all day and just wait for it." Dick's staff knew more about the First Family, as they liked to call the Mulroneys, than most ministerial aides because of the ministry's responsibility for the official residences from 1984 to 1987, when millions of dollars were spent on Harrington Lake and 24 Sussex Drive.

By the end of August, the Wall of Shame was thick with clippings, and Dick's staff knew they themselves were doomed and that they deserved it. There were no safe patronage berths for any of them; they felt like the last Americans in Saigon. "When the government fell," Dick's aide said, "we wanted the helicopters to come and take us off the roof of 24 Sussex."

CHAPTER TWENTY-SIX

MULRONEY, INC.

I T TAKES MORE THAN THE POSSIBILITY OF A CANADIAN PRIME MINISTER as a new neighbour to excite the super-rich of Palm Beach, but in January 1993 the merely wealthy were chattering about Brian and Mila Mulroney's search for a vacation home in the neighbourhood. Thom Smith, the gossip columnist for *The Palm Beach Post*, wrote that the Mulroneys were reportedly looking at properties on Island Drive, an area where prices run from $2.25 million to $3.5 million (U.S.).

It would be hard to top the house they were staying in, the $3-million Seminole Road luxury estate of Charles (Buddy) Jenkins, Jr., an Ocean City, Maryland, businessman. Built in 1932, the two-storey pink-and-white oceanfront home is part of a gated community beside the Seminole Club golf course, where annual fees run to $150,000. Palm Beach residents told *The Toronto Star*'s Tim Harper that Mulroney had offered one resident more than $40,000 in rent for the January holiday period before finding the Jenkins house through the good offices of mutual friends George and Ginger Petty, whose $2.5-million house is part of the same subdivision.[1] Mulroney's staff told Harper that while the taxpayers had flown the Mulroneys to Florida, the prime minister was picking up the cost of renting from Jenkins.

But the Mulroneys had more on their minds than real estate. By mid-January 1993, Mulroney knew he was leaving Ottawa; the matters being discussed now with his most trusted allies were the timing of the announcement of his resignation, the agenda for his last months in office, and, of course, what he would do when he left politics. Others were turning their thoughts to the same subject. In Montreal a small group of old friends were discreetly trying to find a way to help Mulroney return to private life with some security and comfort. An effort began to put together a post-retirement fund to ease the way.

On the evening of February 23, 1993, Mulroney called Deputy Prime Minister Don Mazankowski and House leader Harvie Andre; could they come over? He also called his trusted mentor Guy Charbonneau. When the men arrived, Mulroney told them he'd made his decision to resign on June 25. The next day, on February 24, Conservative Party president Gerry St. Germain issued a press release to confirm what all Ottawa knew, that Mulroney was stepping down. "I am confident that in regard to our major initiatives, the verdict of history will be a supportive one," the prime minister said in his statement. And he asked the party to organize a leadership convention at "the earliest convenient moment."

He wasn't leaving a day too soon. The law required that a federal election be held by the fall of 1993, and even the most die-hard loyalists knew that Mulroney's unpopularity would cost them another Conservative victory if he stayed at the helm. While a number of cabinet ministers and a few backbenchers started weighing their chances in the leadership race, Mulroney concentrated on placing his friends and staff in government jobs, purchasing a home in Montreal, and preparing for an extended farewell tour.

By mid-March the Mulroneys had found a two-storey, four-bedroom greystone house on Forden Crescent in Westmount. Built in the 1950s, it had belonged for twenty years to Montreal lawyer Ivan Phillips and his wife, Lisa; now divorced, the Phillipses had decided to sell it. The house, for which the Mulroneys paid $1.67 million, was more imposing than their old stone cottage on Belvedere Road but far less charming; the garden was small and, built as it was on a corner lot, there was almost no privacy at the front and sides. Still, it had been well constructed and boasted a pool, a large finished basement, an oak-panelled den upstairs, and a maid's room. The closing date was set for April 30.

The couple then turned their attention to the tour. If Mulroney hadn't already been so heartily disliked by most Canadians before the trip began, this jaunt would certainly have done the trick. Pierre Trudeau could have told him that; Trudeau couldn't resist a swing through world capitals on an ambitious "peace mission" before his retirement in 1983, to the almost unanimous scorn of opinion leaders. Mulroney, too, yielded to the temptation. The tour began in mid-April with a trip to Santa Barbara, California, to say farewell to former U.S. president Ronald Reagan and his wife, Nancy. The Mulroneys and their entourage stayed four nights at the luxurious Four Seasons in Los Angeles, then moved on to Houston, Texas, for a goodbye visit to George and Barbara Bush. No matter that the Mulroneys had spent the weekend of January 16 and 17 at Camp David with the Bushes, bidding adieu as the president prepared to turn power over to Bill Clinton; this time it was Mulroney who was leaving office, and the occasion would be appropriately acknowledged. When critics complained that these were just expensive social calls with no national purpose, Mulroney's aides offered a stout defence. Former presidents are influential people, press secretary Mark Entwhistle told *The Gazette*'s Sarah Scott; "you'd be amazed how much business goes on."

The Houston trip turned into a embarrassing débâcle when a storm delayed the Mulroneys' plane, forcing them to land in Corpus Christi, Texas, instead of Houston. They never did make it into Houston; the busy schedules of retirees George and Barbara Bush had no flex for a lame-duck prime minister and his wife. When *Toronto Star* reporter Linda Diebel detailed the comedy of errors that kept the couples from exchanging a last embrace, Mulroney was so angry that he not only telephoned John Honderich, the *Star*'s editor, at home to rant about Diebel's impertinence but persuaded Bush to call Honderich as well. Bemused *Star* readers were treated to the novelty of a letter to the editor from a former U.S. president to complain about a story. Diebel, of course, took the usual round of abuse heaped upon reporters who offended Mulroney; his indignant staff bombarded the newspaper's editors with accusations of malevolence, sloppiness, and inaccuracy.

The humiliating U.S. swing encouraged many Canadians to follow the rest of the tour with a hostile avidity. By early May, the schedule for a nine-day procession through European capitals was arousing a fury among those who knew how lavishly he and Mila liked to travel. PMO spin doctors insisted the trips were crucial; according to Entwhistle, Mulroney "would continue work on several issues of fundamental importance to . . . Canadian foreign policy," and he would be able to "cement relations with Europe, talk about how the world should deal with the former Yugoslavia, and start to lay down the ground for those who will follow him." And, enthused Entwhistle, it was also a chance to say goodbye to foreign leaders who had become "close personal friends." But cynics wouldn't drop their ill-natured carping. The tour was nothing more than a exercise in self-aggrandizement, said some. It's just a way to gather video clips for his farewell tribute from the party, sniped others. He's job-hunting, snickered many.

This was hardly the public relations triumph for which PMO handlers had hoped. Although Mulroney's visits to Moscow, Bonn, London, and Paris went relatively smoothly, disaster struck when the Russians inadvertently released a photograph of a grinning Mulroney against a forest backdrop, his arm around President Boris Yeltsin, and each man holding a high-powered rifle over a pair of dead boars lying at their feet. Brian Mulroney was certainly smart enough to know that this picture — one that showed him in business shoes and socks with his pant cuffs turned up — would be the butt of jokes across Canada. Indeed it was. "Until the dead-boar picture," wrote the *Globe*'s Jeff

Sallot, "Mr. Mulroney's media advisers had always been good at making sure their boss was photographed in nothing less than the most flattering circumstances. But this time something went wrong, and the Prime Minister's critics — animal-rights activists, opponents of trigger-happy diplomacy, opposition politicians unhappy with extravagant farewell tours — have been howling." No Canadian photographers had been allowed near the Yeltsin dacha at Zavidovo, a resort area on the Volga River, but Yeltsin's photographer was there and it never occurred to him that he shouldn't release the picture to the Canadian press. Entwhistle faced a happy mob of reporters all clamouring for details: Did the prime minister pull the trigger? Was it a clean shot? Later, when he was asked directly if he'd shot the boar himself, Mulroney tried an evasive quip: "There was some activity and the boar went down for the count. I don't know who was more surprised, me or the boar."

One of the few journalists who tried to defend the tour was the *Globe*'s William Thorsell, who wearily predicted that reporters would ignore the considerable substance of Mulroney's diplomatic meetings and concentrate instead on covering the expense, the shopping, the photo ops. In a barrage of letters, cranky *Globe* readers let Thorsell know what they thought of his justifications.

The trip was over by the middle of May but it took reporters until January 1994 to find out how much it had cost to transport the Mulroneys and their entourage of seventeen people. Using documents obtained under access-to-information legislation, the Ottawa *Citizen* arrived at a total of $600,000, which included $365,501.41 for travel, accommodation, and per diems; $130,000 for an Airbus from National Defence; $34,287.60 for telephones; $35,737.52 to rent limousines and other vehicles; $20,776.10 for overseas freight services; and $3,905.77 for hospitality. During the trip, video clips were made of foreign leaders saying nice things about Mulroney, and these were featured in the farewell tribute evening that opened the June PC leadership convention. Mulroney's office said the party had covered the cost of filming these bouquets.

The Mulroneys arrived back from Europe shortly after taking formal possession of the new Forden Crescent house. They had hired an architect, Tony Dimiele, designer Céline Laprise, and contractor Lorne Miller to undertake major renovations. The costs involved were substantial and the source of the money to cover them was the subject of endless speculation in both Ottawa and Montreal, even among the couple's close friends. The financing on the house, which is in Mila's name, showed that the couple planned to shoulder a heavy debt load. The Canadian Imperial Bank of Commerce gave them an impressive line of credit (based on a collateral mortgage on the property) of $1.258 million, which suggests either that they made a cash down-payment of about $416,000 or that they paid cash for the full amount and used the line of credit to pay their renovation and decorating bills. If the money was to pay for the house itself, payments on the balance would run between $8,000 and $10,000 a month.

But they did not seem to be short of ready cash. Almost as soon as the house was theirs, the Mulroneys applied to the City of Westmount for a building permit for $600,000 worth of work, and by May 13 a dumpster appeared in the driveway and scaffolding was up at the back of the house. Annabelle King is *The Gazette*'s homes editor, and her sources kept her informed of progress on Forden Crescent; her estimate was that the refurbishing would total not less than $1 million, a figure that included approximately $300,000 worth of upholstery, curtains, carpets, and new furniture. All forty-five windows were being replaced at a cost of $60,000, reported King, and the house would soon have a new kitchen, three new bathrooms — each with its own Jacuzzi — and new offices for Brian and Mila. The house was being rewired for state-of-the-art sound systems, security protection, an elaborate phone system, and smoke detectors. Predictably, some of the residents on Forden Crescent would be inconvenienced by the noise and the mess, so as soon as they returned from the farewell tour, the Mulroneys invited their new neighbours for cocktails at 24 Sussex Drive, sending a bus to provide round-trip transportation. Not everyone accepted, but it was a good-will gesture most of the community appreciated.

This cocktail party was one of the last social events held at 24 Sussex before the leadership convention. All through April and May, moving vans had been hauling away their Sussex Drive furniture, so the Mulroneys prepared to camp up at Harrington Lake, which had also been stripped of most of its furniture, until after the convention. Cheap furniture from a government warehouse ("Stittsville flea market shit," as one servant noted disdainfully) was brought in to replace the Canadian antiques that had filled the farmhouse.

The day the family finally moved out of 24 Sussex, the staff prepared one last lunch for Mulroney and a single guest. "We were told this was a private affair," said one former staff member, "but it had to be done perfectly; it was a very important lunch to the Boss." John LeBlanc, the household chef, was away on vacation, so Mila asked the National Arts Centre's Kurt Waldele to come in and prepare something simple but elegant for the prime minister and his visitor. Waldele suggested grilled fish, a salad, and a dessert, served at the small table in the bay window of the dining room.

In an unusual departure from the norm, the staff were not informed of the guest's identity, so naturally they were curious when a long black Cadillac pulled into the circular drive. "We were all at the windows to see who it was," said one, but they were disappointed when a slender, white-haired man no one recognized stepped out of the car. The two men lunched quietly together behind closed doors. After the visitor departed, everyone hurried to pack up the items they'd need for the next few weeks at Harrington. And then they left 24 Sussex for the last time, too rushed to spare more than a backward glance at the house that had been home to most of them for many years.

Although Sussex Drive was almost empty of furniture, four receptions and one supper party were held there in the last frantic days before the new Tory leader was chosen. Three nights in a row, June 7, 8, and 9, the Mulroneys hosted farewell cocktail parties on the lawns of the residence for 300 to 400 people each, most of them caucus or party members. All over town, the leadership candidates — Kim Campbell, Jean Charest, Jim Edwards, and others — were wooing hordes of hungry, thirsty delegates, but the parties people were talking about were the Mulroneys'. Who was there? Whom are they backing? What are they saying?

On Friday, June 11, the prime minister and his wife welcomed their closest friends to a small family buffet supper at Sussex Drive, catered again by Waldele, before the party convention tribute at the Civic Centre. But this event, meant to be an intimate leave-taking, was itself marred by Mulroney's vindictiveness. Among the invitees were Janis Johnson and her teenage son, Stefan. Johnson was thrilled; it was a peace offering made after a long period of estrangement caused by Johnson's vote in the Senate against the government's abortion legislation; her vote, and those of a few other maverick Tories like Finlay MacDonald, had helped to kill the bill. As luck would have it, on Thursday, June 10, Johnson was among a small group of Tory senators who once again voted against a government bill; this time it was legislation that would have melded the Social Sciences and Humanities Research Council with the Canada Council. It was, the senators believed, a shotgun marriage that had incensed most of the country's academic communities. Soon after the votes were counted and the bill defeated, Johnson received a call from Mulroney's office to tell her that the prime minister could not entertain her and her son at Sussex Drive the next night after all. Johnson minded less for herself than for her son, who was deeply wounded; he and Ben Mulroney were the same age, had known each other since they were infants, and had kept in touch. The estrangement between the parents had made it awkward for the boys, and Stefan was looking forward to renewing a friendship that had meant a lot to him. The story seeped out to a few senior Tories; to minimize the damage, one of Mulroney's associates claimed she'd never been invited in the first place. Johnson icily offered to produce the engraved invitation.

There was another surprising no-show at the party: Johnson's ex-husband, Frank Moores, one of the oldest friends and one of the most powerful Tories of the Mulroney era. Very few people in Ottawa knew that Frank and Beth Moores hadn't seen the Mulroneys for years. He doesn't know why, says Moores today. "I haven't spoken to Brian for four years, almost five. I got dropped off the list. I shouldn't say I'm not unhappy, but it doesn't bother me one way or the other." When asked if it was his notoriety that had caused the Mulroneys to drop him, Moores just snorted derisively. "You've got to be joking," he snapped. "My notoriety's no worse than theirs."[2]

The Mulroneys, their children, and their supper guests arrived at the Civic Centre for the tribute about 8 p.m. Mila had never looked better; she was dressed in a short white piqué suit, and a heavy collar of pearls was clasped around her neck. The family waved to the crowds, watched the video, listened to the speeches, mounted the platform so Mulroney could say his goodbyes to the party, and then, their faces set in fixed smiles, marched out to polite applause. There was no outpouring of emotion, no expression of sadness or regret at the departure of the leader who had brought them two majority victories. The Tories in the arena that night just wanted to get on with the business of replacing him.

There was one last social obligation to get through; back at Sussex Drive 200 friends were waiting to say goodbye. Joe Stewart was there from New Glasgow, and Bob and Trudy Shea from Boston, and the Doucet brothers, and all the gang from Montreal. David Angus had just been appointed to the Senate and couldn't keep a delighted grin off his face. The entire cabinet was in attendance, along with the PC Canada Fund board, Michel and Erica Cogger, Guy and Yolande Charbonneau, and all of Mulroney's staff. Perhaps a few of them spared a thought for the ghosts of happier times, for old friends like Roger Nantel and Rod Pageau and John Grant.

The following morning, in a private room at the National Arts Centre, Mulroney attended his last meeting with the board of the PC Canada Fund. For the previous ten years this hand-picked group had met regularly to ensure the continued success of the fundraising machine that had made their party the richest and most powerful in Canadian history. It may have spent $10 million a year but it always raised far more.

Many of the board's members had wondered if Kim Campbell, the leading candidate for Mulroney's mantle going into the leadership convention, might not actually pull it off, overcoming the Canadian public's deep dislike for the Conservatives and winning a fall election with a minority government. No one dared believe that another majority was possible, but so far the Tories had been able to make the "yesterday's man" label stick to Liberal leader Jean Chrétien. But this morning there was a hint of panic in the room. Campbell's lead over Jean Charest, who was running second, was literally narrowing every hour as her inexperience showed.

Most of the men and women in this room had originally backed Campbell, even Mulroney, as he admitted later to the *Globe*'s William Thorsell. Charbonneau had been raising money for her; so had many of the others. In Toronto, she had the kind of support Mulroney had never been able to win through two campaigns. But at the end of May, Mulroney told Thorsell, his support had shifted to Charest, and by the time David Angus closed the meeting and freed the group to get to the convention, Campbell's support among PC Canada Fund board members had dissipated. A few remained loyal, but most headed for Lansdowne Park with one goal: to rally support to Charest's side. They knew that Campbell had lost the momentum, and that a superhuman effort might be able to turn things around for a candidate who had had greater personal appeal for delegates. It reminded them of the 1984 Liberal leadership when John Turner was so clearly the winner in numbers, but Chrétien had won the delegates' hearts. Although Mulroney and others worked hard on Charest's behalf, it was too late.

Campbell took the leadership by ninety ballots the next afternoon, was sworn in as prime minister on June 25, and then, knowing full well where their loyalties lay, dumped most of the Mulroney cronies on the PC Canada Fund board, including David Angus.

When the Mulroneys left Harrington Lake a few days later, it was to stay for two weeks with George and Helen Vari at their villa at Saint-Paul-de-Vence near the French Riviera before moving on to two more weeks with French president François Mitterrand and his wife at their country home. It was while they were at the Varis' that Mila wrote her letter to Marcel Beaudry cancelling the furniture sale and arranging to return the government's cheque for $150,000.

By early August, the Mulroneys were living in the Laurentians north of Montreal, waiting for their new house to be ready, but they weren't idle. The former prime minister and his wife set up their own company called Cansult Communications Limited. Both had contracts with the Washington Speakers' Bureau, run by Harry Rhoades and Bernie Swain. Mulroney's fee was initially reported to be an astronomical $65,000 a pop, right up there with the price commanded by former U.S. defence chief General Colin Powell; actually it's a mere $45,000 (U.S.). What Mila charges for speaking engagements is not known. Later in the year, Astral Communications Inc., an entertainment company, announced that Mila Mulroney would be joining the board to bring, as chairman Harold Greenberg put it, "an international profile to the company."

At 9 a.m. on Monday, August 2, Mulroney reported to the McGill Street offices of Ogilvy Renault after an absence of seventeen years. This time he moved into a large and newly decorated twelfth-floor corner office. He was not expected to resume his old labour law practice; his job now was to use his international contacts to bring in foreign clients.

Mulroney's remuneration at Ogilvy Renault was a source of much conjecture in the city's business community. Although Ogilvy Renault is one of Montreal's leading firms, with 250 lawyers, its top salaries do not soar to the heights of their counterparts in Toronto, who can expect to earn about $500,000 a year at the top of their careers. The best salaries in Montreal law firms rarely go above $300,000 annually. So even with his parliamentary pension of $33,535 there wouldn't be enough, after taxes, to cover the Mulroneys' jet-set lifestyle, not with mortgage payments of at least $96,000 a year, property taxes of $16,000 a year, a daughter at Harvard, which runs to at least $30,000 a year, and a son at Duke, setting him back another $30,000 a year, not to mention the two younger boys in Montreal private schools at a cost of roughly $15,000 a year. An Ogilvy Renault salary wouldn't be enough to take care of the Mulroneys' clothes budget, nor the jewellery, nor the entertaining. It wouldn't cover the holidays in Palm Beach or the shopping trips to New York.

Even many of Mulroney's cronies wondered how he would do it. "Who paid for the house?" one member of the PC Canada Fund asked a reporter. "We're all wondering." There was talk of a trust fund from the Tory party, but Guy Charbonneau emphatically denied its existence. "There were precedents," conceded Charbonneau. "There was one for Dief and one for Pearson. I understand that some asked Mr. Mulroney if he wanted one and he said definitely not." Stories abounded, especially in Montreal, about gentlemen's agreements to retain Mulroney's services at certain fees as a kind of pension, but again, Charbonneau insists there was no such retirement fund for the former prime minister. "He doesn't need it."

Perhaps he doesn't. Several well-placed businessmen have acknowledged that the campaign begun by close Mulroney friends in the winter of 1992–93 to put together a purse for his security after retirement had been successful. Two wealthy businessmen had led the way, said one knowledgeable source, with $1 million each, while a few others added enough to bring the total up to about $4 million. And since he entered private life, Mulroney has accepted three lucrative board appointments. The first, which he took on in October 1993, was with a U.S. food processing giant, Archer-Daniels-Midland Co., where the minimum retainer is \$37,500 (U.S.) a year, with bonuses for each board committee he joins. The maximum he can earn at Archer-Daniels will be \$100,000 a year. It was the next pair of appointments that ensured his wealth. On November 7, 1993, he was appointed to the boards of Peter Munk's Toronto-based Horsham Corporation and American Barrick Resources Corporation. Once again, the honoraria for sitting on the boards were relatively modest — \$1,000 for attending each Horsham board meeting and \$12,000 a year for Barrick, plus an extra \$600 for each meeting — but the appointments came with 250,000 stock options from each company. Although Mulroney would not be able to cash them in until November 1994, their value has been estimated at about \$1.5 million. On top of this, a Horsham circular to shareholders revealed that the company paid him \$40,125 for advice in 1993.

Before any of these appointments were announced, one of Mulroney's parliamentary associates told an Ottawa journalist that Mulroney could have had a job with an international agency such as the United Nations, but that he didn't want it. Mulroney, he confided, wanted to make money instead. But he didn't want to take on a lot of directorships because he would have to pay tax on the money he earned. Instead, he planned to front various international deals and take big chunks of stock in lieu of payment. Which is exactly what happened with Horsham and Barrick.

When the newspapers ran the stories about Peter Munk appointing Mulroney to his boards and treating him so generously, the penny dropped for the staff who had prepared the very private lunch at 24 Sussex Drive on their last day at the house. The guest was Peter Munk.

A fourth board appointment for Mulroney surprised even the most hard-bitten Ottawa reporters, especially those who still bear the scars of Mulroney's wrath during his years in power. This was the announcement, on December 9, 1993, that an Arlington, Virginia, journalism foundation called The Freedom Forum, established by

U.S. press baron Frank Gannett, had invited Mulroney to join its thirteen-member board of trustees. In an effort to explain the appointment, foundation spokeswoman Cheryl Arvidson acknowledged that Mulroney's relationships with Canadian journalists had been difficult on occasion, but that he was a media junkie who loved to read the papers. Mulroney had told her, Arvidson reported to Southam News, that "he believed one of the most essential freedoms in society is the freedom of the press." In a Freedom Forum press release, issued by board chairman Allen Neuharth, Mulroney was described as a "fixture on the world stage with two other conservative world leaders, former U.S. president Ronald Reagan and former British prime minister Margaret Thatcher." And then it quoted the former Canadian prime minister: "Even politicians who feel the lash of the media from time to time understand that, in great democracies, that is part of the price you pay to maintain a vigilant, effective and functioning democracy. That's just the way it is."

"Brian Mulroney gives us a unique international perspective on the freedoms that we try to foster: free press, free speech and free spirit," Neuharth said. "Not only is he a knowledgeable neighbor, but he also has contacts and experiences around the globe that will enhance our mission." Mulroney was equally complimentary to the foundation. "The Freedom Forum's activities outside of the borders of the United States are far-reaching and very important," he said. "None of us lives in a vacuum anymore, and the walls keep coming down. The internationality of The Freedom Forum is very important." Mulroney said freedom of the press is "one of the most important expressions" of freedom and said he looked forward to working with The Freedom Forum in promoting press freedom around the world.

Canadian journalists stared in wonderment at the story. They had not forgotten his efforts to punish reporters for unfriendly stories, his incessant calls of complaint to editors and publishers and producers when he didn't like the spin. They hadn't forgotten that this was the man who, in his last years in power, gave almost no press confer-

ences. They hadn't forgotten that two magazines, *Saturday Night* —
with its controversial cover story about Mulroney by Mordecai Richler
— and *Frank*, along with John Sawatsky's biography of Mulroney,
had been banned from two newsstands at the 1993 Tory convention.

Mulroney should have looked more closely at The Freedom
Forum before he hopped aboard. A few months before his appointment was announced, *The Los Angeles Times* reported that the organization had admitted that it was under investigation by the New York
State attorney general's office for financial irregularities. (New York
officials had jurisdiction because the foundation was registered in the
state.) Quoting from a journal that covers U.S. charities, the *Times* said
the Forum spent $34.4 million on operating and administrative
expenses in the fiscal year ending the previous May 31, 1993, but took
in only $20.2 million in contributions, gifts, and grants in the same
period. And it paid its chairman, Allen Neuharth, $131,000, more
than ten times the average fee paid to board chairmen of similar-sized
foundations. It also outspent other foundations by a wide margin for
professional fees, travel and meetings, and other expenses. Jacques
Attali would have felt right at home. The foundation is still under
investigation by the New York State attorney general.

There were two potential board appointments that fizzled out for
Mulroney. One, says a knowledgeable source in Montreal, was with a
subsidiary of Bell Canada. When he was approached about a board
position, Mulroney named an asking price about ten times higher than
the company could offer and the proposal went nowhere. The second
disappointment was with Conrad Black's Hollinger Inc. According to
Toronto journalist Patricia Best, Mulroney asked Black for a seat on
the board but was royally snubbed; Black did not find room for
Mulroney on his board, but appointed his wife, Barbara Amiel, Marie-
Josée Drouin of the Hudson Institute, and Peter Munk instead.

Such setbacks were rare in Mulroney's new career. Early in
1994 he accompanied Power Corporation's Paul Desmarais to China
to advise him on the corporation's role in the massive Three Gorges

Dam hydroelectric project with Ontario Hydro and Hydro-Québec, as well as a $60-million real estate development in the Pudong region of China near Shanghai. Mulroney was extremely well compensated by Power Corporation for this assistance. In March, Mulroney persuaded senior Chinese government officials to approve a deal between Power Corporation and American Barrick to develop gold mines in China. An ecstatic Peter Munk told reporters that Mulroney "had been *the* key to the deal, not a key. He opened the door. He, in person, took our proposals to the right people I could never get them to," Munk said after Horsham's annual meeting, held at the Ritz-Carlton Hotel in Montreal on April 27, 1994.

Barrick, say the experts who follow the company's activities closely, takes up much of the former prime minister's time these days, and he was heavily involved in the company's successful effort to take over Lac Minerals in the summer of 1994, calling Toronto headquarters every day for a briefing. Even when he was on a trip to Russia in August 1994, he would telephone daily for an update. Once a Barrick official suggested the line might not be secure. Mulroney assured him there was no more secure phone line in all of Russia; he was calling from Boris Yeltsin's dacha. Whether he and the president had done any boar-hunting during the visit is not known.

Over the last year, Brian and Mila Mulroney have re-entered the close-knit circle of old friends they left behind when they moved to Ottawa in 1983. As soon as they returned from the summer in France, three of Mila's friends threw a surprise fortieth-birthday party for her with all her closest women friends in attendance, including Sally Armstrong and Bonnie Brownlee. The guests presented Mila with a Baccarat crystal caviar set, reported *Gazette* society columnist Tommy Schnurmacher. That same evening, he added, Mulroney and Paul Desmarais spent an hour and a half visiting the Juste pour Rire comedy museum on Saint-Laurent Boulevard. It was good to be back home again, the Mulroneys told their friends.

Among other close friends who have made private life more fun have been Denise and Prentiss Hale, wealthy San Franciscans who move in an international set of movie stars, politicians, and business-men. Denise Hale was once married to movie director Vincent Minnelli and is Liza Minnelli's stepmother. On March 20, 1992, the Hales threw a party for Mulroney's fifty-third birthday at L'Orangerie, the private dining room at Le Cirque, one of New York's most expensive restau-rants. "The highlight of the evening," wrote Denise Hale in a piece recounting the event for *The San Francisco Chronicle*, "was when my stepdaughter Liza Minnelli sang 'Happy Birthday' to Mulroney. Then he sang 'When Irish Eyes are Smiling' and a few more." Hale hired an interior designer to redecorate the dining room for the party; every-thing, including lampshades, chairs, tables, and walls, was repainted or newly upholstered for the event. "Even my jaded New York friends were impressed," Hale told her readers, adding that the guest list included Dwayne Andreas, the chairman of Archer-Daniels-Midland (who was later to bring Mulroney onto his board); Roone Arledge, the president of ABC News; Ahmet Ertegun, the head of Atlantic Records; designer Calvin Klein; actor Christopher Plummer; writers Dominick Dunne and Bob Colacello; Hélène Desmarais; and U.S. ambassador Edward Ney and his wife, Judy.

Both Denise Hale and Mila Mulroney come from Serbian fami-lies, which is one of their bonds, and the friendship is very strong. The Mulroneys returned the Hales' hospitality with a black-tie din-ner at 24 Sussex in June 1992 and another dinner in New York in November 1993. Just before the Mulroneys went to Russia to visit the Yeltsins, the Hales threw another dinner party for them, this time in San Francisco on August 10, 1994. Dubbed "The Serbian Connection," with Serbian entertainers, the dinner was held in a pri-vate room at an expensive restaurant that was redecorated for the event. The guests included such luminaries as former U.S secretary of state George Shultz. And once again, Mulroney sang; this time he entertained the guests with his rendition of "Paper Doll" before mov-ing on to the inevitable "Irish Eyes." Although she found Mulroney an amusing standup comic, the *Chronicle*'s gossip columnist, Pat Steger, was less complimentary about his singing: "It's a good thing he had his law firm to return to after retiring from politics."

One tragic note that marred the Mulroneys' contentment in their return to private life was the sudden death on Saturday, August 28, 1993, of Mulroney's close friend and financial trustee Bruce Verchère, whose wife, Lynne, was chairperson of the Official Residences Council.[3] The couple had been among the small group of Canadians who accompanied the Mulroneys to a black-tie White House dinner on April 27, 1989.

Verchère was a tax lawyer who specialized in investments in Europe; he had been a partner at Bennett Jones Verchère (formerly known as Verchère, Noel and Eddy) and held directorships on a number of Swiss- or German-based boards, including the Swiss Bank Corporation (Canada), which he joined in 1981. Verchère was also close to Canadian bestselling author Arthur Hailey and his wife, Sheila, and served as a director of two of their companies. Over time, he became involved with one of their daughters and they had a serious affair; twin daughters were born to the couple during this period. But Verchère decided to return to his first family. His two sons and Lynne were at home that Saturday when they heard a gun go off. They found Verchère dead in a bathroom. An ashen-faced Mulroney was one of the pallbearers at the funeral on September 2 at Montreal's Christ Church Cathedral but did not return to the house for the reception afterwards; later, when Mila tried to call on Lynne, she was not welcome. Verchère's suicide is still an appalling mystery to his friends and family.

Except for absorbing the shock of Verchère's death, leaving Ottawa has clearly been a happy move for the Mulroneys. Financially they have also fared well. By July 1994, they had refinanced their house with a new CIBC mortgage for $1 million at 7.25 per cent calculated every six months; the monthly payments were set at $7,159.19, about $10,000 a year less than originally budgeted. (That slim financial advantage was offset by the increased value of the renovated house;

now that it is assessed at over $2.2 million, instead of the $1.4 million of the previous year, the Mulroneys' property taxes have risen to nearly $25,000 a year from about $16,000.) Since leaving office, Mulroney has made enough money to pay over $1 million in renovation and furnishing costs for the house and to pay off another $300,000 or so on the original mortgage debt. Given his tax bracket, one former banker estimates his income must have exceeded $3 million in 1993–94 to allow him to pay $1.3 million towards the house and its renovations, as well as cover his family's usual expenses.

Although Mulroney spends much of his time these days travelling abroad, especially to Latin America, on American Barrick business, he has not disengaged himself completely from party politics. He and Mila attended a $10,000-a-plate fundraising dinner for Charest and the PC Party in the summer of 1994 at Doug and Susan Bassett's Toronto home. Mulroney makes a point of keeping in touch with Charest; in August they had dinner together and also enjoyed a fishing trip at Craig Dobbin's camp in Labrador, bringing along George Bush as a guest.

On August 31, 1994, Tory leader Jean Charest met with other senior Conservatives in Saskatoon to try to figure out what to do next, where to go, how to pay for it. Restructuring, rebuilding, renewal: these were the buzzwords. The reality was that there were just two MPs in Parliament and the party was $5.7 million in debt. Traditional western support had been distracted by the Reform Party, and in Quebec, the PC powerhouse for the last ten years, the separatists were in control federally, under Lucien Bouchard, and looked about to take over provincially, under Jacques Parizeau. The only place the federal Tories had any real bench strength, a significant block of parliamentarians with staff, research money, free phone lines, airline passes, and experience, was in the Senate. And with a few exceptions, the senators' loyalty was to the man who put them there: Brian Mulroney. The roll call of senators who had been so close to the former prime minister must be daunting to Charest: David Angus, Eric Berntson, John Buchanan, Guy Charbonneau, Michel Cogger, Trevor Eyton, Dunc Jessiman, Jim Kelleher, Marjory LeBreton, John Lynch-Staunton, Michael Meighen, Pierre Claude Nolin, and Fernand Roberge. These are the individuals on whom Charest must depend, the same people who are, to a great extent, responsible for much of the mess the party is in today.

Maybe there is just too much baggage for a Tory recovery in the foreseeable future. Canadians will never forget words like "There's no whore like an old whore" and "You had an option, sir." There are so many sour memories: the Montreal break-ins, a German strip club, the CF-18 contract, the Sinc Stevens affair, Oerlikon and Airbus, Summerside and Pearson, GigaText and helicopters, stretch limousines and furniture deals and two dead boars. The rogue politicians who ran wild on the Hill have more to answer for than a lost election; they have destroyed the reputation of a proud old party.

1. The PCO, run by the country's top civil servant, the clerk of the Privy Council, is a bureaucratic elite that coordinates the cabinet office activities and serves as the prime minister's public service secretariat, while the PMO is the prime minister's political arm, home to cronies, spin doctors, image consultants, patronage advisers, and speechwriters. Until 1968, the PCO had seconded staff to the prime minister, but Pierre Trudeau wanted a partisan team of his own political advisers, so he split the PCO in two to create a new PMO, whose personnel report to the chief of staff (also called the principal secretary). Trudeau employed between 85 and 90 people in his 1983–84 PMO; by the end of 1985, Mulroney's PMO had a staff of 117. By 1989 the office had ballooned to 146, including people working for Don Mazankowski in the newly created Office of the Deputy Prime Minister.

Over his years in power, Mulroney had five chiefs of staff, each with a unique management style. The first was Bernard Roy, who allowed Mulroney's other senior aides great freedom and direct access to the prime minister. He was followed by senior diplomat Derek Burney, who clamped down on the freedom of the aides and forced them to report through him. The third chief of staff was an old friend, Stanley Hartt, another Montreal lawyer like Roy, who had been deputy minister of finance; as *The Globe and Mail*'s Graham Fraser said, "he functioned like an impresario: impulsive, witty, expansive." Fourth was a clever bureaucrat, Norman Spector, whose cool and correct style was anathema to Mulroney's aides and to Mila. The fifth was Toronto advertising executive and lobbyist Hugh Segal, a funny and likeable man who was determined to make Mulroney more accessible.

2. Moores and Mulroney were associates in various business ventures prior to the leadership campaign. In 1979, for example, Mulroney joined the board of one of Moores's companies, Labsea Inc. On April 24, 1985, Liberal MP Sheila Copps

rose in the House of Commons with documents showing Mulroney had held a corporate directorship in the company for two months after being sworn into office, in direct violation of government conflict-of-interest guidelines. This was at a time when some Tory cabinet ministers were being attacked publicly for ignoring the guidelines. In an effort to defend his ministers, Mulroney had gone after Liberal leader John Turner two weeks earlier for hanging on to his own corporate directorships right up to the day he was sworn in as prime minister. Press secretary Bill Fox said Mulroney had simply forgotten he was on the board because the company had been dormant since its inception. Fox also issued a statement saying the prime minister had received no fees or benefits at any time from Labsea and had never attended any meetings of the Labsea board. Yet documents filed with the federal Department of Consumer and Corporate Affairs in 1988 showed the company was still active, its address the same as Moores's office in Ottawa. The five-person board of directors included Newfoundland businessman Craig Dobbin and Toronto's Latham Burns, the chairman of Burns Fry. It wasn't until 1993 that the company finally disappeared from government records.

Chapter 3   THE MONEY MEN

1. Charbonneau says he asked Lamarre not to buy directly from his wife for the sake of appearances: "I told him I didn't want him to," said Charbonneau. Instead, explained the senator, Lamarre's curator, Leo Rosshandler, made all the arrangements to buy Yolande Charbonneau's paintings: "Everything Bernard bought went through him." Rosshandler refused to discuss the purchases, but an examination of the catalogue of the Lavalin Collection (which has been acquired by the Quebec government) does not show any of her paintings listed among the works by Molinari, Pellan, Riopelle, and other luminaries. The catalogue may, of course, list only works that are displayed.

2. In 1981, when eager investors were pouring money into energy stocks, Gerry and Fred Doucet set up East Coast Energy Ltd. to invest in oil and gas exploration and distribution off the Nova Scotia coast. Premier John Buchanan helped them get the offshore drilling licence they needed. Frank Moores agreed to sit on the board of the new company, and both Michael Meighen and Brian Mulroney promised to invest.

Fred Doucet, the new chairman and chief executive at $70,000 a year, approached Ross Montgomery of McLeod Young Weir, the Halifax broker who was later to help Mulroney raise his leadership funds in the province, to take the company public. But the advice they received from McLeod's president, Thomas Kierans, was that they needed more equity invested in the company. When the brothers beat the bushes for money they found willing investors across Nova

Scotia, from their home town of Grand Étang in Cape Breton to Hollis Street in Halifax. Mulroney put in a cautious $15,000; an even more prudent Michael Meighen hazarded just $7,500. Within a few months the project looked ready to go public and Fred Doucet demanded that McLeod buy East Coast's shares and then sell them at a profit. When wary brokers at McLeod warned that this was too big a risk, given the company's lack of capital, Doucet was furious. After much argument, McLeod's Toronto office stepped in to smooth the way; no one was eager to offend those close to Brian Mulroney, the man they were sure would be the next Conservative leader.

By the fall of 1982, they had a deal. McLeod received its regular commission and stood by its insistence that it only sell the shares, not take the risk of underwriting them. By December, however, the issue was still $3 million short of its target. At this point Walter Wolf entered the picture. Among Wolf's Canadian holdings were two oil rig supply ships, Sea Wolf 101 and Sea Wolf 102, which had contracts with the federally owned oil company, Petro-Canada. As far as he was concerned, East Coast Energy Ltd. was an excellent investment that dovetailed nicely with his supply ships' business.

Doucet persuaded Wolf to take $500,000 worth of shares at $15 each, with the money payable in U.S. funds drawn on the Bank of Butterfield in Bermuda. Within weeks Wolf wanted his money back, claiming he needed it to buy a helicopter. Michel Cogger, Wolf's lawyer, phoned Fred Doucet and McLeod officials every day trying to extract his client from the deal, and finally Tom Kierans settled the matter by offering $250,000 from the firm to Wolf against the value of his shares, shares that had now sunk to $5.95 each. Wolf took it, but he wasn't happy; he was facing the loss of his other $250,000.

A few weeks later Wolf discovered that Cogger had negotiated the McLeod money as a loan, not as a sale of stock. Wolf refused to repay the money to the firm and the brokers sued. The case came to court in Ontario in 1986, and Mr. Justice Eugene Ewaschuk of the Ontario Supreme Court agreed with McLeod, saying Kierans, "a federal Conservative," had given the loan "primarily since the shares had been handled by McLeod and remained unlisted and secondarily since help to Cogger would build up McLeod's goodwill with the federal Progressive Conservative Party." Ewaschuk ordered Wolf to pay the money back; Wolf refused.

Without sufficient capital, East Coast Energy couldn't withstand the buffeting that energy companies suffered during the 1982 recession, especially after paying $17 million (in a mix of cash and East Coast Energy shares) for an Alberta-based company called Petroleum Royalties Ltd. The Doucets sold Petroleum Royalties' assets in Australia, the U.S., and Alberta but later told reporters that the money they earned from these sales didn't equal the amount they'd paid for the company. By the winter of 1982, the Bank of Montreal had petitioned Petroleum Royalties Ltd. into bankruptcy, and in early 1983 East Coast reported a deficit of $18.7 million. By February it was defaulting on payments to its creditors, and by June it was bankrupt, with $3.74 million owing to seven creditors. The bulk of the debt was with the Canadian Imperial Bank of Commerce, which could not have been pleasant for Brian Mulroney, a member of its board. It was a catastrophe for the company's 1,100 shareholders, whose losses added up to $9.4 million.

In October 1985, when Mulroney had been in power for a year, two more unhappy stories surfaced. That month Wolf sued Fred Doucet — by now Mulroney's senior political adviser — for $301,467, the losses he'd taken in his East Coast Energy investment. Then Liberal MPs raised the issue of a grant of $362,761 given to a Wolf company by a joint committee of federal and Newfoundland government officials. One suggestion was that the grant made up for Wolf's losses in the Doucet brothers' energy bubble. Government ministers dismissed reporters' questions on the matter.

The mess with Wolf did not help relationships in Mulroney's circle. Cogger and Doucet were at each other's throats and a distinct, though temporary, chill developed between Mulroney and Cogger. In February 1987, Walter Wolf's lawsuit against Doucet became public knowledge; two years later, on July 11, 1989, Wolf settled with Doucet privately.

3. Shea ran into difficulty in 1984 when the city of Boston paid more than $800,000 in insurance policy commissions on city employees in the fiscal year 1983–84 to Embassy Insurance Agency, a company in which he had an interest. His wife was vice-president of the company. It came to light that in 1980 he and a partner in a separate business called Consultants and Risk Managers, Inc. (CRM), had received a $1-million, three-year contract from the city of Boston to advise it on its insurance needs. CRM had hired Embassy to be the city's reinsurer. The two companies shared the same address and some of the same officials. A grand jury looked at the deal and the case was eventually dismissed for lack of evidence, but city officials were furious. They dumped Shea and Embassy Insurance and announced they were planning to renegotiate CRM's contract. Like Fred Doucet, Bob Shea was dealing with a major business scandal while at the same time fundraising for Mulroney.

Chapter 5   THE BAGMEN AND THE BOSS

1. During most of the Mulroney years in power, the Tories stayed well ahead of the other parties in fundraising. The following table illustrates the Tory money

machine compared with those of the other major parties during the 1980s and the early 1990s. Figures for the New Democrats show combined totals of donations to the provincial and federal parties.

YEAR	PCs	LIBERALS	NDP
1981	$6.9 million	$5.1 million	$5.9 million
1982	$8.2 million	$6.1 million	$7.0 million
1983	$14.1 million	$7.3 million	$8.6 million
1984	$21.1 million	$10.6 million	$10.4 million
1985	$14.5 million	$5.6 million	$10.0 million
1986	$15.2 million	$10.6 million	$13.7 million
1987	$12.8 million	$8.8 million	$12.1 million
1988	$24.5 million	$13.2 million	$17.9 million
1989	$13.8 million	$6.3 million	$13.7 million
1990	$11.0 million	$12.0 million	$14.7 million
1991	$12.0 million	$6.8 million	$19.2 million
1992	$11.5 million	$7.6 million	$13.4 million

Chapter 6 THE TOLLGATERS' PICNIC

1. The author has a copy of the tape of this conversation.

2. Paquin had loaned money to Nantel, giving him a $31,000 mortgage on his office premises and later helping with a mortgage on his cottage.

Chapter 7 ENTER THE MOB

1. The author has interviewed Majeau in six taped, on-the-record discussions over several years, beginning in 1989. The last interviews were done in 1994. There have been dozens of other meetings and conversations over the years as well, many of which were attended by other witnesses, including Rod Macdonell, one of the research associates on this book. Majeau's story has never changed and the facts he gives in this chapter have been verified with many other sources including police officers and lawyers. LaSalle has always denied he was associated with any of Majeau's schemes.

2. The author has interviewed the officer who chased Majeau but he would not go on the record to describe the event. This whole episode is one that the RCMP is very reluctant to discuss.

3. Simard describes Rock's call in his 1987 autobiography, *Le neveu*. To the amusement of Simard and his ghost-writer, Michel Vastel, Rock responded angrily in a column he wrote for the Montreal police tabloid *Foto-Police*, denying he'd ever

offered his services to Simard or promised an early parole. But Simard had not named Rock in the book, something the lawyer seemed to have failed to notice when he wrote the column.

Chapter 8   Breakfast at Nate's

1. During all the speculation about corrupt practices in Mirabel land deals, Quebec Tories were stunned by the contract murder of one of their own, but it proved to be only the first of a number of mysterious and violent deaths to afflict the federal Tories over the next few years. On December 4, 1987, Mario Taddeo, forty-nine, a millionaire Laval businessman and bagman for local Tory MPs such as Vincent Della Noce and Lise Bourgault, was shot dead at his office in the rock quarry he owned in Saint-Antoine-de-Mirabel, about 30 miles north of Montreal. Early in the morning a masked man, carrying a gun in each hand, had calmly entered the office, asked the terrified staff which one was Mario, and then just as calmly shot him. When an employee, Pierre Blanchard, tried to help his boss, the gunman shot him dead as well. Police investigated the murders for six months, interviewed over 200 people, and came up empty-handed. The family offered rewards but no one came forward. To complicate the family's problems was Taddeo's messy personal life; he had left his wife, Geraldine, to live with a woman called Louise Caron — and Caron was his former sister-in-law, who had been married to Geraldine's brother.

   By the time of his death, Taddeo was already under RCMP investigation for a crooked land deal in which a local farmer, Gerard Poirier — whose land had first been expropriated by the federal Liberals for Mirabel Airport and then sold back to him by the Tory government — was being coerced into selling his property to a numbered company owned by Taddeo. Taddeo was after the land and the valuable gravel beds in the area because he had his eye on a big prize: the federal contract to build a new major highway between Dorval Airport and Mirabel, a contract for which he would need to acquire the land in the area and massive amounts of gravel.

   One of Taddeo's proudest possessions was a framed photograph of himself and Louise with Brian and Mila Mulroney at a Tory party event.

Chapter 9   Miss Guatemala et al.

1. Today Schuster admits he knew Séguin, Mitton, and Danis but says he can't remember this delivery.

2. Denis Lapointe appears frequently in this account of the Tories' years in power. He is the same Denis Lapointe who had been asked by senior officers

at Ottawa headquarters to conduct a discreet investigation of the 1984 Montreal burglaries.

3. For an understanding of how money-laundering works in Canada, there is no better guide than Mario Possamai's book, *Money on the Run* (Viking, 1992). A former journalist, Possamai is now an investigator with the forensic accounting firm Lindquist Avey Macdonald Baskerville in Toronto; he is the firm's expert on money-laundering. An Oxford Dictionary definition quoted by Possamai states that the process involves "passing money through a very secret sieve (like a Swiss bank) or through a series of extraordinarily complicated transactions that disguise its true origins or purpose." Possamai adds that the practice is a kind of financial filter. "Funds to be camouflaged enter at one end and emerge at the other with their pedigrees carefully disguised. Concealment, however, is not enough. The ultimate goal is to obscure the origins of those funds so that they can be used without raising the least suspicion. That often involves transferring them to a foreign country and later retrieving them from what seems to be legitimate sources in that country or any other."

And there is a difference in the kind of money that is laundered, Possamai writes. It is either "dirty money" or "black money." The kind of money being laundered at Rockton Consulting's Peel Street offices was clearly "dirty money" — that is, money earned from drug trafficking, extortion, racketeering, and fraud, or money stolen by corrupt officials from public treasuries. Black money, explains Possamai, "is legally accumulated and typically held by otherwise respectable people." It becomes illegal when it is laundered through a foreign country to evade taxes or sent abroad in defiance of a country's laws on exports of money. Black money can also include flight capital, that is, money legally sent abroad to escape "political and economic uncertainties."

4. When a nervous RCMP command in Ottawa cancelled this sting, their targets were politicians, aides, and party organizers, a group of people with the power to end careers and rein in police officers. Four years later, the Mounties organized another major sting operation in Montreal, and the coincidences between the two operations are noteworthy; perhaps the first sting provided the inspiration. The second operation, which ended in dozens of spectacular arrests and drug hauls in early September 1994, lasted four years and was based in an elaborate money-laundering office set up through a registered company working from a Peel Street office and staffed with undercover officers. As the officers helped launder millions of dollars in illicit funds from drug trafficking and other illegal activities, everything that happened was under video and audio surveillance. The major difference between this operation and the Mitton sting was that this time the tar-

gets were only drug traffickers, not politicians. This time the decision from head-quarters was to keep it going.

5. Michael Mitton set himself up as a stock promoter and became a director of seven VSE companies over the next two years. In 1988 he was caught in an investigation of VSE stock promoters and confessed to insider trading and failure to disclose his positions in other VSE companies. On December 21, 1988, he and Janet were barred from trading on the VSE for a period of twenty years, the longest suspension in the history of the Vancouver exchange.

That same year, he was charged by police for defrauding a number of Montreal brokerage houses by writing bad cheques to cover stock purchases. He received a thirty-month jail term but served only a few months.

His former RCMP handler, Denis Lapointe, was implicated in these affairs when the prosecutors claimed that Mitton had offered him stock benefits worth $500,000 and that Lapointe had warned Mitton of the police investigation. On June 2, 1989, the forty-four-year-old officer with twenty years on the force was charged in Quebec Court with accepting a benefit and six counts of breach of trust. Eventually the benefit charge was shown to be completely groundless, and all but one of the other charges — failure to inform his superiors in writing of his legitimate stock investments through Mitton — were dropped. Lapointe was ordered to do 180 hours of community service. Shortly afterwards, Lapointe resigned from the force; today he lives on his RCMP pension. Michael Mitton is a fundraiser for various charitable organizations in the Vancouver area.

Chapter 10   CONFLICTS AND OTHER INTERESTS

1. I am indebted to York University political science professor Ian Greene, who has studied conflict of interest over the years and has shared his research results with me. Much of the historical and statistical material in this chapter comes from research he has prepared.

2. By the end of the Mulroney years, a number of departing ministers had moved quickly into jobs with companies doing business with their old departments. One of these was Energy Minister Jake Epp, who left cabinet in January 1993 and joined TransCanada Pipelines of Calgary in the summer of that year.

Chapter 11   LIFE AT THE TROUGH

1. After Nielsen quit the cabinet in 1986, he was given a seven-year term (at $149,000 a year) as chairman of the Canadian Transport Commission — which he transformed into the National Transportation Agency. "I don't diminish my

own culpability in participating in the system when I was appointed chairman of the CTC," he admits today. "I justify having taken that position on the basis that I was part of the process of designing the legislation that was going to phase it out, and I knew there was an enormous task ahead in dismantling the CTC and setting up the NTA. So it was a great challenge and I took it, and within two years we completely transformed the entire system, to say nothing of decreasing the number of bureaucrats in that system by some 35 per cent. I knew that it could be done there and know it could still be done in virtually every agency and Crown corporation in the country."

2. Citing the pressure of business commitments, Bazin resigned from the Senate on Friday afternoon, December 8, 1989, after a question was put on a House of Commons order paper by NDP MP Rod Murphy. The NDP wanted the details of a Bazin bill for $24,862.86 to the Privy Council Office for work done in January 1988 for the Prime Minister's Office. Although Bazin had admitted the work was done and the bill paid, the PCO refused to give copies of the bill to Murphy, who had applied for it under the Access to Information Act. The PCO told him it did not have the document. As a last resort, Murphy put the question on a Commons order paper, a step that requires an answer from the government, but he never received it.

3. The consultant's report was prepared by Jean Paquin, the brother of Henri Paquin, and was done in close cooperation with Sirois. Because of all the disputes between the Telefilm administration and the board, Paquin's report was a recipe for a coup d'état; it recommended that all administrative powers be stripped from the executive and assigned to the board. All the signing authority of the executive director would be transferred to the chairman. "This was defying the law of Canada," said one close observer of the scene. Sirois leaked the Paquin report to *The Globe and Mail*'s Jay Scott.

Chapter 13   THE POPE OF BISHOP STREET

1. The SFIU, which had just a handful of officers, had been housed in downtown Ottawa in the force's economic crime offices at "A" Division on Cooper Street. In 1985 Simmonds ordered the unit to move into a thirty-person Economic Crime Section in the suburban Alta Vista headquarters where he could keep an eye on them. As former Ontario provincial judge René Marin would note later, in his April 1991 report on the ethics of the RCMP operation, "the motivation for the change appears to have been a desire to bring the sensitive investigations undertaken by the Unit more directly under the control of headquarters."

2. The names of Charbonneau and Vidosa were blacked out in the copy given to the press, but the author has confirmed independently that theirs are the names being concealed.

The author has also corrected some minor typographical errors in the report.

Chapter 15   GIGAMESS

1. The members of Mulroney's "kitchen cabinet" during the 1988 federal election campaign were Waschuk, Fred Doucet, Pat MacAdam, Frank Moores, and Gary Ouellet; while they might not have been directly involved in the campaign, they were trusted friends with excellent networks across the country. They frequently dropped in at 24 Sussex in the evenings for a chat.

2. There is a curious connection here with the Glen Kealey case. While Kealey was lobbying for federal money to support his "smart" office building, he hired Dr. Douglas Young to advise him.

3. The story of Cogger's lobbying for GigaMos was revealed in the transcripts of his 1992 preliminary hearing in Montreal.

4. Later, when the *Gazette*'s Rod Macdonell called Mazankowski's office to find out why the minister had not warned the Saskatchewan government, Mazankowski's press secretary, Tom Van Dusen, told Macdonell there was no record of his boss having received the letter. When Macdonell pressed Van Dusen for an explanation, Van Dusen uttered a profanity and hung up the phone. Macdonell was not able to find out whether any subsequent warning from the federal government might have enabled the Saskatchewan officials to recover the bulk of their funds from Montpetit.

5. David Angus denies having had any role in raising money to save Cogger's farm.

Chapter 16   LEASES R US

1. Bourque bought out Gerry Doucet's interest when Doucet left the firm in 1989 to set up a new lobbying company with his brother, Fred. Unless Bourque was actually lobbying himself, the rules did not oblige him to register as an owner of the company, especially when he had MacAdam on board to represent his interests.

2. MacAdam also had a business connection to Bourque, Jr., one he had established on December 23, 1988, when the two incorporated The Birkenhead Group Inc., a company that sold fax machines.

3. Researcher Ken Rubin discovered that the lease agreement required Perez to pay $500,000 annually in ground rent, an amount that increases every four years until it reaches $1.8 million in the sixty-sixth year. Perez also pays a percentage of gross revenues.

Chapter 17   SELLING SUMMERSIDE FOR A SONG

1. Robert Foster was Kim Campbell's choice as chief party bagman when she became prime minister in the summer of 1993. Foster was replaced a few months

later, soon after Charest took over as interim party leader.

Chapter 19   IT PAYS TO ADVERTISE

1. Cossette was also supposed to get the Air Canada advertising contract, then split evenly between an English firm and a Quebec firm. "My marching orders are that it's to go to Cossette," said one senior Tory on the board of the PC Canada Fund to a friend. Only the intervention of Air Canada's president, Claude Taylor, prevented the move.

2. Three or four years later, during their investigations into Cogger's finances, the RCMP obtained the written statement from Charbonneau and then told Scott about it. This was when Scott found out that Cogger's story did not match Charbonneau's recollection of events.

3. Blue Thunder was the Quebec Conservatives' name for the group of advertising companies pulled together to produce the ad campaign in the province for the 1984 federal election. Roger Nantel was in charge, aided by Jean Peloquin. (In Ontario a similar group of companies that came together for federal campaigns for the Liberals was always called Red Leaf Communications.)

4. On October 12, 1989, Henri Paquin, the Montreal developer who had backed Michel Gravel and Eddie Desrosiers and loaned money to Roger Nantel, left his office just before 7 p.m. in his black 1987 Mercedes-Benz and drove west on Rue Thimens towards the suburb of Saint-Laurent. Behind him was Guy Therrien, the vice-president of Paquin's Société de Gestion DHP, in his BMW. Therrien noticed that his boss was talking to someone on the car phone as he drove. Suddenly, at five minutes to 7, there was a sharp explosion in Paquin's car. Out of control, the Mercedes swung sharply into a row of parked cars and shuddered to a stop. At first, when passersby and the police approached the smoking car, they thought it was possible that the driver was still alive. He appeared to be sitting upright, uninjured. But as soon as they opened the door, they could see that the bomb had detonated under his seat, and there was nothing left of the body below the waist.

     Paquin had been murdered in a contract hit by someone who had triggered a bomb by remote control, the police said later. The word on the street was that Paquin was connected to organized crime and that his death had been ordered by the Mob. "My father was not a part of the Mob," said Paquin's son Marc, in a statement issued two days after his father's death, "but maybe his involvement in Saint-Laurent went against interests that were bigger than his." The police were unable to solve this crime.

     To counter the rumours of Mob membership, six months later Paquin's family offered a reward of $150,000 to anyone who could help them find the hit man. "We have taken this unusual action because we want our father's killer to be caught and, more importantly, because we want his name cleared," Marc Paquin told the *Globe*'s André Picard. "It is not easy for us to live with these events, but it's worse to live with the insinuations that he was a member of the Mob."

5. An inquiry into the Kemano Dam project is under way; its findings are expected in 1995.

Chapter 22   PIE IN THE SKY

1. In the spring of 1994 an extraordinary scandal blew up in Germany when it was revealed that Franz Josef Strauss had helped an intimate friend and benefactor, Edward Zwick, evade German income taxes of close to $90 million and had also advised him to flee to Switzerland to escape the police. German newspapers and magazines have been publishing stories ever since that show how the tax evasion scandal has enveloped other senior German politicians. Zwick, a multimillion-aire owner of luxury German spas now in exile in Lugano, Switzerland, had showered Strauss with valuable gifts and benefits over the years, benefits that included the use of an executive jet with Strauss's initials on it. It was discovered that Strauss had doubled his annual income by illegally paying himself 300,000 Deutschmarks a year from a trust he helped administer. And Germans found out Strauss had extensive land holdings in South Africa, another bombshell.

From April 1994 through the summer, European papers were full of the revelations about the corrupt Strauss administration, and Germans, who had revered the politician and named Munich's airport after him, shook their heads sadly. Now an angry and frightened Edward Zwick has started to speak publicly about his old friend's business affairs because his son, Johannes Zwick, has been imprisoned by German authorities for becoming involved in the tax evasion plot. As he threatens to tell everything he knows about Strauss's Swiss bank accounts and his other financial secrets, Zwick has become a major embarrassment to the Kohl government. The fiasco is being called "the fall of the house of Strauss" by *The Daily Telegraph*, which has pointed out the damage it is doing to the political ambitions of the Strauss children, especially Monika Strauss, who is a senior politician in her father's old party.

What Germans do not yet know about are the extensive business interests of the Strauss family in Canada, business interests managed by Strauss's friend Karl-Heinz Schreiber and represented by Government Consultants International until it folded in 1994. To this day Fred Doucet's lobbying firm still lobbies for Bitucan, the company partly owned by the Strauss family. What connections there may be between Strauss's personal business interests here and his chairmanship of Airbus, both represented by the same Ottawa lobbyists, may yet be explained by a frightened old man in Switzerland.

Chapter 26   MULRONEY, INC.

1. George Petty, a good friend of Mulroney's, has been a munificent donor to the federal Tories for many years, both personally and through his pulp and paper company, Repap Enterprises Inc., which in turn has been the recipient of generous federal support. Petty was an adviser to the Mulroney government during the Canada-U.S. free trade negotiations.

2. People who know Moores well say the rift was caused by Moores's suggestion to Mulroney in 1988 that he should leave politics, rather than lead the party into another election.

3. One indication of how closely Verchère was linked to Mulroney was that he included an order for Gary Mulroney's business cards as Manicouagan constituency manager in a printing job for his own law firm.

INDEX